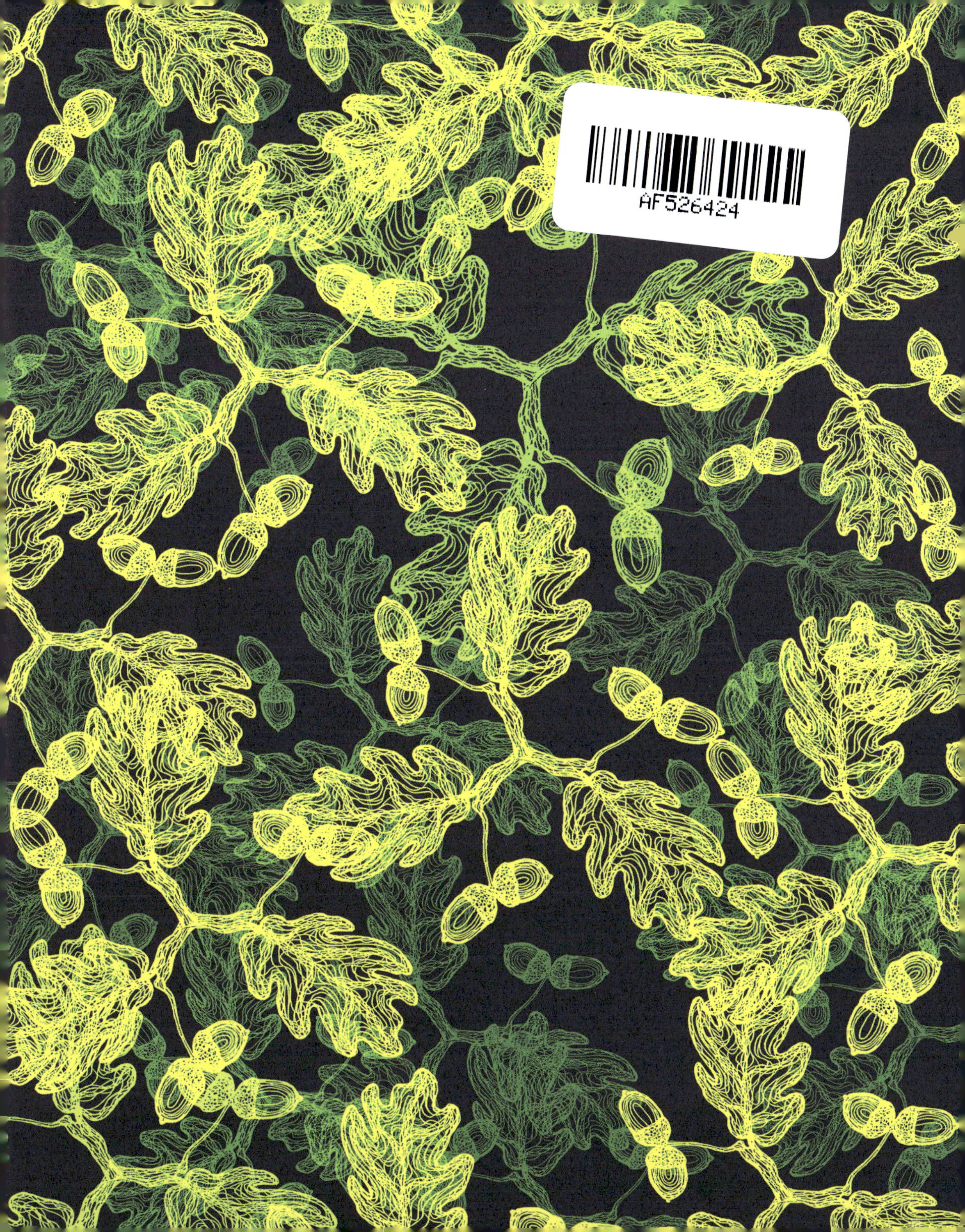
AF526424

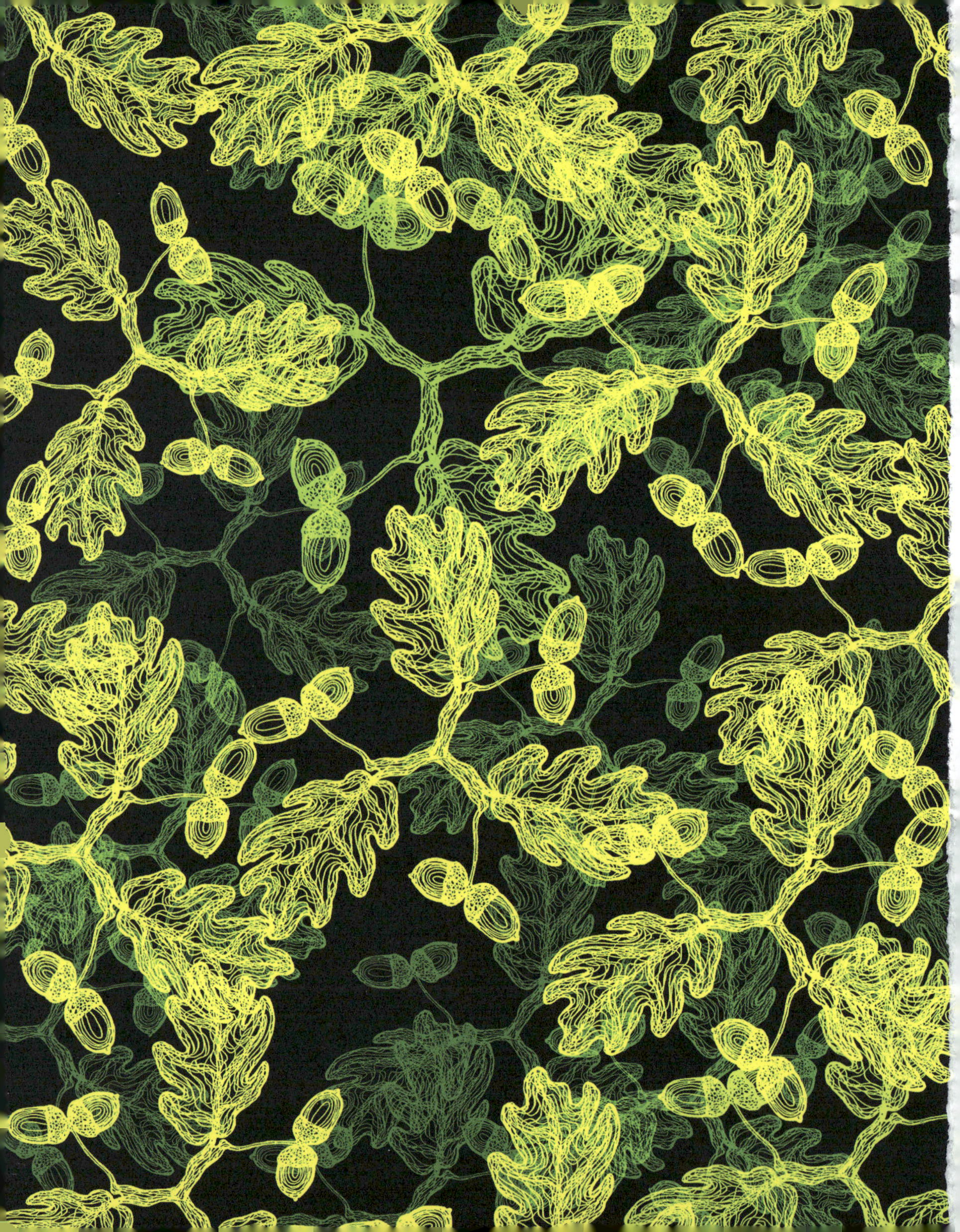

TIME FOR MAGIC

TIME FOR MAGIC

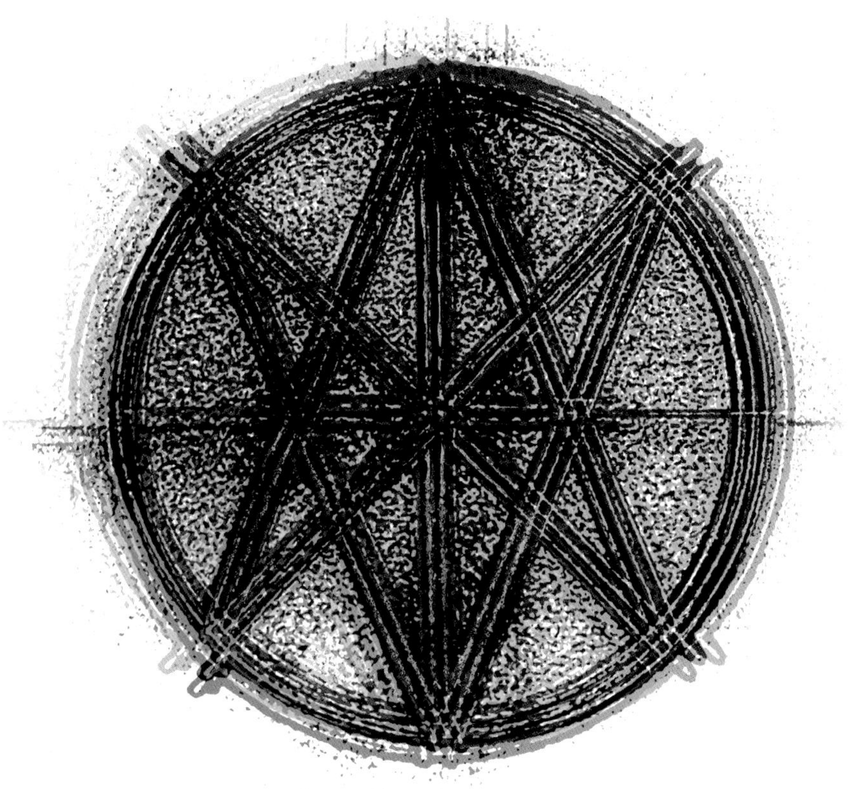

JAMIE REID

PHILIP CARR-GOMM

STEPHEN ELLCOCK

JOHN MARCHANT

TIME FOR MAGIC

First published in the UK and USA in 2024 by
Watkins, an imprint of Watkins Media Limited
Unit 11, Shepperton House, 83–93 Shepperton Road
London N1 3DF

enquiries@watkinspublishing.com

Publisher	**Fiona Robertson**
Designer	**Atelier Pickard**
Head of Design	**Karen Smith**
Editorial assistance	**Maisie McGregor**
Proofreading	**Kelly Thompson**
Indexing	**Edward Gauntlett**
Additional photograhy	**Glen Wilkins**
Production	**Uzma Taj**

A CIP record for this book is available from the British Library

ISBN 978-1-78678-848-1

10 9 8 7 6 5 4 3 2 1

Typeset in Garamond Premier Pro
Clarendon URW
Custom Woodblock

Printed in Bosnia and Herzegovina
Colour repro by Rival Colour UK

www.watkinspublishing.com

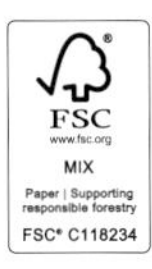

IMAGE SELECTION	**Stephen Ellcock**
STEPHEN ELLCOCK & JOHN MARCHANT ON JAMIE REID	**Stephen Ellcock & John Marchant**
A BIOGRAPHY OF JAMIE REID	**John Marchant**
CAPTIONS	**John Marchant**
THE EIGHTFOLD WHEEL OF THE YEAR	**Philip Carr-Gomm**
CHAPTER INTRODUCTIONS	**Philip Carr-Gomm**
NOTES FROM HELIGAN	**Alasdair Moore**

CONTENTS

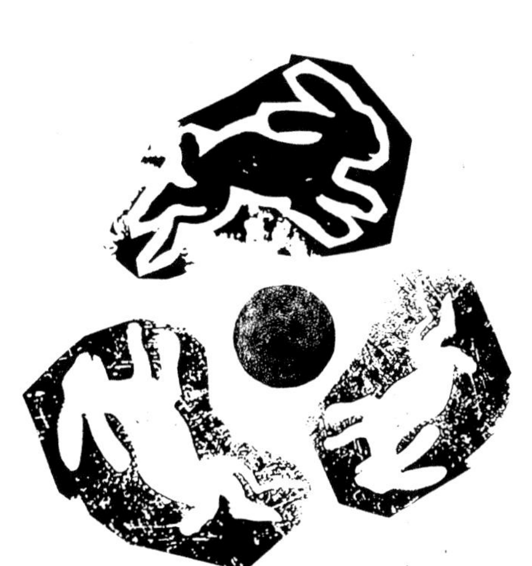

A BIOGRAPHY OF JAMIE REID

JOHN MARCHANT

British artist Jamie Reid (b. 1947 Croydon, d. 2023 Liverpool) was an iconoclast, anarchist, punk, hippie, rebel and romantic, infamously connected with the Sex Pistols and the DIY aesthetic of Punk. At its heart, Punk was both romantic and political, and Jamie was the acknowledged driving force of rage against the monarchy, the state and the status quo.

He grew up in suburban Croydon, under the parental influences of Druidry and social protest. As a boy, he joined the Aldermaston marches against nuclear weapons on UK soil, and was greatly impressed by an older brother who was a member of the Campaign for Nuclear Disarmament and involved with radical protest actions. Jamie's great-uncle, George Watson MacGregor Reid, had been a member of the Golden Dawn and a scholar of Eastern mysticism, taking on the mantle of Chief Druid of the Druid Order in 1909. He was photographed being hauled away from Stonehenge by police after a solstice protest.

By May 1968, Jamie and his art college friend Malcolm McLaren had become greatly impressed by the revolutionary events in Paris and by the actions and slogans of the Situationist International. They tried to make it to the Left Bank in time for the rioting but found only the smouldering ruins and accompanying graffiti – '*La barricade ferme la rue mais ouvre la voie*', '*Soyez réalistes, demandez l'impossible*' and, best of all, '*Vite!*'.

After a stint as a semi-professional footballer and gardener, Jamie co-founded an independent, agit-prop press group called Suburban Press. Croydon at that time was in the process of being carved up and ransacked by property developers and corrupt councillors, and through six issues and various collaborations with other radical groups, Jamie honed his skills with scalpel, glue and Xerox machine to create punchy protest graphics that looked as good on bedroom walls as in the papers.

Radical cyclists hammered Rolls Royces, goods were handed out free to kids in Selfridges – anarchy was building in the UK. The country and its youth were ripe for a radical act, and Reid and McLaren knew exactly what they were doing. The Sex Pistols smashed their way into the public consciousness with their attitude, sarcasm, energy and wit, as well as their image as violent rebels against the ultra-conservative values of the mid-1970s. Those who were touched by Punk felt an electric charge that continues to inform our culture to this day. Much was written about Punk at the time and much has been written about it since, some of it true. It was a smash-and-grab raid. It was intelligent, funny, violent and essentially romantic. It couldn't last.

Following the untimely end of the Sex Pistols project in a welter of misunderstanding, vitriol and death, Jamie and his then-partner, the actor Margi Clarke, decamped to Paris to escape the misery and chaos. Penniless, they convinced a record company to buy their songs, or rather the rapidly recalled lyrics to traditional Irish rebel ballads. Returning to Brixton in time for the riots of 1981, Jamie started visual work again, now developing a mad, picaresque multimedia extravaganza. The *Leaving the 20th Century/How to Become Invisible* cycle embodied artworks as well as a musical, with the latter enjoying a single performance in Liverpool at the end of the 1980s, after years of on/off development. In the mid-1980s, Jamie had become a visiting part-time lecturer at the Liverpool School of Art at the invitation of Colin Fallows, and began to produce the printed and painted textiles that would be further developed throughout his career.

By this time, Jamie was working with graphic designer Malcolm Garrett at Assorted iMaGes, on Curtain Road, in Shoreditch, London. He'd been given a space to work in and a brand-new tool to play with: a colour photocopier. He began copying, collaging, tearing and pasting, creating work for a disparate group of musicians, including Boy George and Transvision Vamp. He was now acknowledged as an important contemporary artist, his work an integral part of an influential exhibition on the Situationist International – an exhibition that travelled from the Centre Pompidou, in Paris, to the ICA in London and in Boston, US. He had also picked up a paintbrush again, beginning his explorations into sacred geometry and colour magic on rough canvas.

It was at this point that another resident of the rambling Victorian warehouse in which Jamie worked commissioned him to refurbish his burgeoning complex of recording studios. Ten years later, Jamie and accomplice Mike Nicholls finished work. The Strongroom Studios was his largest-ever project, the entire interior brimming and alive with his colours and glyphs.

Through the 1990s, Jamie was engaged with protest movements, against the Poll Tax, Clause 28, the Criminal Justice Bill, English Heritage and more. By now he had relocated to Liverpool on a permanent basis, finding it to be more comfortable yet also more alive than anywhere else. He immersed himself in the local arts scene, notably with the radical arts group Visual Stress, with whom he collaborated on street actions, rituals and parades, principally directed at confronting the city's awful legacy from the slave trade. A major survey of Jamie's work called *Peace Is Tough* opened in New York in 1997, travelling to Japan, Ireland and Greece.

Through the early years of the 21st century, Jamie continued to paint and draw, including creating huge banners for Druidic rituals. He began to mine the possibilities of limited editions of his artwork, enjoying this fast and cheap method of getting his work on walls, rather than struggling with a cynical art establishment. In 2009, a collaboration with Japanese fashion icon Rei Kawakubo for her company Comme des Garçons brought Jamie's work back to the catwalk, thirty years after his graphic work had made Vivienne Westwood's Seditionaries line notorious. Meanwhile, he continued his involvement with important protest groups, such as Occupy, Pussy Riot and Extinction Rebellion.

The natural world was a constant for him, from walking in Scotland and Wales to sowing and harvesting on his allotment in Liverpool. When he was given the chance to create a piece of land art at Heligan in Cornwall, he decided to create his renowned OVA symbol in a newly-sown wildflower meadow, and to hold earth-based, community events there throughout the year to celebrate the passing of the seasons.

Always moving forwards, always quick with a contrary opinion, and forever the free-thinker, Jamie was in his later years an integral part of the Florence Institute community enterprise, in Toxteth, Liverpool. Known as the Florrie, this art space–community kitchen–refugee resource represents many of his dearest interests. It is in this human compassion where Jamie's greatest strengths as an artist lay; what he wanted to do more than anything was to encourage others to fulfil their potential. And that's Punk.

Jamie MacGregor Reid is survived by his wife Maria, daughter Rowan and granddaughter Rose.

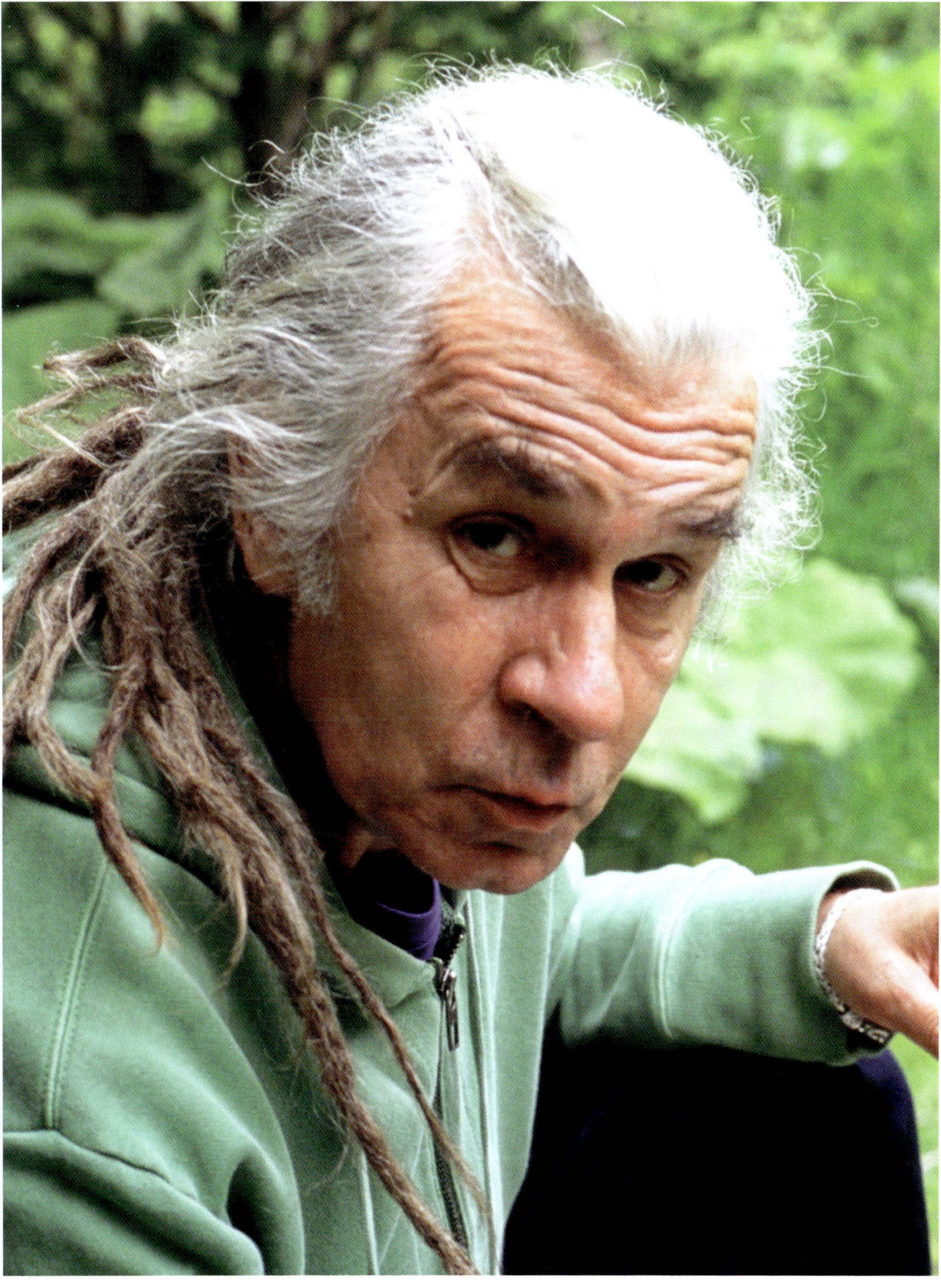

STEPHEN ELLCOCK & JOHN MARCHANT ON JAMIE REID

STEPHEN ELLCOCK

I've always believed that Jamie Reid will come to be regarded as one of the most important and influential figures in British culture of the past fifty to sixty years. People still haven't really come to terms with his extraordinary body of work or with his legacy. His energy, dynamism and uncompromising, unflinching commitment to his art were absolutely remarkable.

The fact that Jamie Reid tends to be synonymous with just one phase of his career – the Sex Pistols – is a deep shame. Punk has had a phenomenal cultural impact, but his legacy is far, far more than that. The work he was doing throughout his career resonates today and in the situation we're facing now, it's increasingly important. His legacy will endure. A comprehensive retrospective of his work would give you the history of British counterculture of the last fifty-five years, from the art school strikes and Situationism, to Punk, to the miners' strikes and rave culture, to sacred-site access and environmentalism. Jamie is an example of an artist who engaged with society with a burning desire to transform it. He made art without compromise. And his work is alchemical and transformative. Jamie was undoubtedly a mage and a seer, following in the illustrious footsteps of many of the greatest artists that these islands have produced.

JOHN MARCHANT

Yes, he was part of the visionary tradition of radical dissent from Wat Tyler onwards, through people such as William Blake and Gerrard Winstanley. Jamie's thing was never just visual; it was always about politically engaged language for the people. In fact, we have a beautiful piece from 1976 in Jamie's Pistols archive that actually states 'we don't care about the music'. Jamie's partner at the time, Sophie Richmond, told me that they wouldn't have got involved with the Pistols if it hadn't been a political movement. The politics was the whole point.

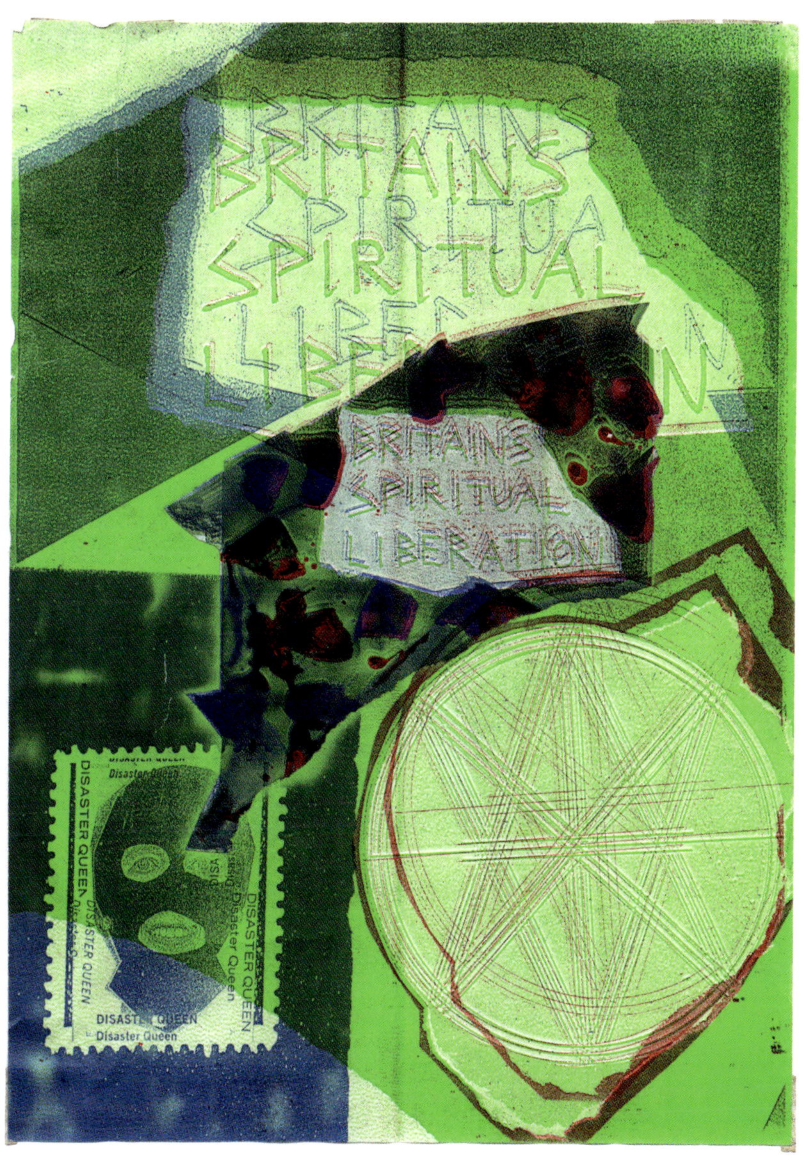

Britain's Spiritual Liberation / 1990

This colour Xerox collage was produced at a time when the then-Prime Minister Margaret Thatcher (for it is she under the mask) was desperately seeking to cling to power, and there was an ongoing struggle for the very identity of the country following years of strife, such as the miners' strikes and the Poll Tax riots. Jamie felt that an embrace of spirituality was needed, as a new direction and a release from the dark Thatcher years.

What is missing nowadays is this kind of social engagement from visionary people. There are a few artists and musicians who are politically engaged, but few have achieved the seismic impact Jamie had, particularly in his work with Malcolm McLaren. Leaving aside the impact of the Sex Pistols' music, Jamie and Malcolm's legacies as pranksters, shape-shifters, provocateurs and iconoclasts are secure and will endure.

Yes, there's no doubt the Sex Pistols stuff overshadows the rest of Jamie's work, but that's only because it's so powerful. If you took out what Jamie achieved in those three years from his career, you'd still have an extremely interesting artist.

Absolutely, the influence of Jamie's agit-prop and Pistols-era work, together with the graphics, texts and ideas arising from fellow Situationist agitators and troublemakers, can still be spotted everywhere today, not just in graphic design or art but in the wider culture. We can, of course, trace a direct line between the Situationists and Jamie's work.

People say all the time how influenced they have been by this work.

It's significant that in his later career Jamie collaborated with people like Shepard Fairey. Personally, the cumulative impact of seeing Situationist-type graphics in the underground press when I was growing up probably changed the course of my life. Many of these relics of '60s and '70s counter-culture, are, in retrospect, deeply problematic, and with the benefit of hindsight can seem incredibly gross. Often the prevailing attitudes were horrendous – sexism and racism were rife – but in terms of graphics, style and attitude, this graphic work had a huge, lasting impact on so many people.

As far as I was concerned, the combined effects of a couple of whiffs of joss sticks and patchouli, being gobsmacked by Hawkwind's *Space Ritual* on multiple occasions at multiple venues, a hidden stash of *Oz*, *It*, *Frendz*, *Black Dwarf*, *Peace News*, *Nasty Tales* etc, a copy of the *Last Whole Earth Catalog* shoplifted from the Japetus bookshop, Birmingham (for which belated apologies), a police truncheon whacking me in the small of the back at the Windsor Free Festival, in 1974, along with many other formative adolescent experiences, virtually guaranteed that I would never pursue the life, goals and aspirations preordained for me… and this was before the events of 1976 and 1977 dashed any remaining ambitions and put paid to any hopes of a steady life and pension plans for good.

One of Jamie's key objectives in life was to remove the scales from people's eyes, and what you're talking about is that very thing. And then empowering people to take things forwards, in their own direction. Punk is often seen as being negative or even nihilistic, but actually it was a very positive agenda. The lyric 'There's no future' implies that the trajectory we're currently on is not good for us as human beings, and we have to change it.

People tend to overlook that and think of the angry, vicious, spitting, inarticulate stereotype. But Punk was empowering.

Jamie stayed in the vein of protest until his dying breath. He was always pushing that forwards; he never tired of it. Although his body gave out in the end, his mind was sharp and full of protest right to the last moment. He had this phrase that he'd trot out quite regularly: 'Who the fuck are the English anyway?' He had all sorts of things to say about the British, about the royal family, about the ruling classes. The class system was something he really thought needed dismantling. It's not unusual to want to root for the underdog and Jamie most definitely did that, but he helped to empower the underdog as well.

He'd be the last person to want to talk about Punk though. Ask him any questions about this and he'd deflect instantly. He'd say, 'Yeah, what we did with Megatripolis was much more important'. The Access to Stones campaign was really important to him, too. People were saying, 'Having access to these places is our right. These sacred sites belong to us; they shouldn't be taken away from us by the government'.

The most significant aspect of British history has been the enclosure of the commons since 1066. We are where we are today because of it, and it has informed everything from the rise of capitalism to the migration of population from the rural to the urban. People were divorced from their past and deliberately made rootless, their insecurity encouraged by divide and rule.

And a thousand years later, it continues to be so; a vast proportion of land in this country is owned by a tiny percentage of people.

The history of British radicalism goes back to the Norman invasion. I can't remember who it was that said that in the 11th and 12th centuries, a group of nobles hired mercenaries to seize the land from the people, rewarded their sycophants and basically seized power and disenfranchised everybody. And that's been the situation ever since. A bunch of thugs took over, mafia basically. And Jamie stands in the tradition of those that have protested against this.

One of the things that came up when I visited the headquarters of the Druid Order to look through their archive for pictures for this book, is the fact that the two most important events of the 18th century, the French Revolution and the American Revolution, were inspired primarily by one person: Tom Paine. And he is in a long line of mystical radicalism, a kind of proto-Druidism with a mystical element. And obviously Blake is a hugely important figure in terms of political radicalism combined with a transcendent vision of universal unity. In terms of the Druids, Jamie's great-uncle shows how they combined a luminous and syncretic vision of nature, pantheistic almost, with political engagement.

Yes, Jamie's great-uncle, George Watson MacGregor Reid, first gained notoriety for agitating on behalf of dock workers in New York and Boston. He got thrown out of the country, returned to England and became an initiate of the Golden Dawn, in the pre-Aleister Crowley era. He was given the name 'MacGregor' by Samuel Liddell MacGregor Mathers as an indicator that he was part of the inner circle. Then he became involved with the Druid Order and was chosen as Chief Druid in 1909. Yet at the same time, he was very interested in politics and stood for Parliament.

George would attract huge crowds to mass rallies on Clapham Common and elsewhere, advocating radical causes and basically stirring up trouble.

He was charismatic enough to draw the crowds. He was very invested in personal empowerment, the social side as well as the spiritual side. He put up striking miners at his house in Clapham in the 1920s. He was a fabulist and told all sorts of extraordinary stories about himself, that he'd walked across the Tibetan steppes, for example. He was also a serial bigamist!

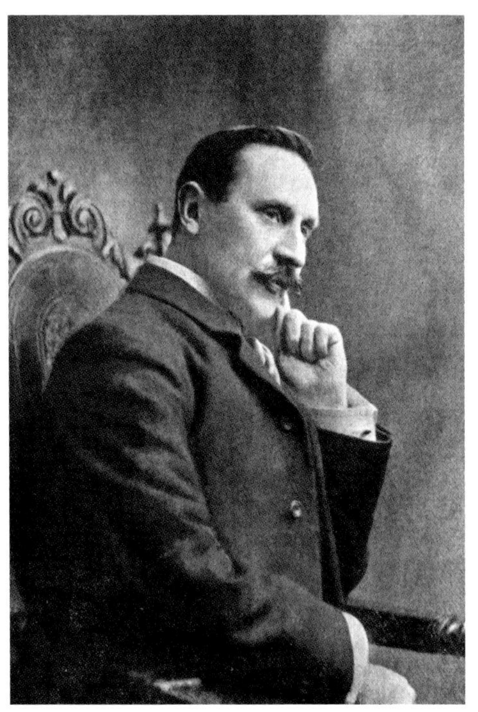

George Watson MacGregor Reid / *c.*1912
Jamie MacGregor Reid's great-uncle, George Watson MacGregor Reid, was an extraordinary man: Chief Druid of the Druid Order, socialist, campaigner, occultist, fabulist, author, publisher, adulterer. His year of birth is unknown (probably around 1860 on the eastern seaboard of Scotland) and his death in 1946 was just months before the birth of his great-nephew Jamie. 'The Old Unc' cast a spell over the family with his interests in the radical empowerment of all peoples. He is pictured (below) at the gates of Stonehenge, demanding entry without paying a fee, as was – he felt – his right, and the right of all. George later annotated this image of himself in white, alongside the straw-boatered private owner of the stones and 'the Servants of Sir Edmund Antrobus', i.e. the police: 'We come to worship according to our faith and you meet us as if to praise God was a crime.'

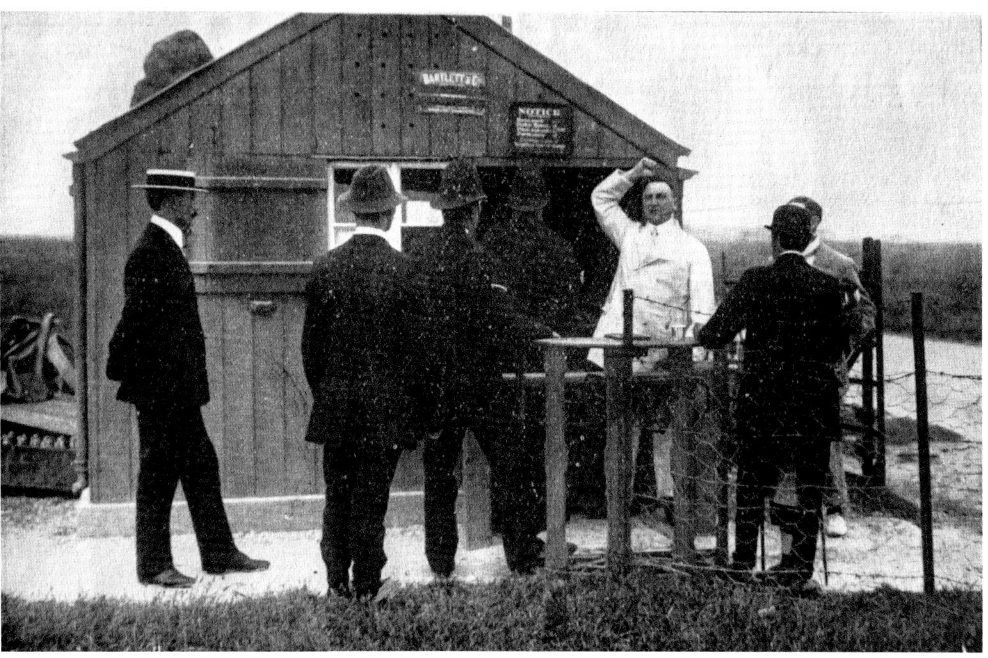

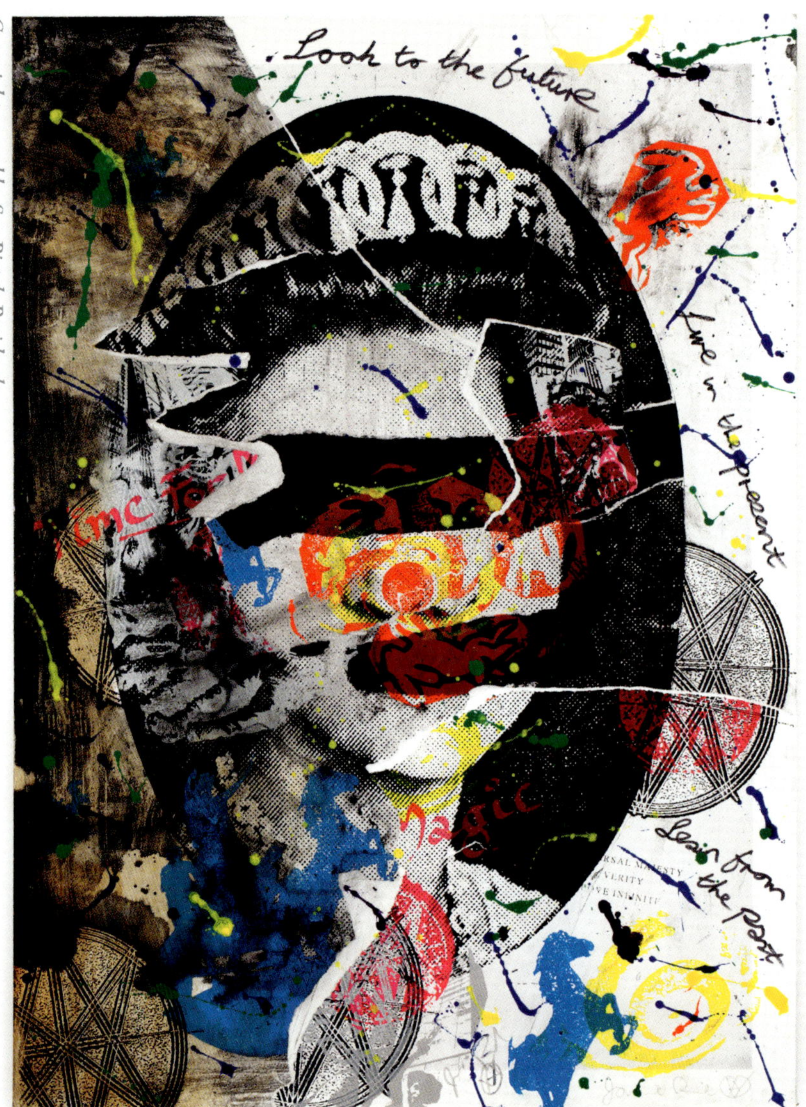

Learn from the Past, Live in the Present, Look to the Future / 2011

Jamie was fond of quoting the statement in this title and essentially lived by it. Here, he has collaged versions of what is arguably his best-known image of Queen Elizabeth II with overprinted designs from what he often considered his most satisfying work – the interior design of the Strongroom recording studios in Shoreditch, London. Also present are a hare, both a symbol of free thinking and a 'familiar' of artist and ecological campaigner Joseph Beuys, as well as Boudica in her chariot, shaking her spear in defiance of Empire, Jamie's OVA symbol (see also page 61) and a portion of the phrase 'Time For Magic'.

Wasn't he an early advocate of things like yoga and vegetarianism?

Yes. George was also one for encouraging people to trespass, where appropriate. In the 1920s, Stonehenge was privately owned. George encouraged storming of fences to gain access to the stones, much to the landowner's chagrin, and the police would show up. There would be scuffles, and George would be there, cursing the police. George was a huge figure in the Reid family. Jack, Jamie's father, had been raised by George. The story is that Jack's father died of wounds sustained running guns for the Chinese during the Boxer Rebellion. Another story is that George may actually have been Jamie's grandfather rather than his great-uncle. Who knows? He died not long before Jamie was born.

So this is the very interesting soup that Jamie grew up in. The family was very involved with the Campaign for Nuclear Disarmament (CND) and, as a child, Jamie was taken on the Aldermaston marches. These two strands of politics and spirituality are important because these are also two aspects of his artwork. Most people struggle to combine them, but when politics and spirituality come together, you get something seismic.

Yes, you do. That's what I was trying to do when I was going through Jamie's vast archive to select images for this book, and I hope we've succeeded in fusing those two strands.

So we started with this body of work that Jamie created around the eight festivals of the Wheel of the Year. Jamie was involved with the Order of Bards, Ovates and Druids, and was very good friends with Philip Carr-Gomm, who was then Chief Druid and who has written about the Wheel of the Year for this book. Jamie observed the Eightfold Year himself. He had an allotment right on the banks of the Mersey, and his principal activity there was watching; he would just watch the birds and observe the seasons turn. There was a group of people on the allotment site who followed the Eightfold Year and they would all hold rituals together. Jamie would provide a lot of hangings, and they would make a ritual space and celebrate the festivals of the Wheel of the Year as a group.

Some years ago, Jamie put out a small book called *Eight Fold Year*, which included paintings to illustrate the eight important festivals of the year – the two solstices, the two equinoxes and the four cross-quarter celebrations of Imbolc, Beltane, Lughnasadh and Samhain. We decided to expand it for this new edition and bring in a much wider body of work, including his earlier work from different eras and also pieces from a series of 365 postcard-sized paintings, one for each day of the year.

In selecting the images for this book, I wanted to emphasise the continuity and integrity of Jamie's work and to highlight how his work evolves organically over the years; there is a direct line that can be traced from his early art school days to the Eightfold Year paintings of his later years. His work is a continuum, with all the essential elements, obsessions, recurring motifs present throughout the decades. The style and vocabulary may change but the essential message remains the same.

I think it's an absolute disgrace that no mainstream publisher has published a book of Jamie's work since *Up They Rise*, almost forty years ago, although he is one of the most important artists and cultural figures of the last few decades. There are currently no books available that encompass his entire career. I wanted to try to do justice to that, and instead of just chucking things together, there was this great structure of the Eightfold Year to play with.

Once I'd gone through hundreds and hundreds of images, a sequence and a natural order revealed themselves and certain images seemed to fit naturally into certain phases of the year. There is a thread that runs through Jamie's work. His paintings of the days of the year don't contain text and they're not overtly political, but they offer a transcendent vision of life, of the natural world, that is, in itself, political.

That was part of the driving force behind the project we started at the Lost Gardens of Heligan in Cornwall, where we installed Jamie's OVA symbol, 100 metres in diameter, in a field, surrounded by seeds that grew into wildflowers. We wanted to fuse politics and the natural world. Jamie was deeply concerned about the disengagement of people from nature, which is not only problematic for the natural world but also for us as human beings, because we're part of nature and we don't realise it. He liked observing the Wheel of the Year because it makes you cognisant that the year is turning. As soon as you celebrate one festival, then six weeks later there's another one coming up, and you become much more aware of nature changing through the year.

I think that the Heligan Project is absolutely extraordinary. It's beautiful in its simplicity, but it's also something that I can imagine

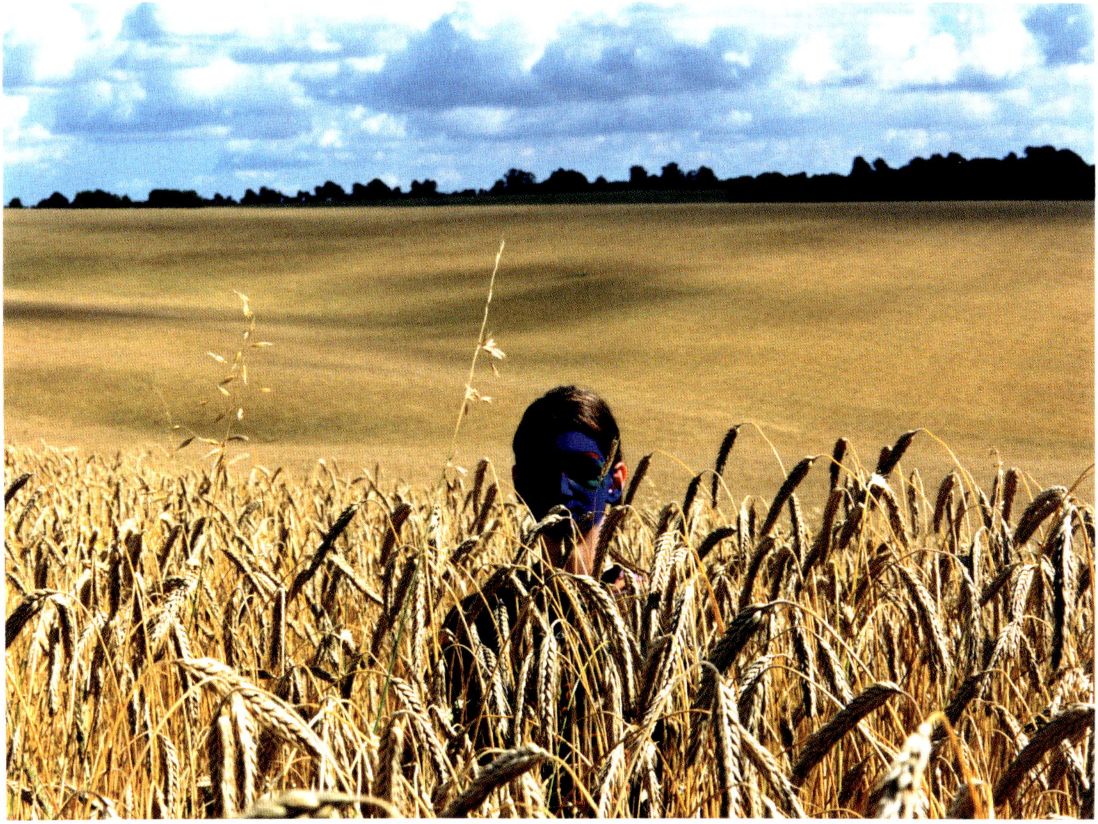

Modern Woad / 1990s

NOTE ON THE EIGHTFOLD YEAR ARTWORK

Jamie painted hundreds of postcard-size images linked to the seasons of the Eightfold Year. Many of these can be found in their relevant chapter, all untitled and undated. He also did a series of eight titled larger paintings – Winter Solstice, Imbolc, Spring Equinox, Beltane, Summer Solstice, Lughnasadh, Autumn Equinox and Samhain – which can be found on pages 38, 56–7, 92, 116, 122–3, 144–5, 184 and 203.

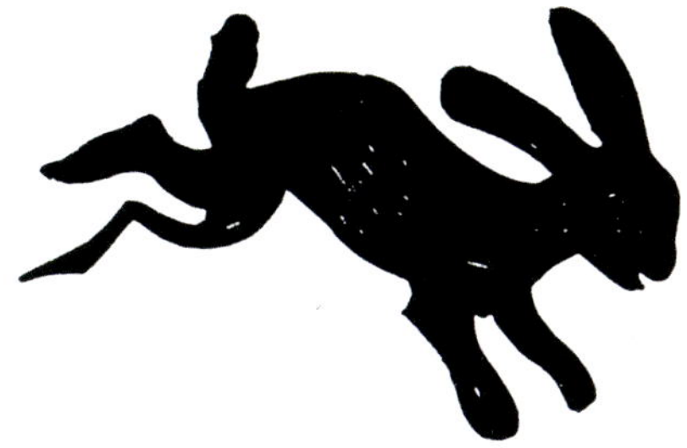

anyone would appreciate, be they a National Trust garden visitor or an environmental activist. Whoever they are, they're going to find it beautiful and moving. It's one of the most extraordinary works of conceptual art that I think I've seen in recent years, on a par with the great works of land art like Robert Smithson's *Spiral Jetty* or Nancy Holt's *Sun Tunnels*.

Jamie was offered a wildflower meadow at Heligan to do something in and, very quickly, we came to the idea of installing the OVA shape with the tip of the A, for Anarchy, pointing north.

And that was the emblem that appeared again and again in his work. Can I just clarify, does it also directly reference the CND symbol?

It didn't directly reference CND but there was a connection to it. In the OVA, there's a circle for compassion, an A for Anarchy and a V for Victory. Like the CND emblem, Jamie's OVA is supposed to be something simple and easily recognisable that could go on the back of a jacket or on a badge. If you extend the horizontal line of the A to the circle, which Jamie did in earlier versions, you have the eight points of the Wheel of the Year.

The tip of the A, pointing due north, is where we celebrated the Summer Solstice at the Lost Gardens of Heligan. In 2022–23, we went round the eight festivals of the year, doing an event on each date. Jamie wasn't well enough by then to attend, sadly.

Is it intended as a permanent addition to the landscape of Heligan?

It was supposed to be a one-year project but we extended it into a second year, switching from wildflowers to Emmer wheat, which is a heritage wheat that needs no fertilisers and no herbicides. So that was scoring a point against agribusiness. The wheat was harvested and ground for bread. And I've been talking to people in Croydon about redoing it there. If they give us the land, we'll do it.

A great example of Jamie's legacy of political engagement is his work with the Florrie, in Liverpool. It's such an inspiring place.

Yes! Jamie had been a resident of Liverpool since the '80s. The Florence Institute (now known as the Florrie) was originally a Victorian social club for boys but had burned down and was just an abandoned shell. Jamie was integral in its restoration as a community centre, offering support in terms of publicity and funds. They'd asked Jamie if they could do an exhibition of his prints in the community centre. We went to have a meeting and I remember turning to Jamie and whispering in his ear, 'Why don't we do a full retrospective here instead?' Instantly Jamie said, 'Yeah, let's do it.' So we brought the whole archive to the Florrie and installed this big retrospective in 2016 called *Casting Seeds*. Every invitation had a little wildflower seed packet attached. I think they had something like 10,000 visitors to that show in just four weeks.

I know that art was reinstated as a subject in one of the local schools as a result of that exhibition. And it cemented Jamie's relationship with the Florrie. He got a studio there, and he would go two or three times a week just to be there, talking to people, being part of the fabric of the place. They really looked after him and he really gave a lot to them too, helping with fundraising and raising the profile.

Jamie was always happy to support a protest movement, whatever it was. Actually, his very first published work was in *Sanity*, which was the CND paper. And he was particularly happy to be involved with the Occupy movement in London. He did a big piece of artwork which was used as a fundraiser for them, and, later, he did another fundraiser for Extinction Rebellion.

I think it's probably important to mention how the book changed because of Jamie's death.

He didn't fiddle with it!

I think I became more conscious of just how necessary this book could be, and of the need of creating something that could stand as a fitting tribute to Jamie's life and legacy.

We started working on this book when Jamie was still with us and I'm sure he would be thrilled with it. Maybe we shouldn't say this, but Jamie did often moan about things that upset him, usually corrupt politicians, certain artists (not naming names) or his beloved Fulham FC not winning. But I think he would be really pleased with this. He always wanted people to see his paintings and understand he wasn't just about the Pistols.

We've given people the opportunity to see the vast corpus of Jamie's work. To me, that's hugely important. Most people won't have seen most of this stuff before. Obviously we've included images from the Sex Pistols era, but that's a tiny part of the book.

And it's still only part of the story. There's still much to be told. I think this book is going to open up this huge body of work to people. Jamie was ahead of his time and it's all there waiting to be discovered.

And when you see it, his work is transformative. The paintings he did inside the Strongroom recording studios, in Shoreditch, in the late '80s are extraordinary – a complete immersive environment. They're incredible. But no one gets to see them. They should be open to the public on some days.

He was really proud of his installation work at the Strongroom Studios. He would say, 'People always want to talk about the Pistols, but the Strongroom is the most important thing I did'. He was also immensely proud of his official role as artist for Afro Celt Sound System, which was born from a meeting between Baaba Maal, musician Simon Emmerson and Jamie at Strongroom.

I think underlying the title of this book – *Time for Magic* – is the idea that there's potential for change. And that's key to Jamie, really. The idea that things can be different – more beautiful.

More just.

Yeah. More nurturing, more harmonious. I think that's the essence of it: there's always time for magic.

Time for Magic should be seen as a visual manifesto for a better world, an antidote to complacency and nihilism, a call to action and an instruction manual for the re-enchantment of the planet.

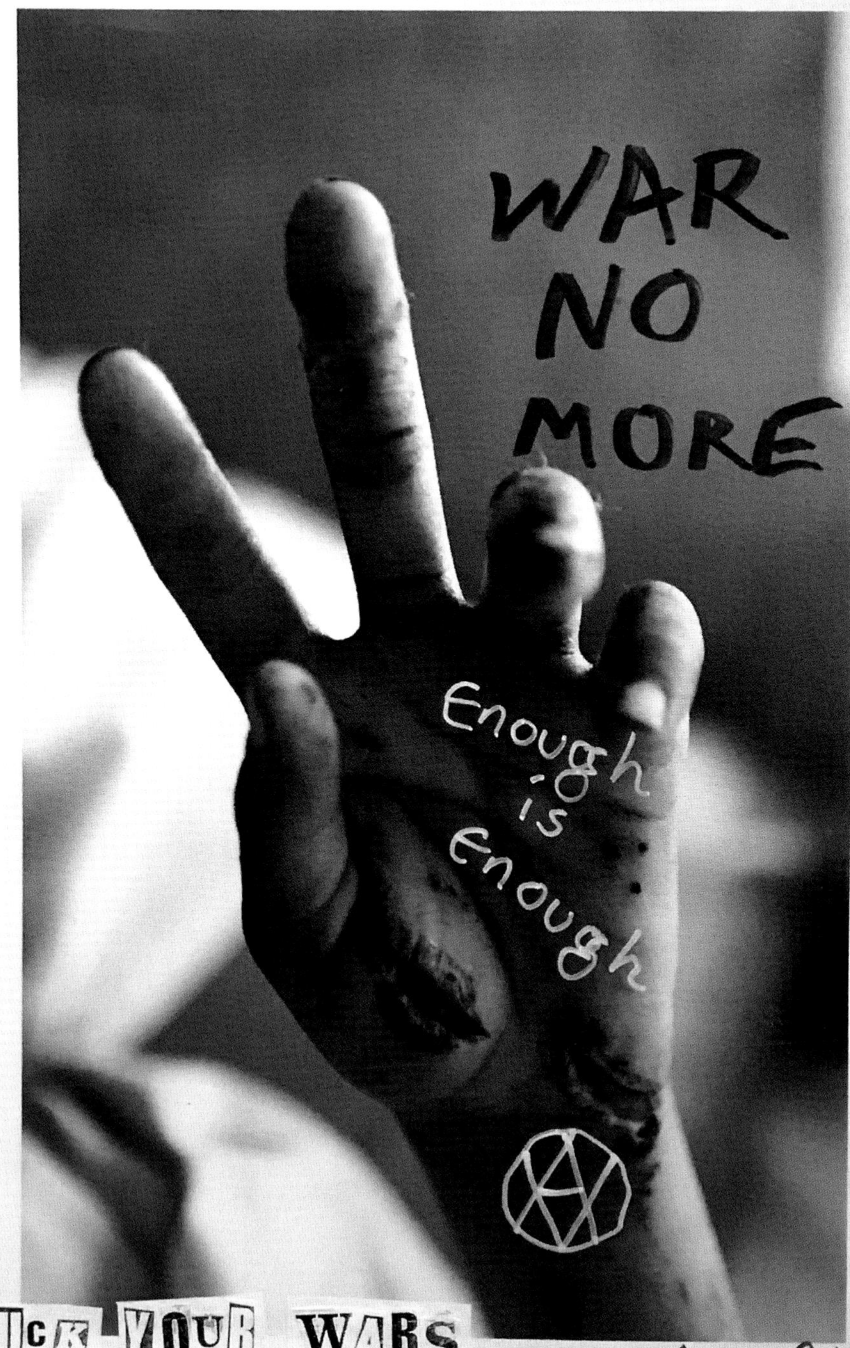

Enough Is Enough/Fuck Your Wars / 2019

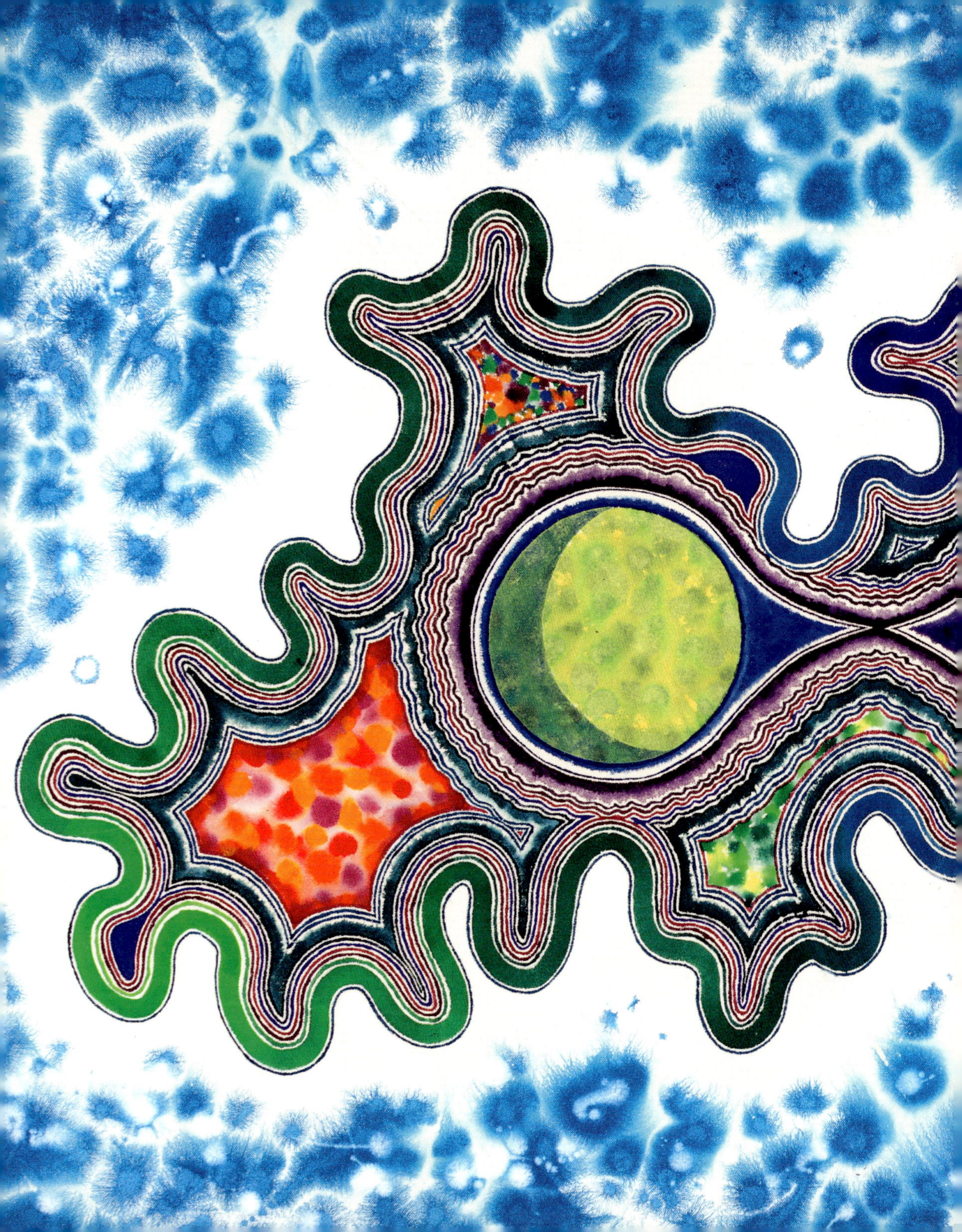

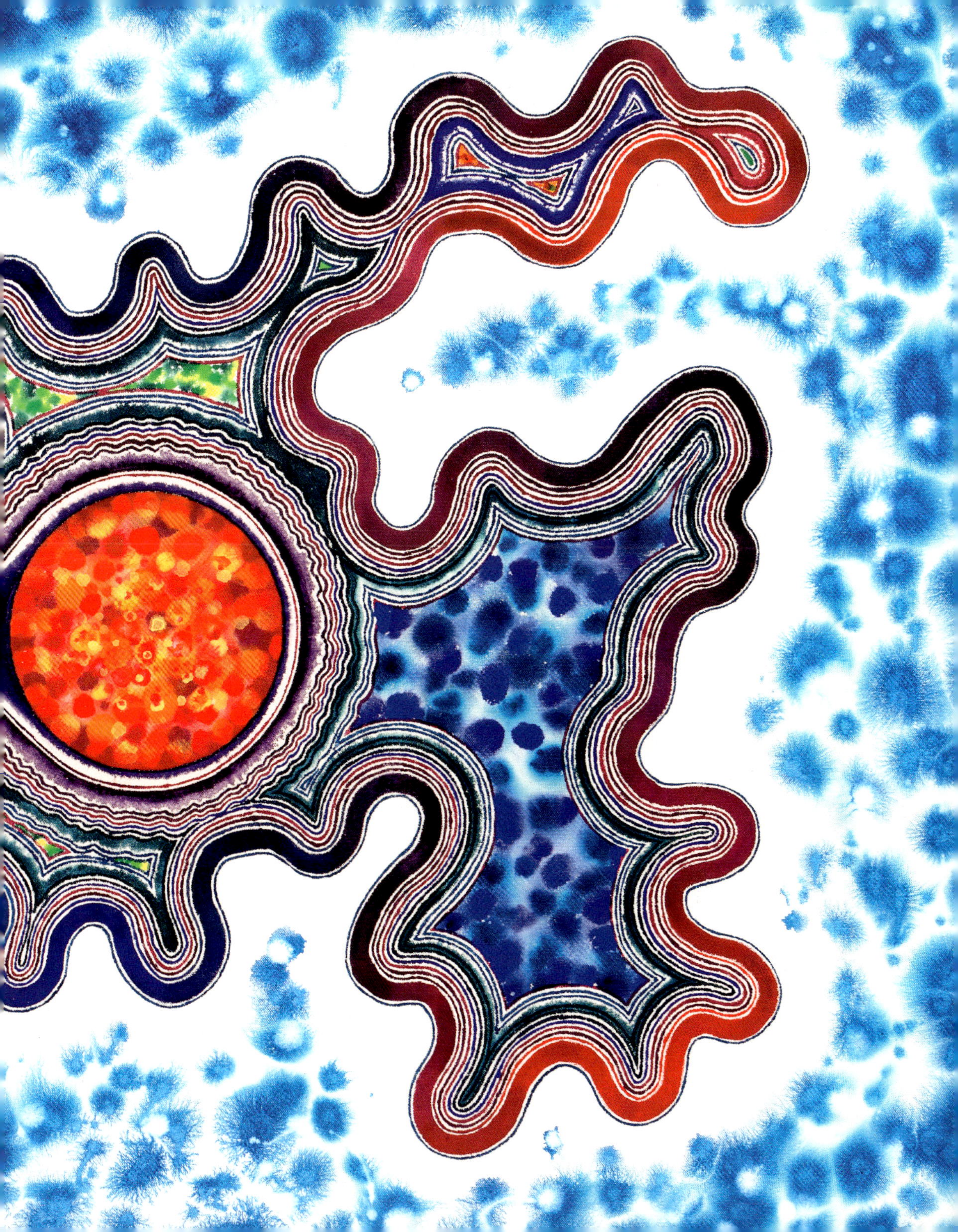

THE EIGHTFOLD WHEEL OF THE YEAR

PHILIP CARR-GOMM

Time for magic! It's all around us: we exist in a dancing world of colour, movement and change. But pause to observe this kaleidoscope, and a pattern starts to form: a Catherine wheel with eight spokes. Spring, summer, autumn, winter, and the times in-between, around and around they go: everything going in circles all the time. The earth spinning both on its own axis and around the sun. The sun herself spinning, and the galaxy turning endlessly.

We dance and spin around this wheel, around this cycle of the seasons and the cycle of our own lives. Sometimes it can feel like we spin around too much, but the whirling dervishes of Sufi tradition find deep peace and stillness – the Source of all Being – by spinning around and around in their dances. Maybe going around in circles holds a secret or two.

Magicians cast a circle to work their magic, and modern Pagans, witches and Druids celebrate their rites in circles. Central to their practice is a cycle of worship and celebration that is also depicted as a circle: the Eightfold Wheel of the Year. This way of working spiritually, of celebrating eight festivals around the year, is rooted in the distant past and yet it only came into being in its modern form quite recently: in the middle of the 20th century, when a witch and a Druid began exploring the relevance of the old ways for a society ravaged by two world wars. Gerald Gardner, who initiated the birth of modern witchcraft, and Ross Nichols, who founded the Order of Bards, Ovates and Druids, probably began by talking about the solstices and equinoxes that they already celebrated as members of the Ancient Druid Order, which held ceremonies for the Summer Solstice at Stonehenge and for the equinoxes at Tower Hill and Primrose Hill, in London.

They would then have explored the folklore and history associated with the cross-quarter festivals of Imbolc, Beltane, Lughnasadh and Samhain, which came to be known as the Celtic Fire Festivals. With the help of two inspiring women – the witch Doreen Valiente and the Druid Vera Chapman – they introduced

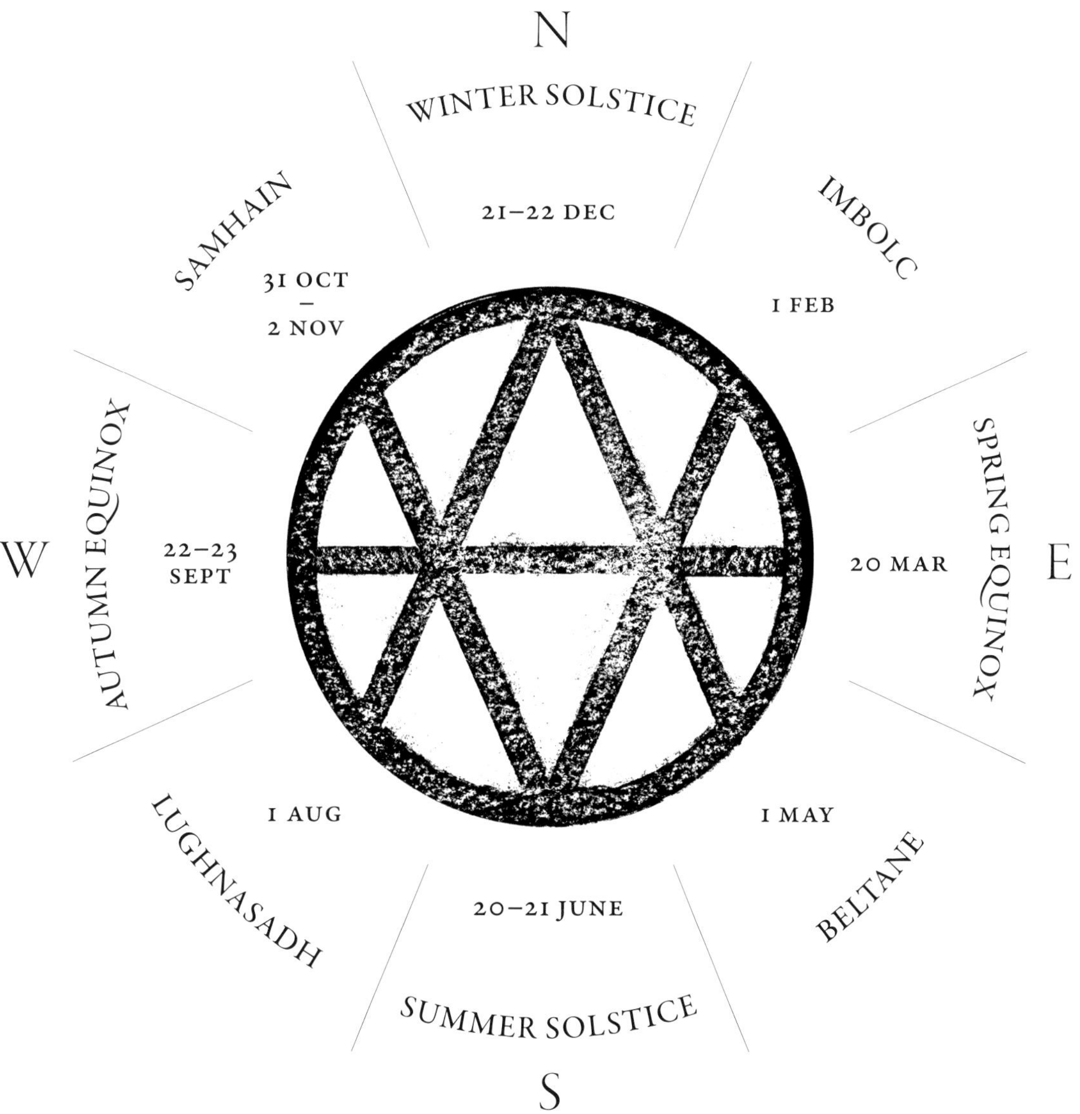

The Wheel of the Year
The Druidic Wheel of the Year, also known as the Eightfold Year, includes eight festivals: the two solstices, two equinoxes and four Celtic cross-quarter festivals of Imbolc, Beltane, Lughnasadh and Samhain. Each festival has its own character and energy, and is observed in its own way. Following the ever-turning Wheel of the Year, you are never more than six weeks away from a celebration.

rituals to mark these times, and, in doing so, managed to enrich the fourfold scheme of solstices and equinoxes to offer a celebration every six weeks or so, creating a ritual cycle rooted in heritage and tradition that soon came to be known as the Eightfold Wheel of the Year.

And that's how the Druids, witches and Pagans began to celebrate this cycle in the modern era, drawing on folklore and tradition to devise ceremonies that honoured these particular moments in the turning of the year.

Up until the 1990s these celebrations were confined to the fringes of mainstream culture. From the '60s onwards, in addition to Druids and Wiccans, you could find some hippies involved, and festival-goers loved the Druids' Summer Solstice ceremonies at Stonehenge. But the numbers of people who actually followed the eightfold cycle numbered in their hundreds, not thousands. This started to change as the 20th century drew to a close. The urgency of the environmental crisis had started to become clear, at least to those with their ears and eyes open. The forecasts of the Club of Rome's report *The Limits to Growth*, published in 1972, had been largely ignored, but, by 1990, with the continuing pressure of environmental groups, the outrage caused by the 1989 Exxon Valdez oil spill and fires burning out of control in US parks, such as Yosemite, it was becoming harder to avoid the conclusion that we were in serious trouble. One consequence of this changing awareness was a turning towards the earth with an increased sense of reverence and care, as more and more people realised how much we were abusing her.

Honouring the seasons, demonstrating our love for the earth and trying to get back in touch with her cycles was no longer the concern of a few eccentrics. An interest in the folklore, history and celebration of the seasonal festivals spilled into the mainstream. In the US, the Burning Man festival that attracts thousands each year was started as a Summer Solstice ritual in San Francisco. In the UK, thousands gathered for the solstices and equinoxes at Stonehenge, for the Beltane celebrations at Calton Hill, Edinburgh, and for Imbolc in places like Marsden, West Yorkshire. The BBC began offering poems for the solstice; and the AA guide to coastal walks suggested good places to watch the solstice sunrises.

But, even if celebrating some, or all, of the Eightfold Wheel of the Year has been becoming more popular, is this of any real use as we hurtle towards our potential destruction through ecological collapse?

The eco-crisis is so massive and serious that we need to find its root causes. Why did we start it, and how can we stop it?

No one would consciously try to destroy their species and the world, so how is it that we now find ourselves on the path to doing so? We must have got here unconsciously, by believing and behaving as if we were separate from nature, as if everything were not connected. This belief has resulted in the runaway greed and exploitation that has led us to this catastrophic point in our evolution.

If this is the cause of the problem, the first remedy must be to consciously attempt to free ourselves from this belief and become aware, instead, of being part of the web of life that holds every living being together. Hence the need for practices like celebrating the seasonal cycle, to weave our awareness back into the fabric of nature.

Since observing the festivals invites us to come together and physically enact ritual, we engage not just our minds and hearts but our bodies too. This may feel like no big deal. After all, what difference can us becoming more attuned to nature make to the insane mess that we're living through?

For every one of us who heals our sense of separation, of disconnection from the natural world, it is going to make a difference: to us, and to those around us. And from a sense of care and connection to the earth, we can start to act differently. Observing the Eightfold Wheel can act as an encouragement and as a channel for this. Druid Dana O'Driscoll's *Sacred Actions: Living the Wheel of the Year through Earth-Centered Sustainable Practices* promotes an integration of the spiritual and social value of seasonal celebrations with specific actions we can take. She suggests practices related to each festival that work with these qualities: at the Winter Solstice, restoration; at Imbolc, re-skilling; at the Spring Equinox, resilience; at Beltane, regeneration; at the Summer Solstice, re-visioning; at Lughnasadh, reverence; at the Autumn Equinox, receptivity; and at Samhain, release. The eightfold scheme is used to foster a renewed sense of connection to nature and a greater engagement with sustainable living.

In addition to the environmental crisis, we are also living through a mental health crisis. Connecting to nature, having a religious worldview or sense of spiritual meaning, and feeling part of a community have all been shown to have a positive effect on mental health. And celebrating the seasonal festivals supports all three of these things. Although you can celebrate the eight festivals on your own, there is an implicit invitation in the Wheel

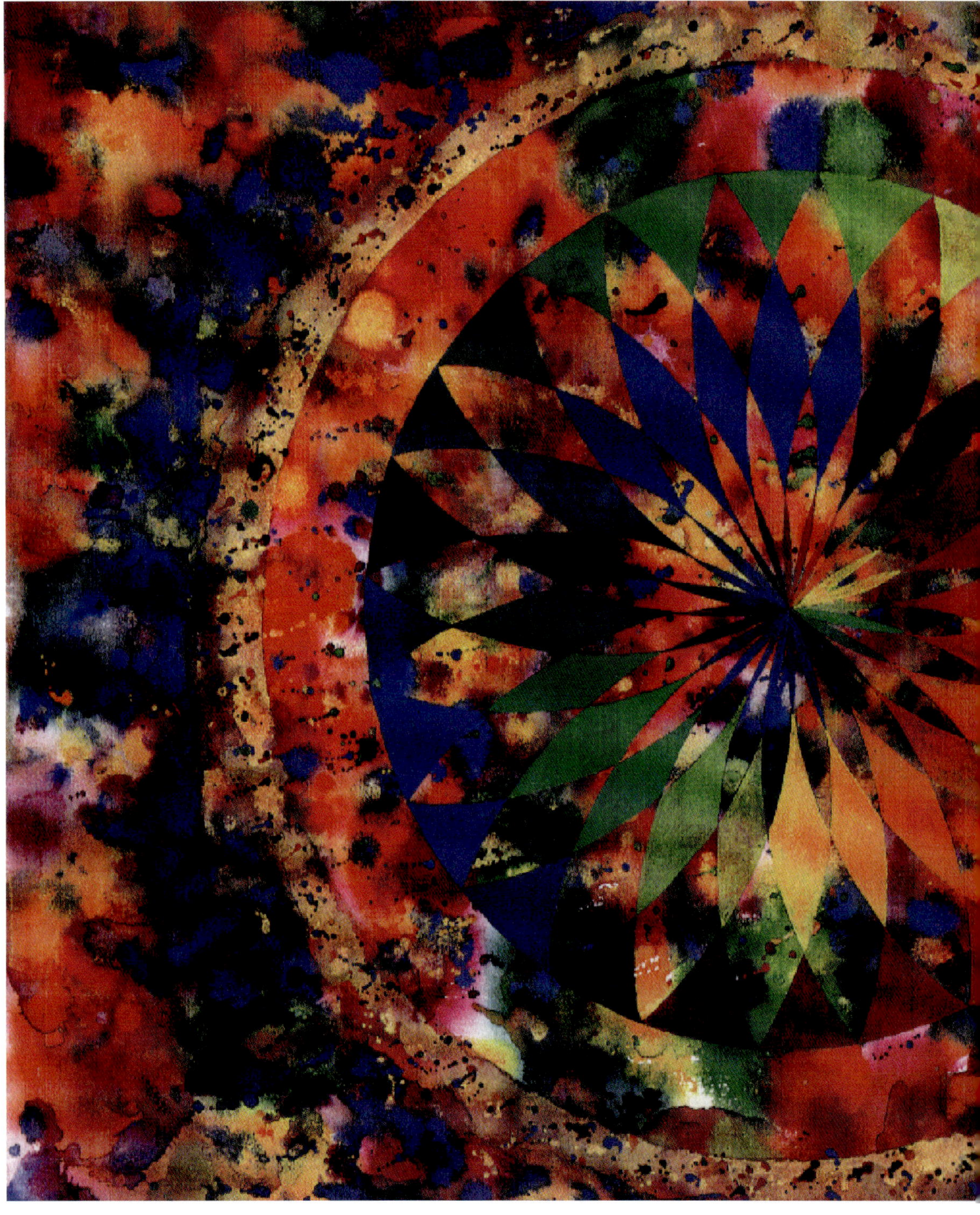

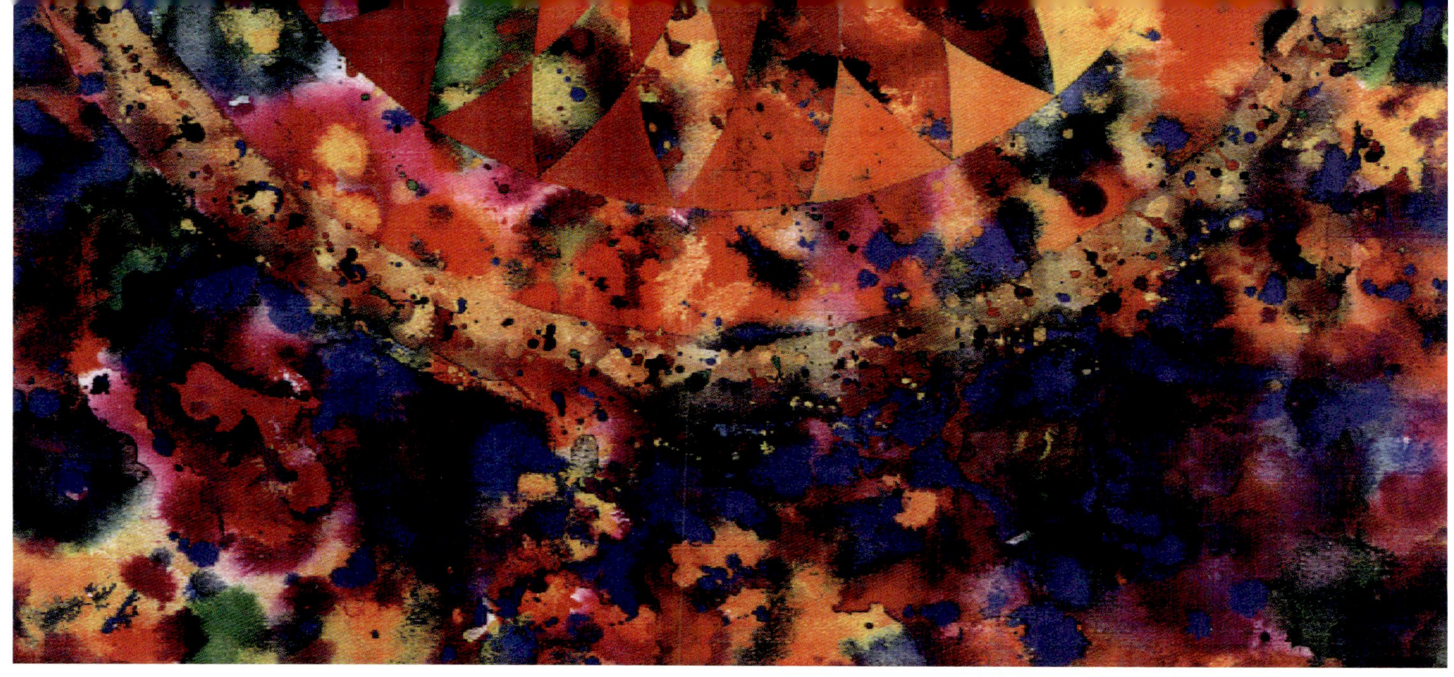

to bring people together. Whenever we think of celebrating the Summer Solstice, for example, we think of people coming together – gathering in special places: on hilltops, in stone circles.

Attuning to the Wheel not only brings more connection to nature and community, it can also help to deepen our sense of connection to whatever you want to call deity – the Divine, Goddess, Spirit. The eightfold cycle doesn't just connect you to the pageant of the changing seasons as we cycle around the year. At the heart of the celebration of the turning of the year is an invitation to go deep and to connect with Source – with the still centre of Being – like the whirling dervish who finds stillness as she spins.

You start off thinking you're tied to this wheel. You celebrate these festivals every year. Around and around you go, year after year, until something gets you off the wheel – a car accident, illness, old age, whatever it is. But here's the secret – it's the one spoken about by the Daoists, who say: 'When yin peaks, it turns to yang, and when yang peaks, it turns to yin.' Within the heart of everything lies its opposite. Within the discipline of celebrating the festivals lies freedom. In following this cycle, in attuning to the rhythms of nature, in going around and around, each time you're actually being invited to move towards the still centre: to open up to the changeless within change, to the timeless within time.

The invitation is to find freedom in limitation: freedom in the commitment to stop eight times a year, to be mindful, to open up to where you are, to what's happening in the landscape, and in your heart. To tune in and take notice of the changing world, and at the same time, to open to the changeless within you.

And one of the great things about celebrating the Wheel is this: it isn't just about you. It's like dancing with the whole tribe to celebrate the wonder and the strangeness of life. When you jump over the Beltane fire or light the central candle in your Winter Solstice ritual, you're doing this in the company of friends, and in the company of ancestors and future generations. You're celebrating a moment, but also a rhythm, a continuity.

As Chief of the Druid Order, Jamie Reid's great-uncle, George Watson MacGregor Reid, was the first whose solstice ceremonies at Stonehenge were reported in the newspapers. And Jamie then carried on the tradition by celebrating the festivals with his art – inviting us all to join in. He understood the radical, political implications of following the wheel.

It's time for magic.

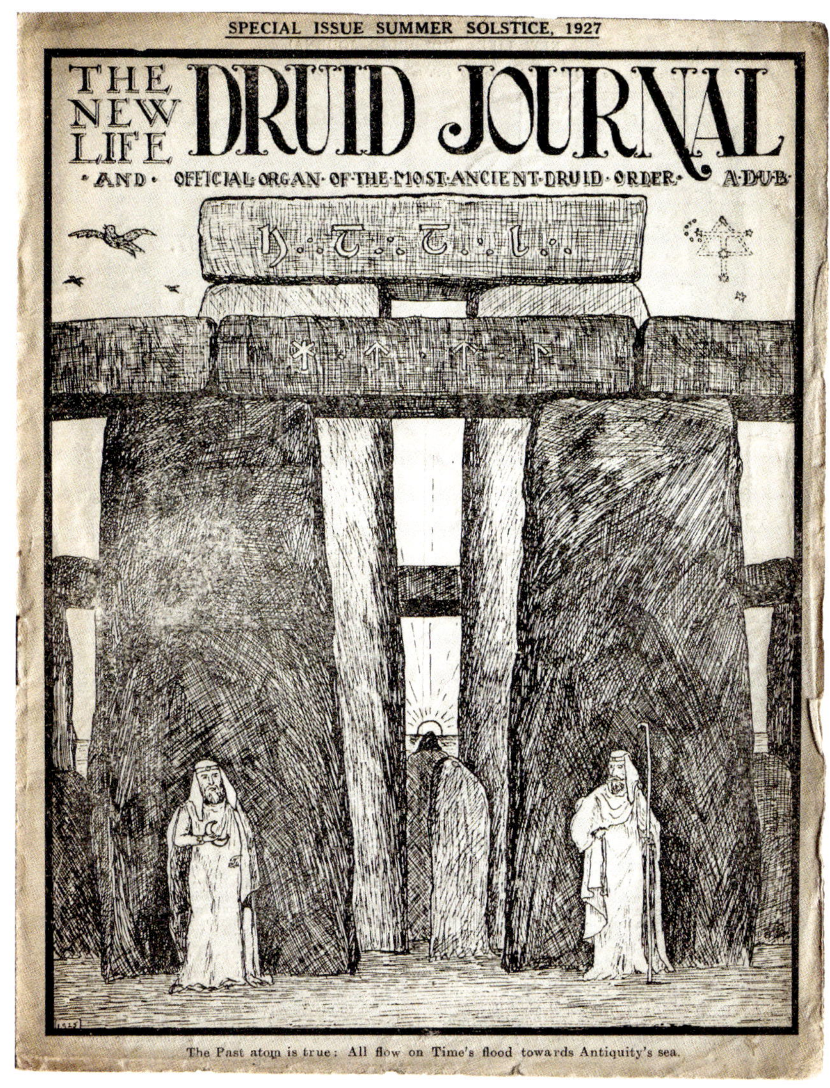
SPECIAL ISSUE SUMMER SOLSTICE, 1927

THE NEW LIFE

DRUID JOURNAL

AND · OFFICIAL ORGAN · OF THE · MOST ANCIENT · DRUID · ORDER · A·DUB·

The Past atom is true: All flow on Time's flood towards Antiquity's sea.

The New Life and the Druid Journal / 1927
A special combined edition of George Watson MacGregor Reid's publications *The New Life* and *The Druid Journal*, produced to celebrate Summer Solstice in 1927. The cover illustration may be by George's son, Robert, who took over as Chief of the Druid Order in 1946. There are pronounced stylistic similarities with another illustration known to be by Robert – and, curiously, also with Jamie's drawing hand.

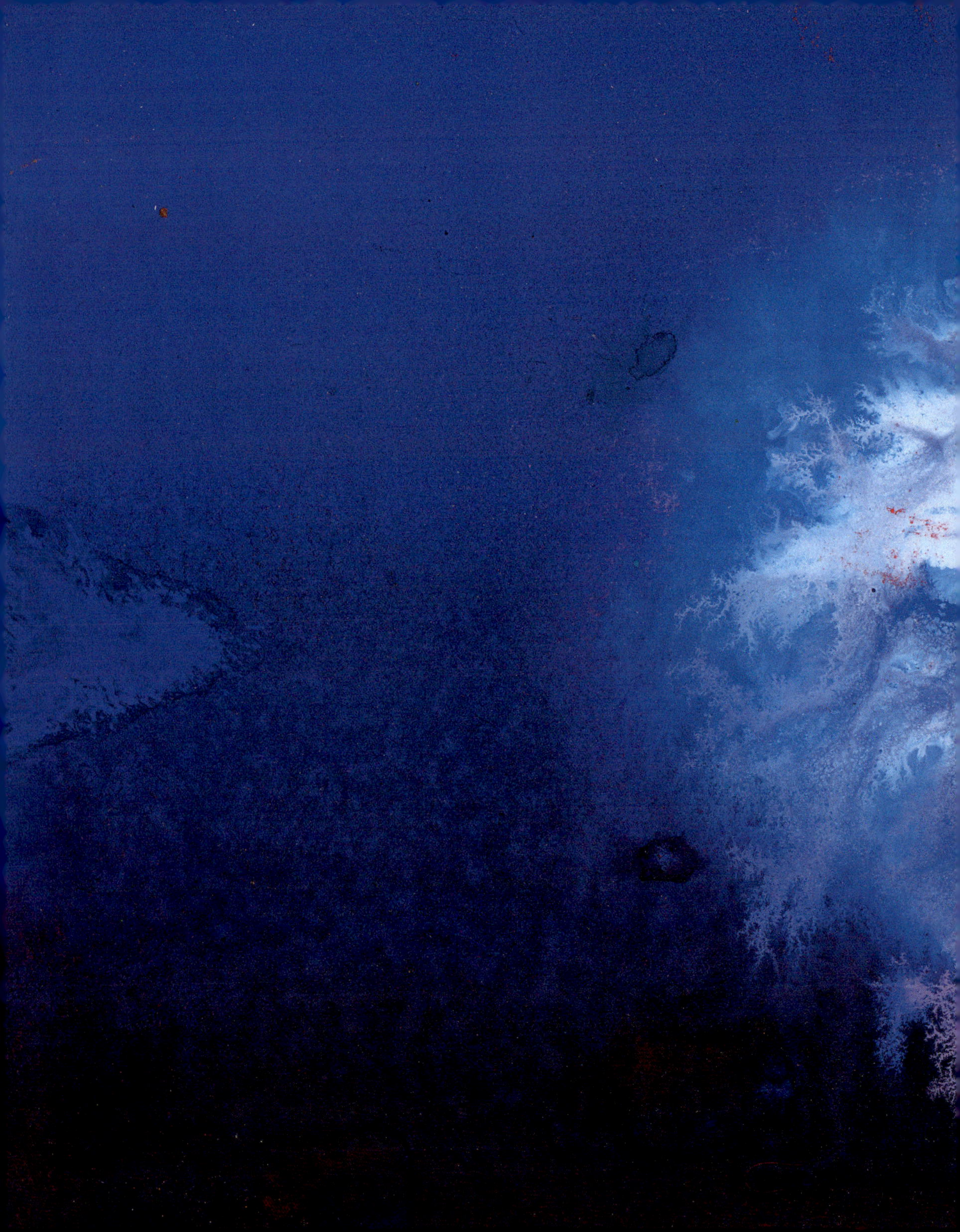

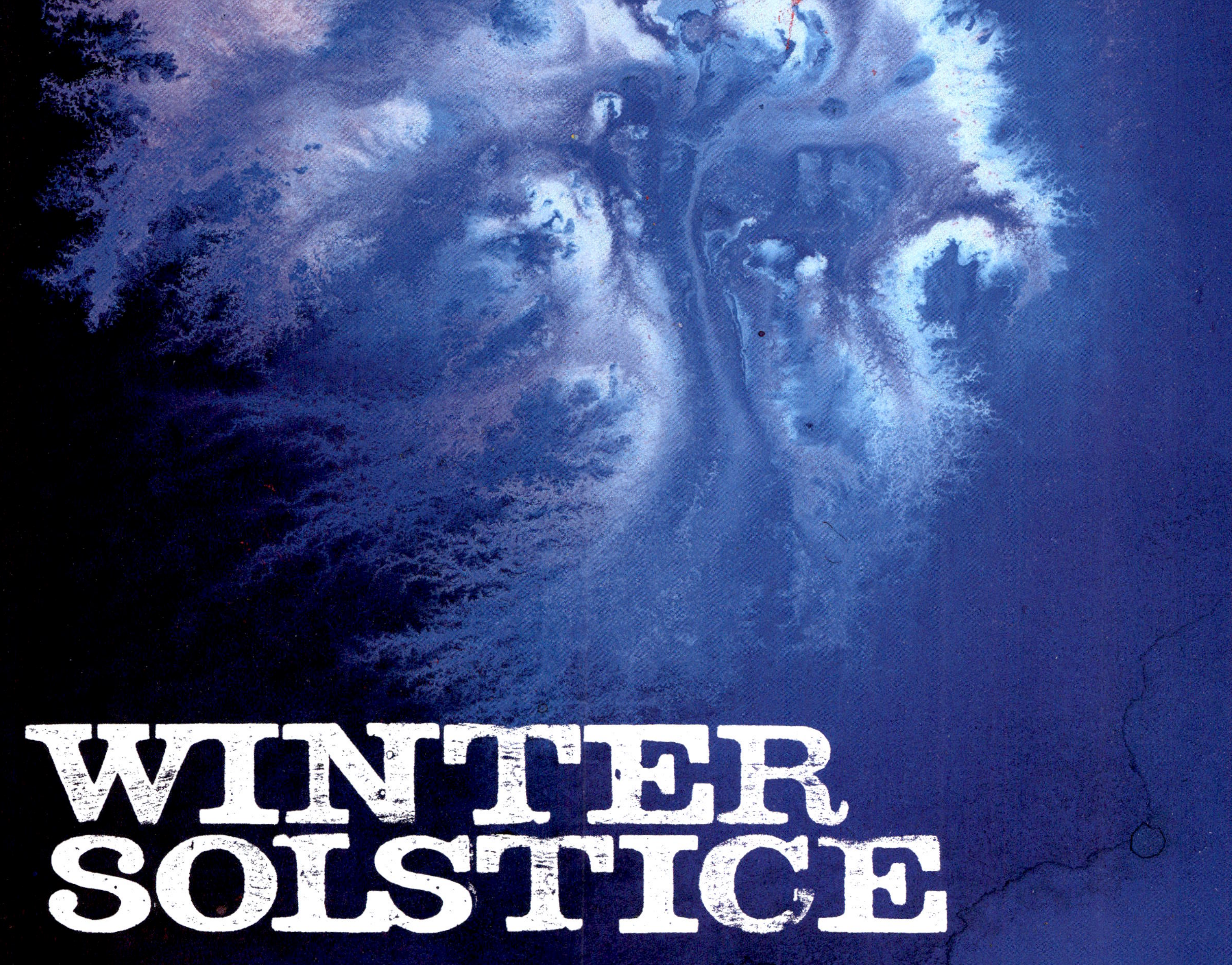
WINTER
SOLSTICE

WINTER SO

It's dark and cold and miserable. The Wheel of the Year is stuck in the mud, and the idea of it helping us change seems impossible. How can anything want to grow or move at this time of year? How can any change come? Nothing is going anywhere.

But then, at the darkest moment, when the Earth is tilted at its further point away from the Sun, something pulls, and it's the pull of the New Year. Not the New Year of the Romans' Julian calendar, but the real astronomical New Year. It's quintillions of tons of molten rock hurtling through space at 483,000 miles an hour that's pulling and saying: 'Wake up! A new year is beginning. You thought it was the end. But we've only just started. Again.'

And so the Druids, witches and Wiccans, the shamans and Pagans light their candles and their bonfires and welcome the rebirth of sunlight in the world. The days are going to get longer now. That was just the darkest night before the dawn. In the meantime, although many hate this season, we can love it too, and embrace this time of resting, letting go, sinking down, allowing the new ideas to come.

Winter Solstice is associated with the fostering power of darkness, the star-spangled night sky, and with neither age nor youth. We are suspended in time, preparing for rebirth. Maybe it's the real you who emerges now; the smiling public front you put on in spring and summer has fallen like autumn leaves, and you are bare in the ground, like a seedpod. Now is a time of clarity and simplicity. In the night sky, the bright Pole Star reminds us that we can continue to steer true, however lost we may feel.

This moment of dawning light is a celebratory one. No wonder prehistoric people built monuments to honour the midwinter sun, its piercing ray reaching deep into the heart of immense stone burial chambers: Maeshowe in Orkney; Newgrange and Knowth in Ireland. Places to reinspirit the bones of the ancestors. We can imagine initiates staggering reborn out of the earth, enlivened with the visions they'd experienced in these stone wombs. At Stonehenge, the sarsen stones are aligned so that the setting of the midwinter sun could be watched from inside the circle through the pillars of the Great Trilithon, and feasting took place at nearby Durrington Walls at this time.

Later, the Romans observed the festivals of Sol Invictus and Saturnalia in late December, and then, later still, Christmas took over; certain traditions that may have roots in ancient times, such as hanging up mistletoe ('all-heal') to kiss under, and burning a Yule log, remain with us today. The practice of wassailing, which involved toasting good health by drinking from a communal cup, or was carried out as an orchard-blessing ritual, has been revived and is enthusiastically practised by many today; and mummers' plays are once again being performed at midwinter.

Try sitting in darkness in a solstice ceremony and lighting a candle in the centre of the circle. It represents the birth of the year, the birth of the sun-child, the beginning of the 'revolution towards all things good', as old Archdruid MacGregor Reid once wrote. And then let's each of us take a candle of our own and light it from the central candle, so we all have our own light as we sit together around the mother light, the sun. Nothing to do but be together here, feeling the pull of the tide towards the summer, towards doing and being in the world.

This solstice dawn doesn't mean energetically plunging into life. The winter world is still a sleepy place, the light of the sun weak, though growing stronger every day. You can carry on dreaming, waiting for the next turn of the Wheel. If Winter Solstice is when your spirit is reborn, it is the next festival, Imbolc, that will wake you up properly and push you out into the world.

NOTES FROM HELIGAN

'A cold, misty morning. At sunrise, torches were placed and lit on all eight points of the OVA, and a brazier was set in the middle. Torch smoke drifted eastwards across the OVA as the new light of the solstice lifted across the leafless trees, and the thin sunlight caught the stems of the dead flowers. As with all of these wonderful celebrations, the gifts of this project with Jamie have been both unexpected and deep. All too often we run through the year without really considering our place in the cycle, but this year we've been so much more engaged with the celestial calendar, which is what Jamie had intended.'

Alasdair Moore, Head of Gardens and Estate at the Lost Gardens of Heligan, and his team collaborated with Jamie to create the OVA symbol in a wildflower meadow. Month by month the installation changed – as seeds were sown, plants grew tall and then died back, and different seasonal rituals were held.

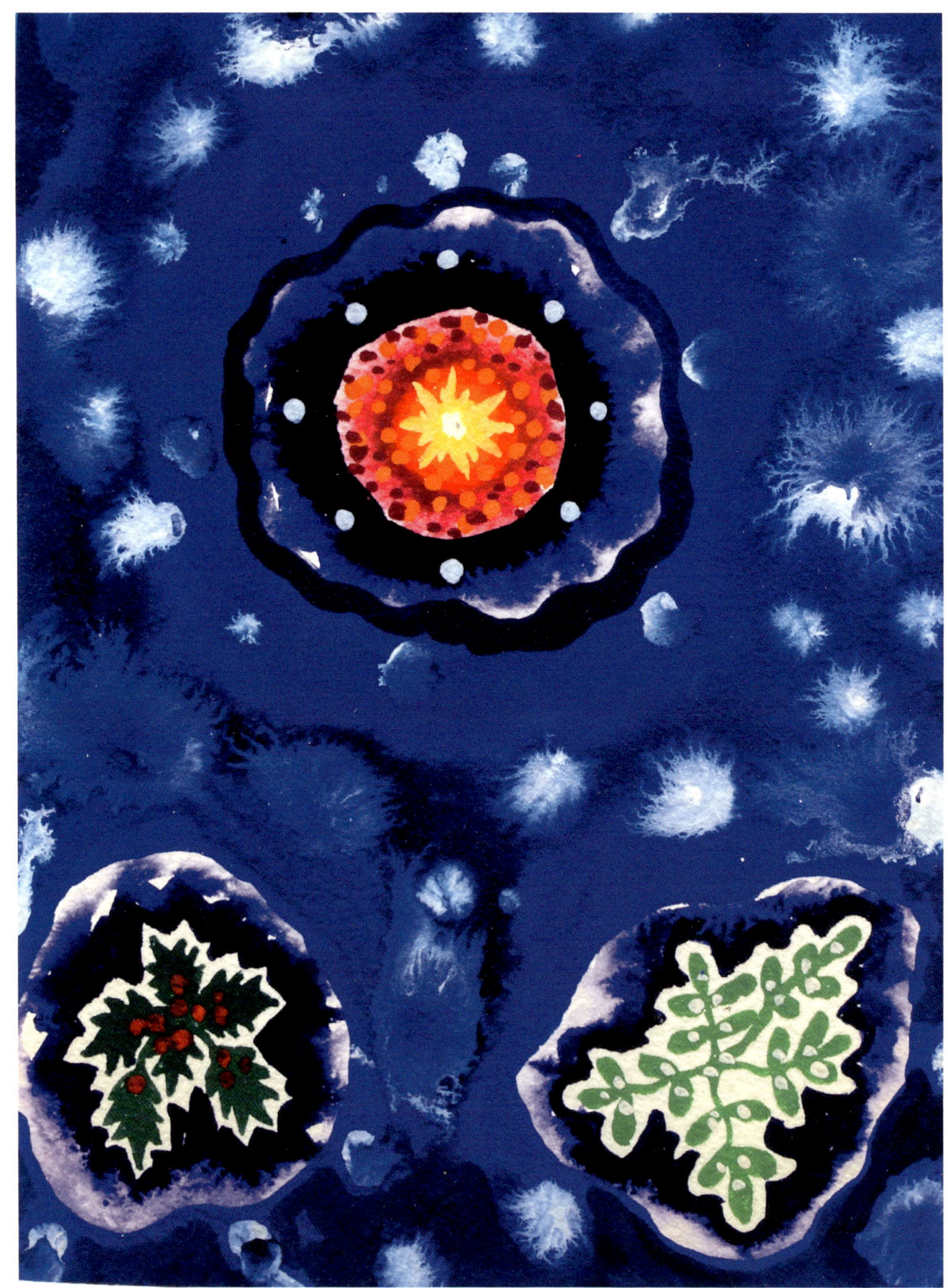

Winter Solstice / 2010

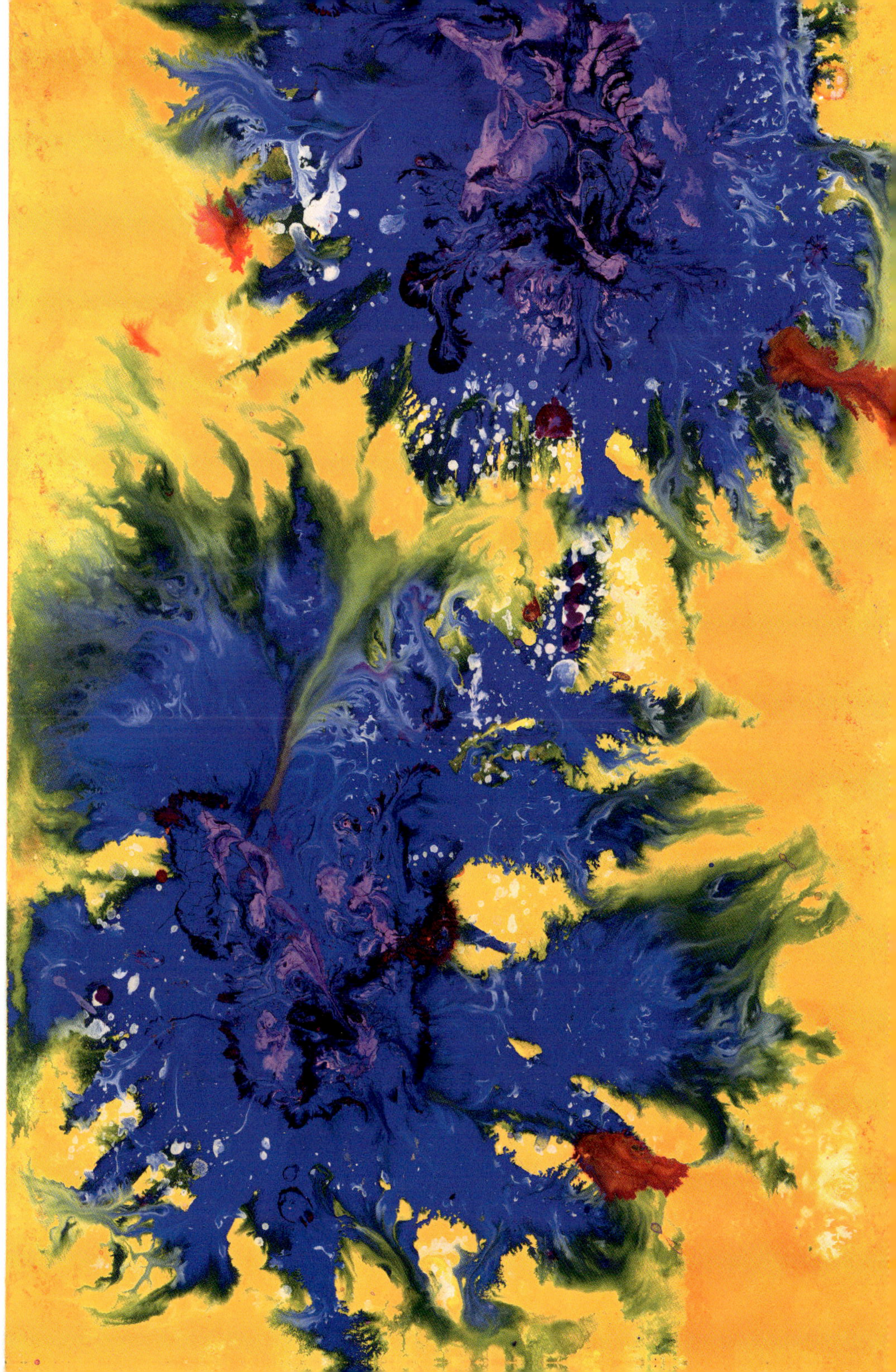

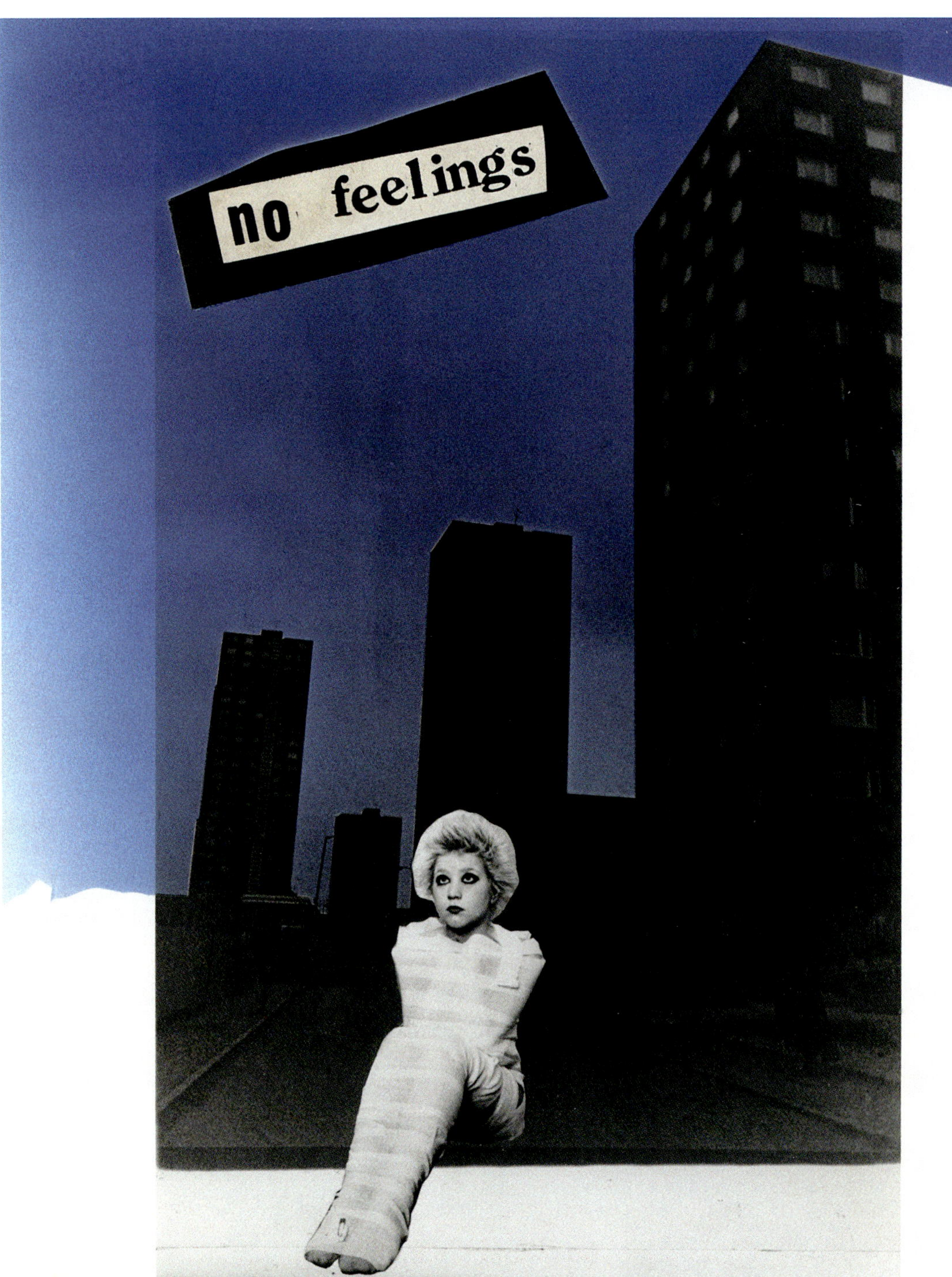
no feelings

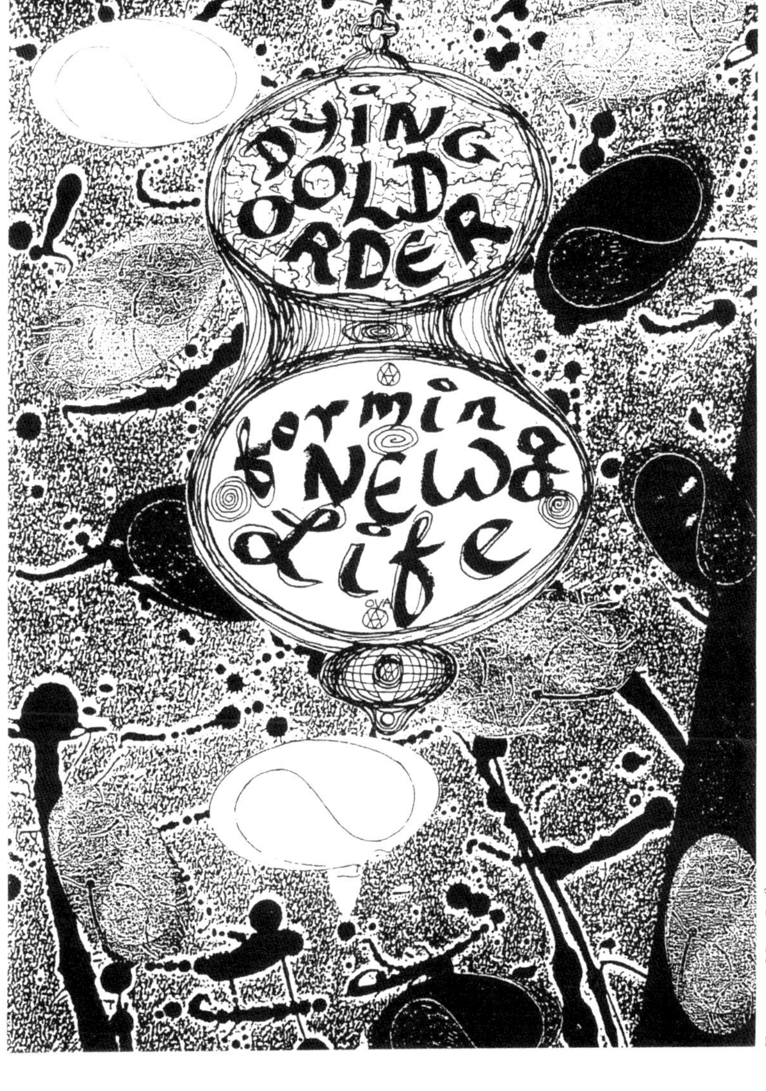

Forming New Life / 1988

No Feelings / 1977

This work was one of a series of graphics produced to illustrate each song on the Sex Pistols' album *Never Mind the Bollocks, Here's the Sex Pistols*, for inclusion in a promotional poster insert. The original collage of this poster now hangs at the V&A, while *No Feelings* is in the permanent collection of the Tate. This piece features the prominent Pistols' entourage member Little Debbie, also known as Debbie Juvenile, wrapped and stranded in a state of alienation and boredom.

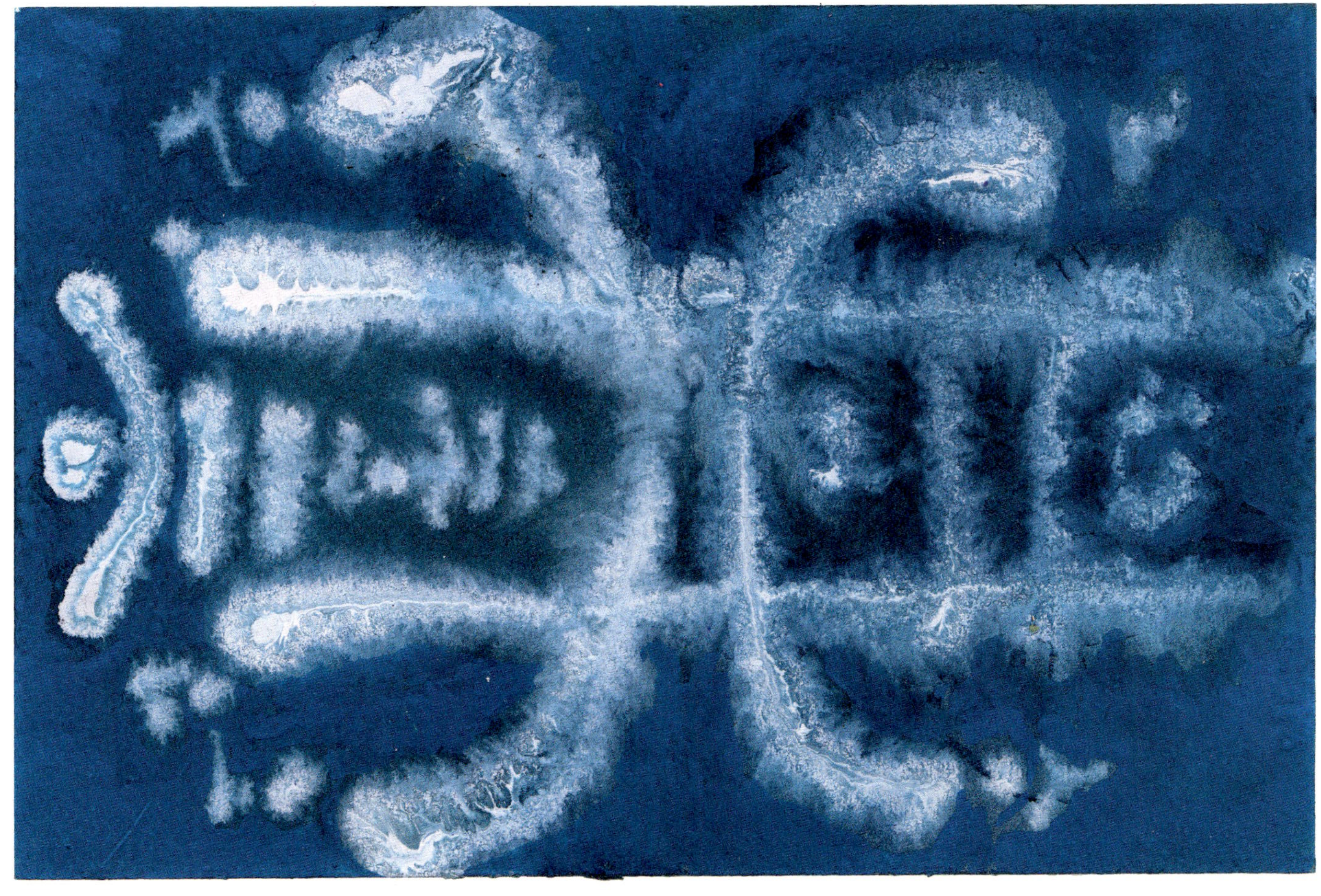

Snowfall on the Balcony / c. 2010

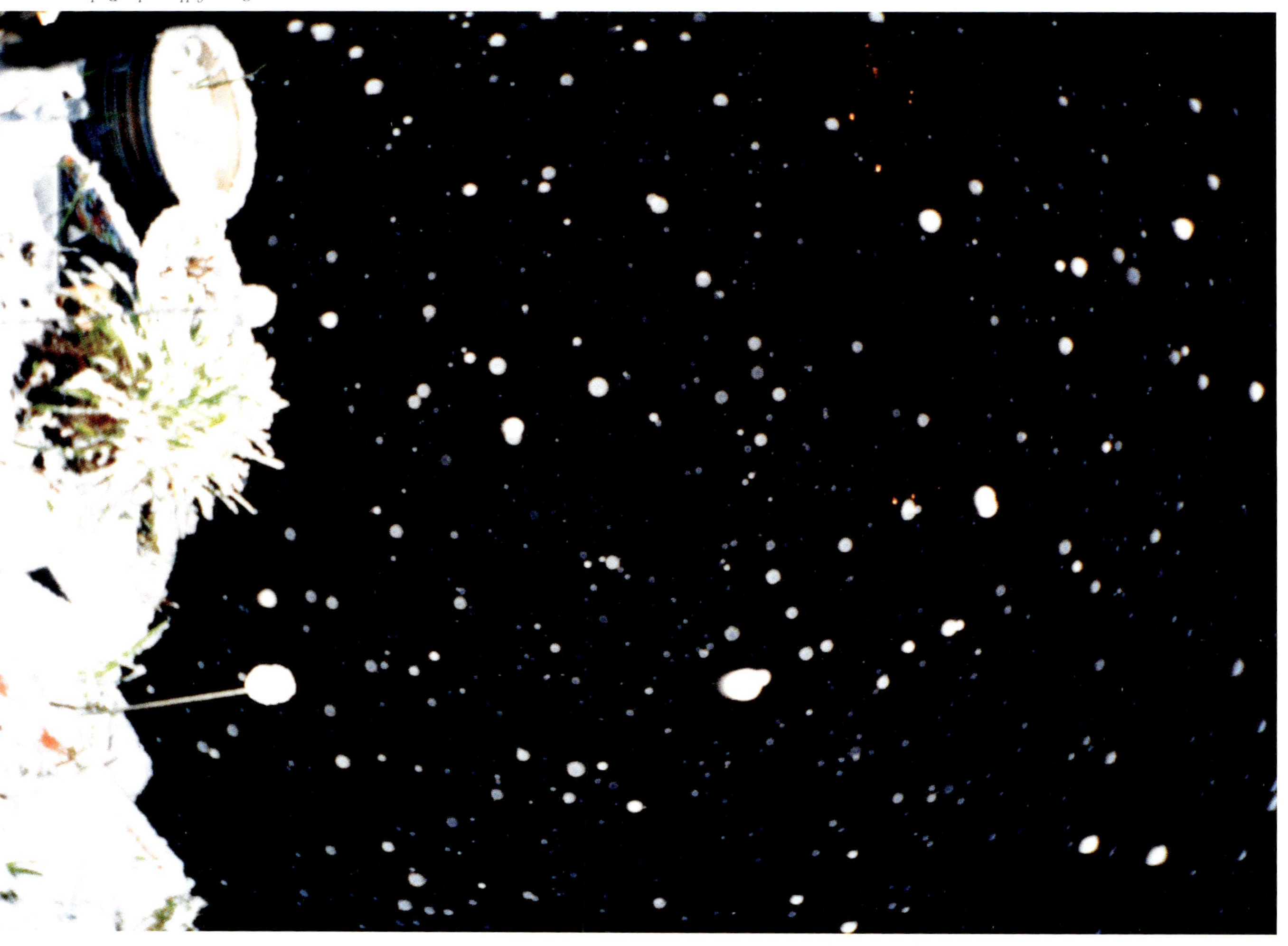

The two pillars

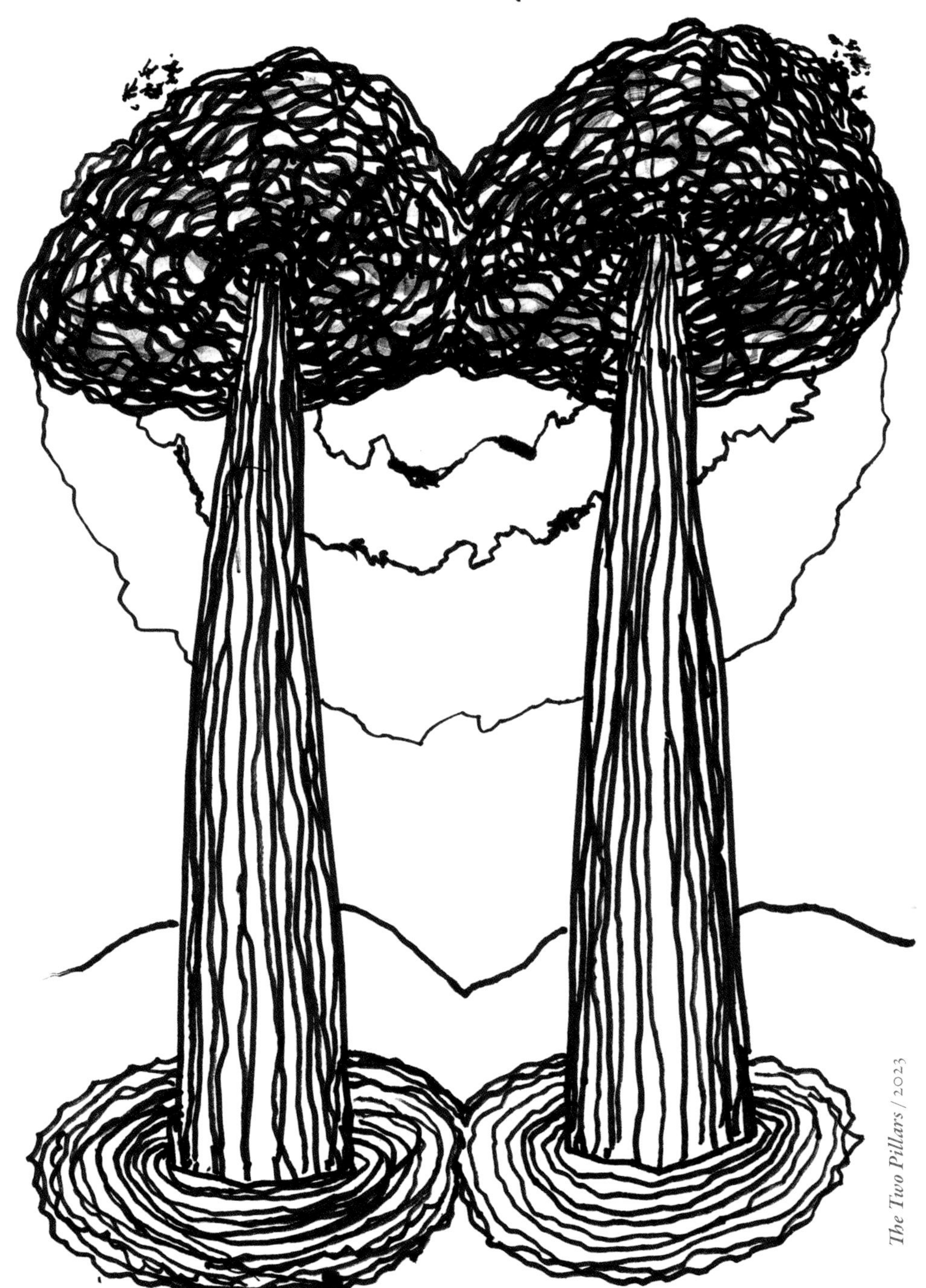

The Two Pillars / 2023

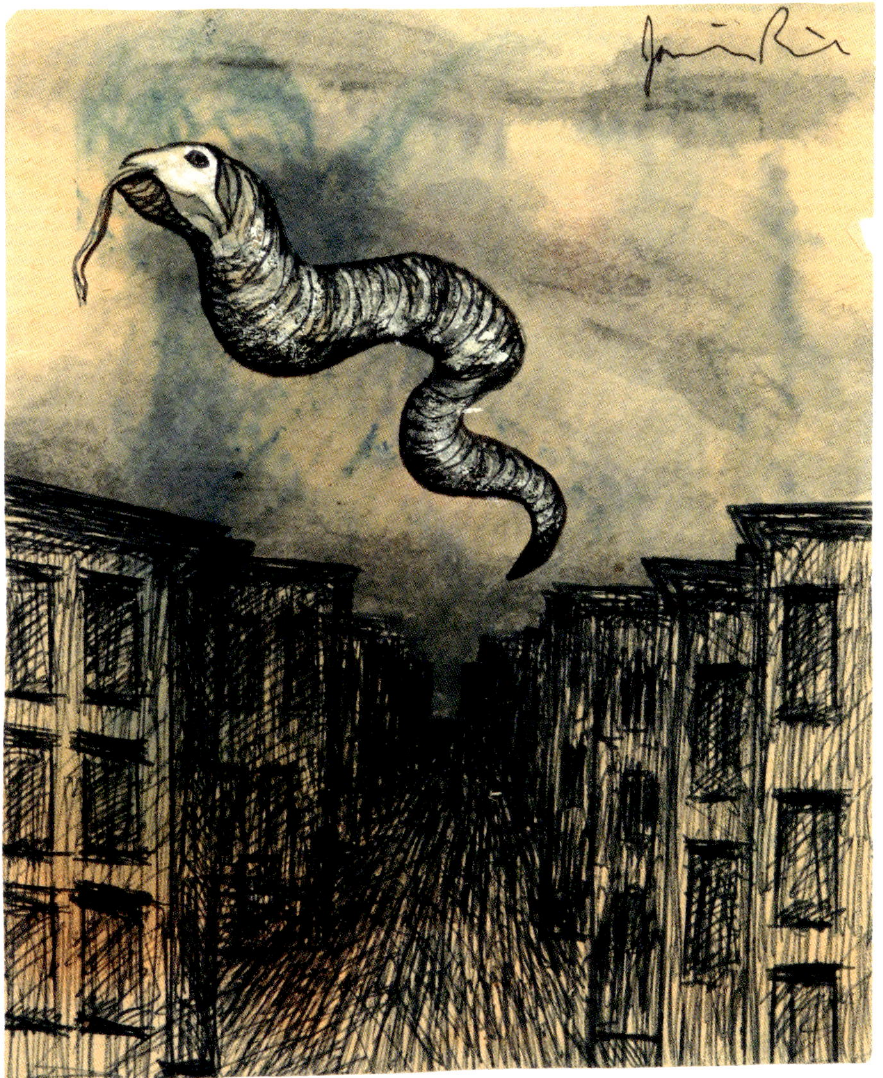

Flying Snake / 1970
Jamie was a great admirer of William Blake. This image has an echo of Blake's Urizen as he surges through his creation – the darkness, misery, squalor and exploitation caused by the Industrial Revolution. Thomas Paine, Mary Wollstonecraft and the wider Romantic movement were introduced early to Jamie by his parents, who imbued him with a sense of radicalism, as well as wonder at, and reverence for, the natural world.

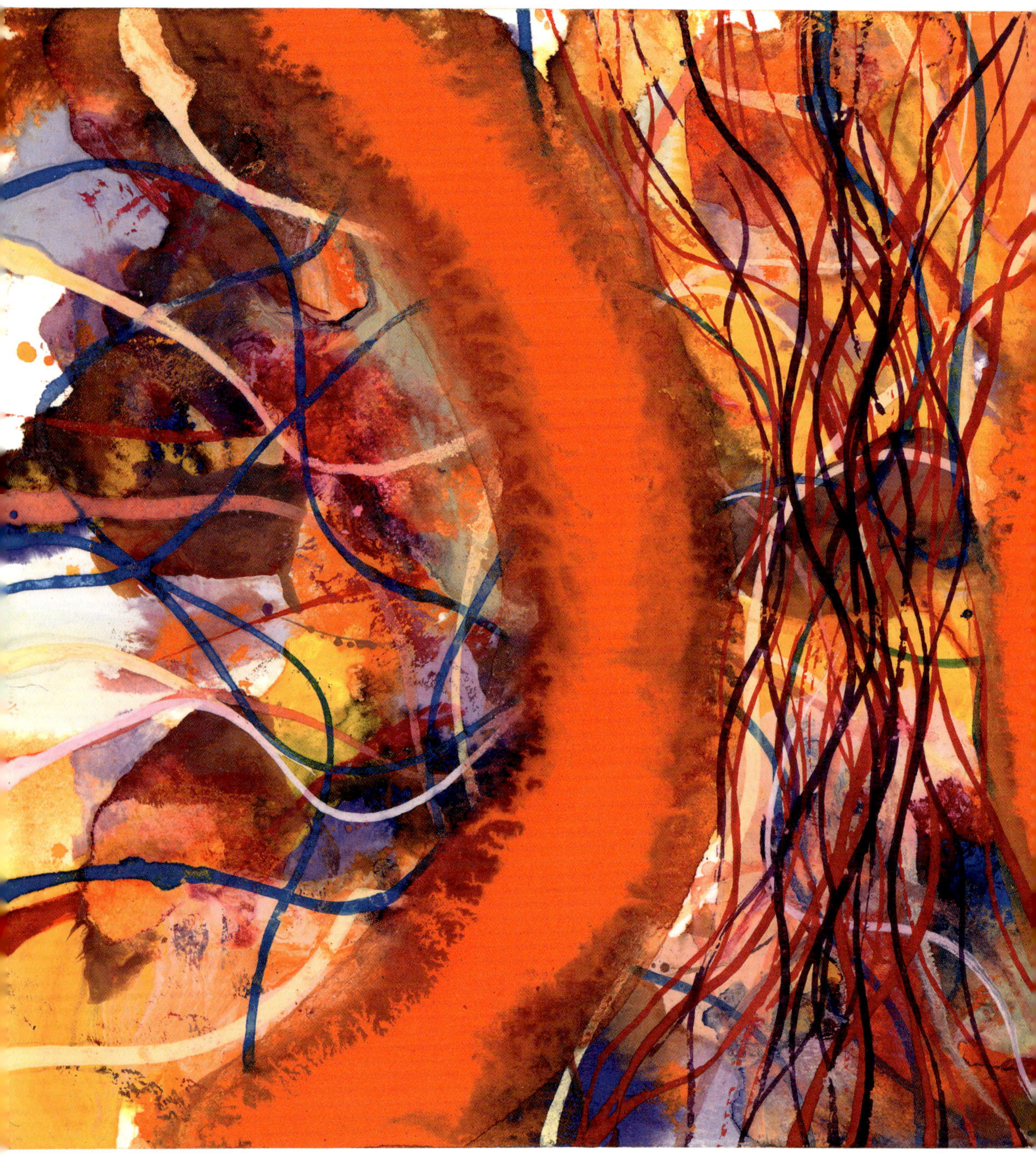

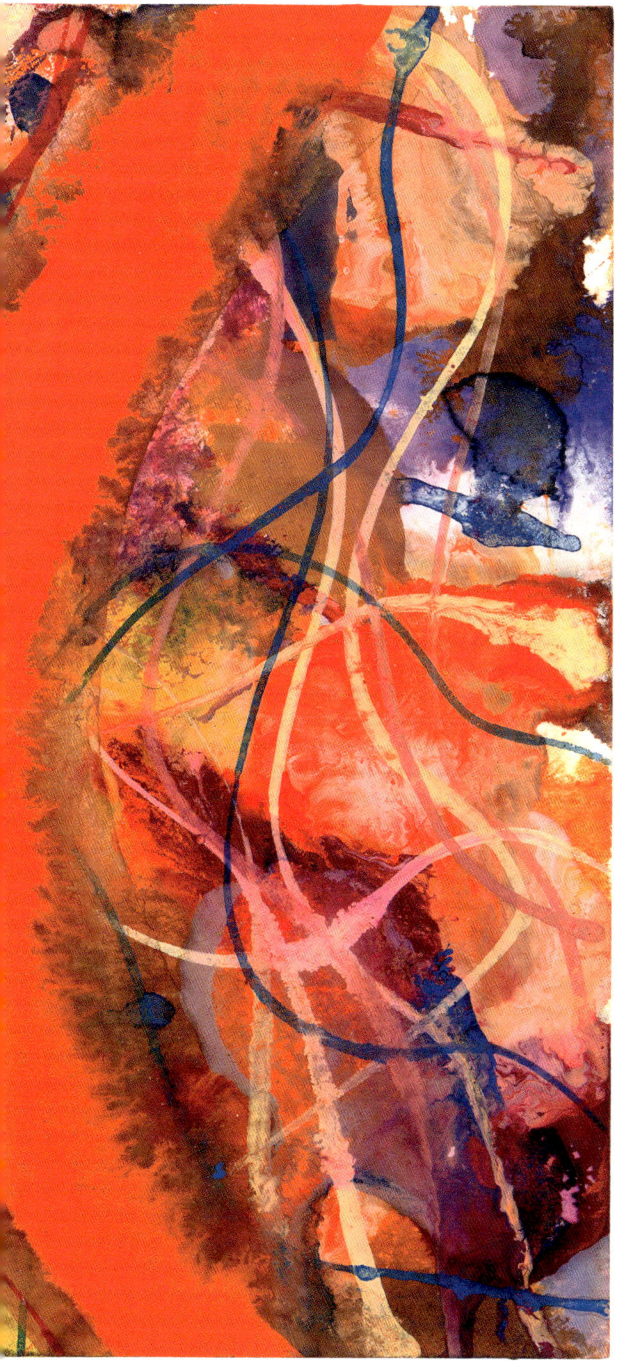

365 Eightfold Year Cards / *c.* 2010

Jamie produced hundreds of small-scale paintings in his home studio in Liverpool. He would usually work on the floor, kneeling or lying on his side, mixing colours in dozens of plastic cups, the years of creativity layering his floor with paint spatters. As he worked, he would listen to his favourite jazz musicians, such as Charles Mingus or Alice Coltrane, or to the Test cricket. One primary project was to produce a group of 365 cards, one for each day of the year. These cards are painted in a variety of styles, some carefully structured, some nominally figurative, many entirely free. All are gouache on A5 card. For Jamie, this project was closely linked with his interest in the turning Wheel of the Year, and many of these images can be seen throughout this book, untitled but placed in the season in which they were created. Jamie also created larger paintings for each of the festivals of the Eightfold Year, and each of these is shown in the relevant chapter.

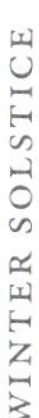

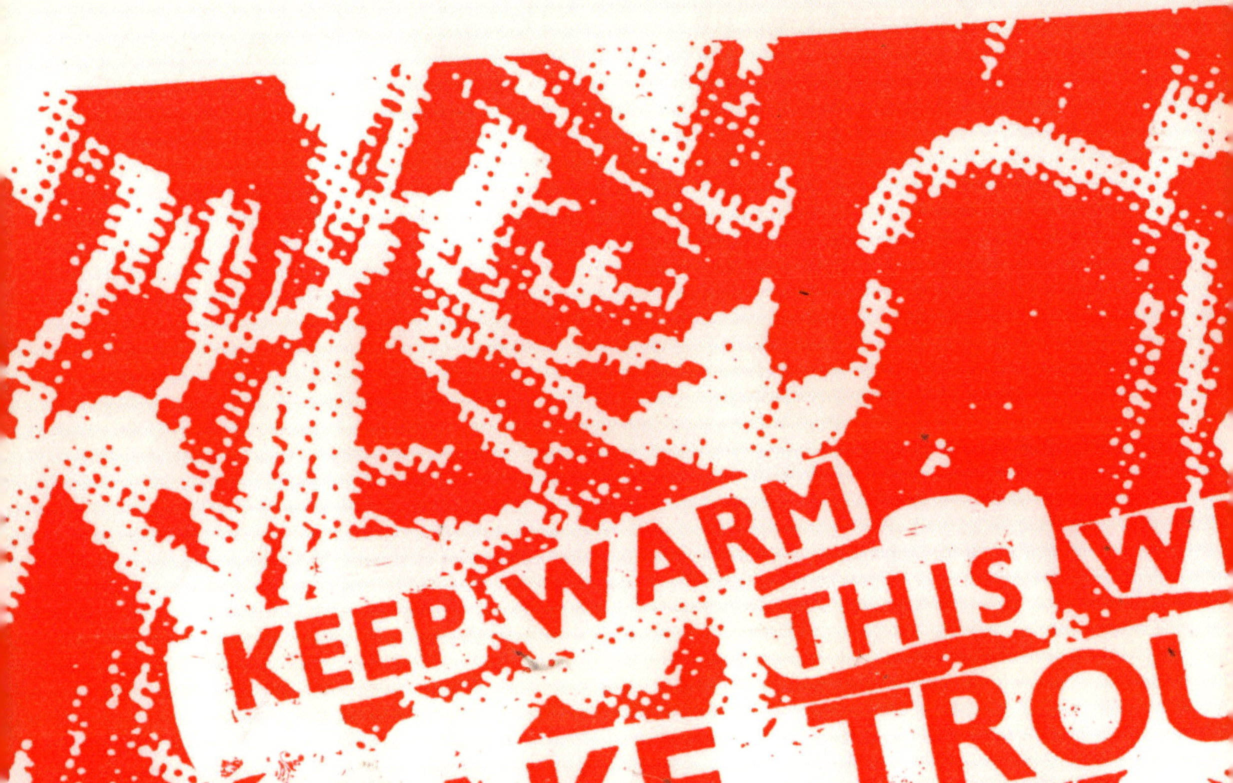

KEEP WARM THIS WI

MAKE TROU

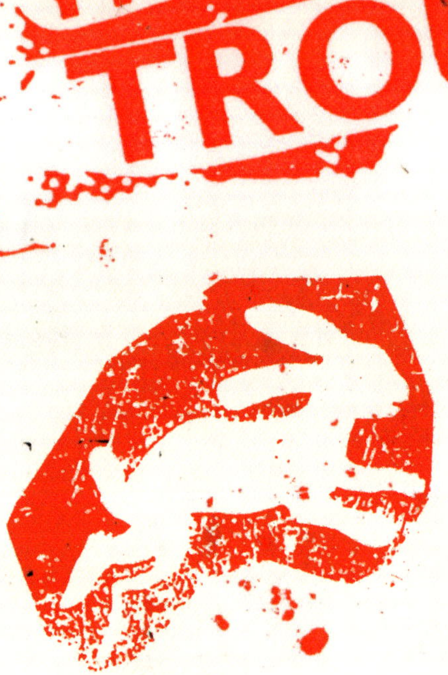

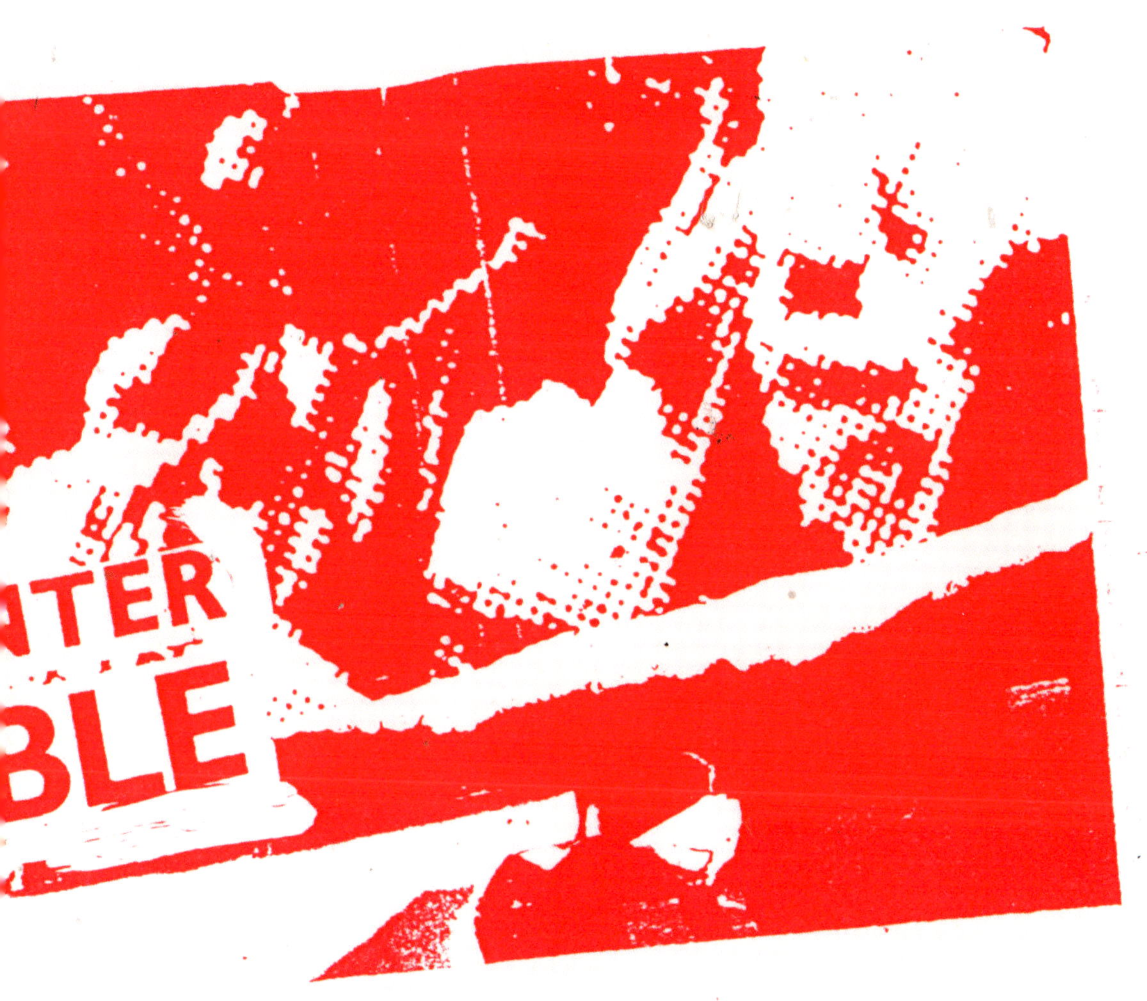

Keep Warm This Winter (Make Trouble) / 1974
Jamie's Croydon-based print collective, Suburban Press, collaborated with other press collectives in the UK and abroad, printing and distributing agit-prop material. This visual started life as an sticker for one such group, Wicked Messengers, and was later incorporated into the Sub Press/Jamie Reid canon, much like *Nowhere Buses* (page 118). Such materials were often distributed through countercultural bookshops, such as Public House in Brighton and Compendium in London. This one was produced during a period of austerity, when Edward Heath's Tory government enforced energy shortages and the three-day week.

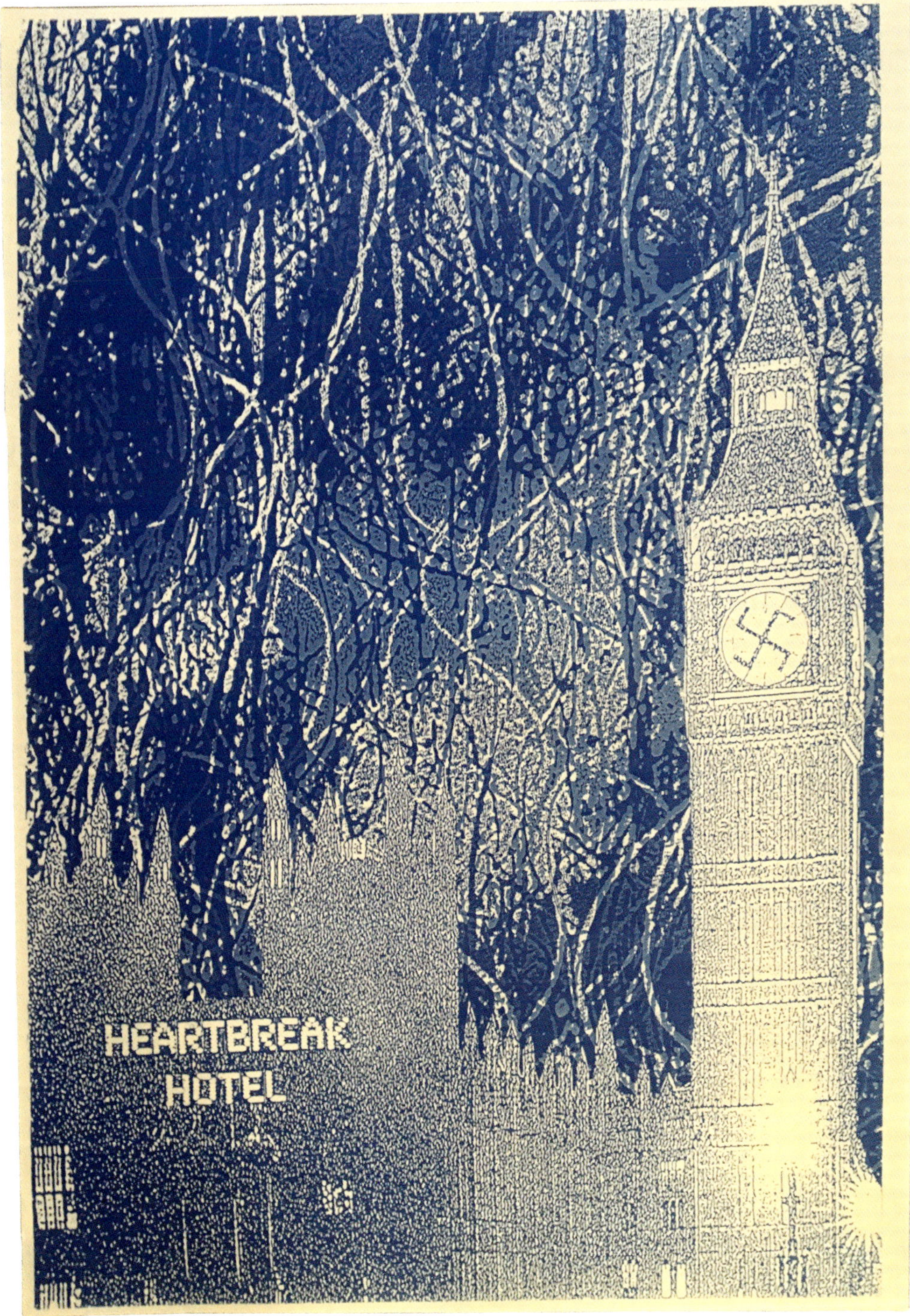
HEARTBREAK
HOTEL

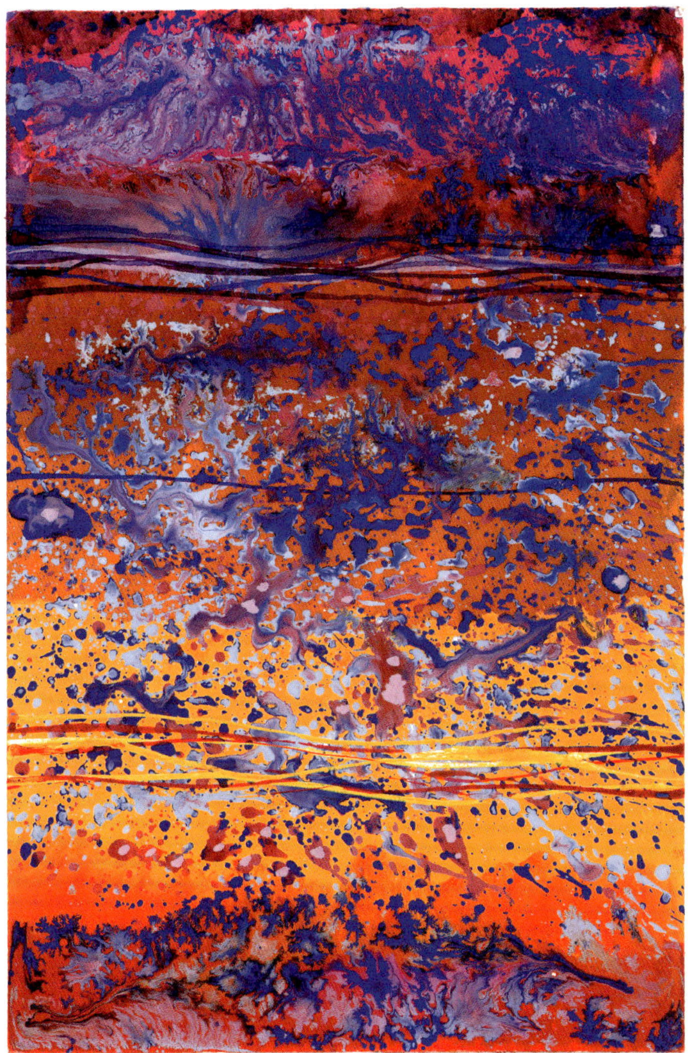

Heartbreak Hotel / 1988

This collage was produced in 1988 as part of a wider campaign, including a graphic package for Boy George's 'No Clause 28' single, to protest draconian anti-LGBTQ legislature being drafted by Margaret Thatcher's government to, in the words of the act, 'prohibit the promotion of homosexuality by local authorities' in the UK. This version repurposes one of Jamie's 1960s college-era paintings for background, and replaces the hands of the Great Clock of Big Ben with a swastika. Jamie had previously used this offensive graphic to attack the Sex Pistols' record company, Virgin, for tasteless exploitation of the death of Sid Vicious.

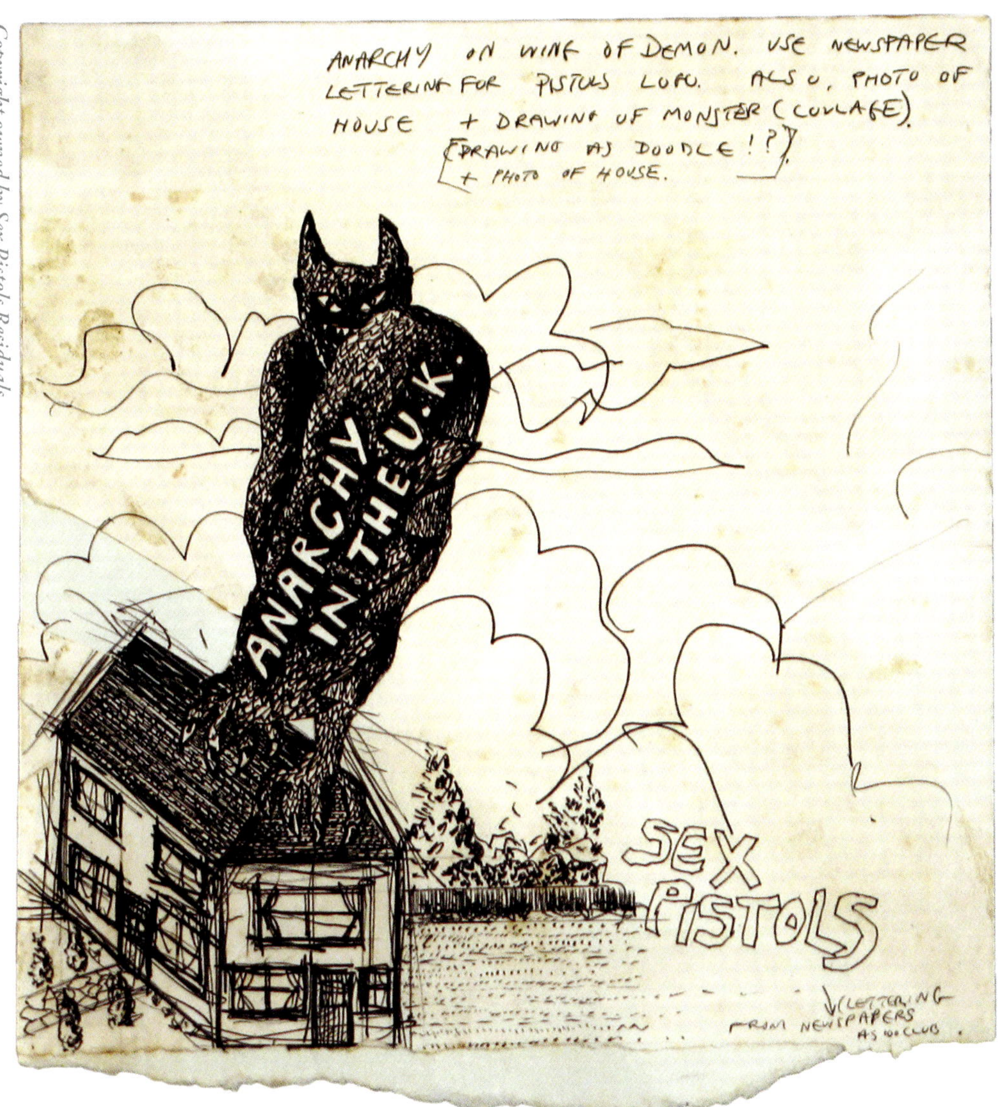

Anarchy in the UK / 1976

This draft, rejected artwork for the Sex Pistols' first single 'Anarchy in the UK' is a hand-drawn version of a painting from *The Cat Book* (1972). Jamie's college confrère Malcolm McLaren had gone on to manage the Sex Pistols, and it was he who rejected this draft as 'too romantic'. Jamie was usually left to produce artwork for the band with no interference. Everyone was free to play their part during the short creative life of the Sex Pistols, which Jamie referred to as 'three magical years'.

Switch On Something for the Miners / 1974
This Suburban Press sticker was funded by the National Union of Mineworkers President Arthur Scargill, with money taken from a tin of petty cash kept under his desk. It was produced during the miners' strike of 1974, in direct opposition to the government's plea for energy-saving as a means to break the strike. The miners were striking for safer working conditions as well as better pay, but were portrayed as being at odds with the public good.

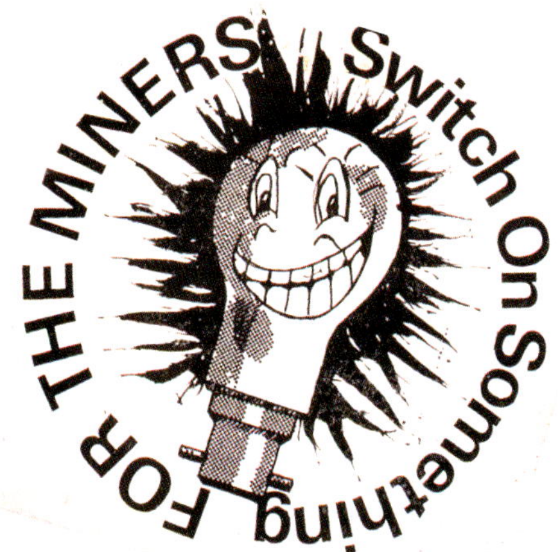

Rhys on the Slate Mountain, Llanberis / 1992

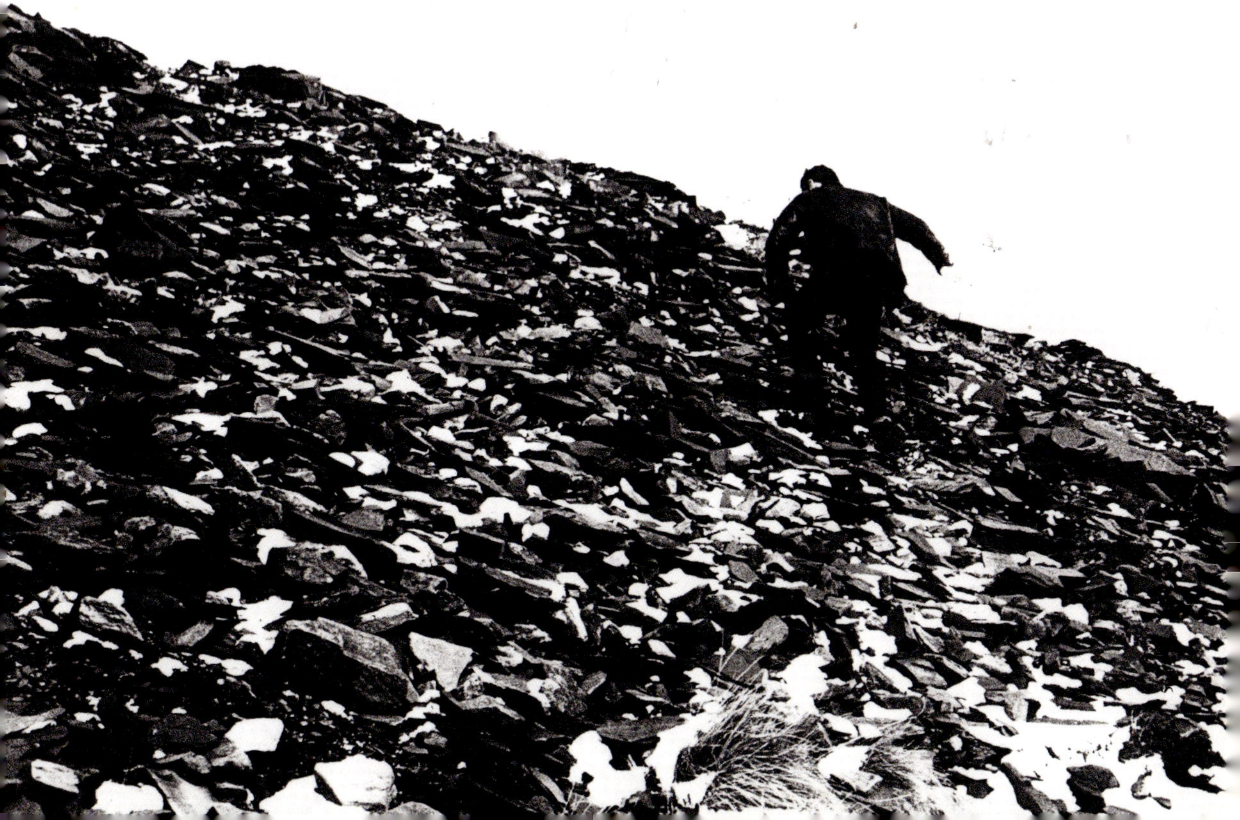

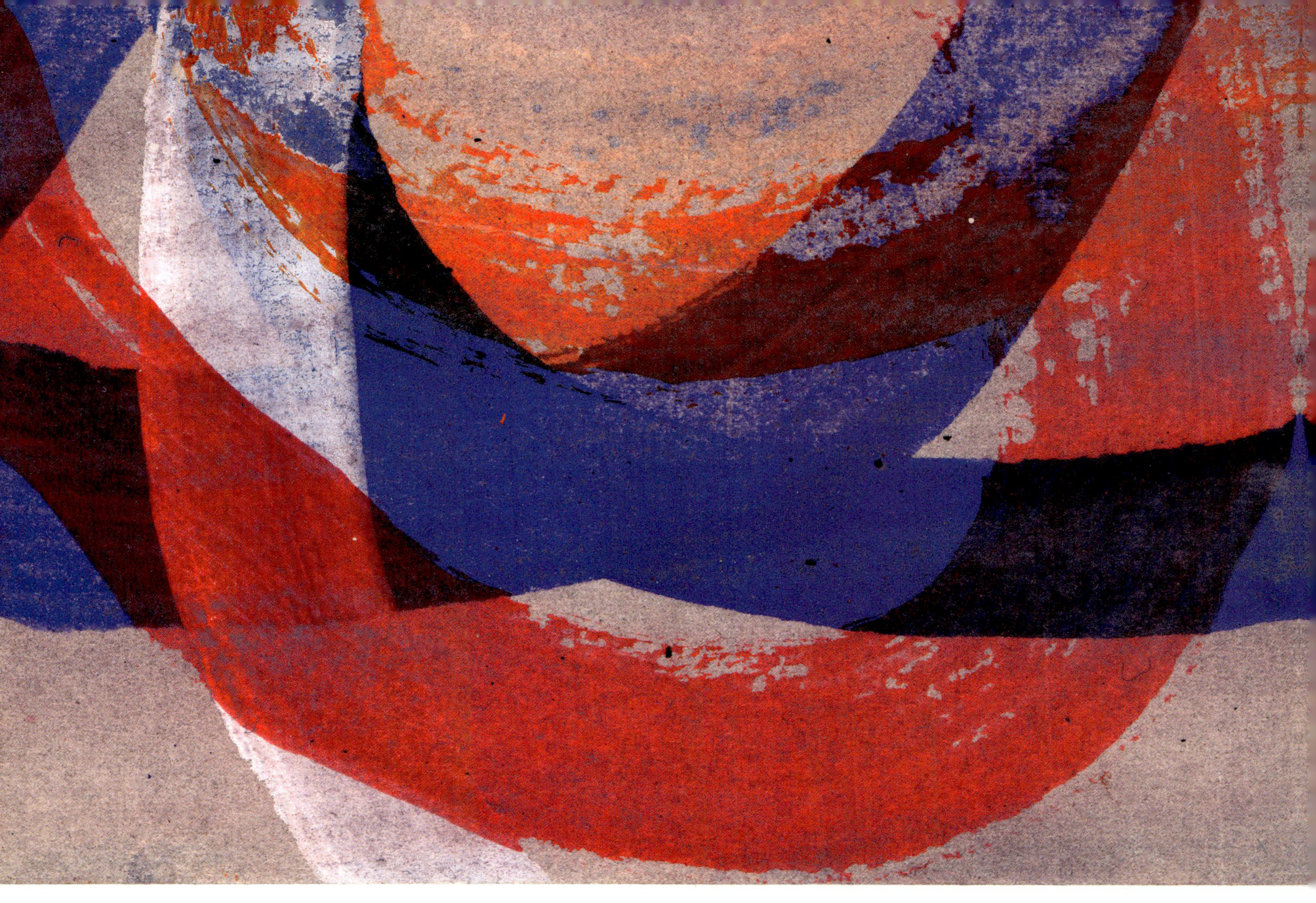

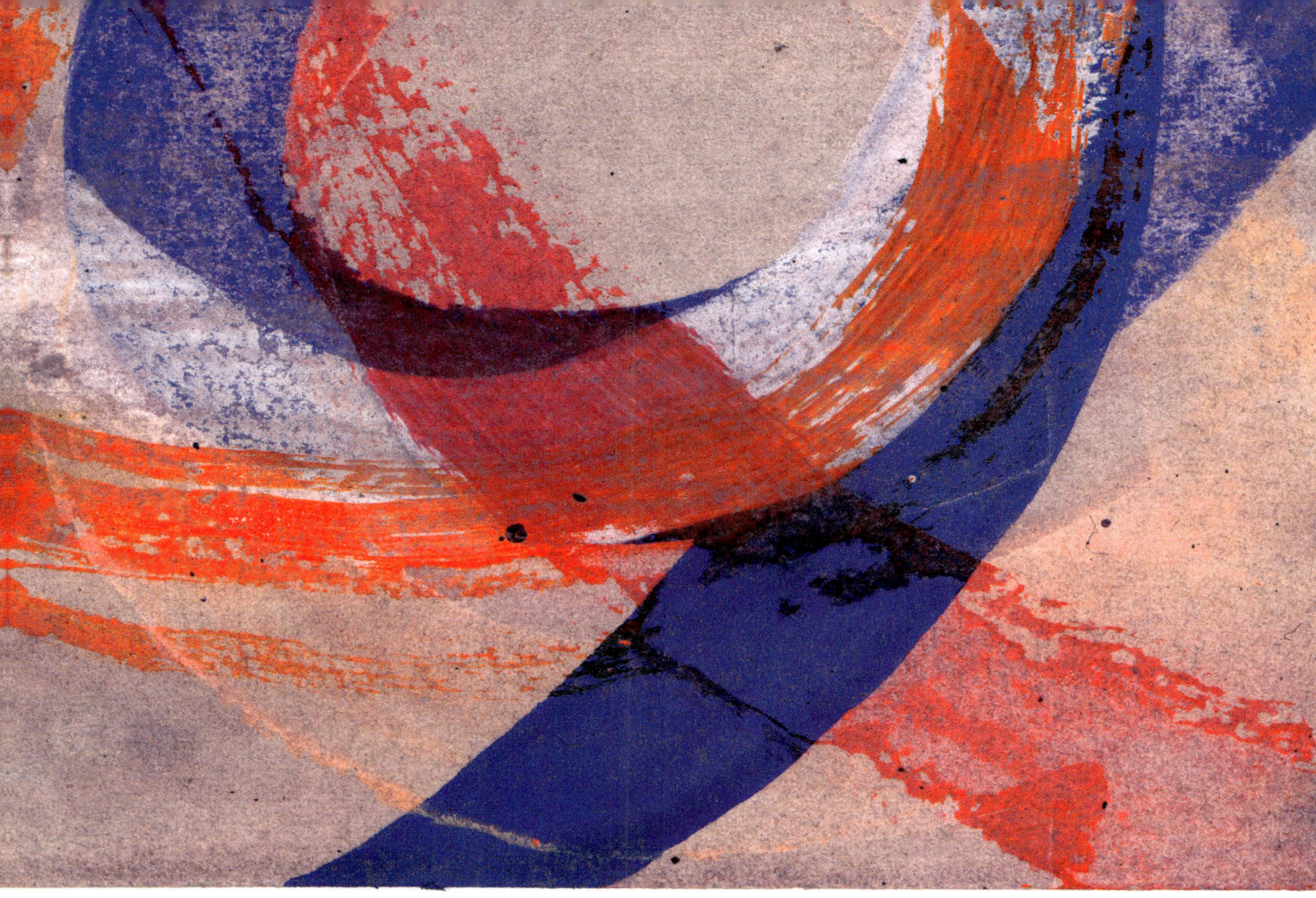

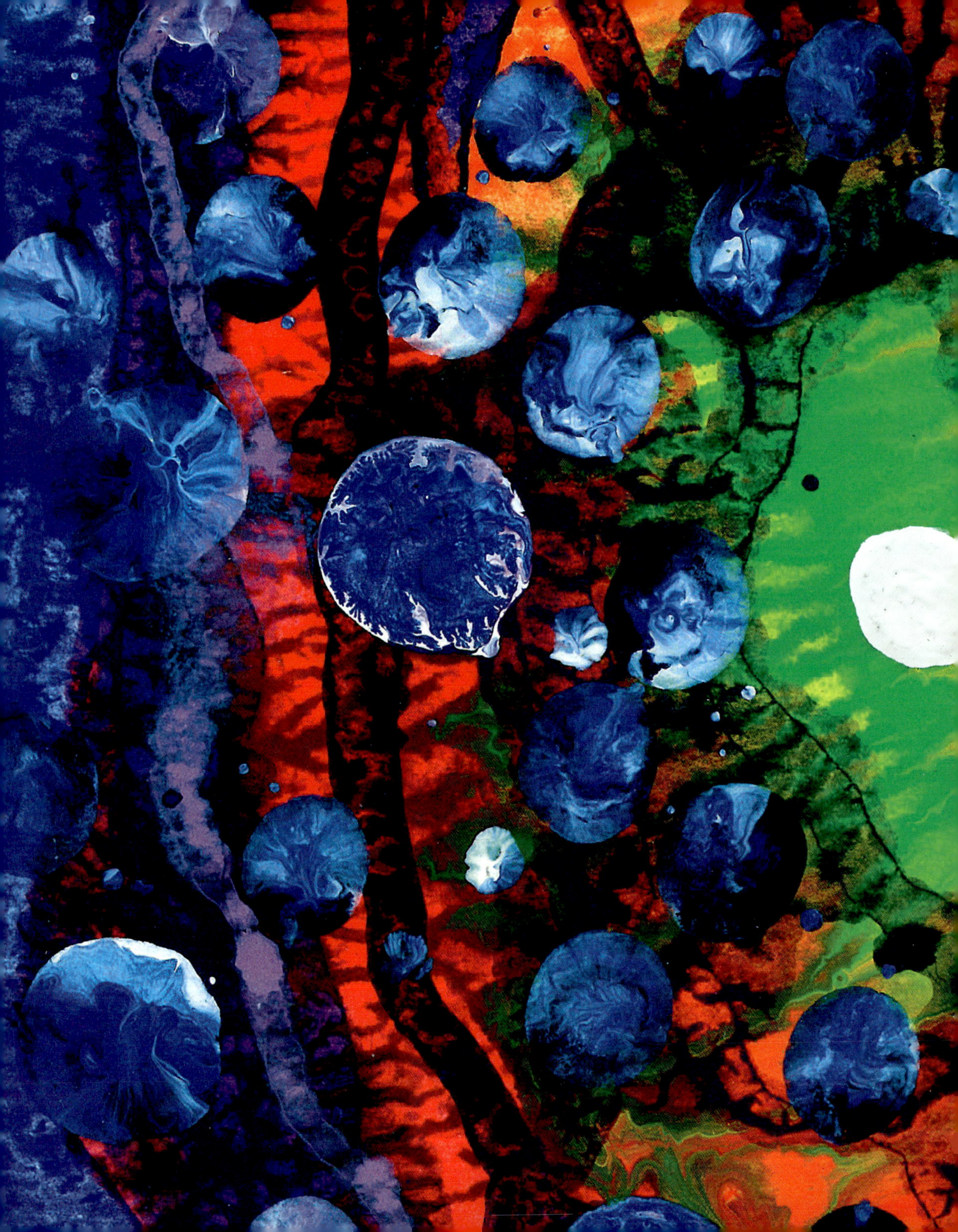

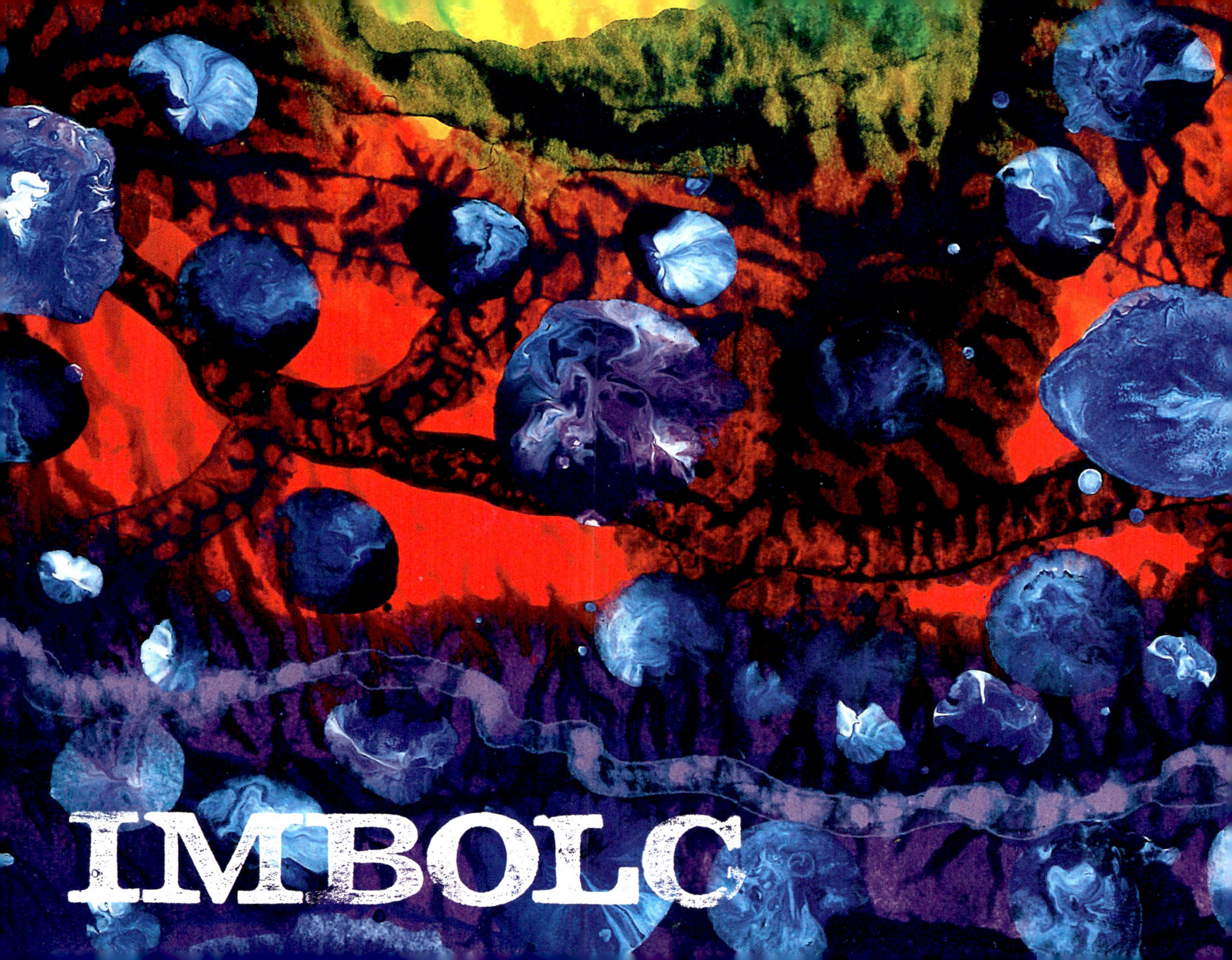
IMBOLC

IMBOLC

Previous pages
Imbolc / 2010

Birth isn't instantaneous; it's a process. The labour has been going on since the solstice, and it's now, at Imbolc, that we emerge from the womb of winter. The nights continue to be long but the snowdrops are pushing up through the cold earth and soon it will be time for the departure of the Cailleach – that old severe goddess of darkness who we both love and hate.

But, as at Samhain, at the other side of the Winter Solstice, this is a liminal time. We wake up and then our head falls back again on the pillow and the dreams go on for a while. Brighid, also known as Bride or Bridie, the Pagan goddess who later became a Celtic Christian saint, whispers: 'Fire or Water, which do you want?' And the answer is both, of course, as the snow melts and the streams run clear again. This is a time that is strangely calm despite the great forces rising up beneath the earth's surface.

Brighid was the goddess of the forge, of poets and bards, of storytellers and musicians, and of crafters of iron and silver, who bring beauty and 'awen' – the elixir of the Druids that gives inspiration – into the world. In the forge, fire and water combine in alchemical union to work their magic on the raw materials of art. Now empathy and intuition unite to feed our creativity.

We wash our faces and turn to clearing away the litter of winter. Imbolc is a time for making plans, setting intentions, looking ahead to the planting season, when the inspirations and intentions formed in the long, dark months can start to take root and grow as the days lengthen. This is the time to check that our wishes align with our needs, not our greed, and to check that we don't fall into the trap of desire for desire's sake – the trap that is closing around the whole world today.

In Druid ceremonies we light eight candles – to signify the Goddess and her Eightfold Wheel – and float them on water, symbolising the way in which Brighid unites fire and water. Her name means 'fiery arrow', and it's said that the nuns at her monastery in Kildare kept an eternal flame burning in her honour.

With the coming of Christianity, Imbolc became known as Candlemas, and was dedicated to the time when Mary took the infant Jesus to Jerusalem, for her ritual purification as a new mother, according to Jewish tradition. The beginning of February is considered significant in cultures all over the world. The rising energies of the earth, like a sleeping dragon awakening, mark the start of the Chinese New Year. In Japan, it's Setsubun, when people drive away the misfortunes of the old year and welcome in the energies of a new spring.

In addition to her other roles, Brighid is also the patron of midwifery; she helps the year be born and can support our creativity, too. It was once believed that she would visit homes on the eve of Imbolc to bless the inhabitants. People used to leave out cake, or bread and butter, on the windowsill for her, or make plaited crosses of straw or rushes and hang them up to welcome her. We can ask Brighid in our Imbolc rites to bless our creativity, to help us give form to our dreams, to help us fashion a life that can bring gifts to others.

Now is the time in the turning of the Wheel to pause in the stillness of February days and nights, and to appreciate the miracle of birth, the strong and nurturing power of the Goddess.

NOTES FROM HELIGAN

'Jamie had ordered boxes and boxes of snowdrops "in the green", with their bulbs and leaves attached. We gathered at dawn to plant these at each of the eight cardinal points on the OVA. Outside the OVA, Valentine's Field was already as green as the snowdrop leaves. In the woods below us, a male pheasant's call echoed through the trees. A robin hopped around as we dug in the cool earth. In the huge expanse of the field and the great span of the OVA, each snowdrop flower seemed so tiny, so delicate. But late winter is their time to bloom and they can push through the frost. Peace is tough.'

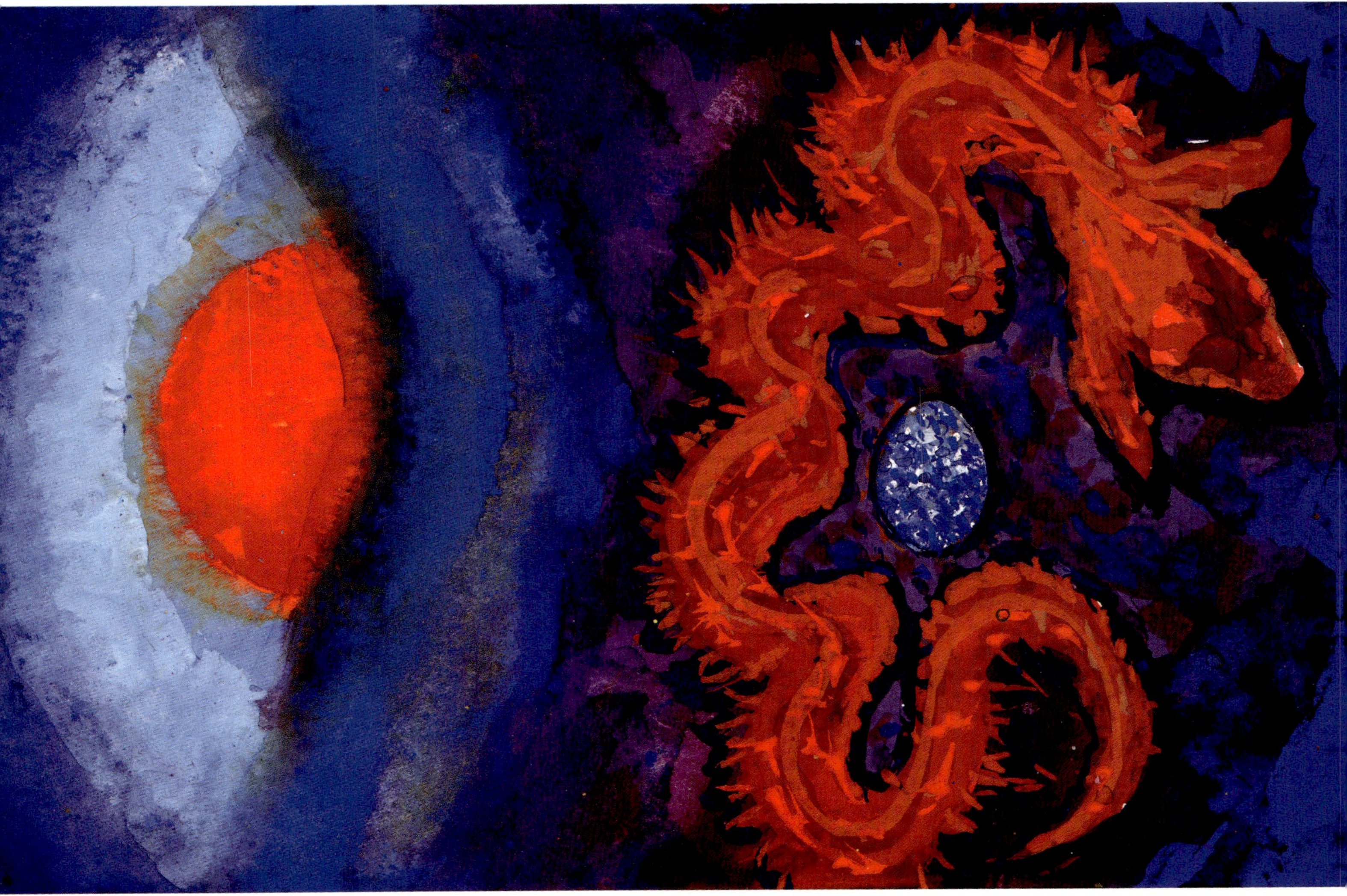

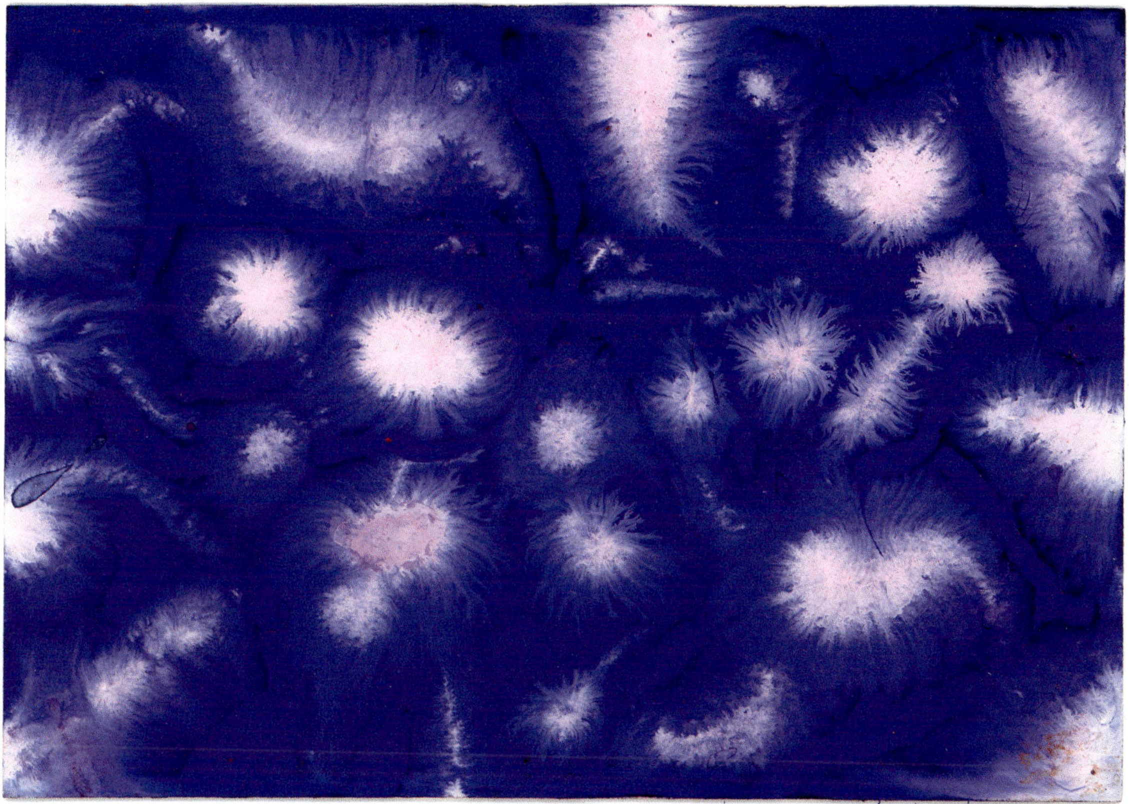

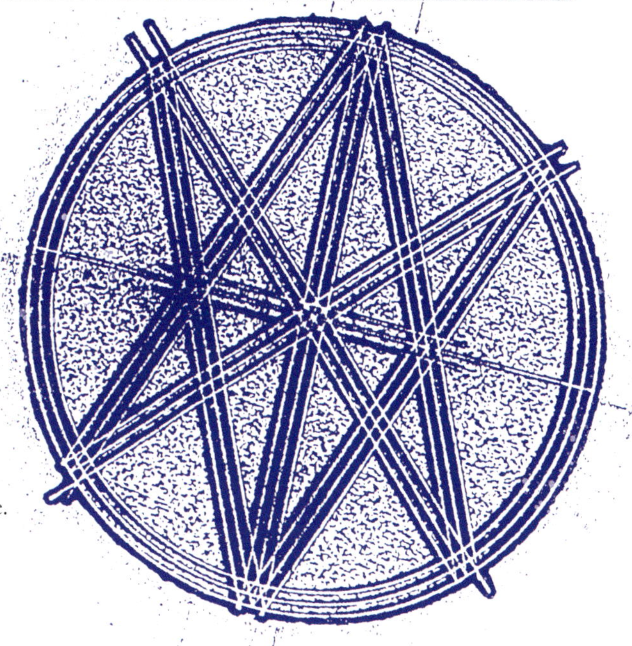

OVA / 1980s
Conflating an A for anarchy with a V for victory and an encircling O for compassion, the OVA symbol also represents birth and rebirth, and refers to the ovates of the Order of Bards, Ovates and Druids – conduits to universal consciousness through Mother Nature. Developed by Jamie in the late '80s with the assistance of Assorted iMaGes designer Garry Mouat, the symbol often found its way into Jamie's large-format paintings, collages and drawings, and was even added as part of his signature. The OVA is now synonymous with both Jamie and with a spiritual anarchy that places people before governance or capitulation.

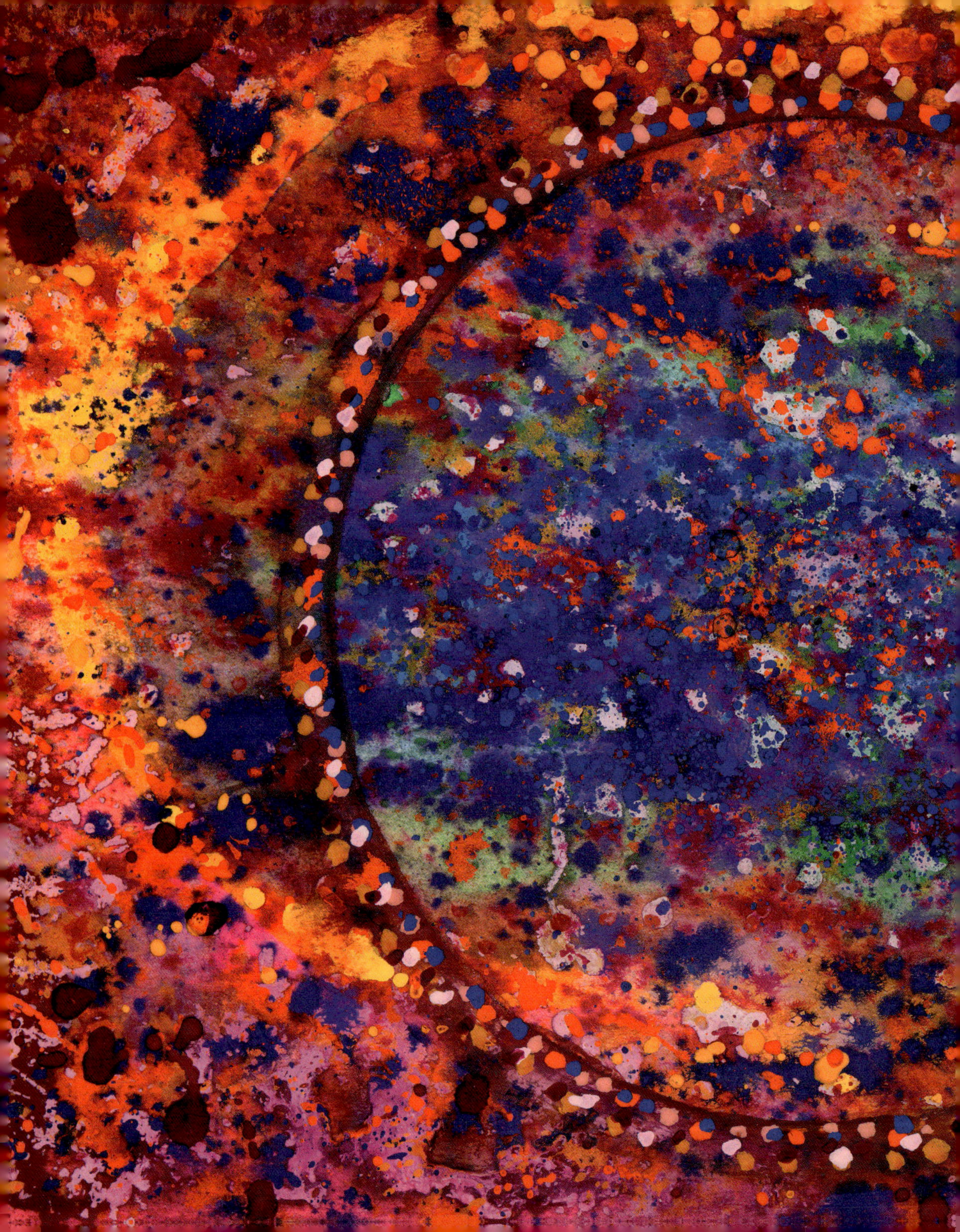

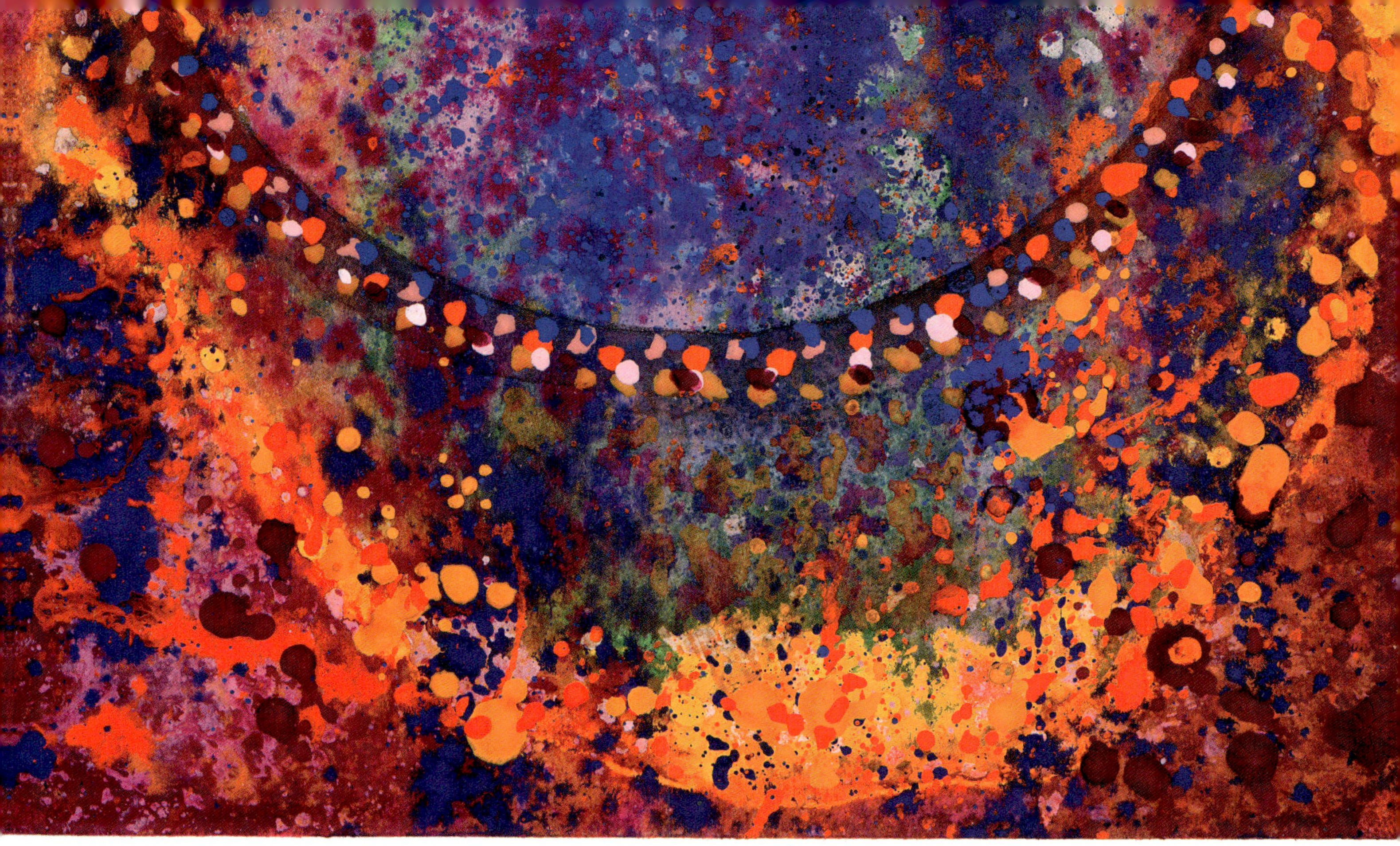

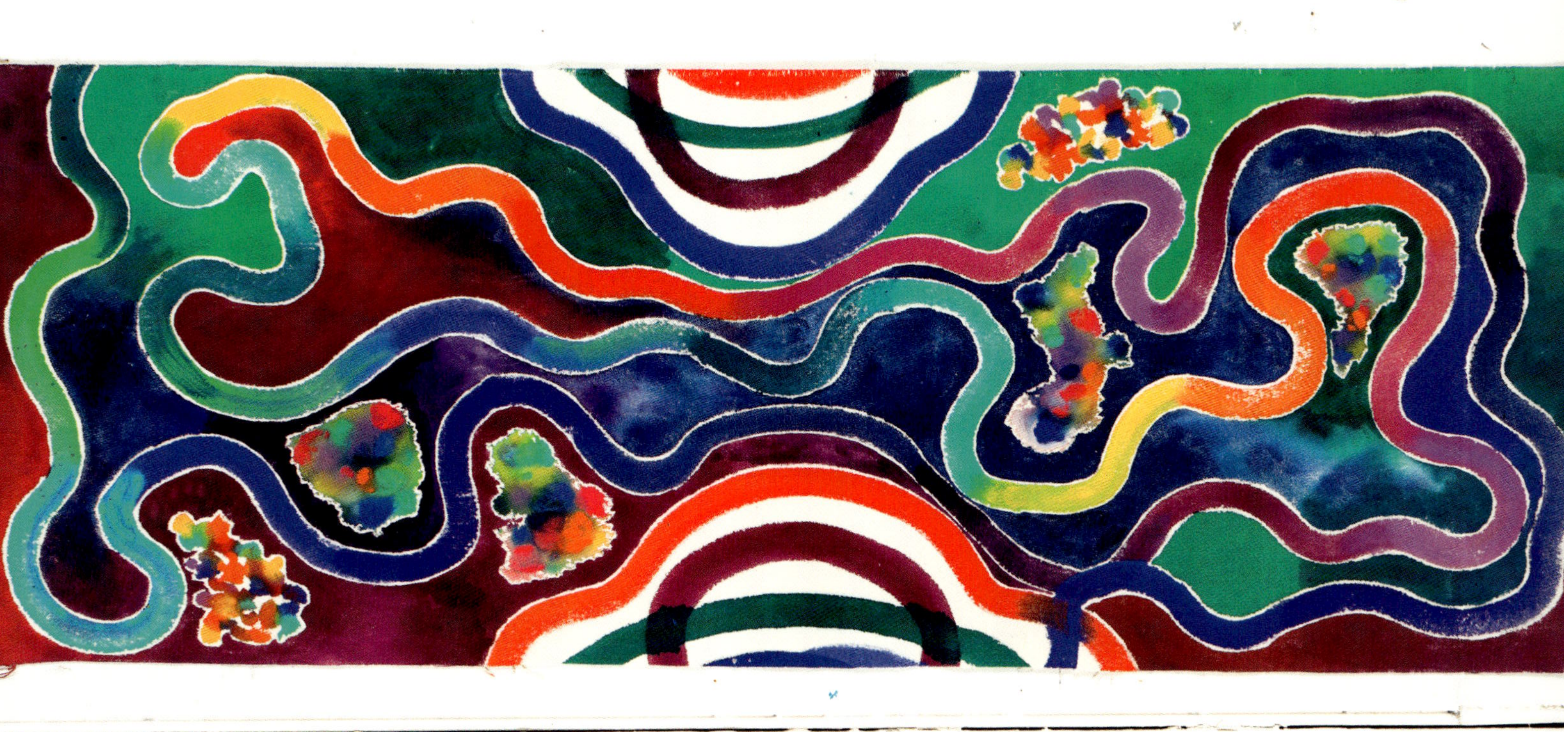

Untitled on floorboards / c. 2012

NURTURE NATURE

The rights of man — Thomas Paine (woman)
all our basic birth rights have been eroded in recent history ... bit by bit piece by piece ... workers rights gone.
education a comodity you have to pay for.
rule of fear (based on lies be it terroism or pandemic
keep people in obedience do what your told.
racism & gender inequality
the rich get richer & the poor get poorer.
destroy the domintor culture.
aborigal revenge

the levellers
Boudica.
William Blake.
Mary Wollstonecraft. (Wollstonecraft)
Frida Kahlo
Leonora Carrington
society of the spectacle
Gaia payback

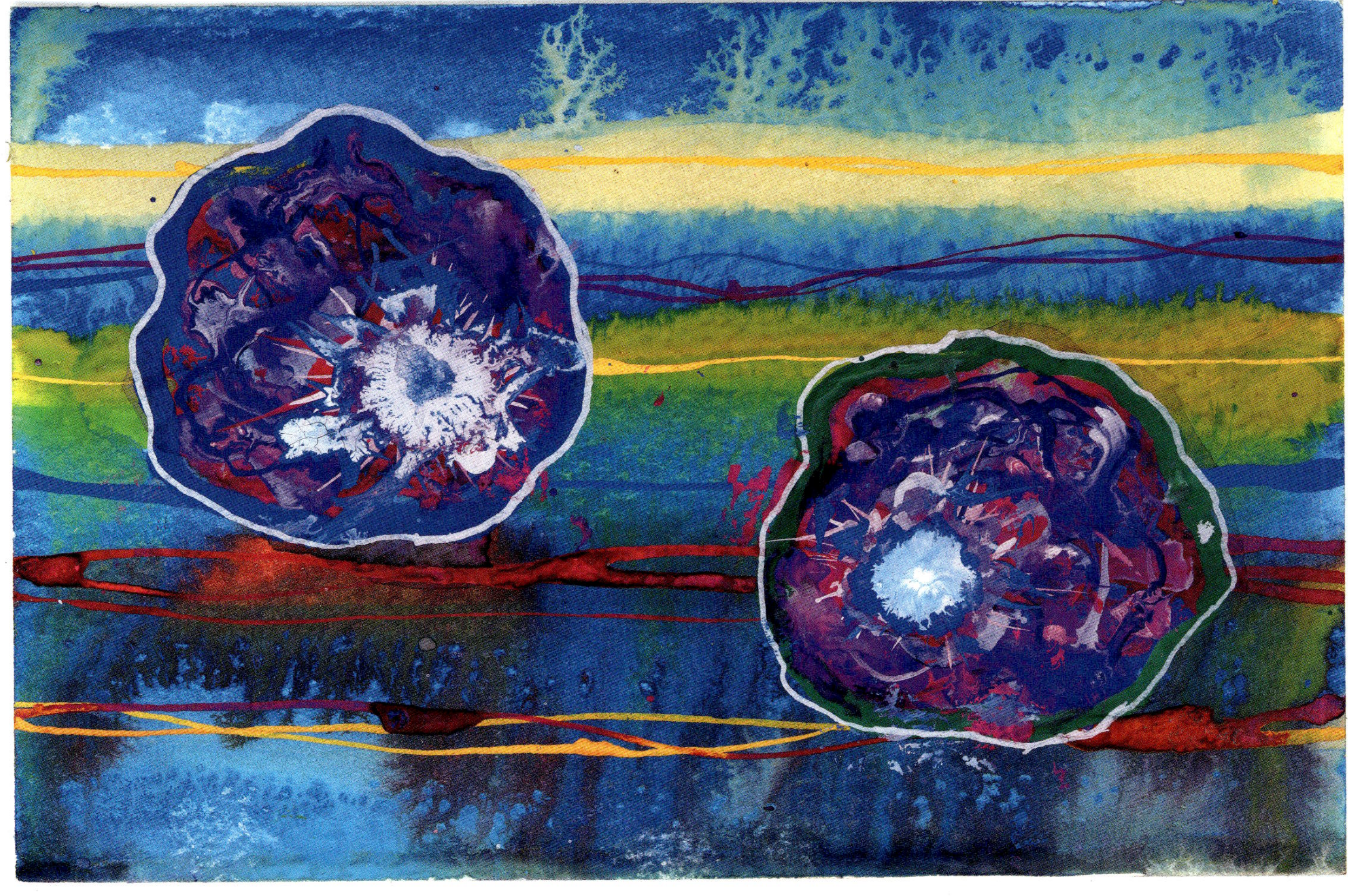

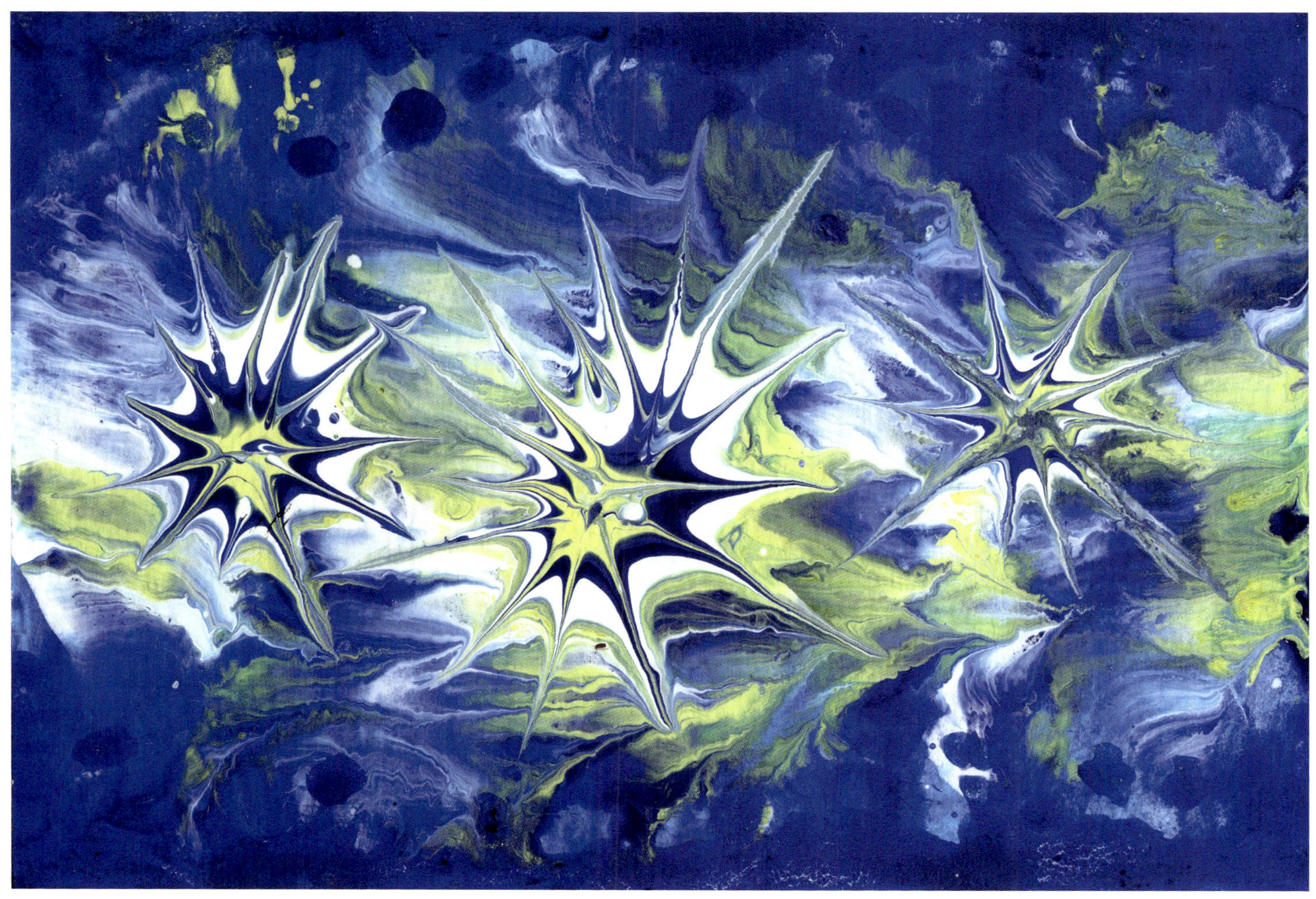

SPECIAL WINTER NUMBER, 1913. Two Shillings and Sixpence, Net.

THE NEW LIFE

WALTHER DUTTKE

Published for the Proprietors by THE TRIBUNE PUBLISHING CO., Great Turnstile Chambers, Great Turnstile, High Holborn, London, W C.

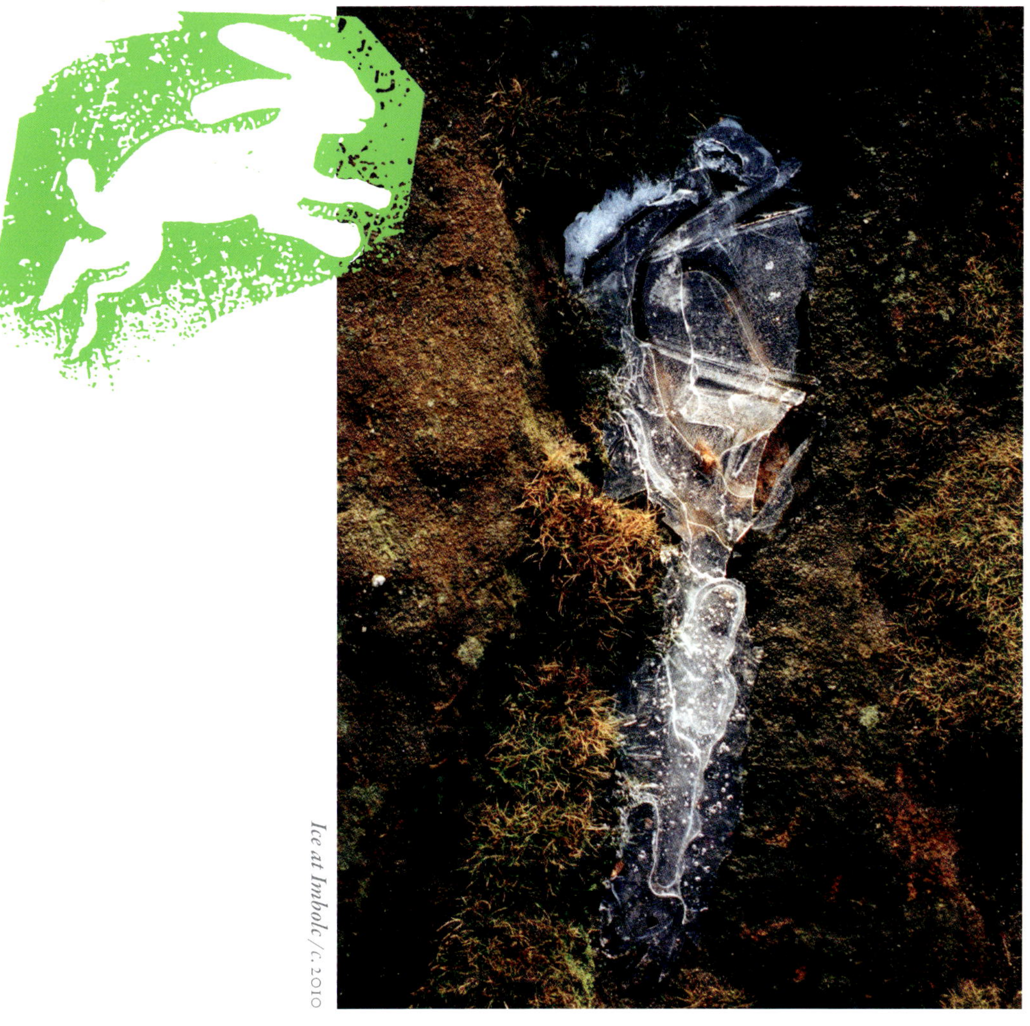

Ice at Imbolc / *c.* 2010

The New Life / 1913

The magazine *The New Life* was produced by Jamie's great-uncle George Watson MacGregor Reid when he was Chief of the Druid Order. Both this and the similar *Nature Cure* publication were vehicles for his writings (often pseudonymously credited), as well as offering advertising for products from dietary supplements to camping equipment rental schemes.

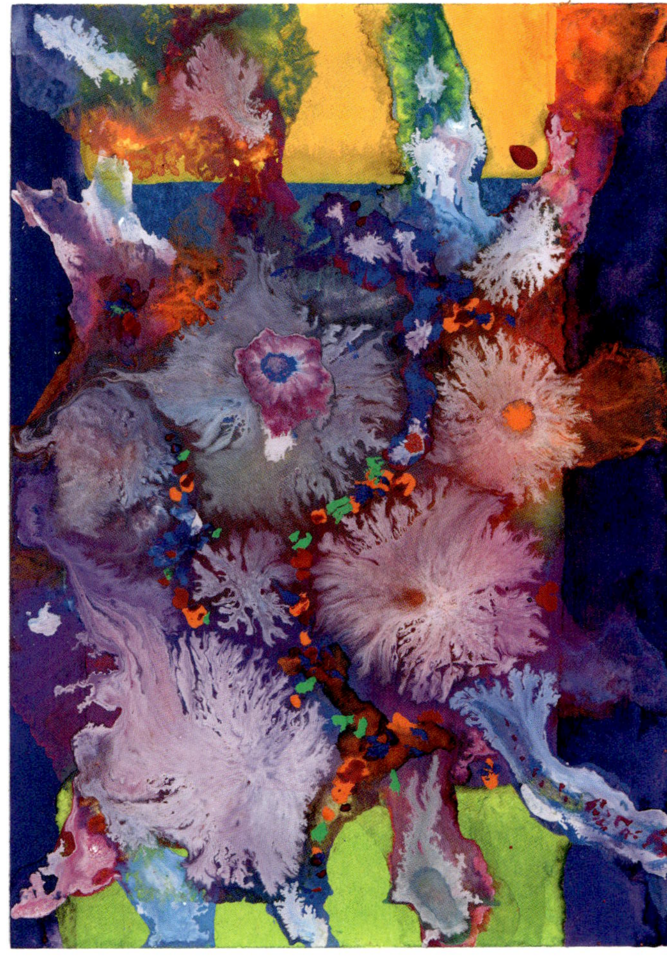

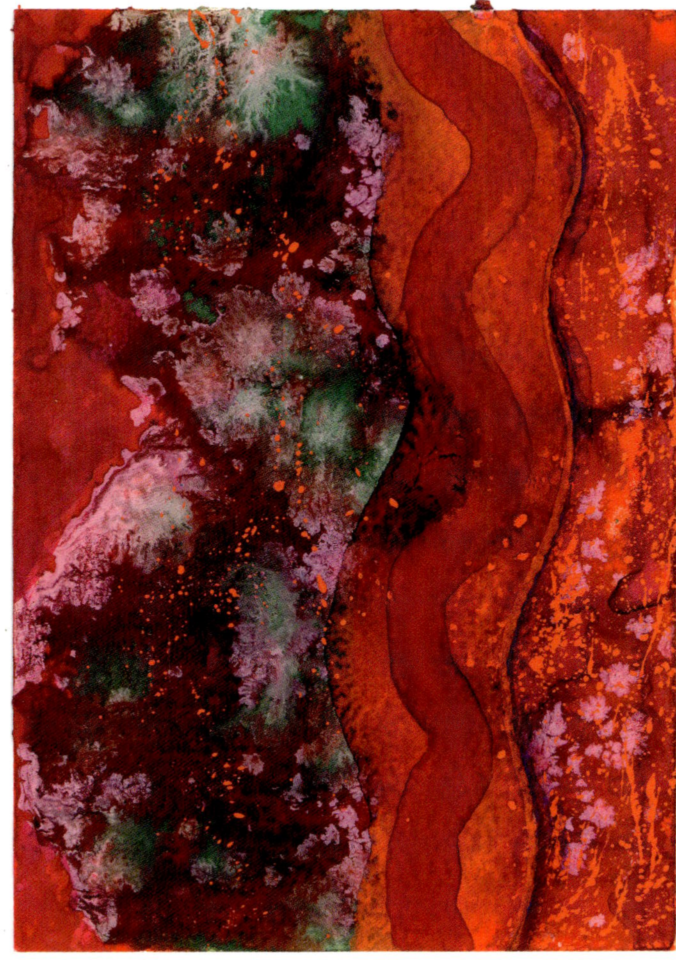

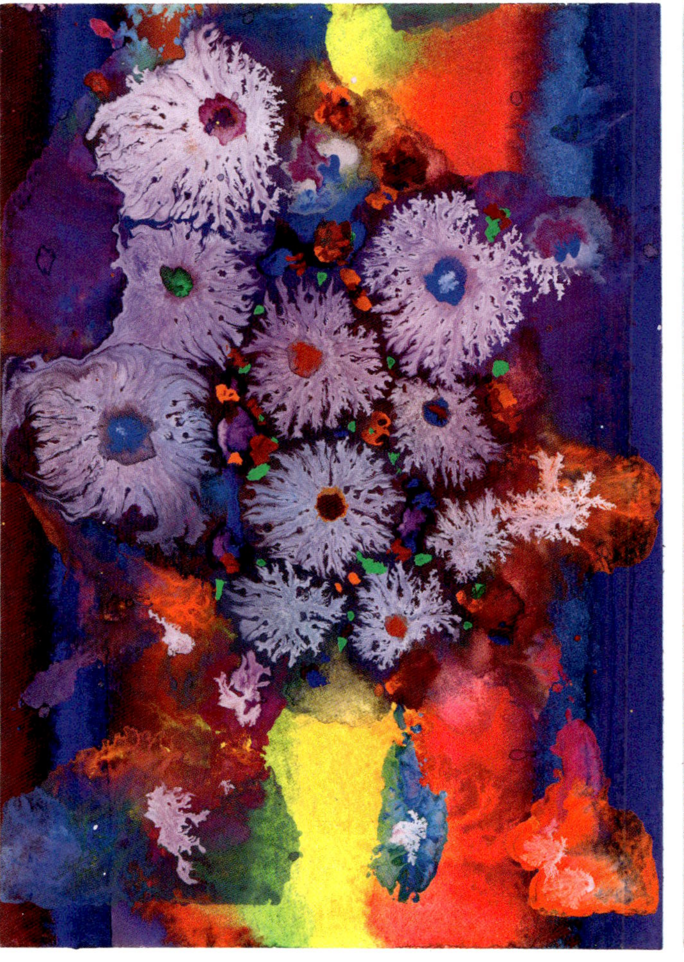

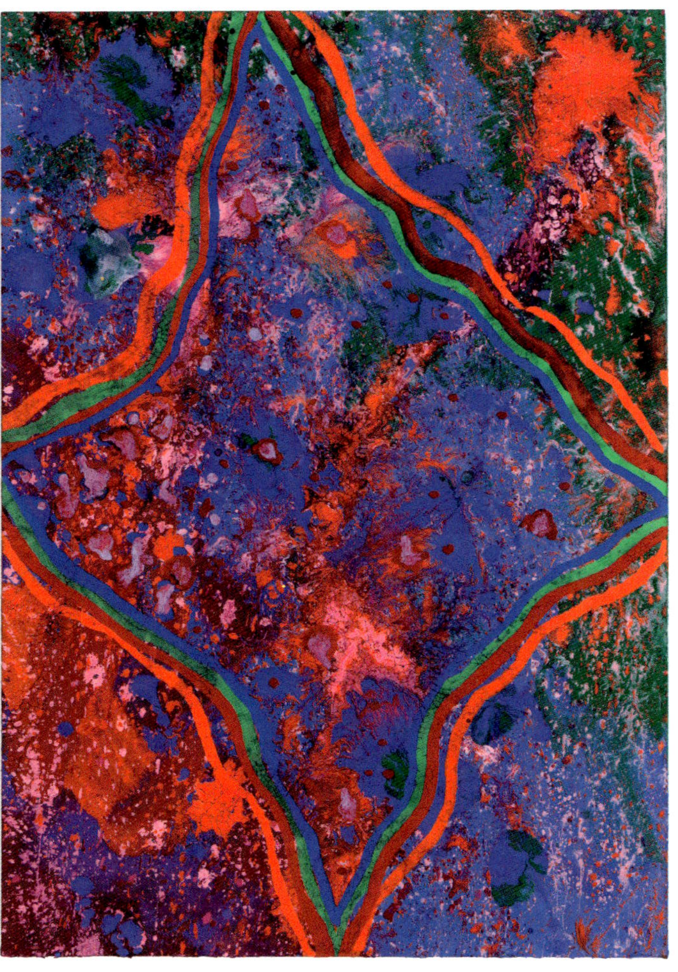

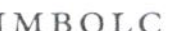

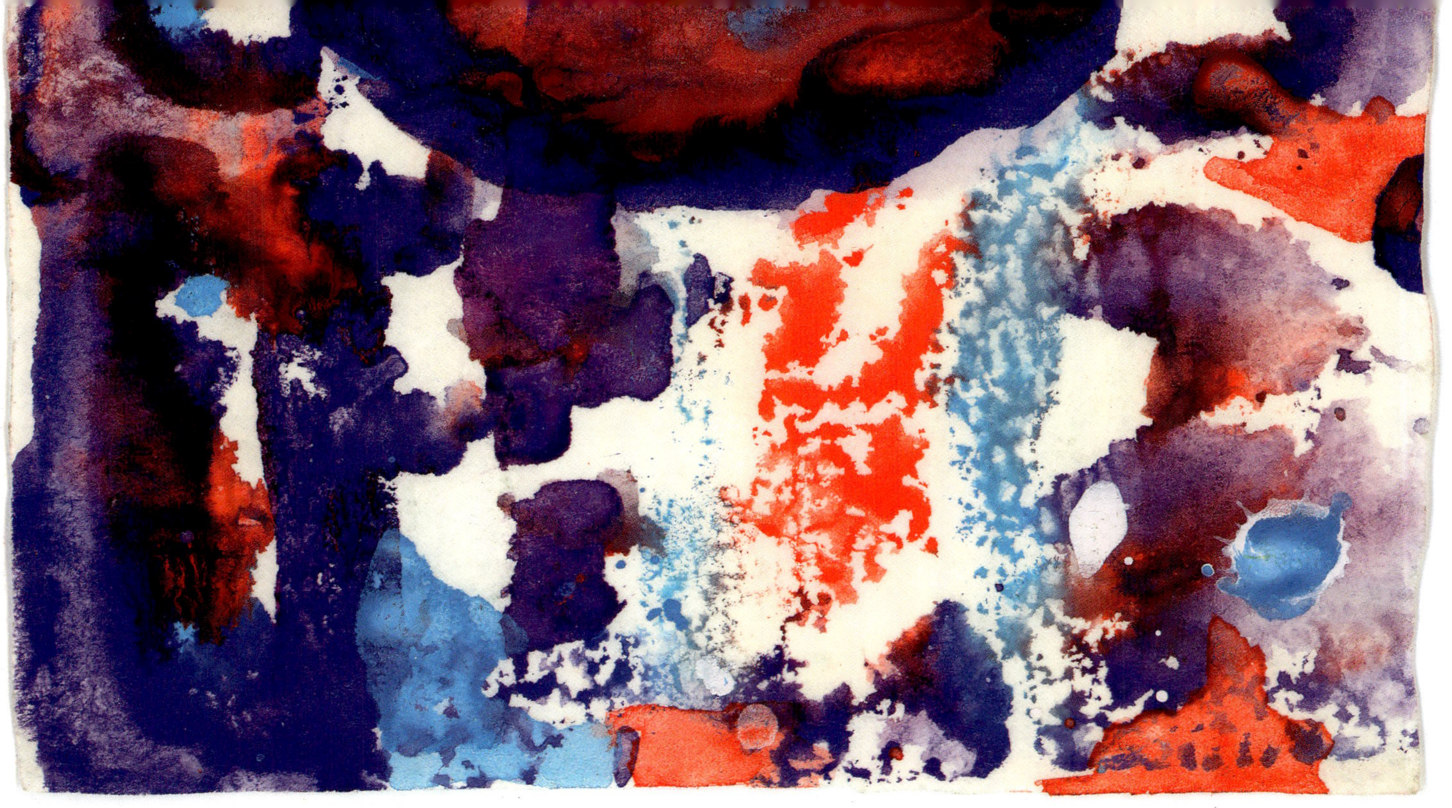

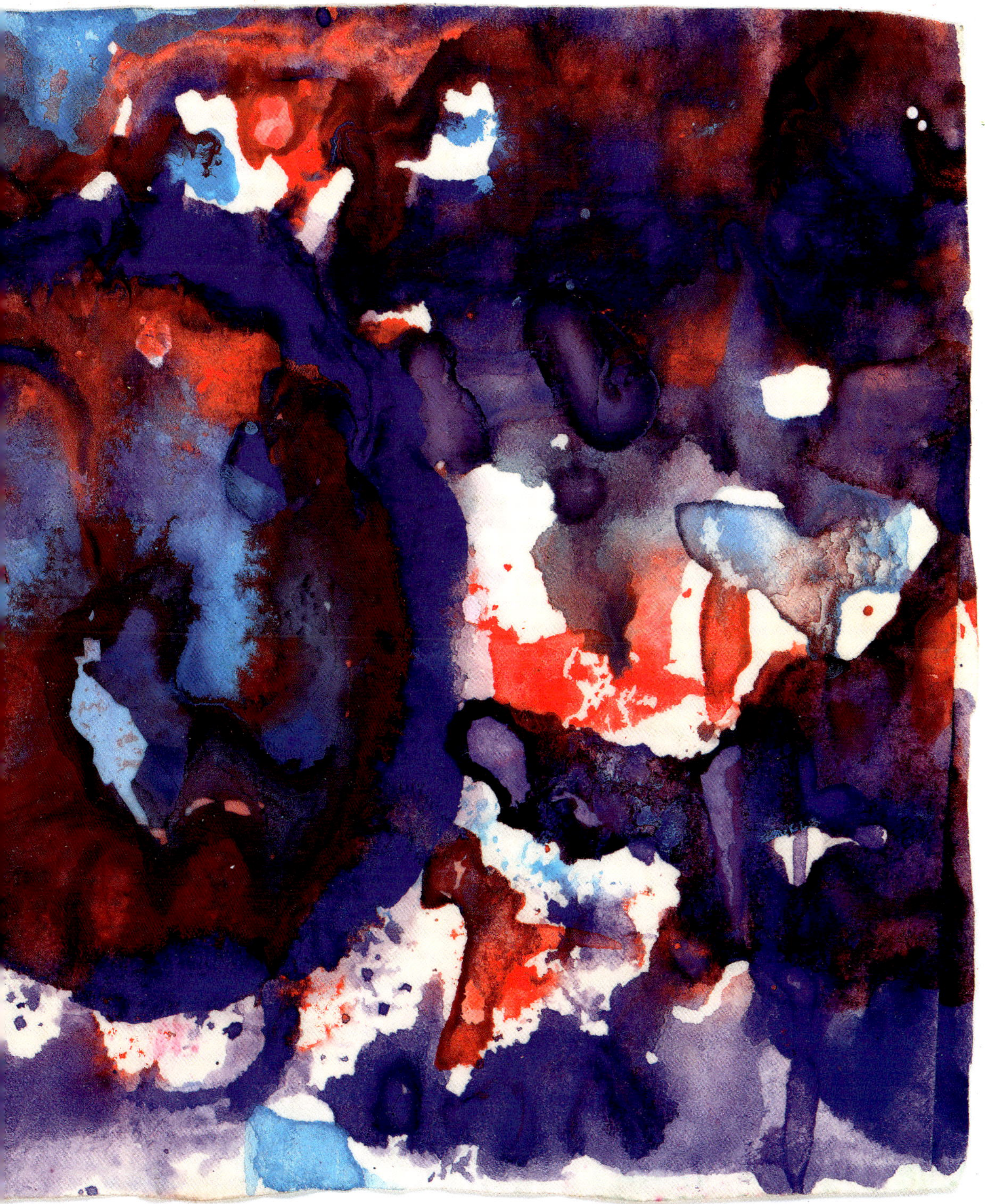

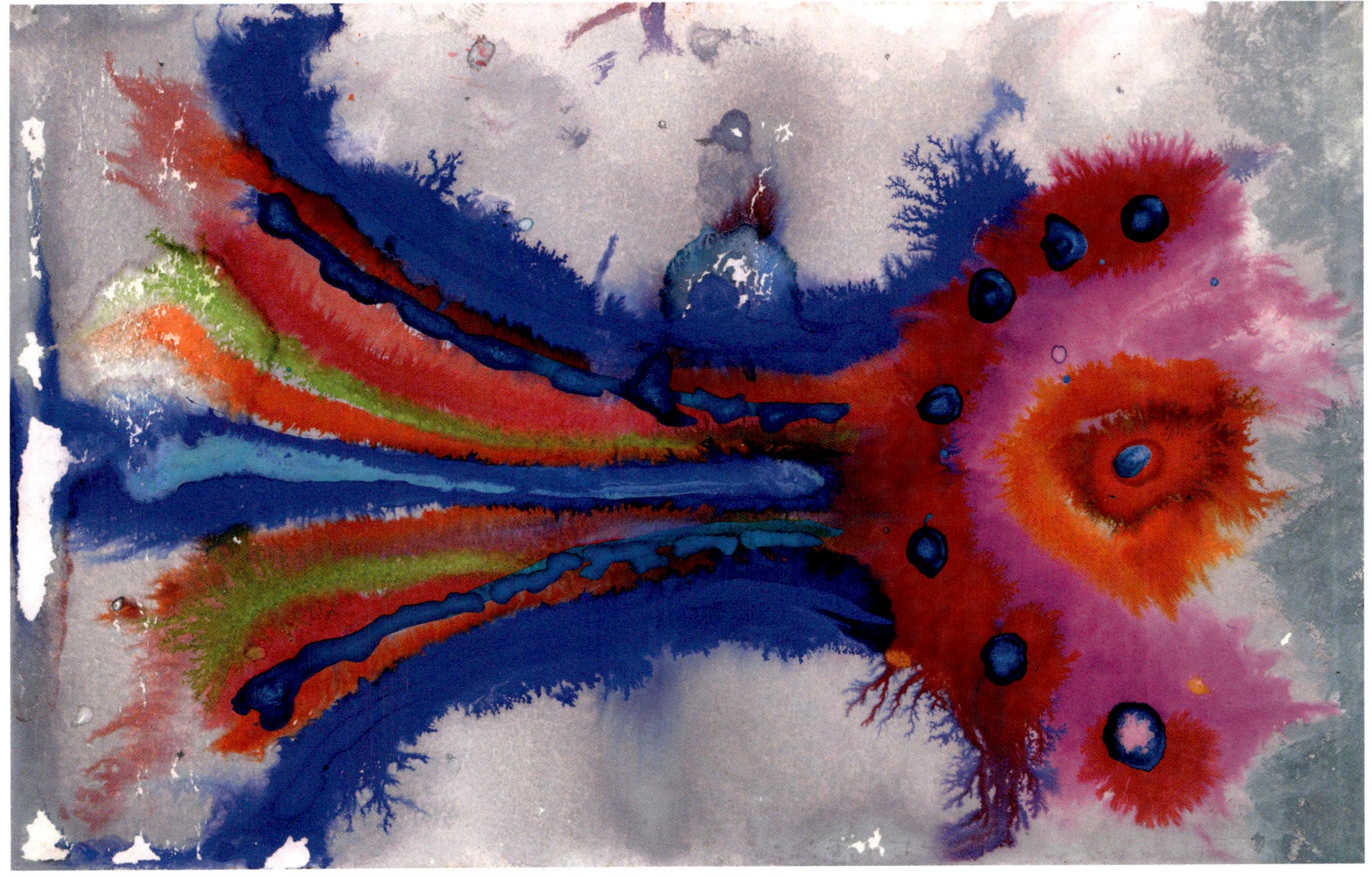

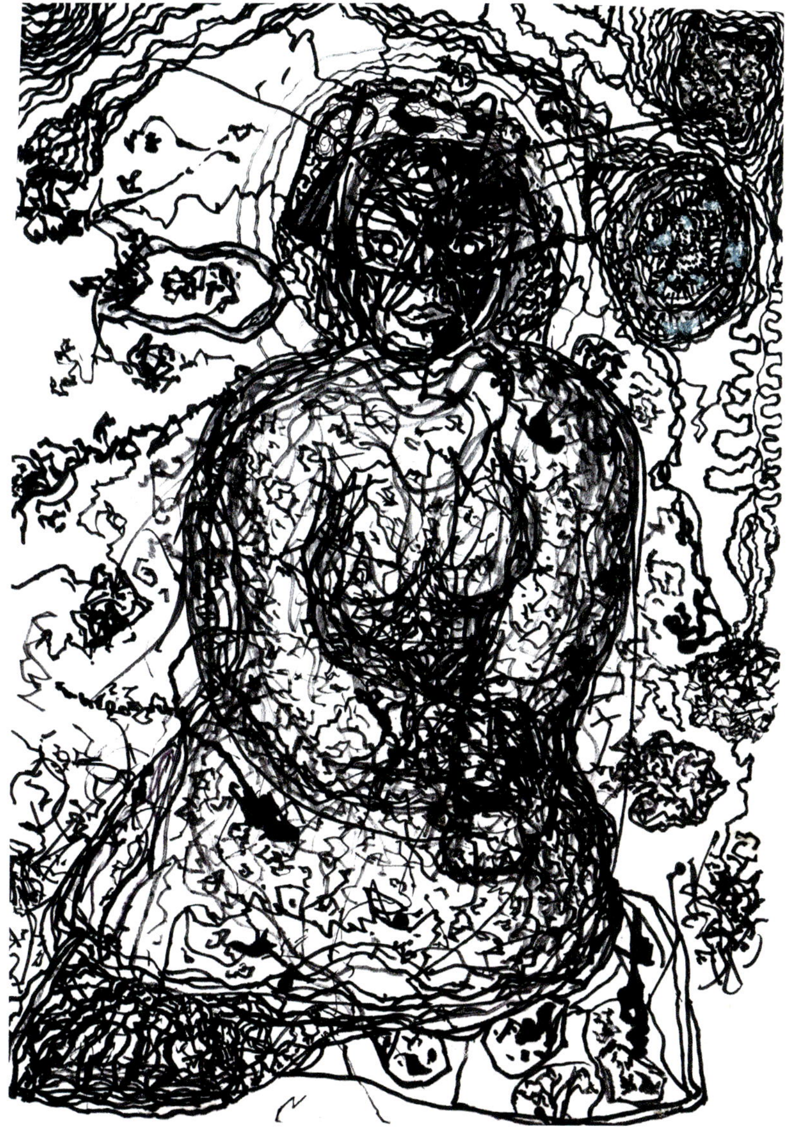

Untitled (Drawing of Seated Woman) / 2022

In his latter years, Jamie's physical limitations meant a shift from painting to drawing, which became a daily practice. Jamie was pleased that he still had a facility for drawing, although it had not meaningfully exercised for some decades. Hundreds of drawings and text-based works appeared, sometimes within a narrative framework whose details were left to chance.

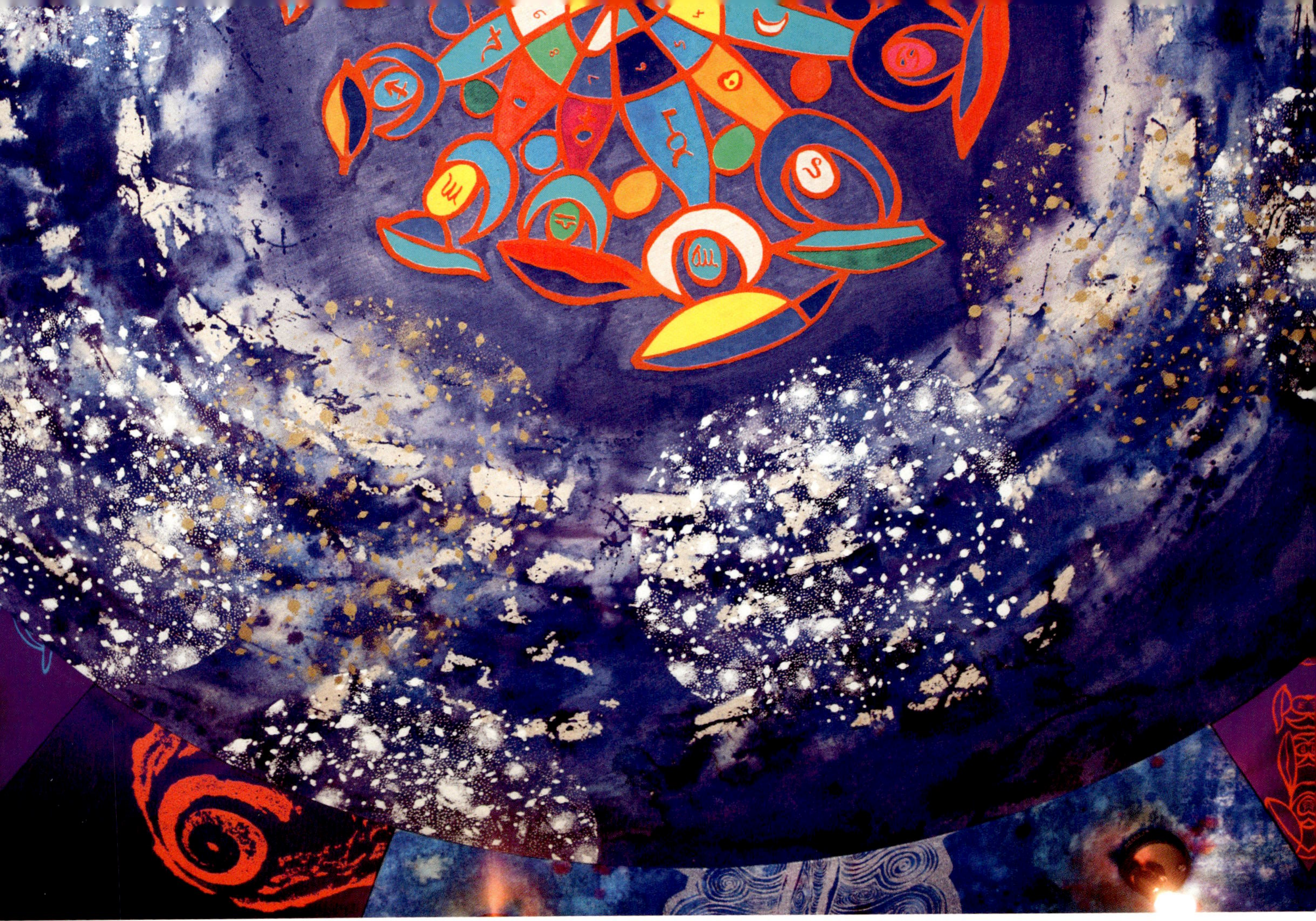

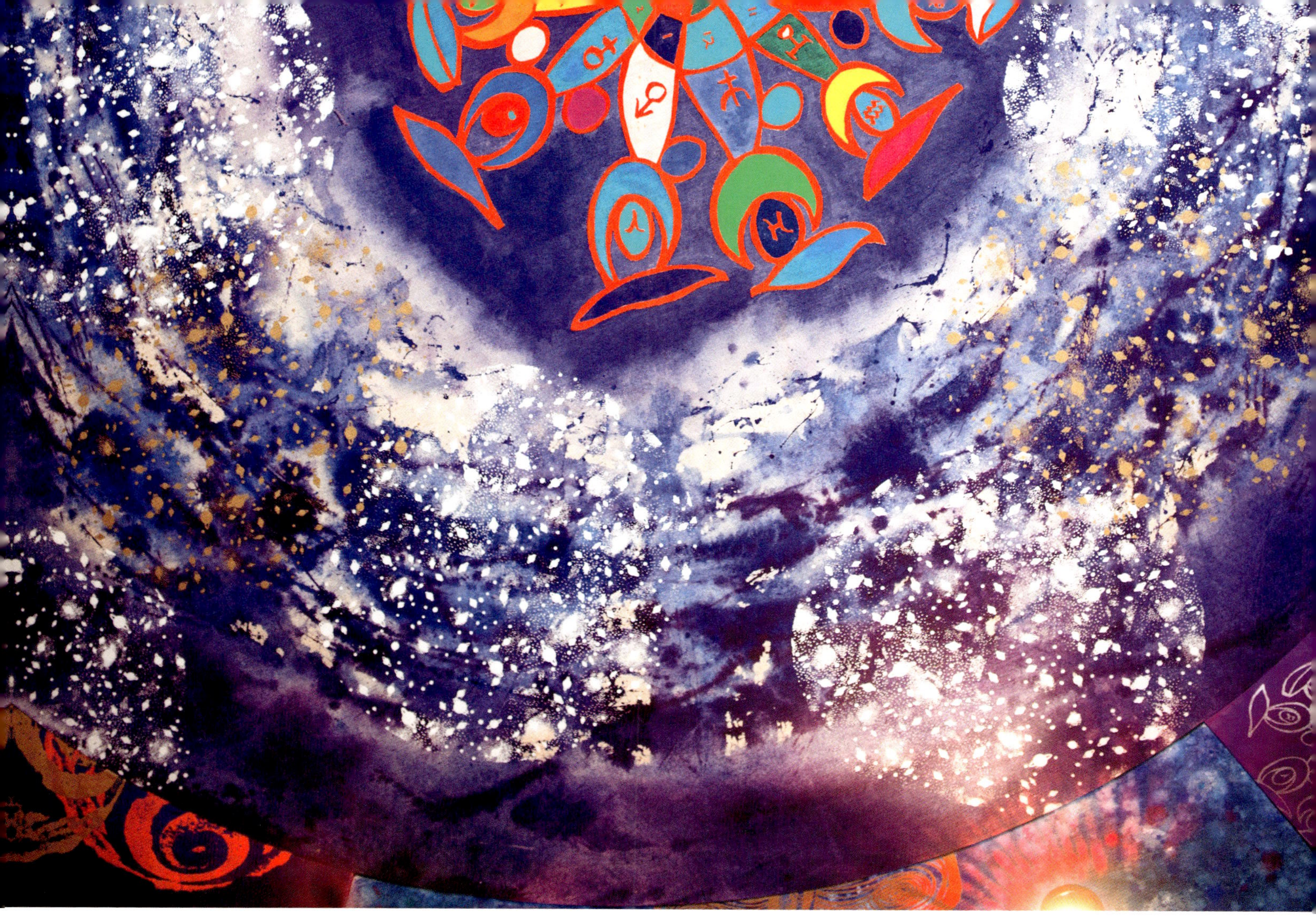

Strongroom Studio interior (ceiling) / 2018

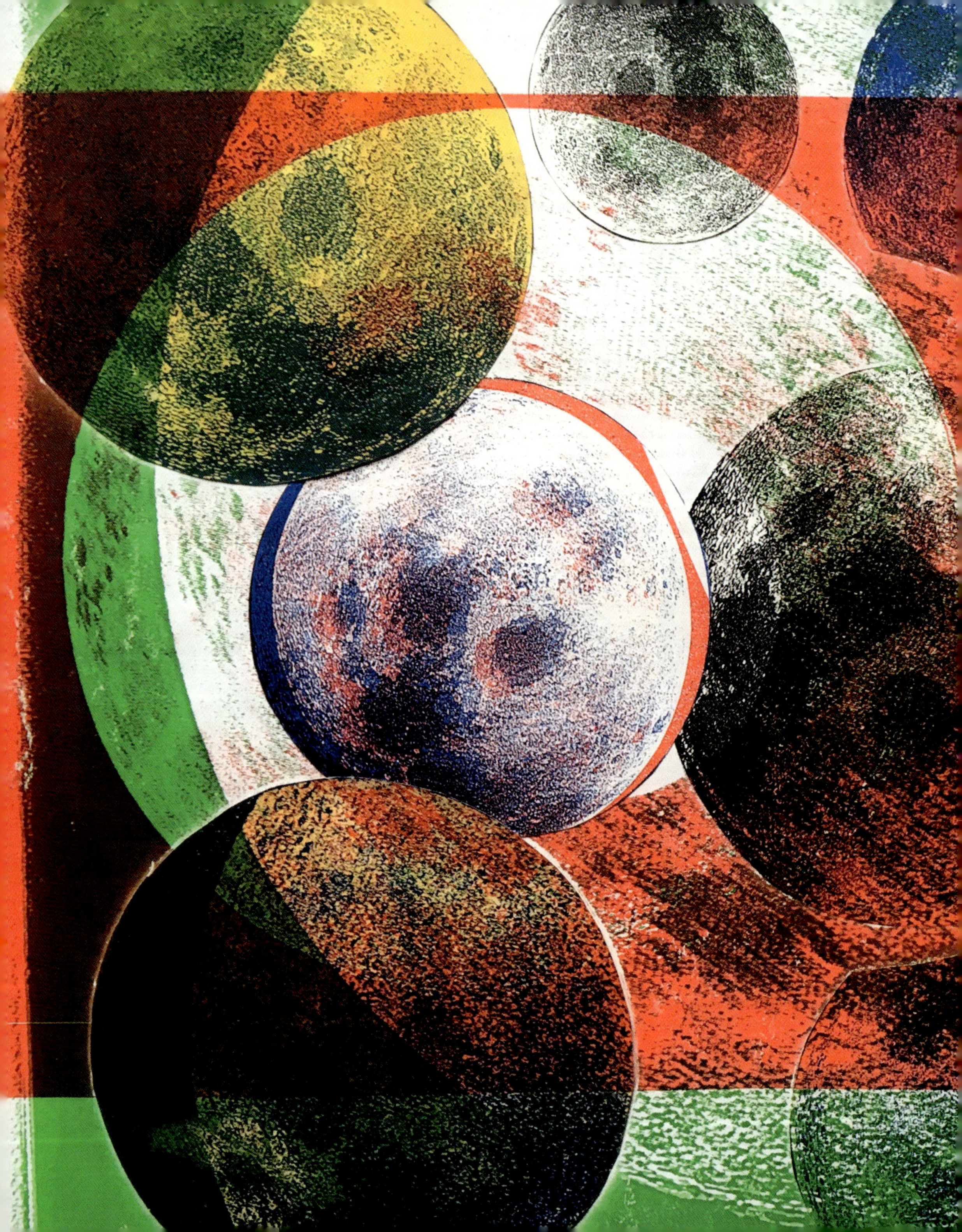

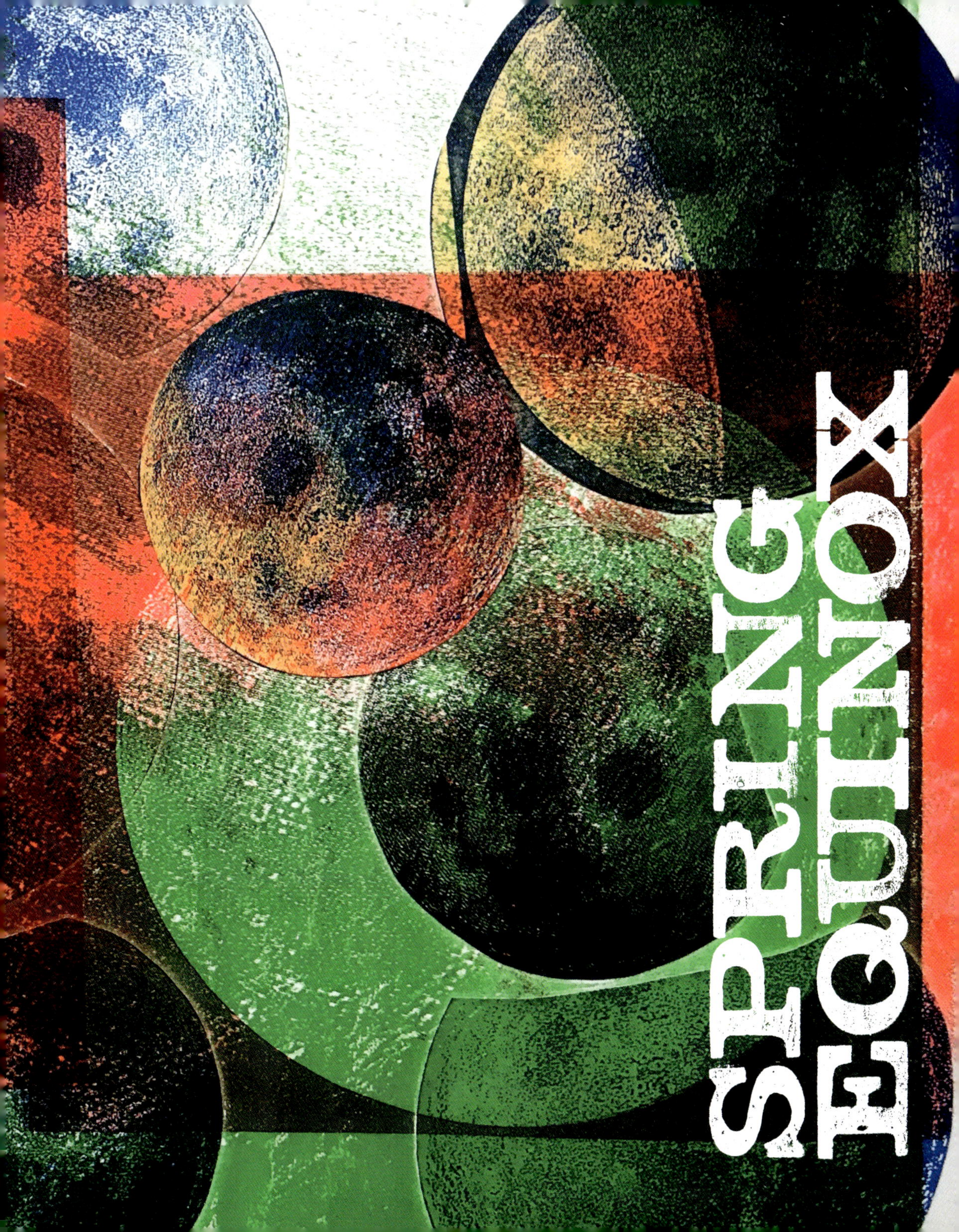
SPRING
EQUINOX

SPRING EQ

The year is trying to crack us open like eggs! Who can really believe that spring is here when the March winds scour, and stinging rain hits you in the face? But she is, and the primroses, crocuses and gorse are flowering to herald her arrival.

Each of the year's four seasons is associated with three festivals. The first and last of each trio are Celtic fire festivals that celebrate two seasons at once. At Imbolc, we bid farewell to winter and welcome in the first glimmers of spring; at Beltane, we celebrate the height of spring and also the start of summer; at Lughnasadh, we dance for summer and lean into autumn; at Samhain, we bid the autumn fires farewell and turn to face winter.

The Spring Equinox is at the midpoint of spring's three festivals, at the place of balance between the light and dark halves of the year. From tomorrow the days will grow longer than the nights and we will enter the bright times. But for now – just for a moment – we can stand at this gateway into the light half of the year and experience a sense of balance.

The Spring Equinox is associated with the rising sun, with the energy of the growing child, with developing an increasing sense of engagement with life and with other people. It's the time when ideas strike and a new energy flares up, a vitality that gets things done. It's time to clear the decks for action because, once the sluggishness of winter is gone, you'll be thrown full tilt into a year that won't pause for another breath until the next equinox, in September. This equinox is calling you to action. It requires you to work, to make something of your life. It's time to break out of your shell and burst through your own defences.

In the Druid tradition, this festival time is known as Alban Eilir, the Light of the Earth, and now is the time to honour the earth in all her potential. The soil with all its richness and promise lies waiting for the sowing. Even though many of us may now live in towns and cities, and go about our lives without thinking much about the land and its cycles, this springtime potential still provokes a feeling of joyful anticipation.

This can seem the most elusive of the festivals to tune into, a season of shape-shifting. The hares that stand on their hind legs and box at this time are themselves shape-shifters – witches in animal form, people used to say. There are many folktales of a hare shot at night and a local, strange, old woman found to be injured with a shotgun wound the next day.

Hares sleep in shallow scrapes in the ground that are known as forms and look like lapwings' nests. As lapwings' nests are filled with eggs in March, over time the belief grew that hares laid eggs. And the egg, of course, has always been a symbol of new life. Children used to paint them and roll them down the hillside to celebrate Easter. Over time, the hare became our Easter bunny, and the eggs are now made of chocolate.

On the opposite side of the Wheel is the Autumn Equinox, the year's other point of balance, when the sun will once more rise due east and set due west, and day and night will be equal again. Then the promises will be fulfilled, our hopes affirmed, and we will reap what we sowed. Our projects realised – or not. Winter will be calling to us, not summer, and we will have to accept the decline of our energies as the Wheel continues to turn.

For now, the arc of the year is upwards. Cold March days disguise the wonders of death and rebirth.

NOTES FROM HELIGAN

'The performance group The Pillars Of Wonder took over the proceedings for the final ritual of our first year at Heligan – Spring Equinox. Processing down to Valentine's Field and in and around the OVA, the people taking part carried banners and placards featuring Jamie's slogans and drawings. The Holly Man appeared, antlers in his hands and his head wreathed in holly, and yellow smoke billowed from a censer. Four loudspeakers were placed at the cardinal points of the OVA to emit drones in the key of E, and then we all walked into the centre, bringing everything together. It was a wonderful way to celebrate the completion of the OVA's first yearly cycle, with laughter and a sense of togetherness with Mother Nature. Soon the time will come for the sowing of seed. Spring is on its way.'

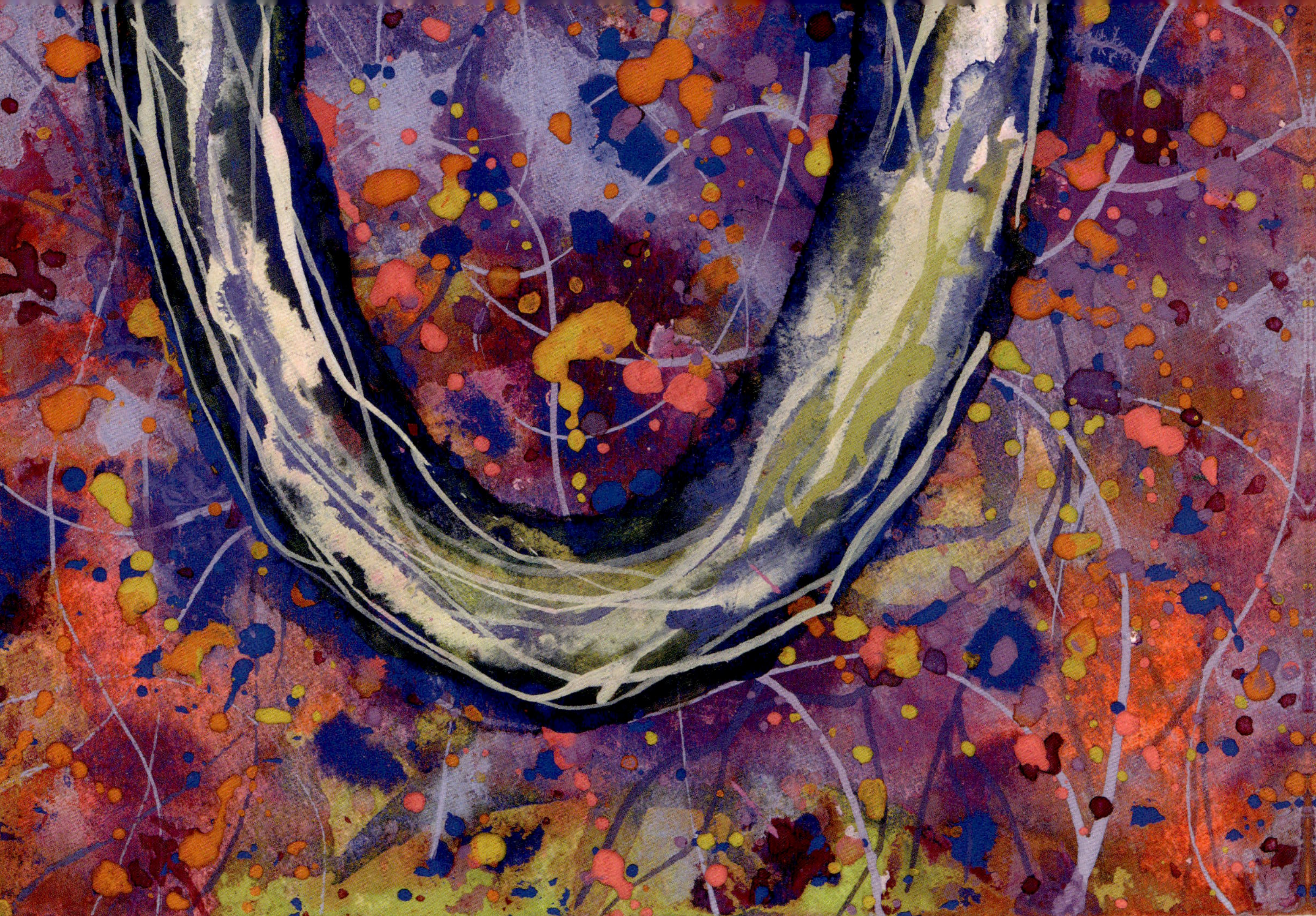

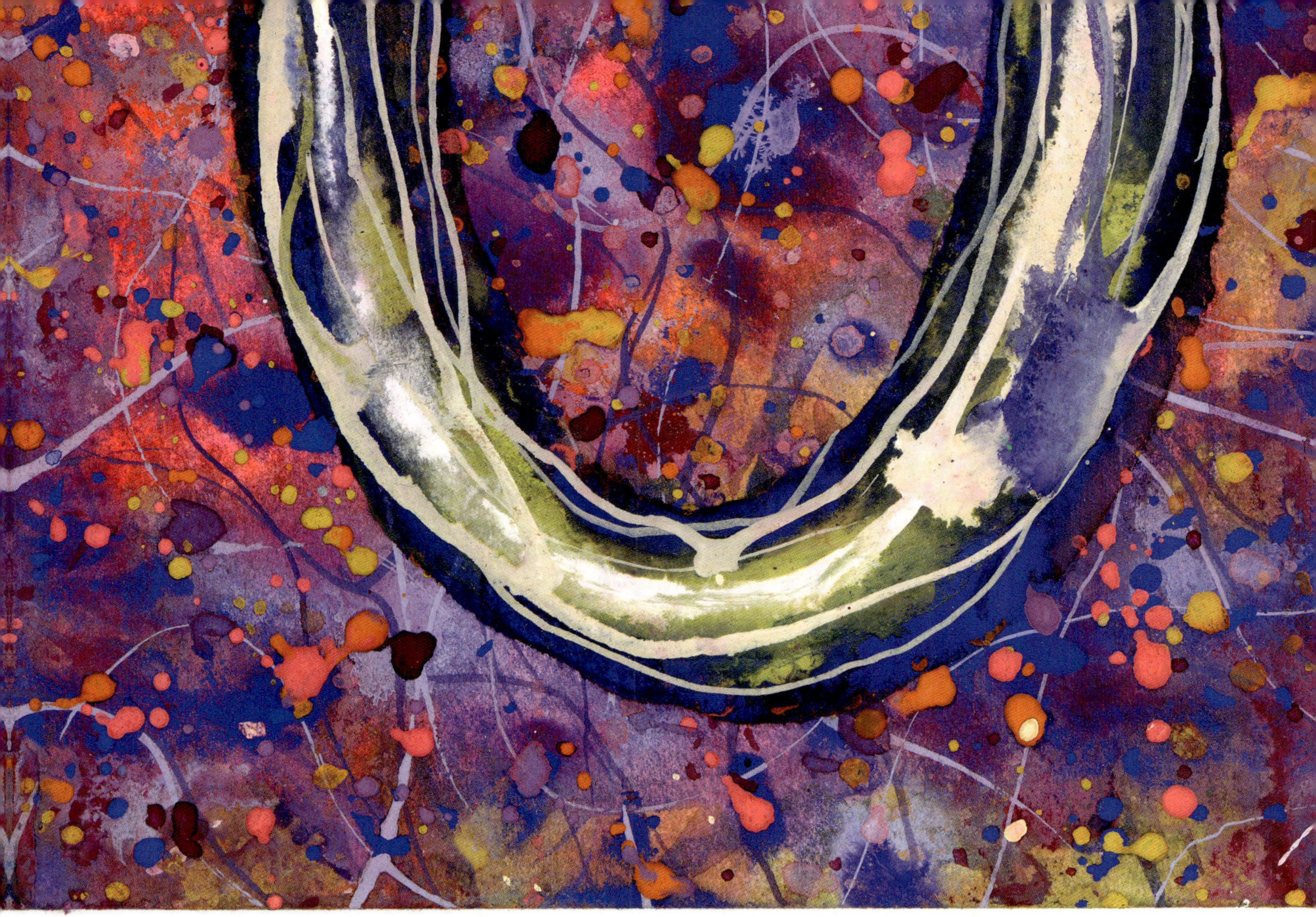

CELTIC SURVEYOR

Universalist
Spiritual Liberation
Soul Wash
Soul Death
Gypsy
Root Race
Shaman
Cultural Crossover
OUT OF
DARK AGE
OVATE
Buddhist
Leaving The 20TH
INTO LIGHT AGE.
Druid
NEW MILLENIUM
Love
All for One
One for All
Pre History Tomorrow
AWAKENING
HOMEOPATHY
DREAM POWER
Mind over Matter
ENERGY FIELDS
Astrological
MAGNETIC
QUARTZING
OPENENDED.
CIRCLE THE SQUARE.
SCHEIHALLION CLAN
WEALTH REDISTRIBUTION
GOLDEN SECTION
COMPASSION
ACCESS TO KNOWLEDGE
DRAIN THE POISON
Serve The GODESS
TRIBAL
To hell & back again
COLLECTIVE
OPEN SOCIETY
UNDERWORLD
MIDDLE WORLD
UPPER WORLD
GLOBAL COMPASSION
GLOBAL GARDENER
CREATURE WISDOM
Learn from The Beasts
CARING
BARTER.
SWAPS
SUPER SENSE.
Money is ACURSED CONCEPT
The Greening
EAST IS WEST IS NORTH IS SOUTH
COMMON WEALTH.

Celtic Surveyor/1991

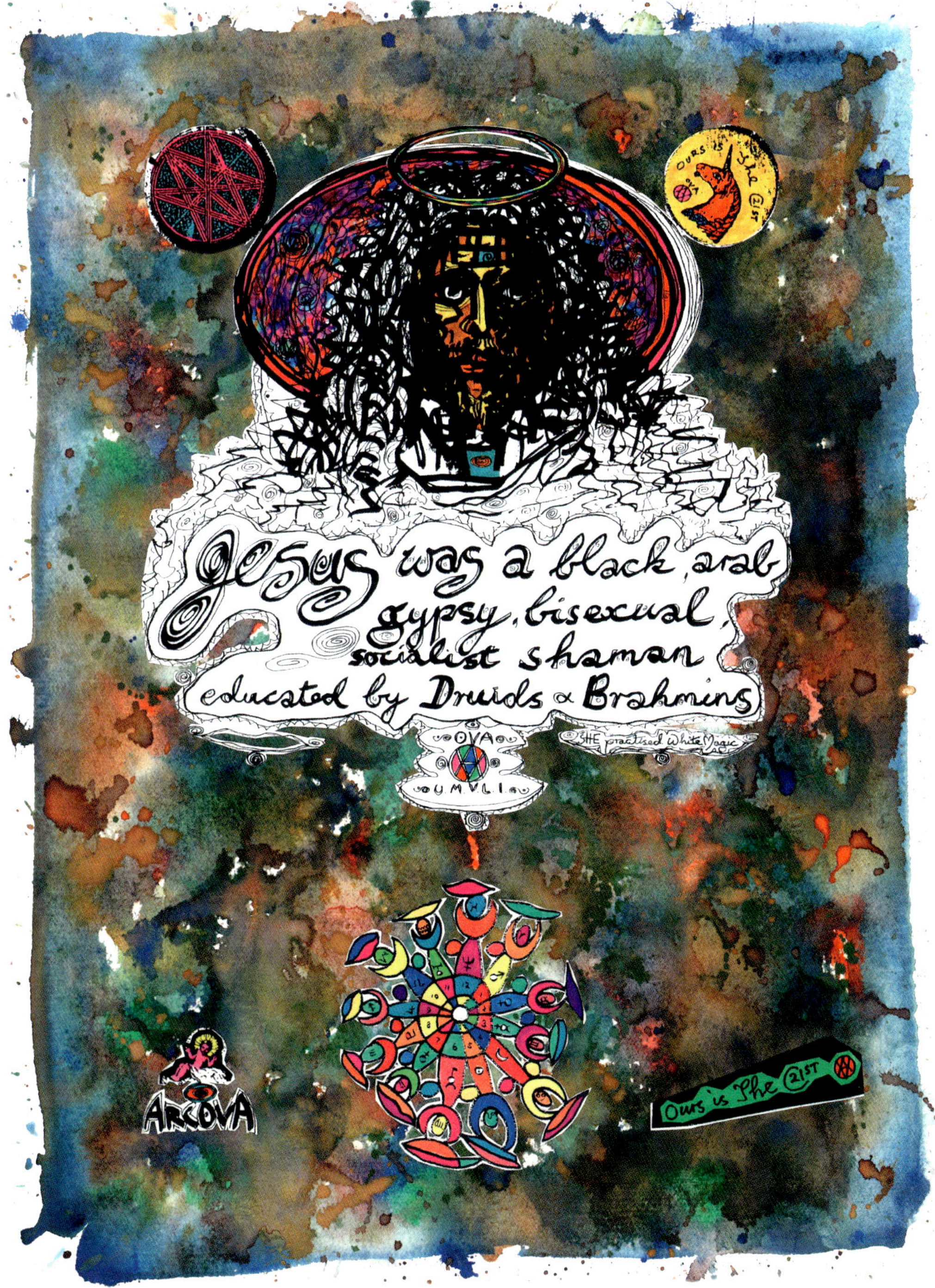

Jesus Was a Black Arab Gypsy Bisexual Socialist Shaman Educated by Druids and Brahmins / c.1994

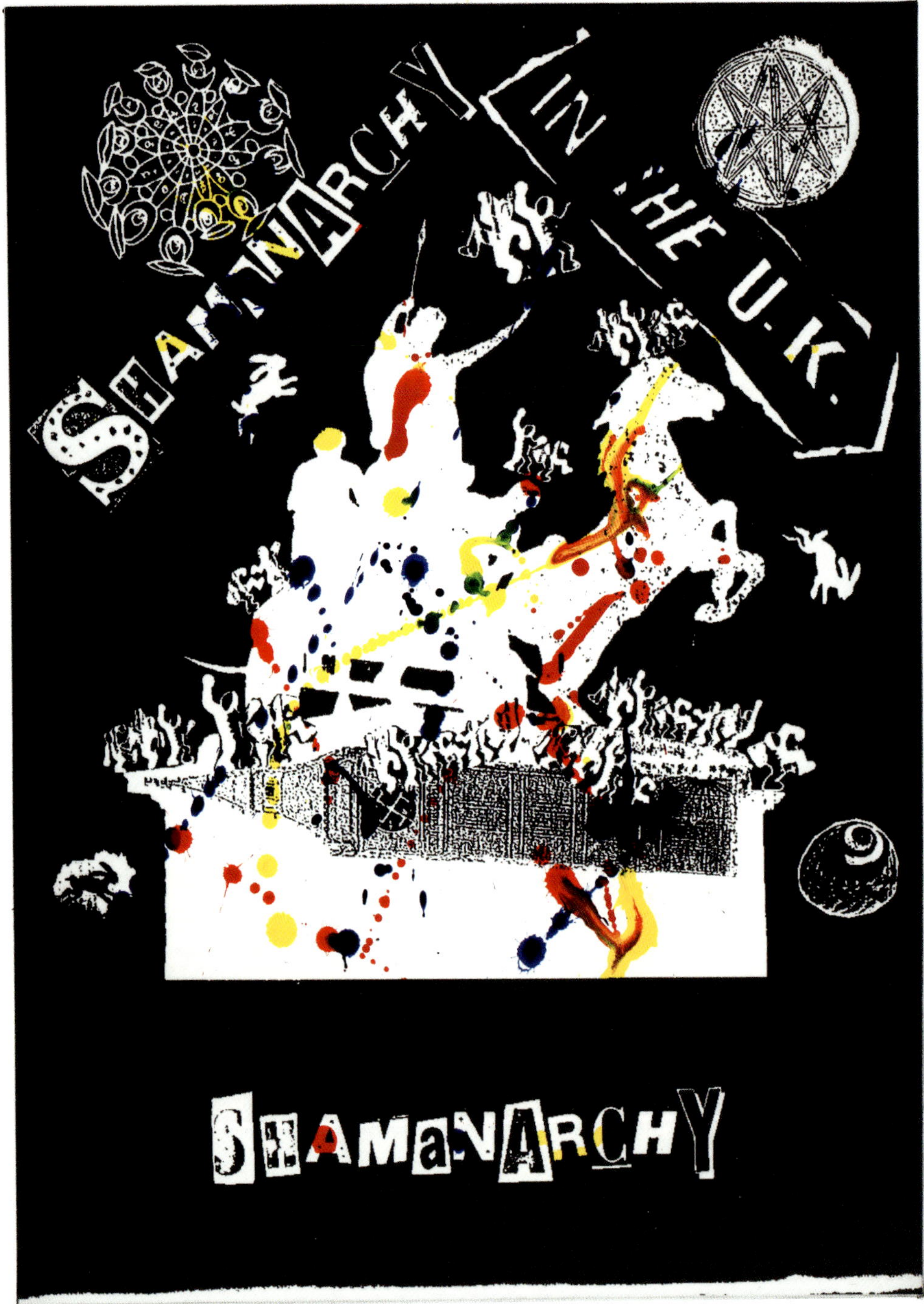
IN
U.K.
SHAMANARCHY

Shamanarchy in the UK / 1992

Obviously riffing off the famous Sex Pistols' song title, *Shamanarchy in the UK* was created for an album produced by Fraser Clark's Megatripolis movement. This festival-like club night in London fused rave and ambient music with New Age thinking offered by in-person or satellite-linked speakers, such as Allen Ginsberg, Terence McKenna and Timothy Leary, to forge an ideology that wasn't above either pranksterism or extensive drug use. This visual includes the silhouette of a statue on the Thames Embankment of Boudica raising her spear at the Houses of Parliament. The source image was taken by Jamie on a visit with Fraser Clark to talk with amenable MPs about the impending Criminal Justice Bill, which would enforce further constraints on the already legally beleaguered rave scene.

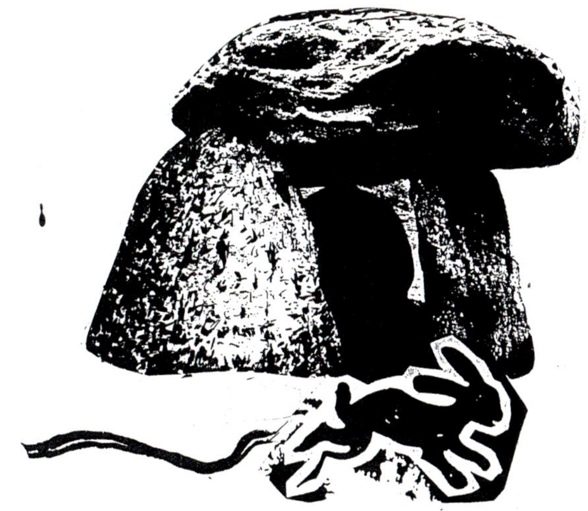

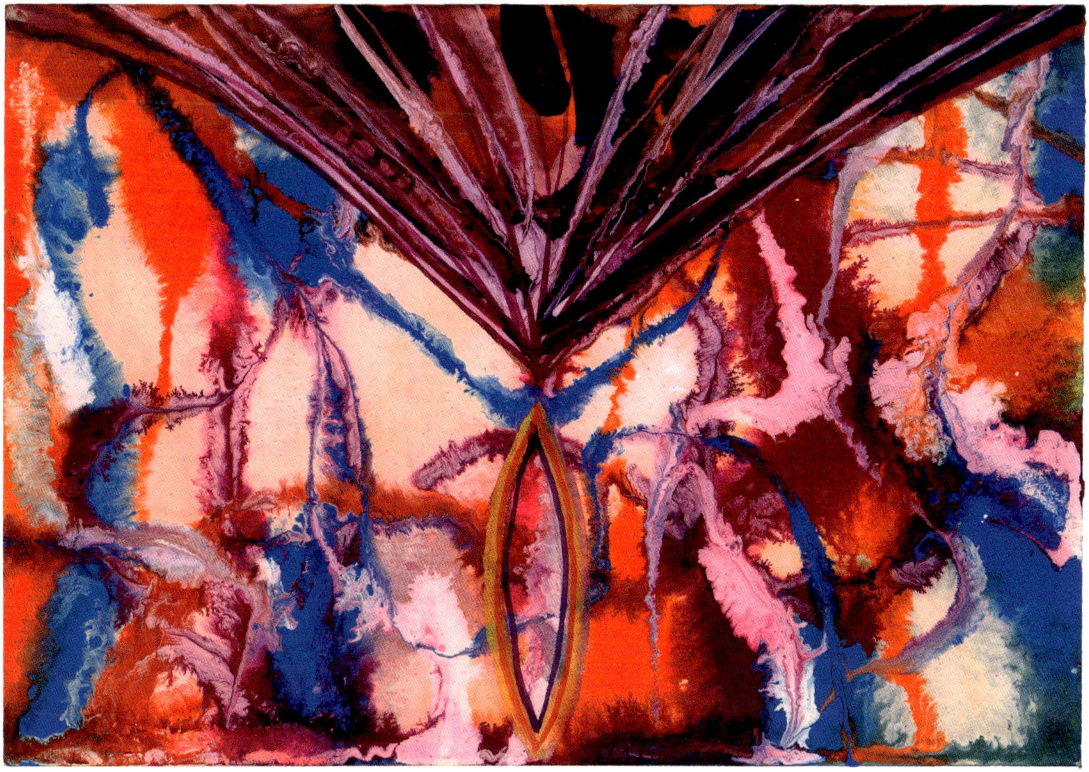

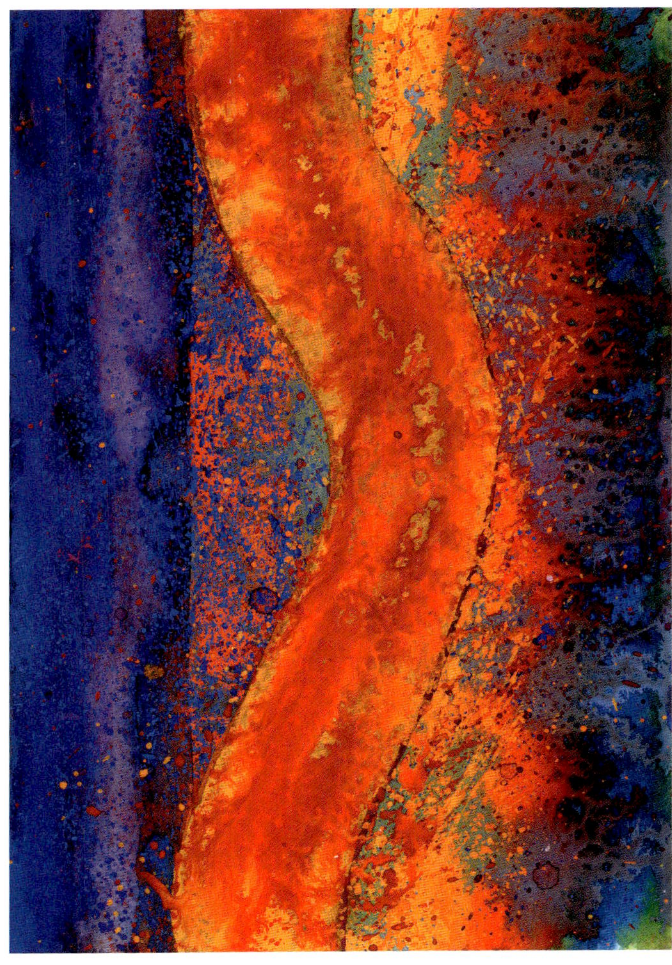

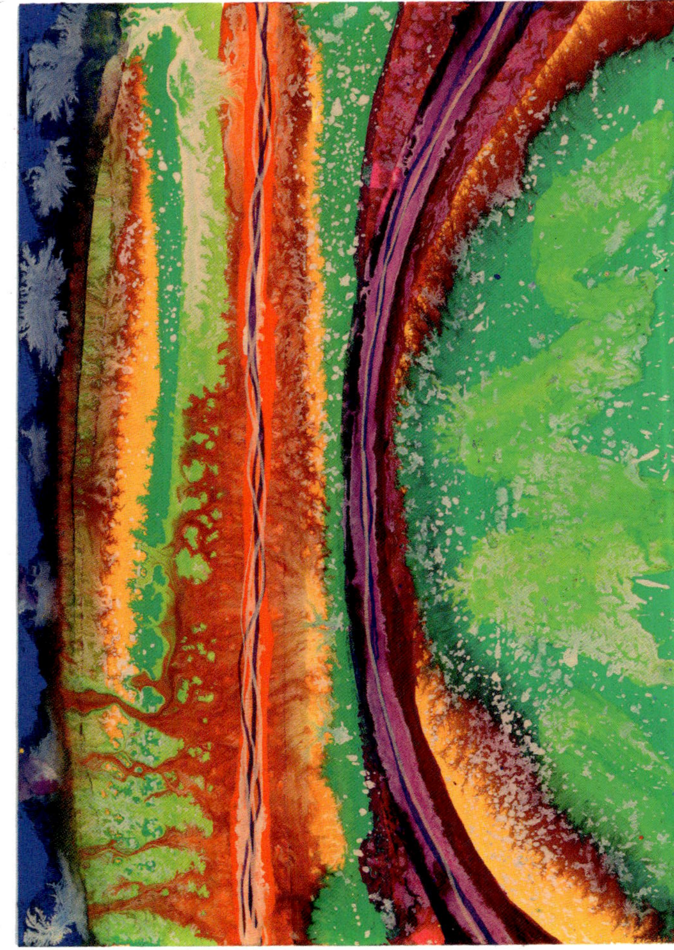

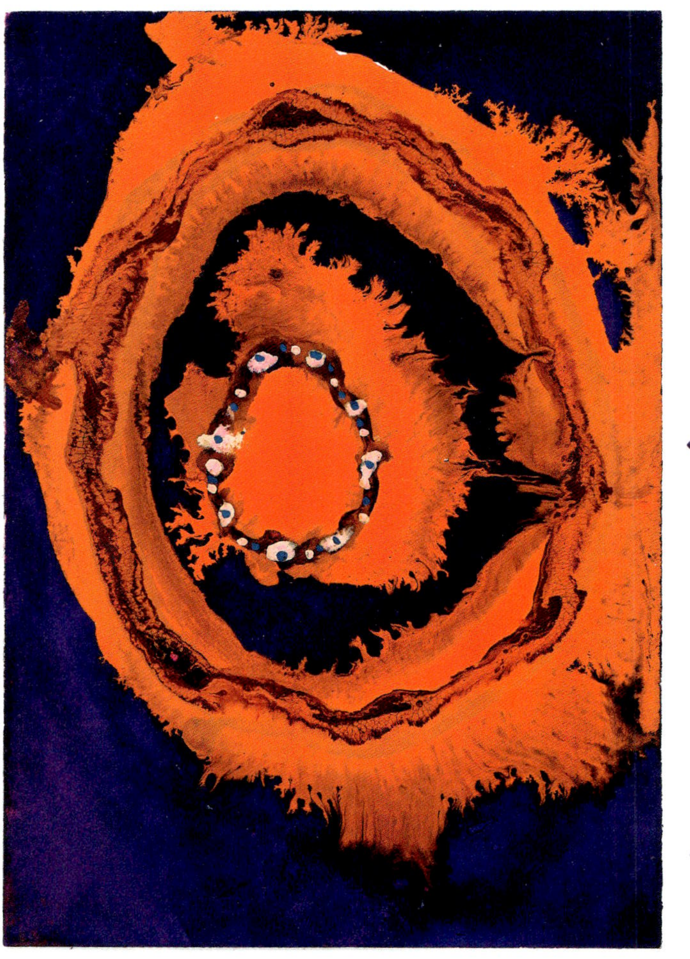

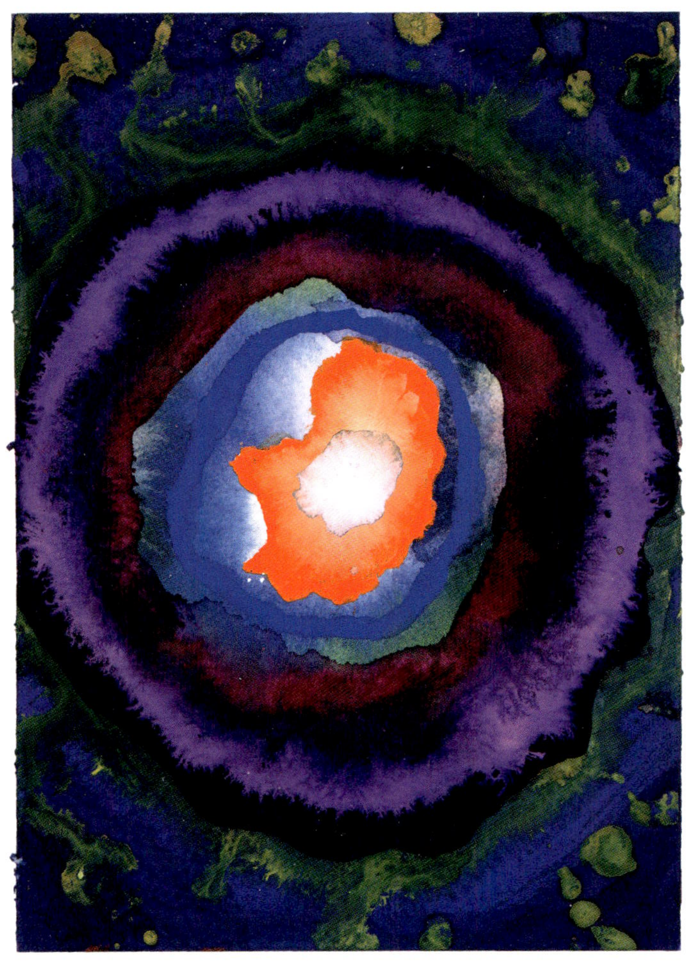

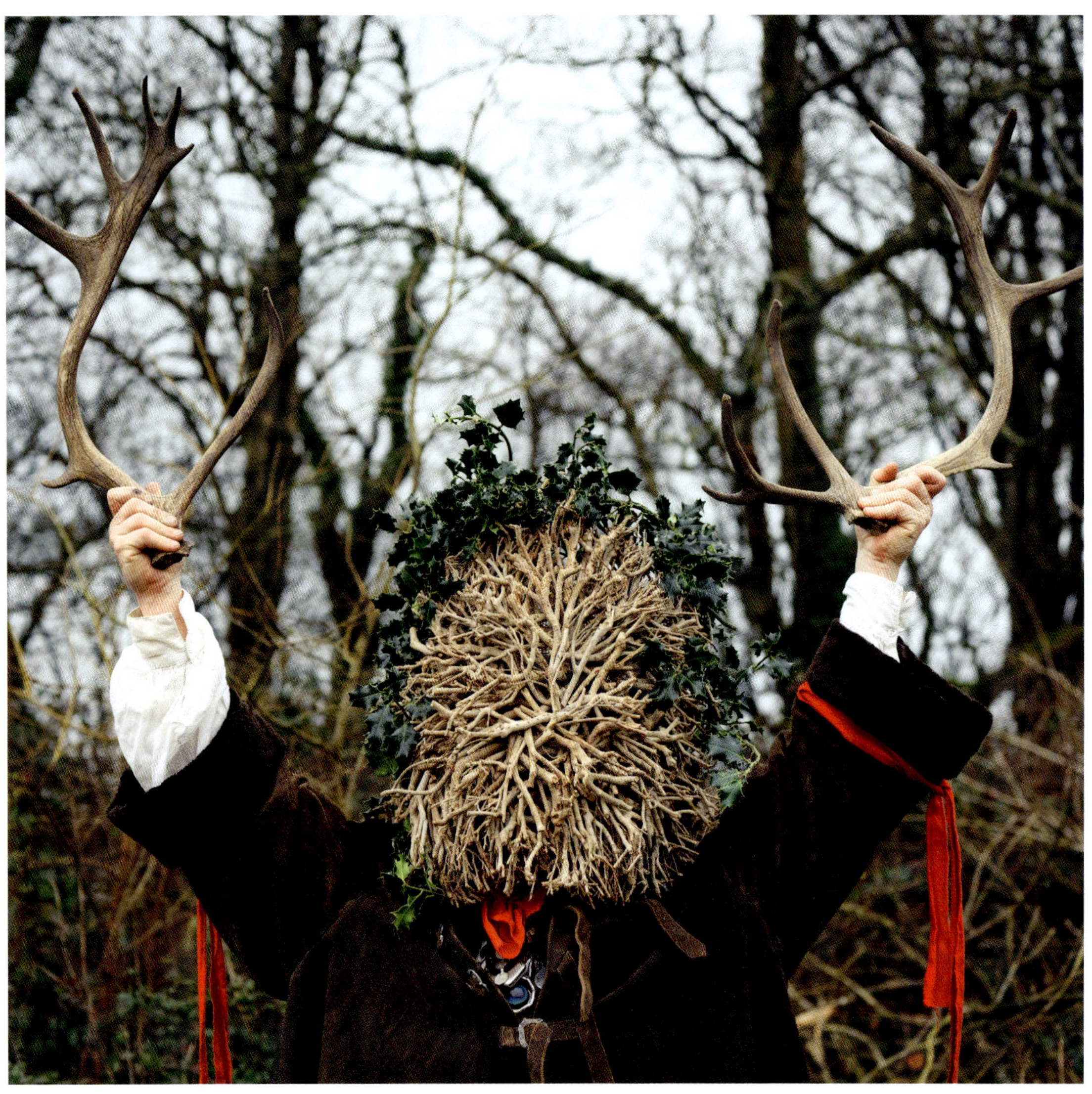

The Holly Man / 2023
The Holly Man appeared at a Spring Equinox ritual at the Lost Gardens of Heligan in 2023. Arranged with a performance group called The Pillars of Wonder, of which Jamie was a founder member and which included musicians Richard Norris and Matthew Shaw, this particular event involved procession, tonal drones, banners and a lot of yellow smoke!

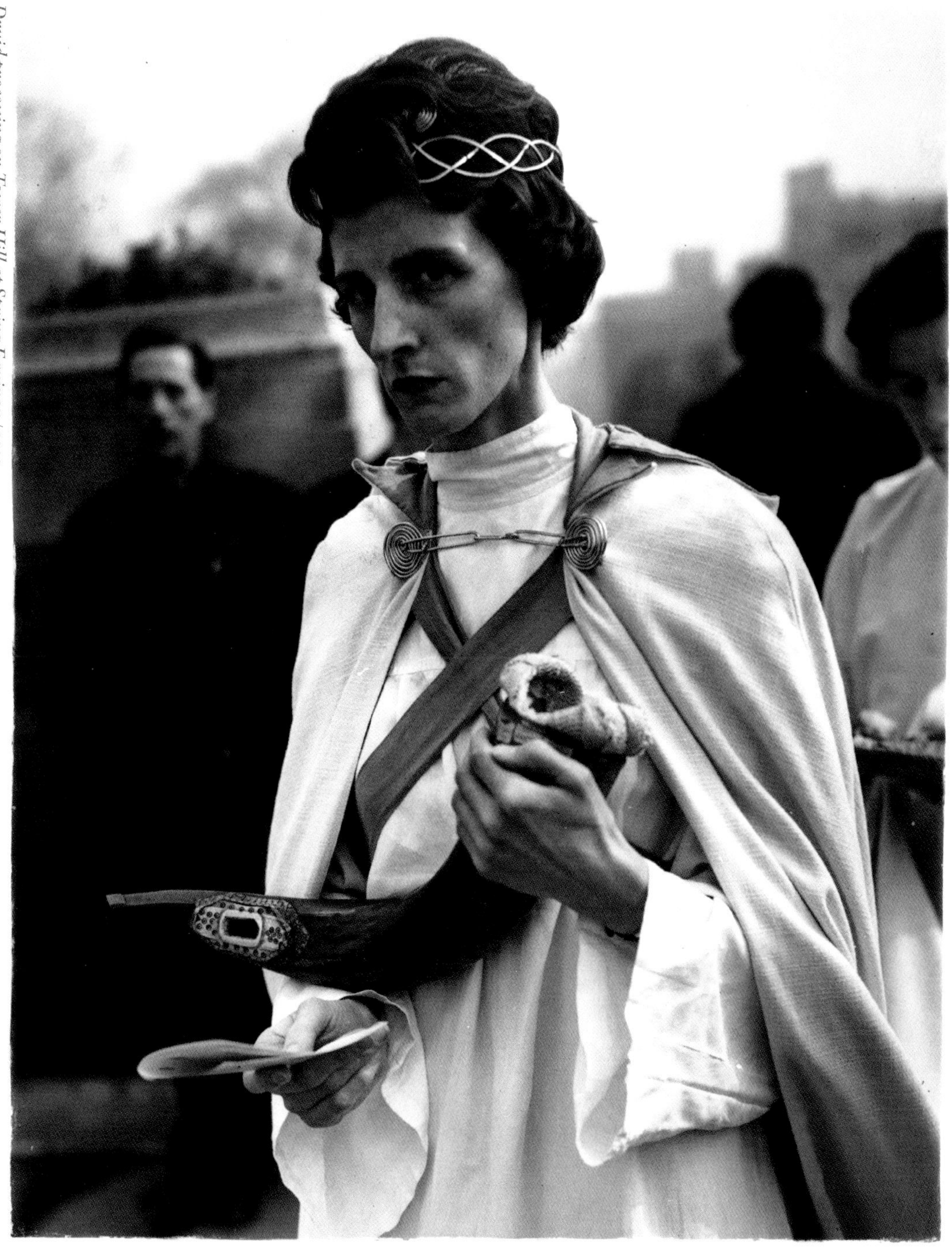

Druid processing on Tower Hill at Spring Equinox / 1959

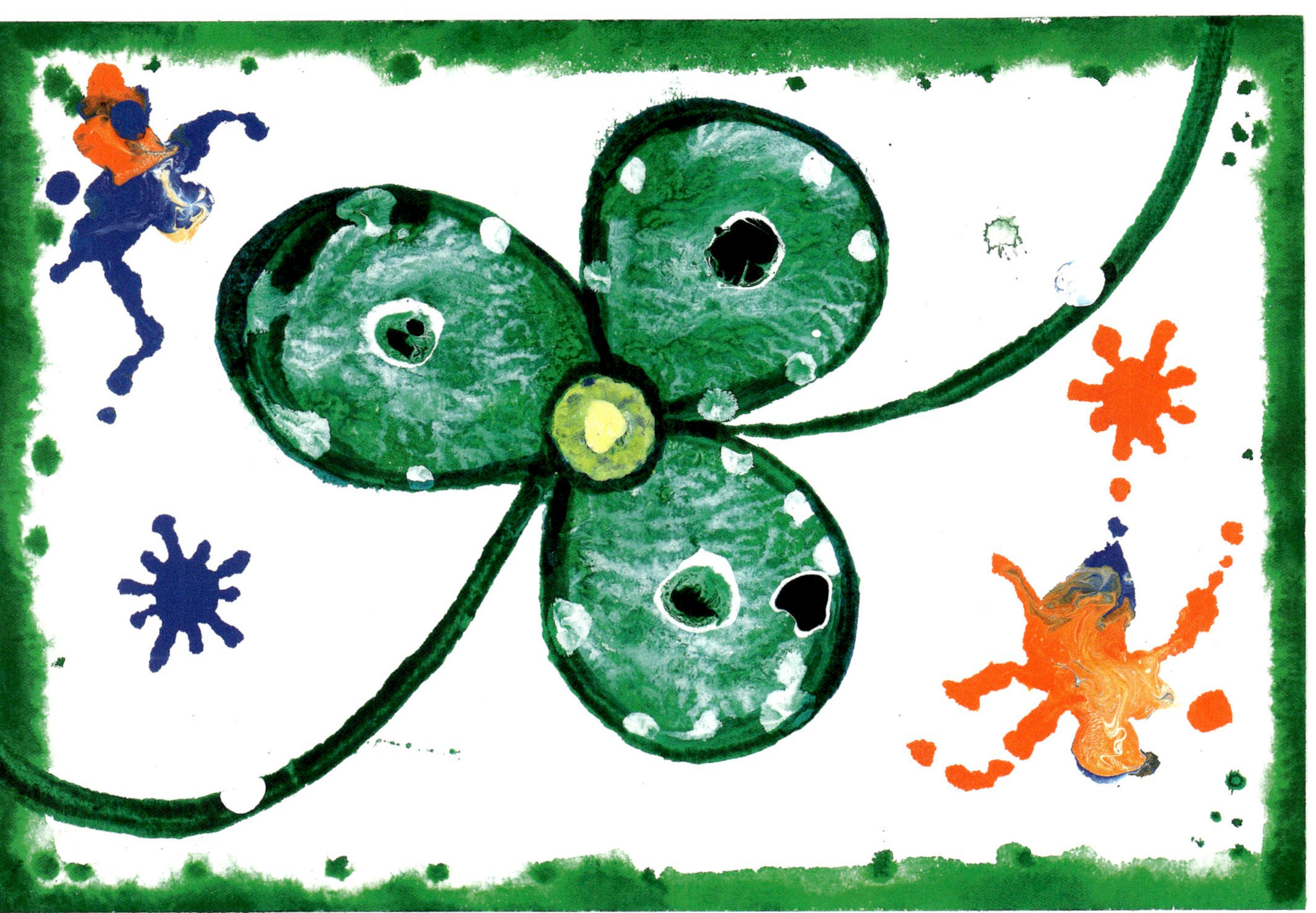

Spring Equinox / 2010

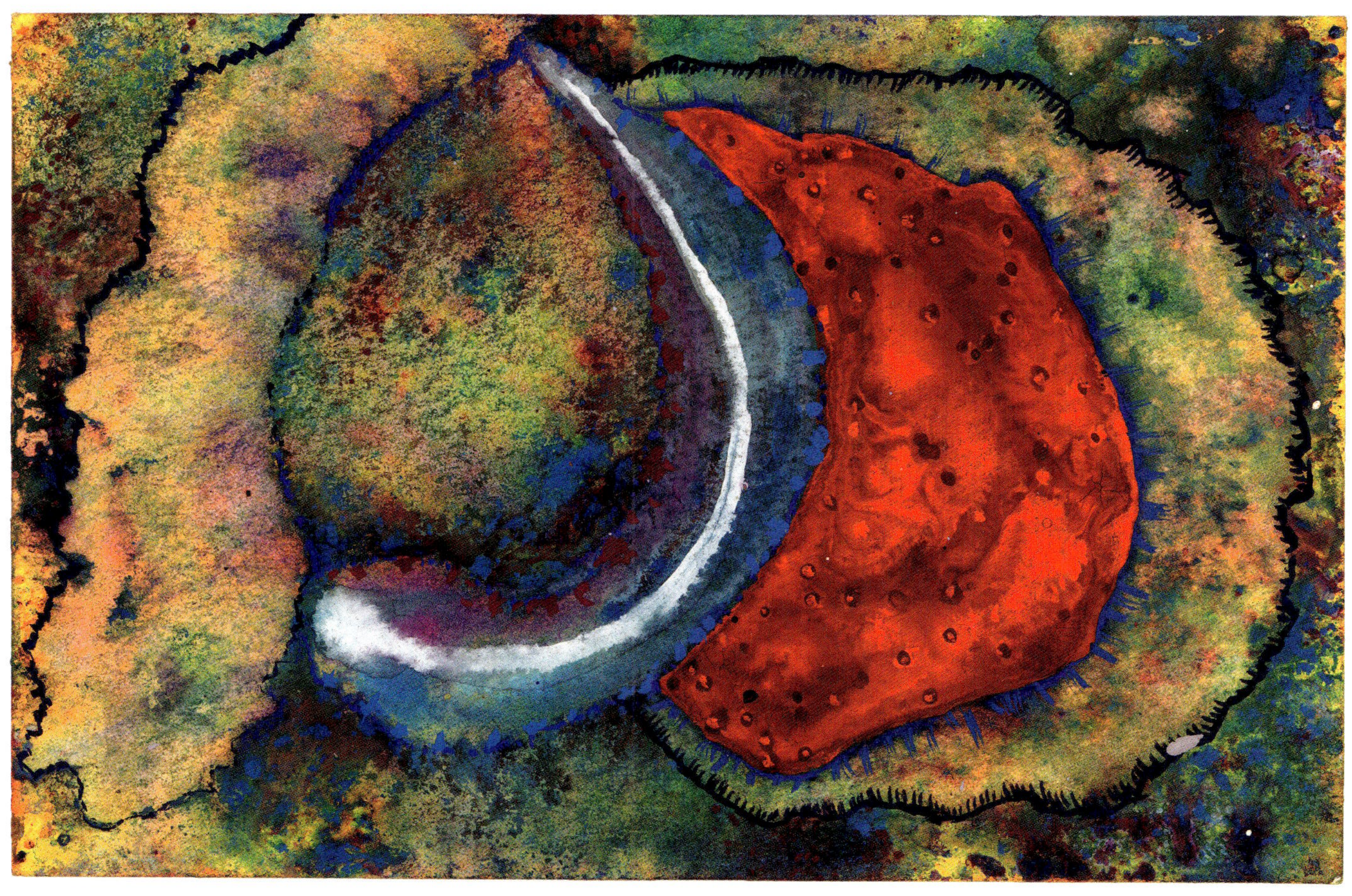

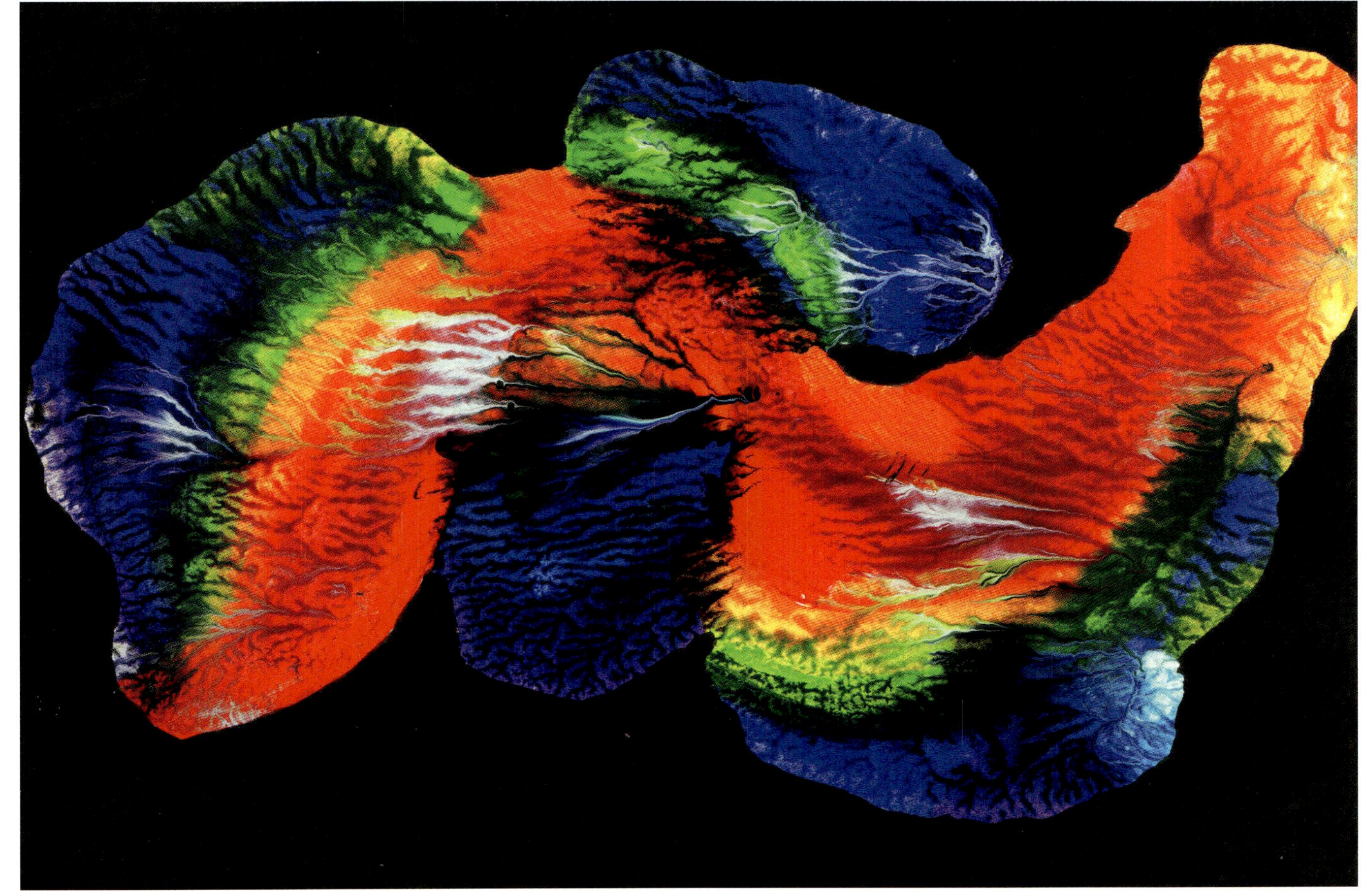

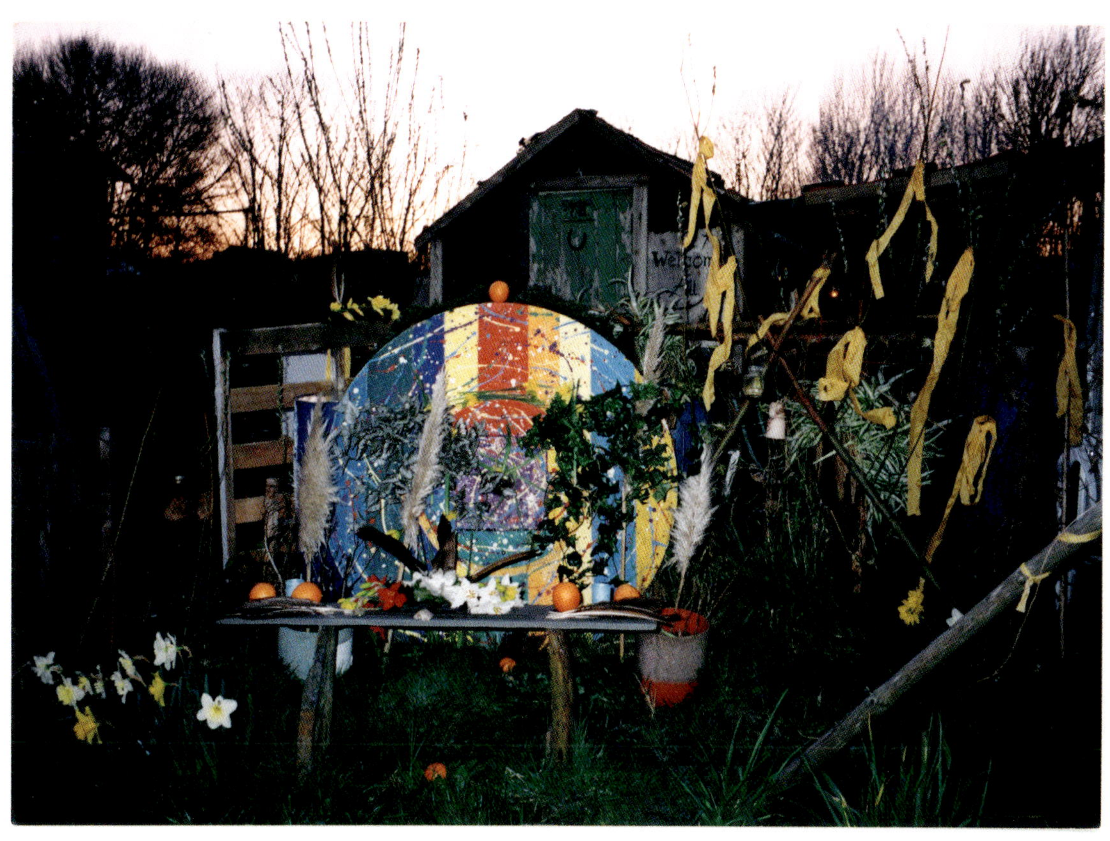

Ritual at Jamie's Allotment / *c.* 2002

For Jamie, his allotment near the banks of the Mersey was a place for observation and thought, for watching the birds and the turning of the seasons, as much as a place for growing food. Along with other allotmenteers, Jamie would regularly celebrate the rituals of the Eightfold Year, either on site or travelling to the hills of North Wales for larger gatherings that were often decorated with his large, painted hangings.

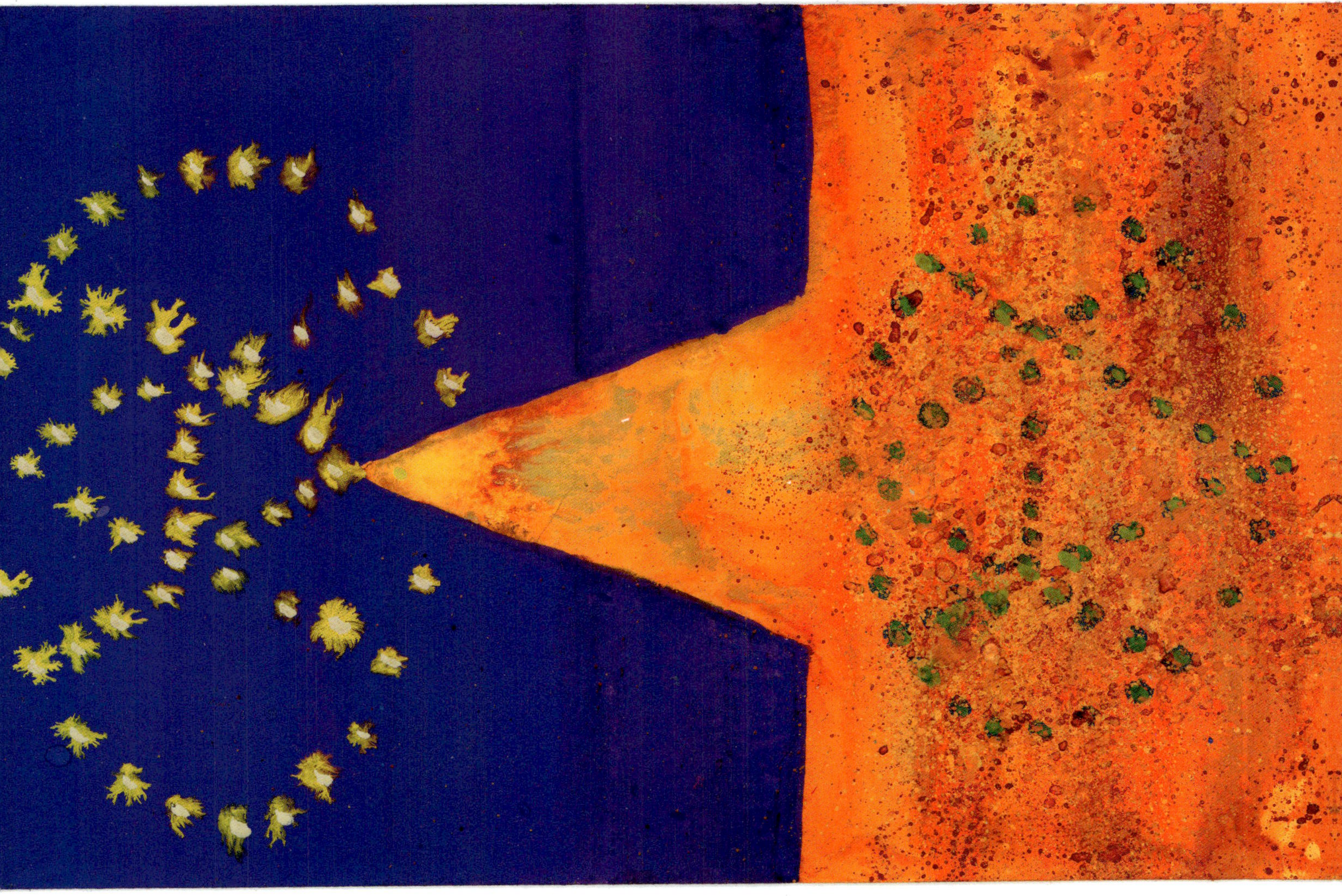

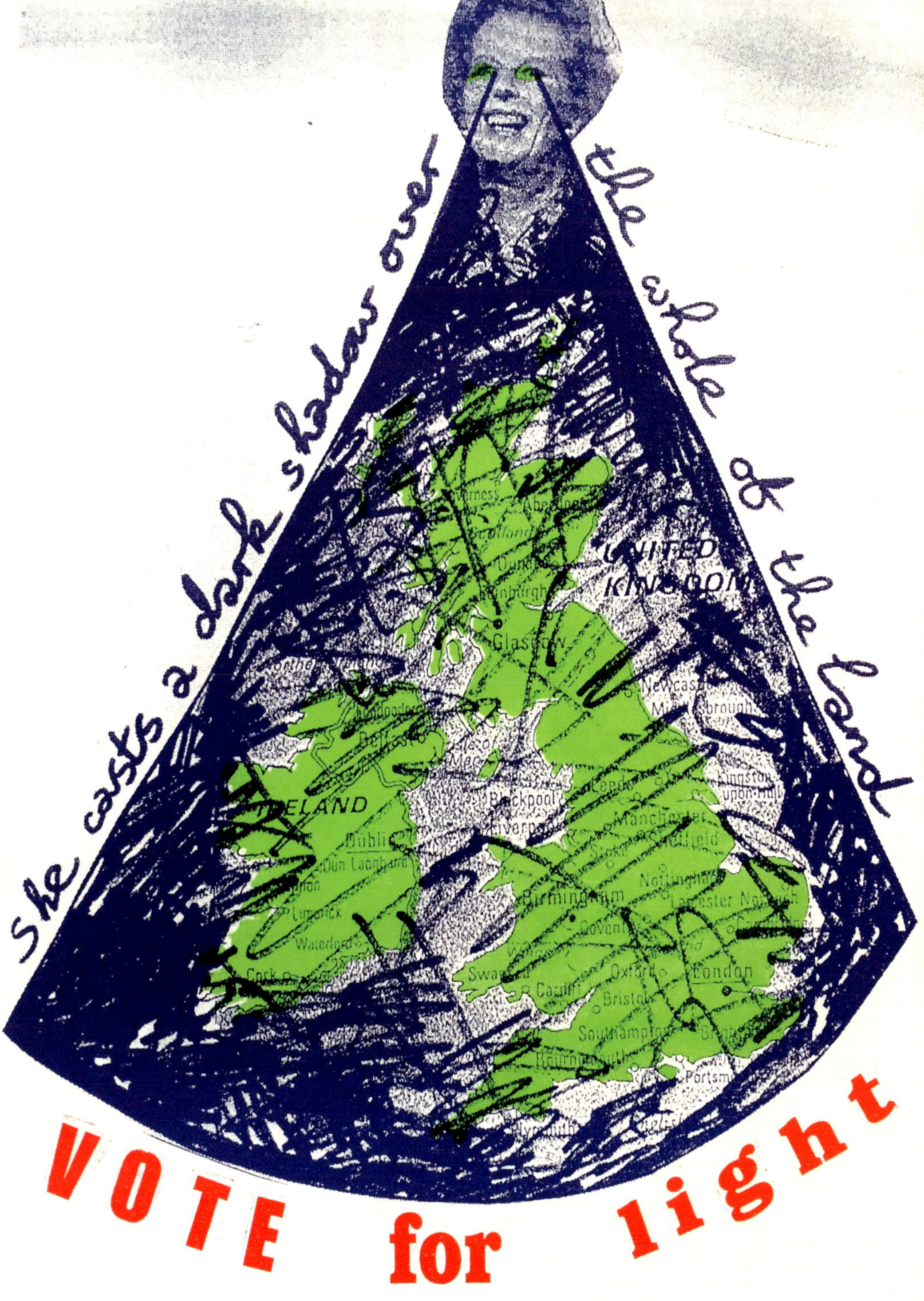
she casts a dark shadow over the whole of the land
VOTE for light

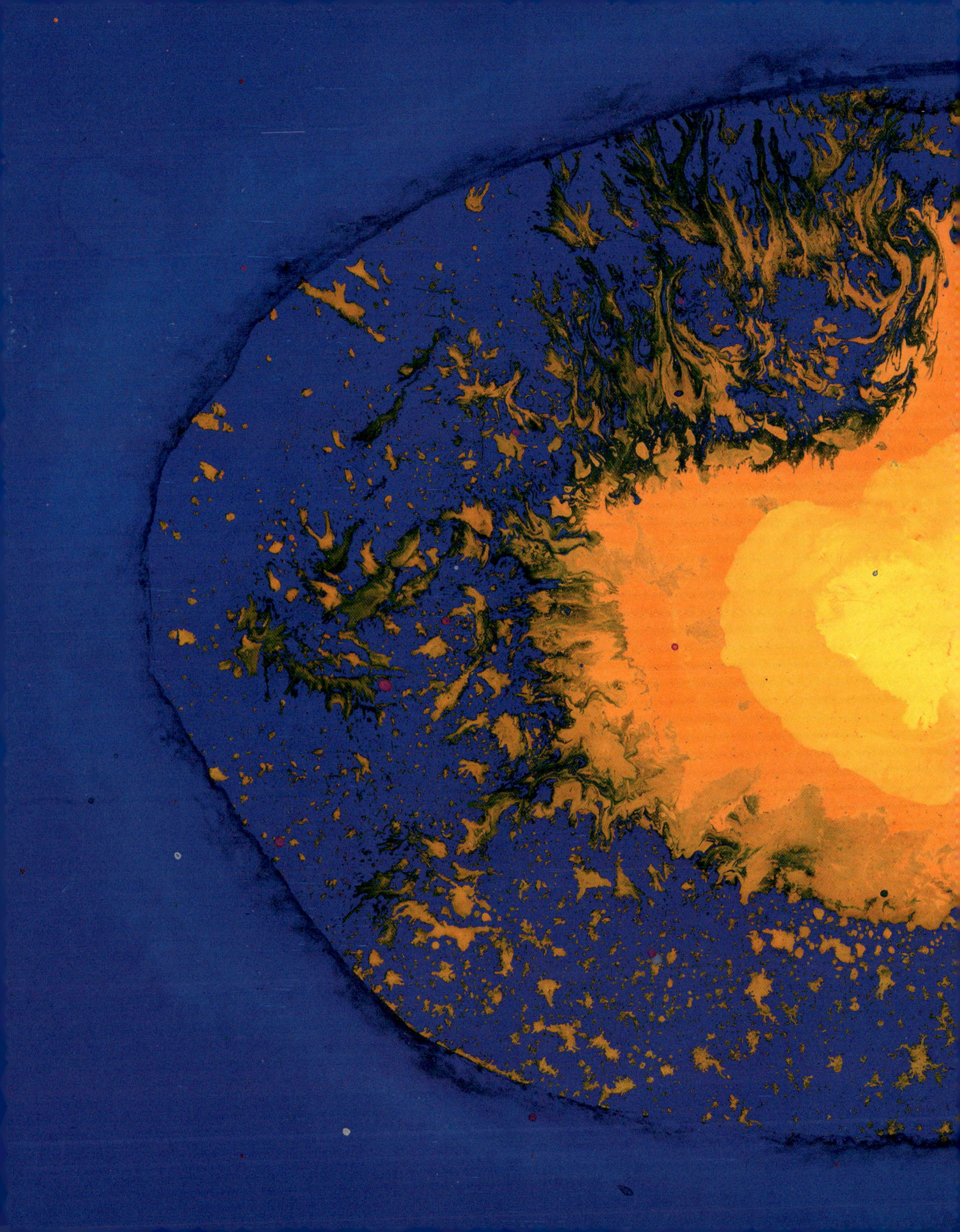

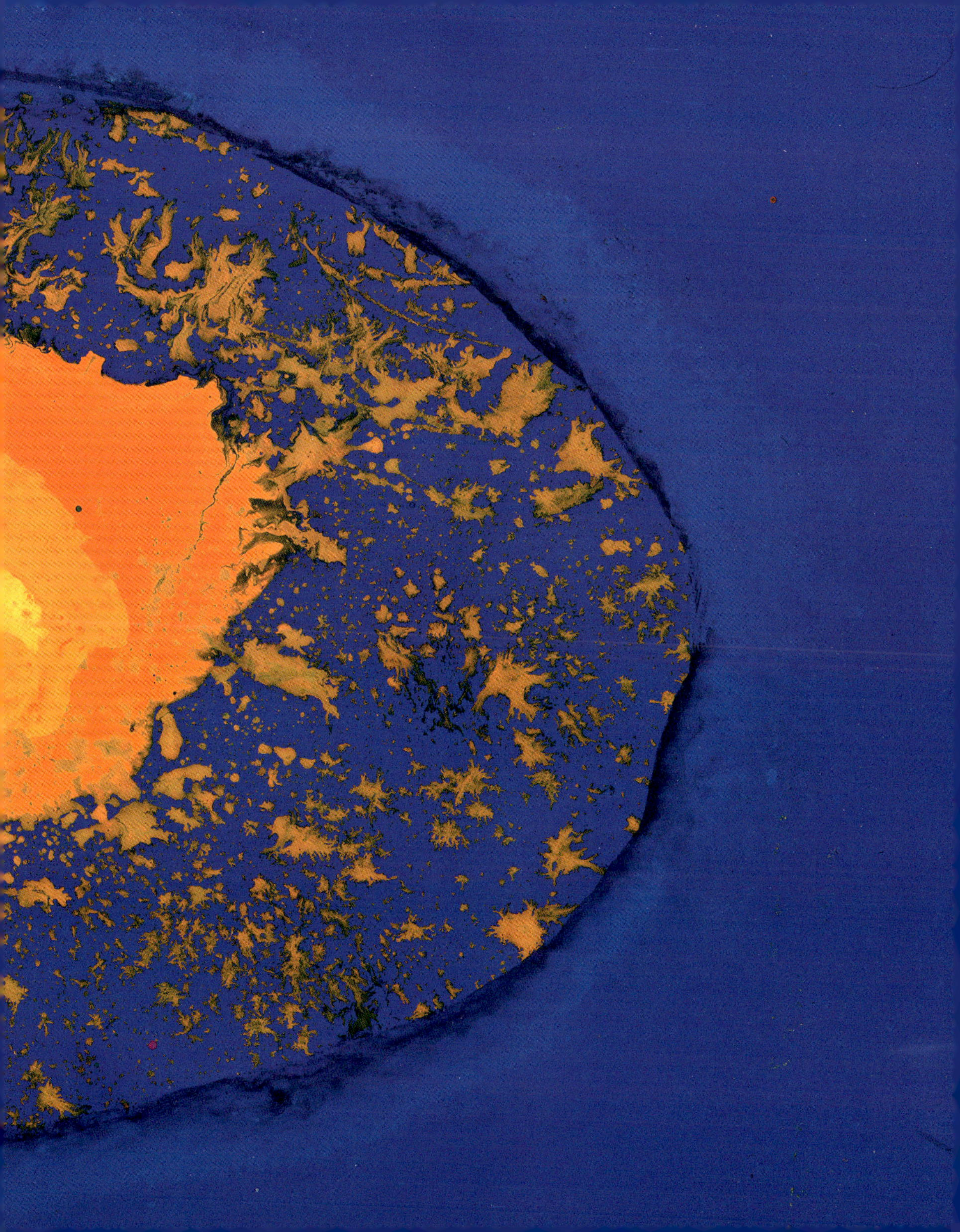

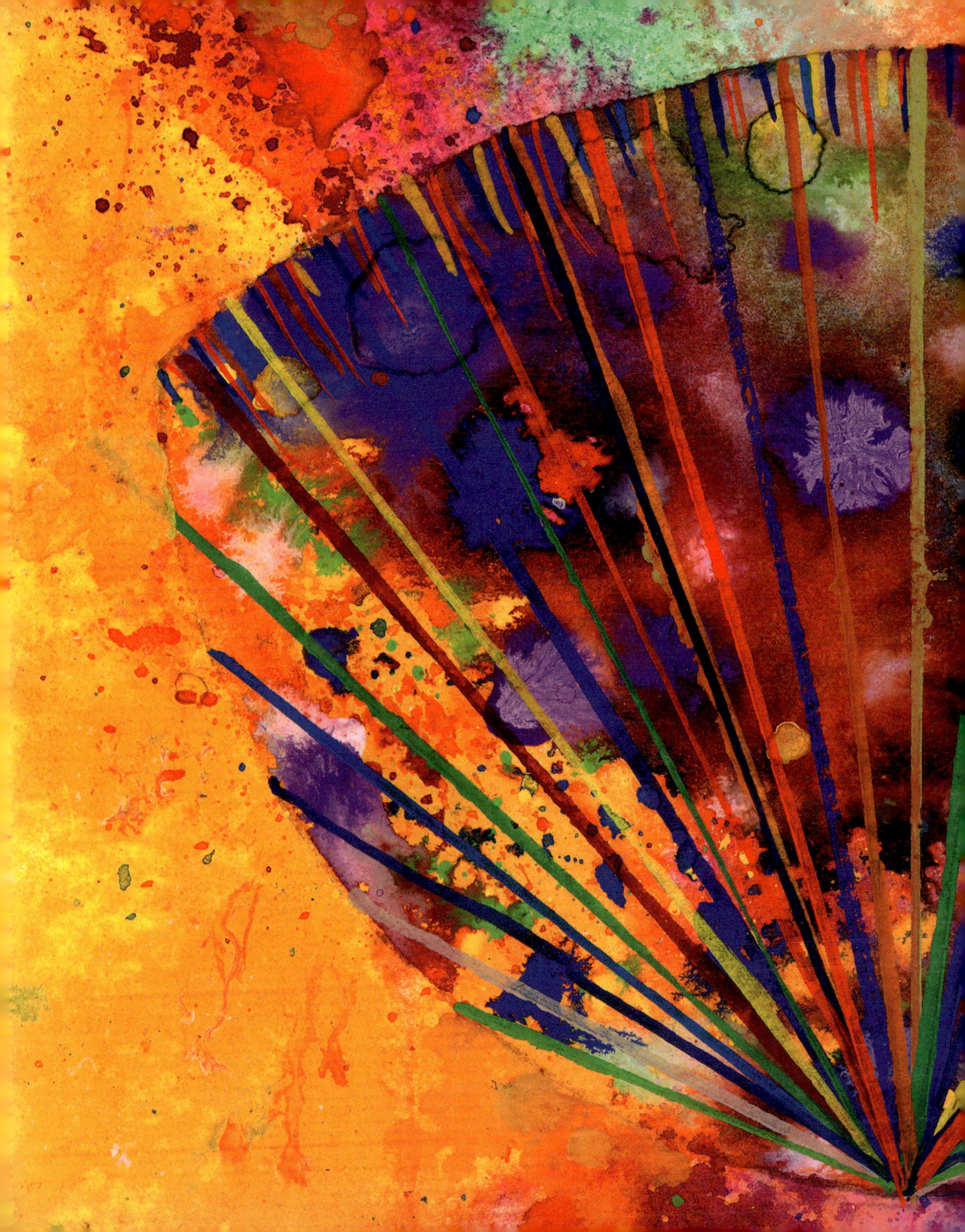

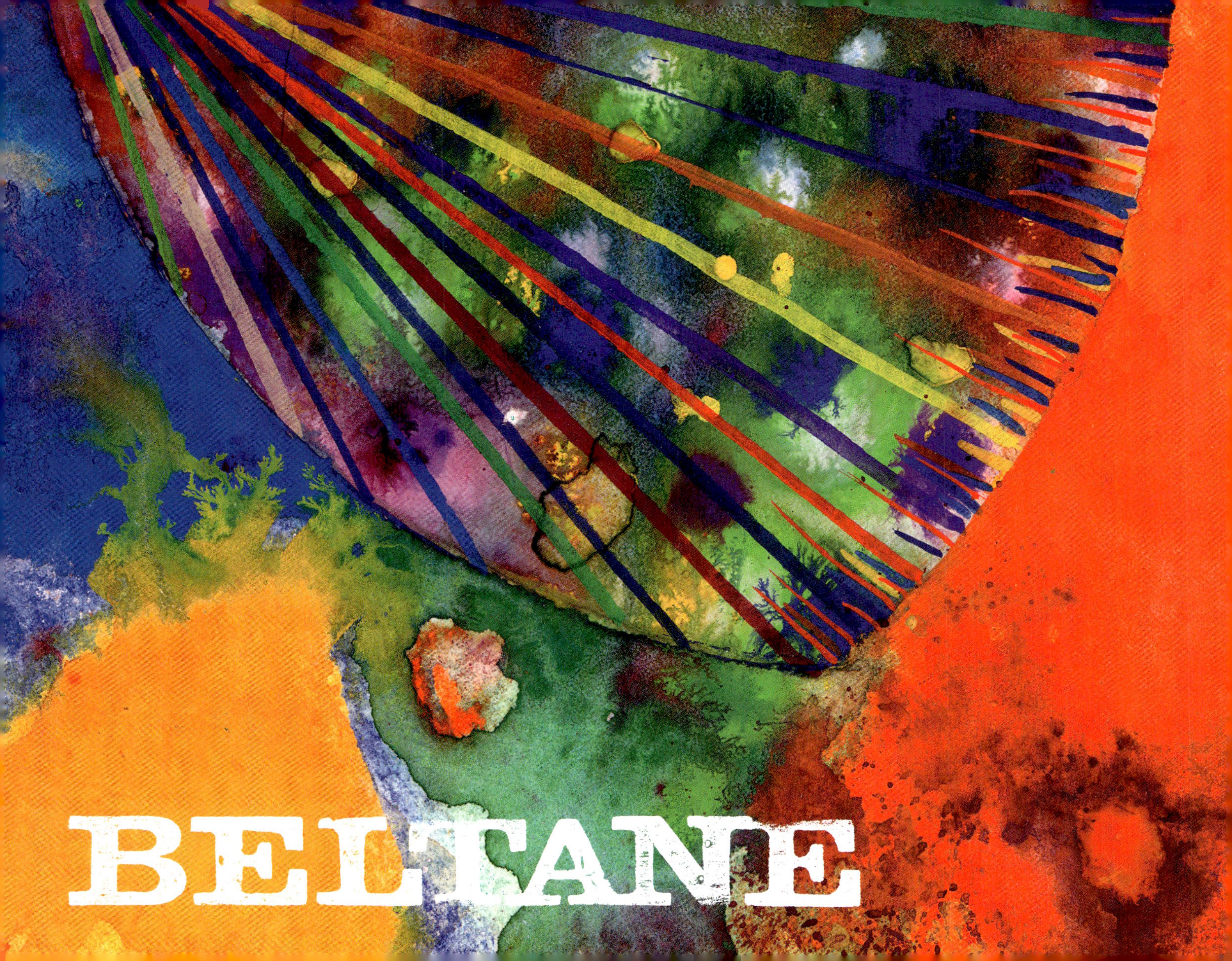
BELTANE

BELTANE

By Beltane you can really start to feel that spring is here, even that summer is on its way. It's a fiery time. Traditionally, out in the countryside two great bonfires would be lit and the cattle passed through them to protect them from witches and fairies and keep them healthy before they were taken up to the summer pastures.

When the fires died down people would jump over them, or walk in circles around them, or leap backwards and forwards over the flames three times to bring them luck. Young women would jump over the embers in the hope of finding a good husband, pregnant women in the hope of a good birth; children were carried over to protect their health; and each household would take some embers home to kindle a new fire in their hearth, while the rest would be cast on the sprouting crops to encourage their growth.

The earliest written records of this custom come from a 9th-century Irish text that describes Druids at this time lighting two 'lucky fires' with great incantations. Records survive, too, of the custom taking place in Scotland, the Isle of Man, and places in England such as Cumbria, Devon and Cornwall. From Wales in the 1830s there is a vivid account of May fires being lit by nine men using nine different woods that were piled together and lit by rubbing sticks of oak together.

In Scotland, the old tradition of baking a Beltane bannock, or oatcake, continues, and for the past thirty-five years Beltane has been celebrated in a dramatic way in Edinburgh, with a procession up Calton Hill led by a Green Man and May Queen, who announce the birth of summer by lighting a huge bonfire.

Now there's a sudden blooming of flowers, including a splash of white hawthorn blossom, or 'May', across the countryside, and an almost palpable sense of rising sap. There's been an upsurge of interest in May Day festivities, from 'bringing in the May', or decorating the home with hawthorn boughs, and dancing around maypoles to Morris dancing and mass parades such as the 'Obby 'Oss festival in Padstow, Cornwall. In Hastings, the Jack in the Green festival has been attracting crowds for almost forty years, with two days of music and dance in the streets and a procession through the town led by a Green Man. This leaf-covered, twig-strewn, green-faced figure appears in Beltane celebrations across the country. People see him in the carved foliate heads of medieval churches, and though these old stone images may not, in reality, represent a Pagan deity surviving into the Christian era, the Green Man is a thriving folkloric icon today – an emblem of wild, untrammelled nature.

The Morris dancing season traditionally opens on 1 May with dawn gatherings to 'dance up the May'. Morris dancing has in recent years been reinvigorated by performance groups such as the all-female Boss Morris, who are reinterpreting folk dance for the 21st century, rejecting nationalistic tropes in favour of a fresh, inclusive approach to an ancient art.

The spring energy of Beltane brings with it the power to generate: not only life, but also positive, creative ideas that, in their turn, can give birth to new initiatives. As the forces of nature regenerate with the spring, we can turn our attention to what we need in our lives and to co-operating with the flow of nature. It's the perfect time for turning our hands and minds to rewilding the environment around us, as well as our own lives.

NOTES FROM HELIGAN

'The first celebration of a new OVA at Heligan: a day of sowing seed. It was cool and cloudy but the gently rolling field glowed with the lustre of freshly-turned soil, ready for the seed. A gaggle of gulls waddled across the soil, looking for worms. The outline of the OVA had been carefully laid out by Heligan's Mark Davies. To complement the wildflower seed from last year's harvest, Richard Scott of the National Wildflower Centre had brought along sacks of corncockle, corn chamomile and cornflower seeds. Local Druid Lynda Moss led proceedings with a recital of 'A Blessing for Spring' by Maria Ede-Weaving. John Marchant was there to represent Jamie, who was unable to attend due to illness, and to help distribute seed to folk who came to sow. Cornflower is one of the most distinctive wildflower seeds, each one like a tiny shaving brush. Once common in fields, it is now a rarity.'

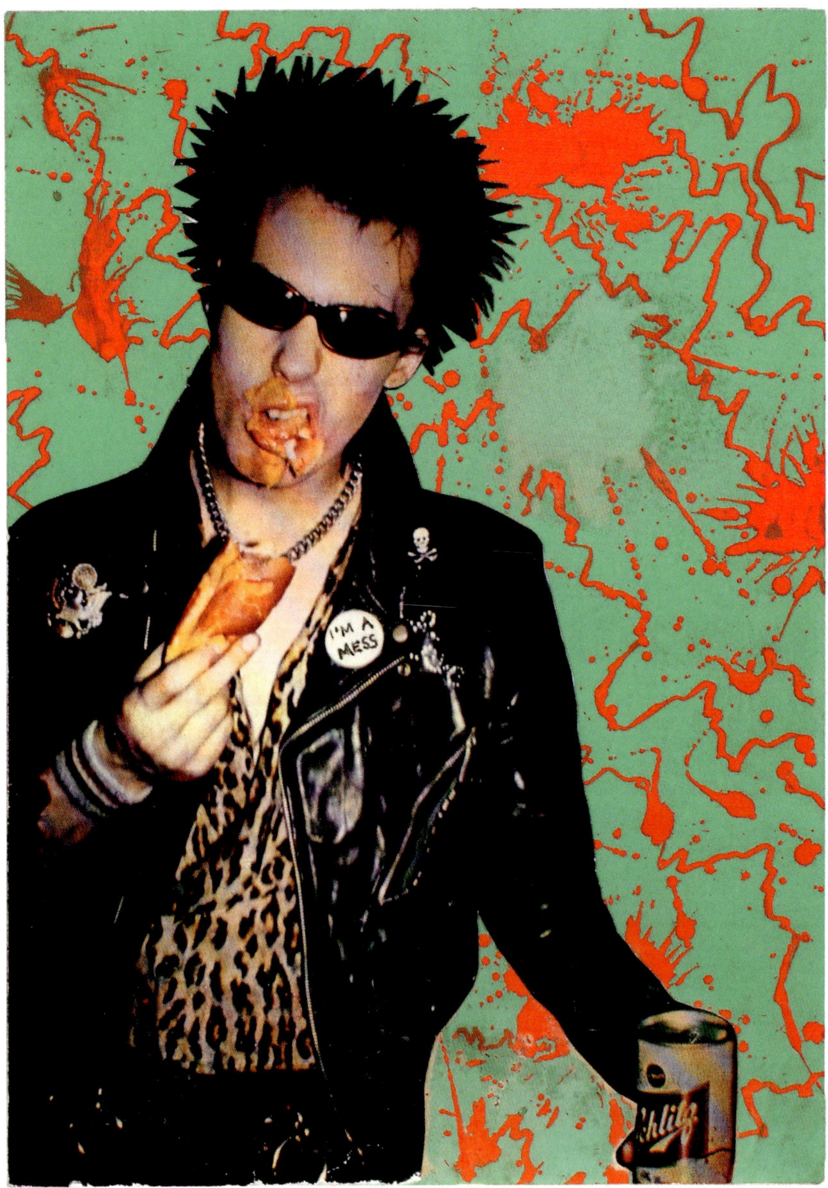

Sid I'm a Mess / 1978
Jamie was very fond of Sid Vicious and felt that his death had been exploited by his record company for profit. He made works such as *Viciousburger* and a Sid Action Man in a little coffin to highlight the hypocrisy. This collage, however, uses a Bob Gruen image taken on the Sex Pistols' tour of the US, and combines it with a hand-painted ground to really push the image forwards. Jamie has re-lettered Sid's badge in ink.

Boy George as Putto / 1989

This piece was done for Boy George's 'No Clause 28' single, protesting against the prohibition of the promotion of homosexuality by local councils. The collected artworks also featured Thatcher in a balaclava mask, and George as the children's character Noddy.

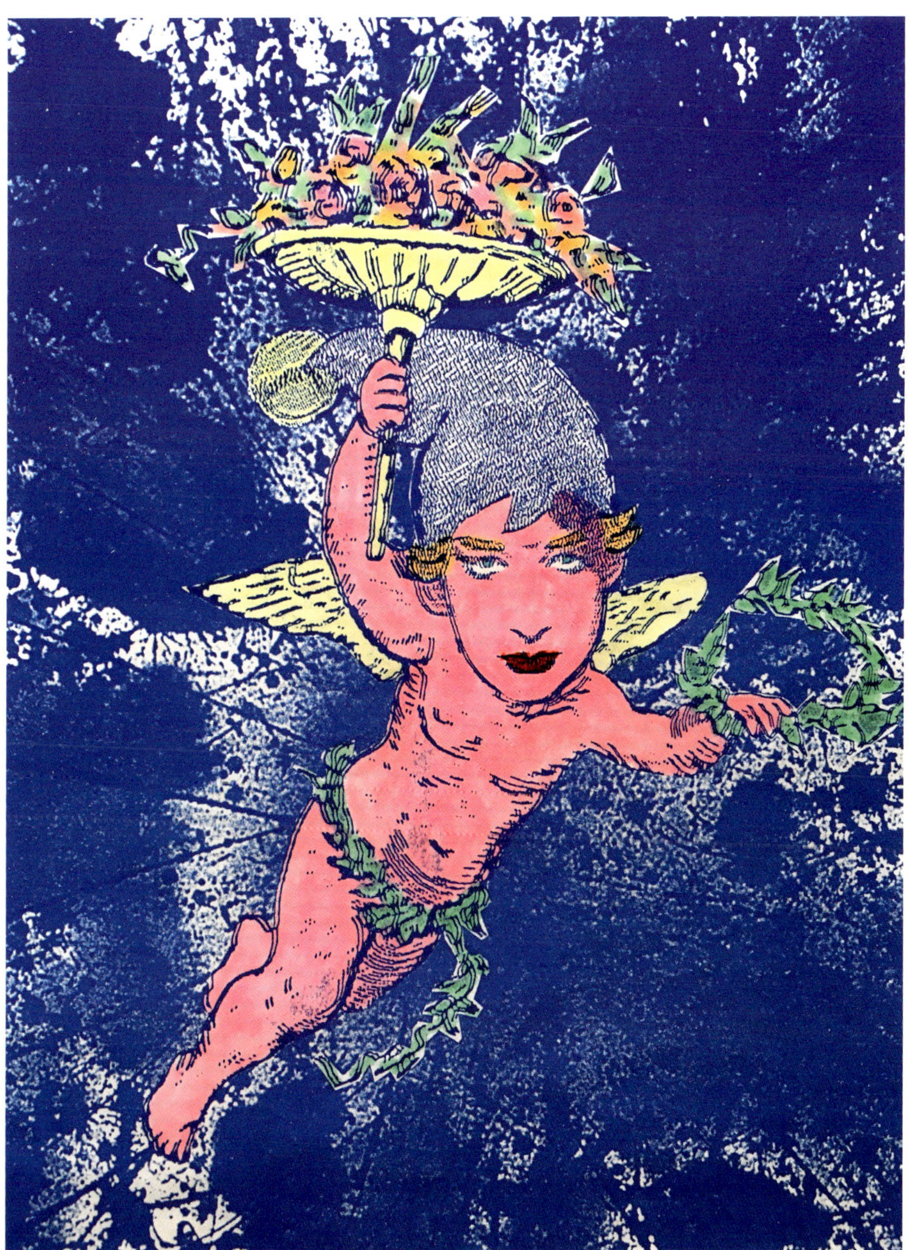

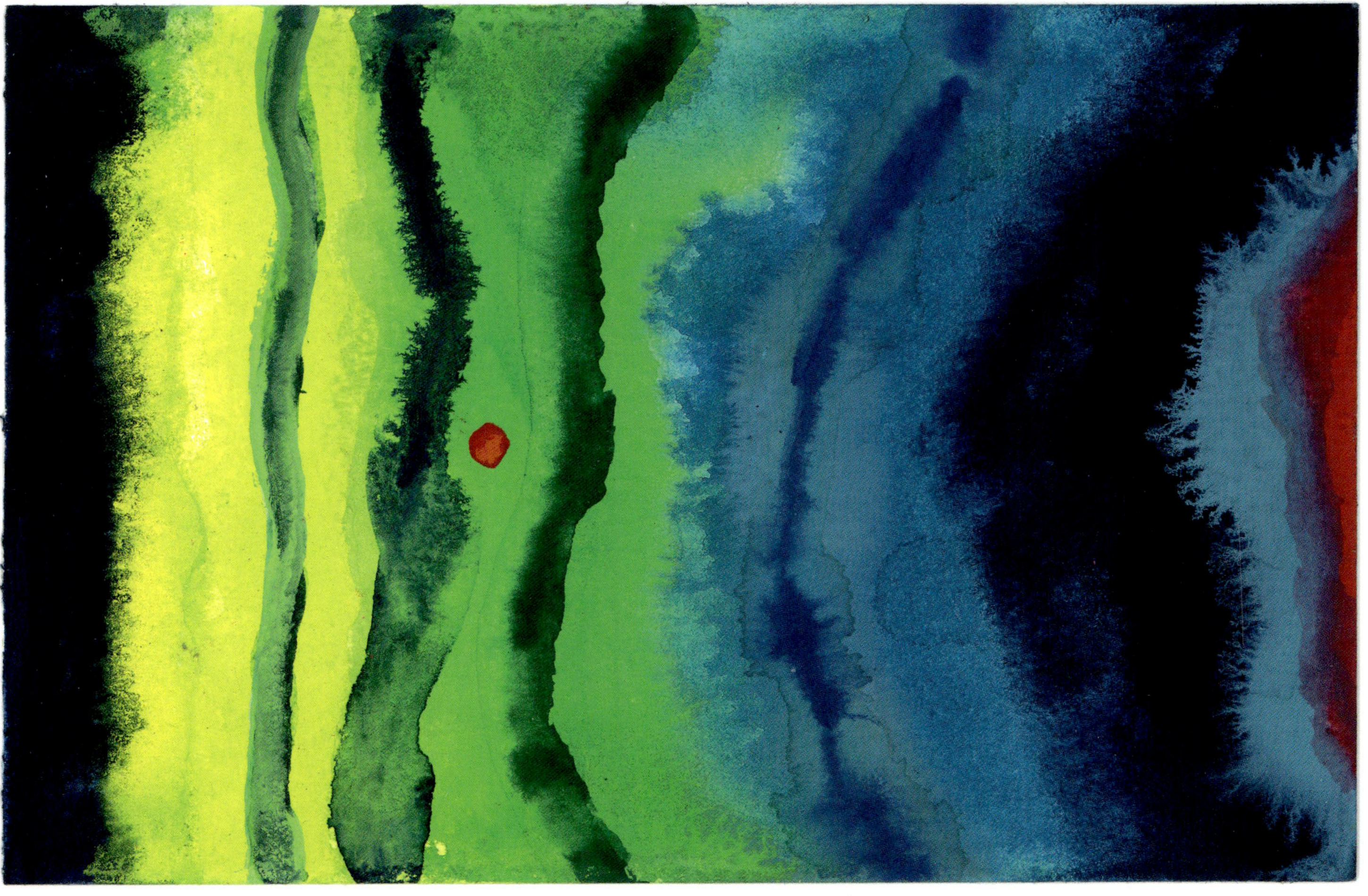

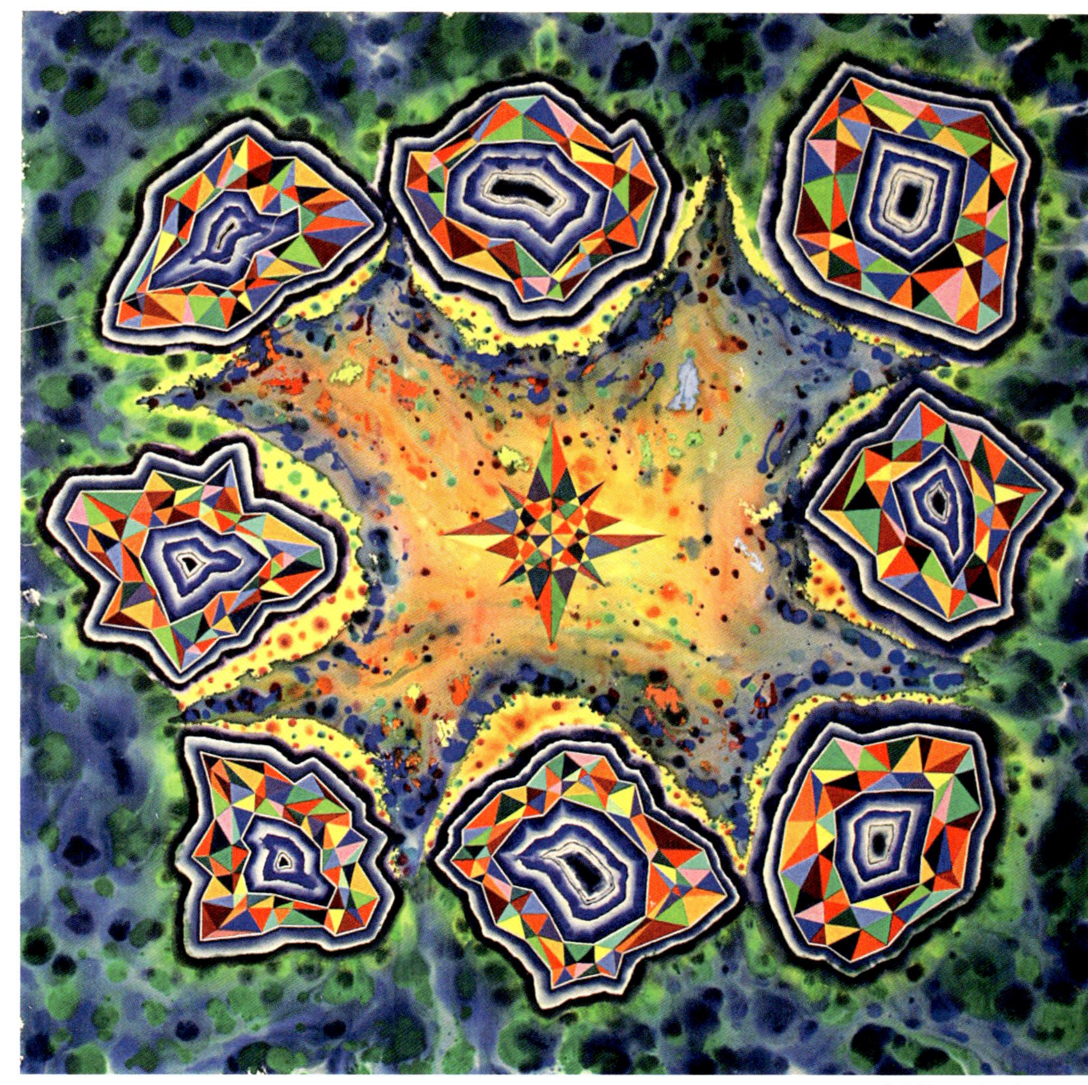

Untitled (Out There) / c. 2010

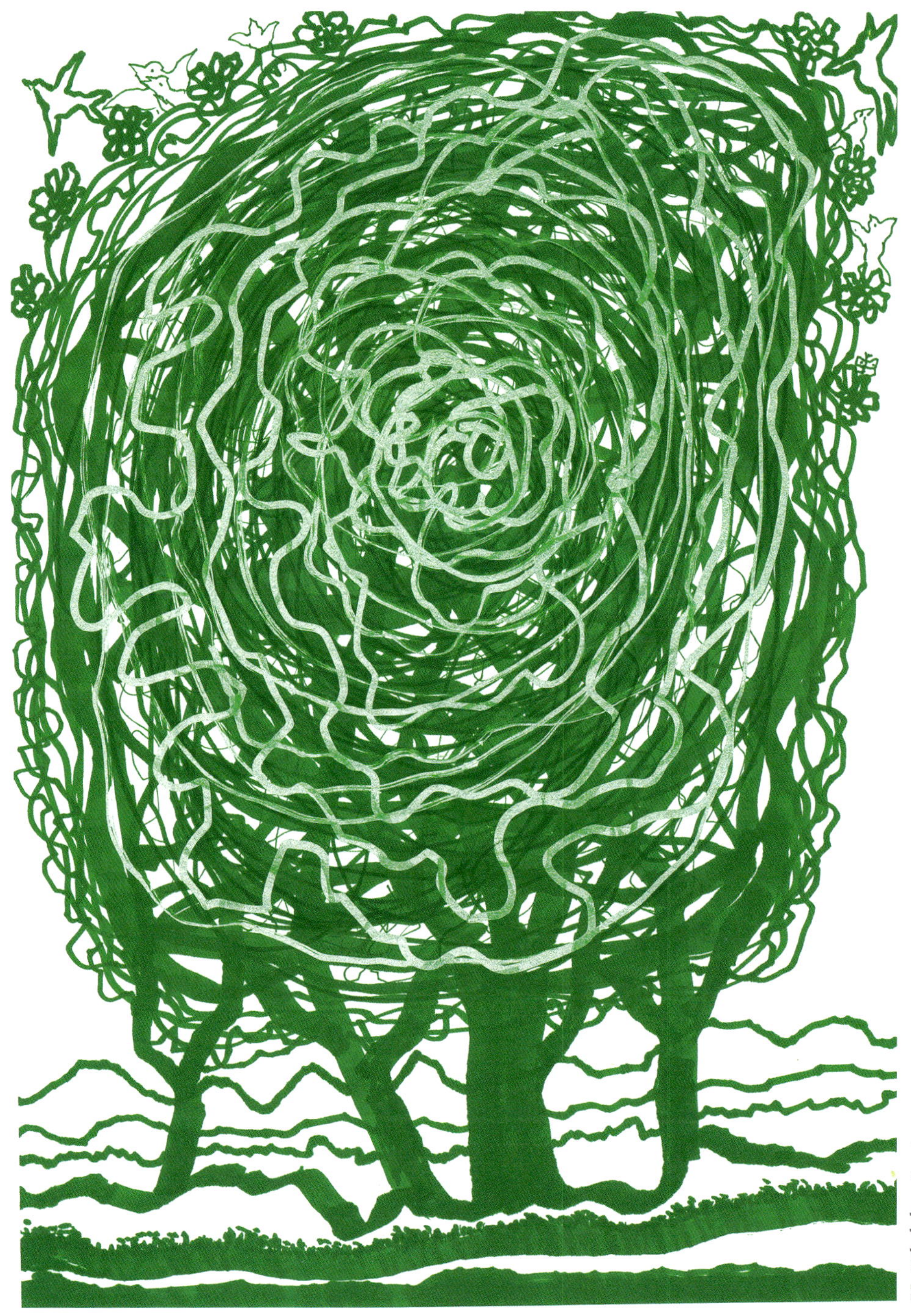

Untitled drawing / 2022

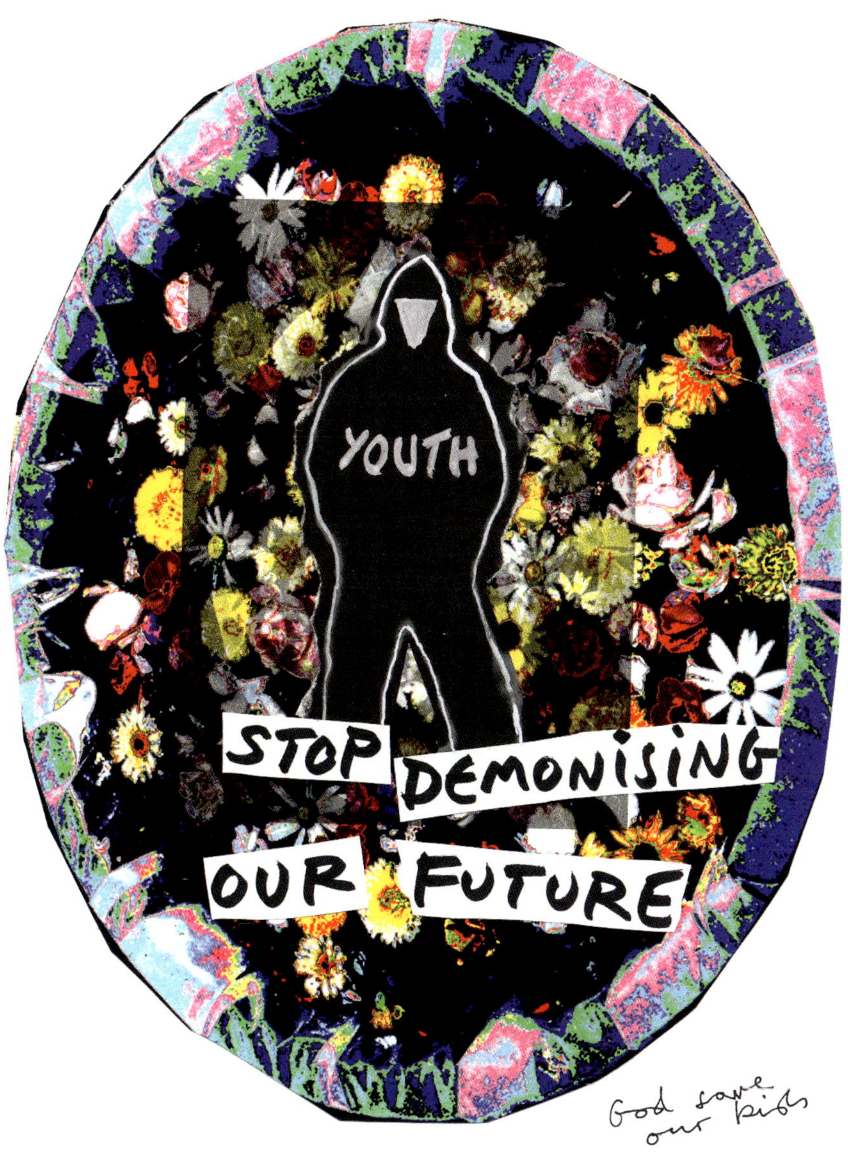

Stop Demonising Our Future / 2010
This artwork was produced on commission from the *Guardian* at a time when young people were being demonised – and arrested – for wearing hooded sweatshirts. As with Punk, fashion had created a confrontation with the establishment that many found unsettling, but was ultimately just an expression of disaffection. Jamie overlaid the outline of the young person on an image from a ritual offering he had made at his allotment in Liverpool, giving the piece a feeling of uplift and radical positivity.

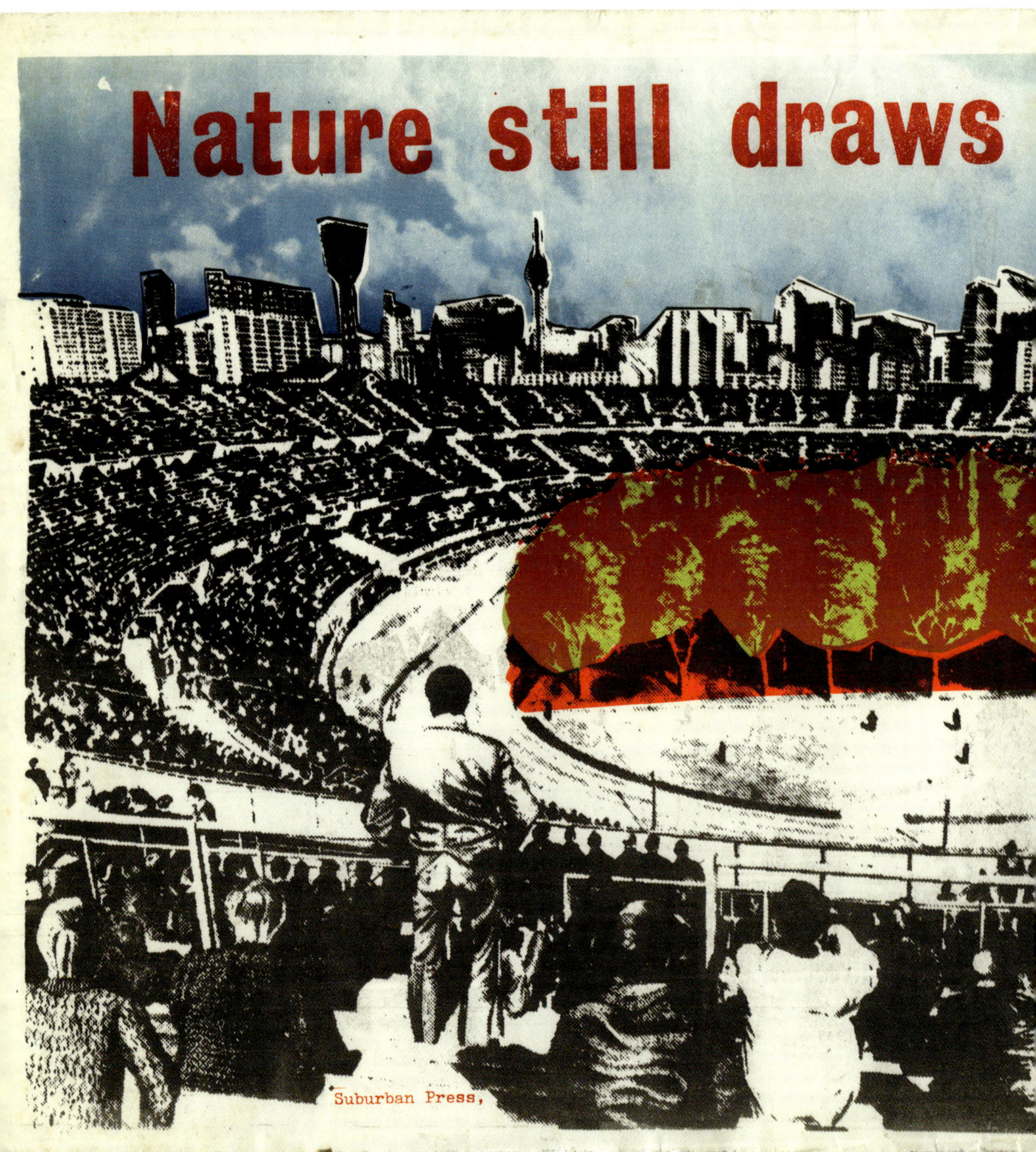
Nature still draws
Suburban Press,

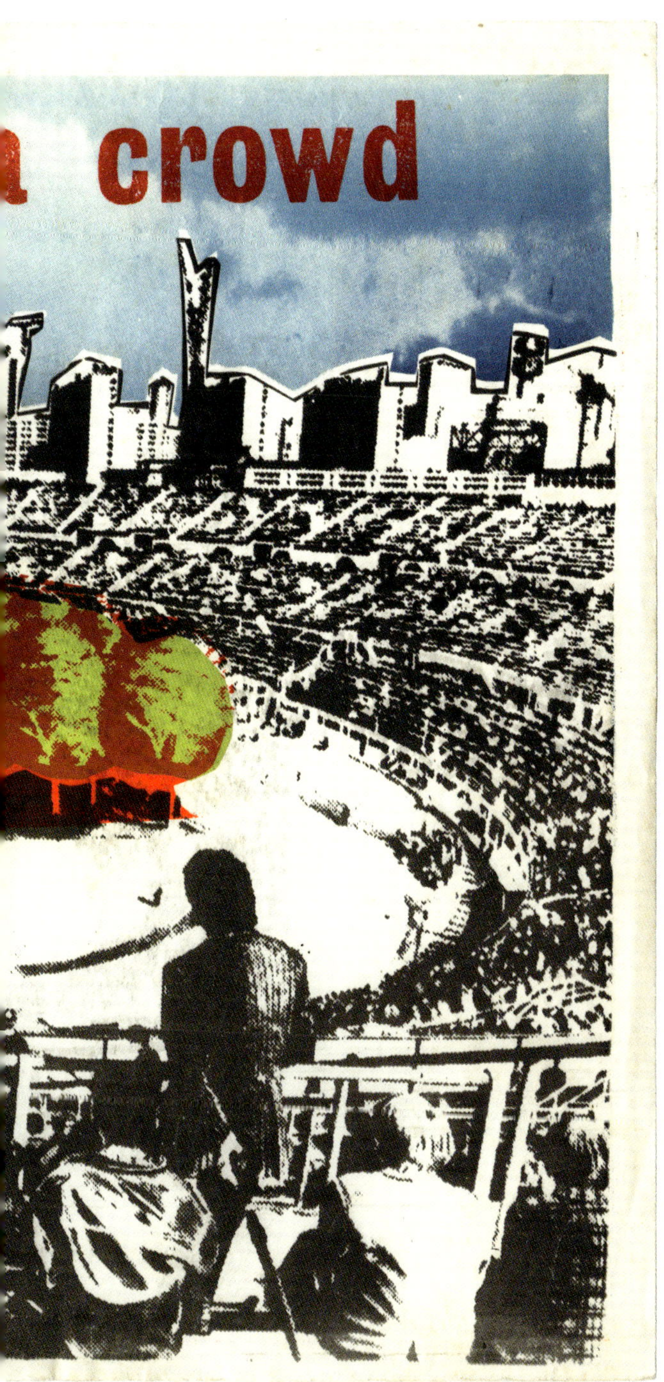

Nature Still Draws a Crowd / 1974
This image appeared in the final production by Jamie's Croydon-based, agit-prop print collective Suburban Press in 1974. The *Poster Book* was a collection of provocative images principally lifted from previous issues of their publication and designed for bedroom walls. The image was inspired by the inclusion of entirely gestural planters within the sterile commercial development of Croydon's then-new Whitgift Centre. The planters had swiftly become depositories for cigarette butts and other detritus. Here, the idea has been extended to reduce nature to a merely entertaining spectacle, to be experienced at a distance. It should be noted that during the opening ceremony for the 2012 Olympics, director Danny Boyle brought this very concept into the Olympic stadium, placing trees on the centre pitch.

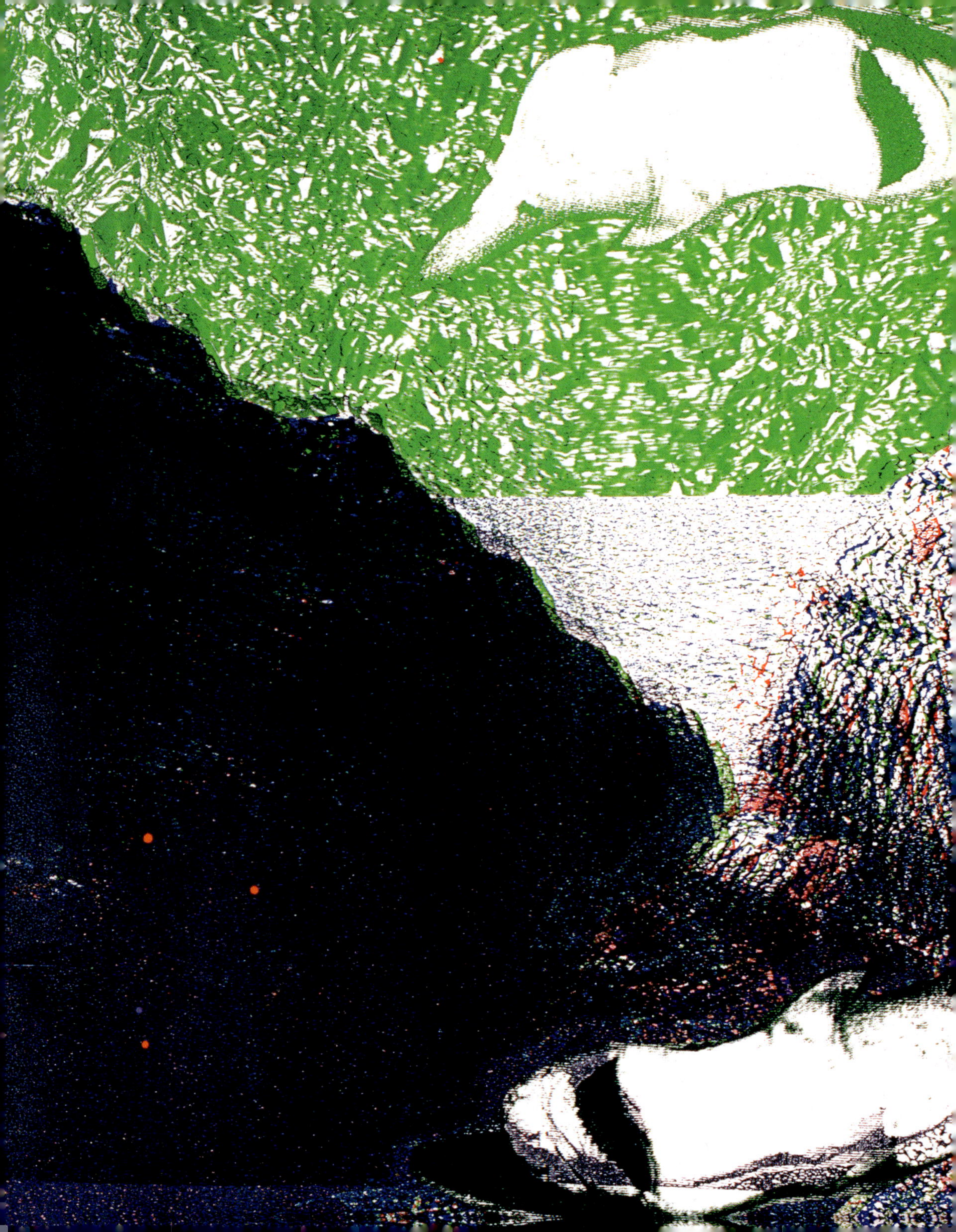

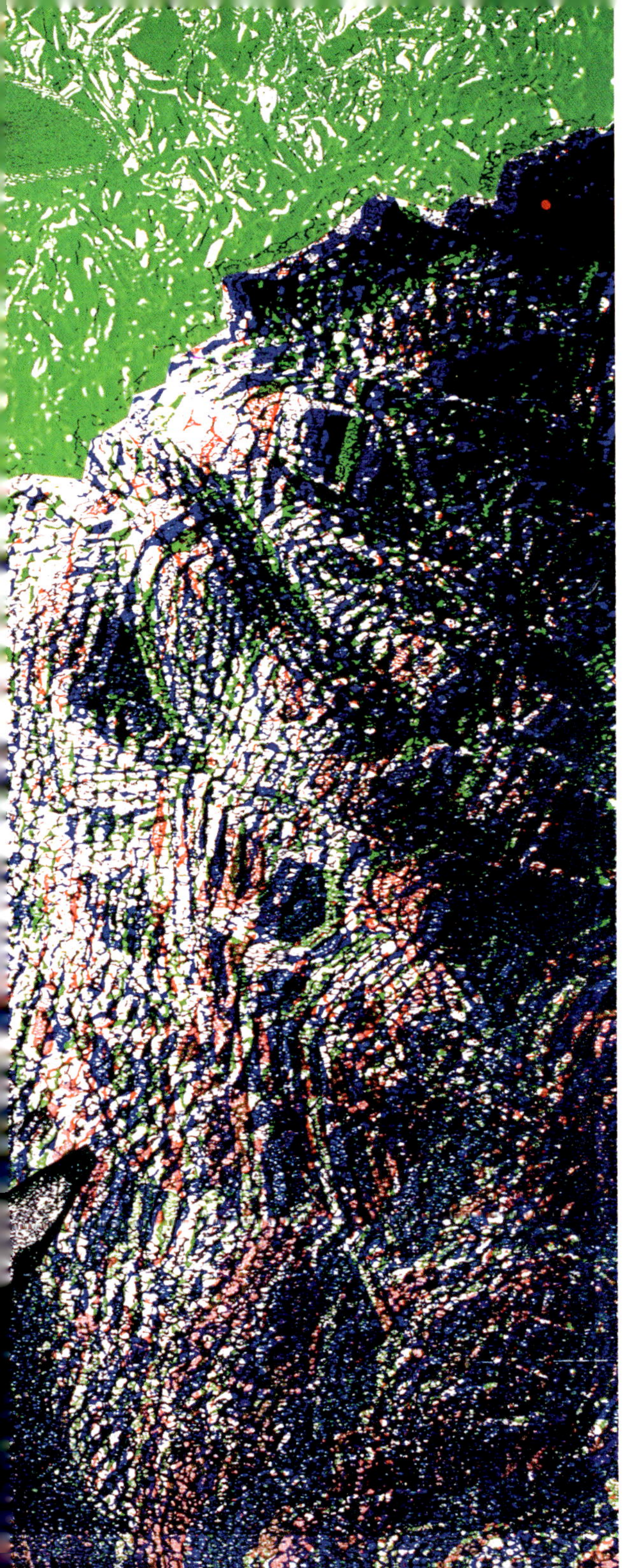

Ear Trumpet Sharks / 1987
This record sleeve visual was produced during a particularly productive spell in the late '80s when Jamie was working at Assorted iMaGes in Shoreditch, London (in a building later taken over by the expanding Strongroom Studios, which Jamie was to spend a decade refurbishing). This particular piece was created for Ear Trumpet, a short-lived and intriguing group, which featured Steven Severin of Siouxsie and the Banshees, and Bruce Gilbert of Wire.

Up They Rise / 1968
This early painting features Jamie himself and his college friend Malcolm McLaren, with his striking curly, red hair. Here, they are playing with the elements of possibility around the tower blocks of Croydon – 'a playground for the juggler'. Jamie and Malcolm remained friends right through the Pistols period and on until Malcolm's death in 2010; Jamie always insisted that Malcolm was a genius. Some years later, in the middle of the night, Jamie accidentally tuned in to hear Malcolm's voice. For an hour or so Jamie lay in the dark, listening to his dear friend speaking through the ether.

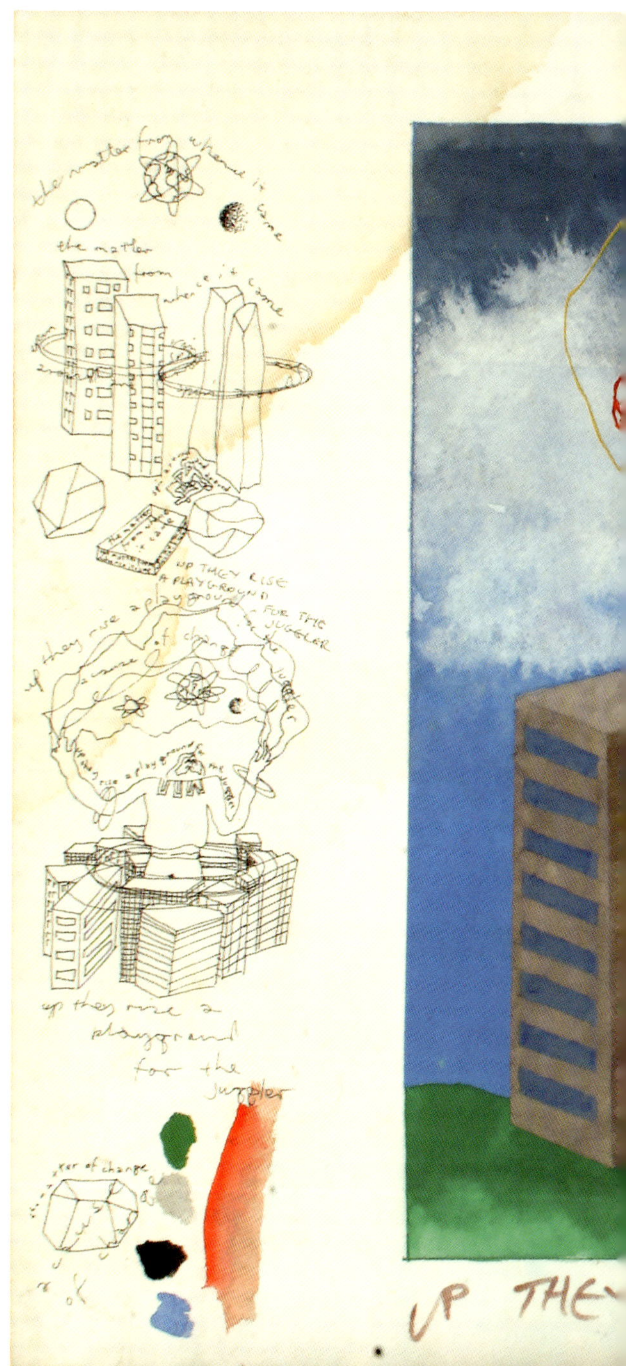

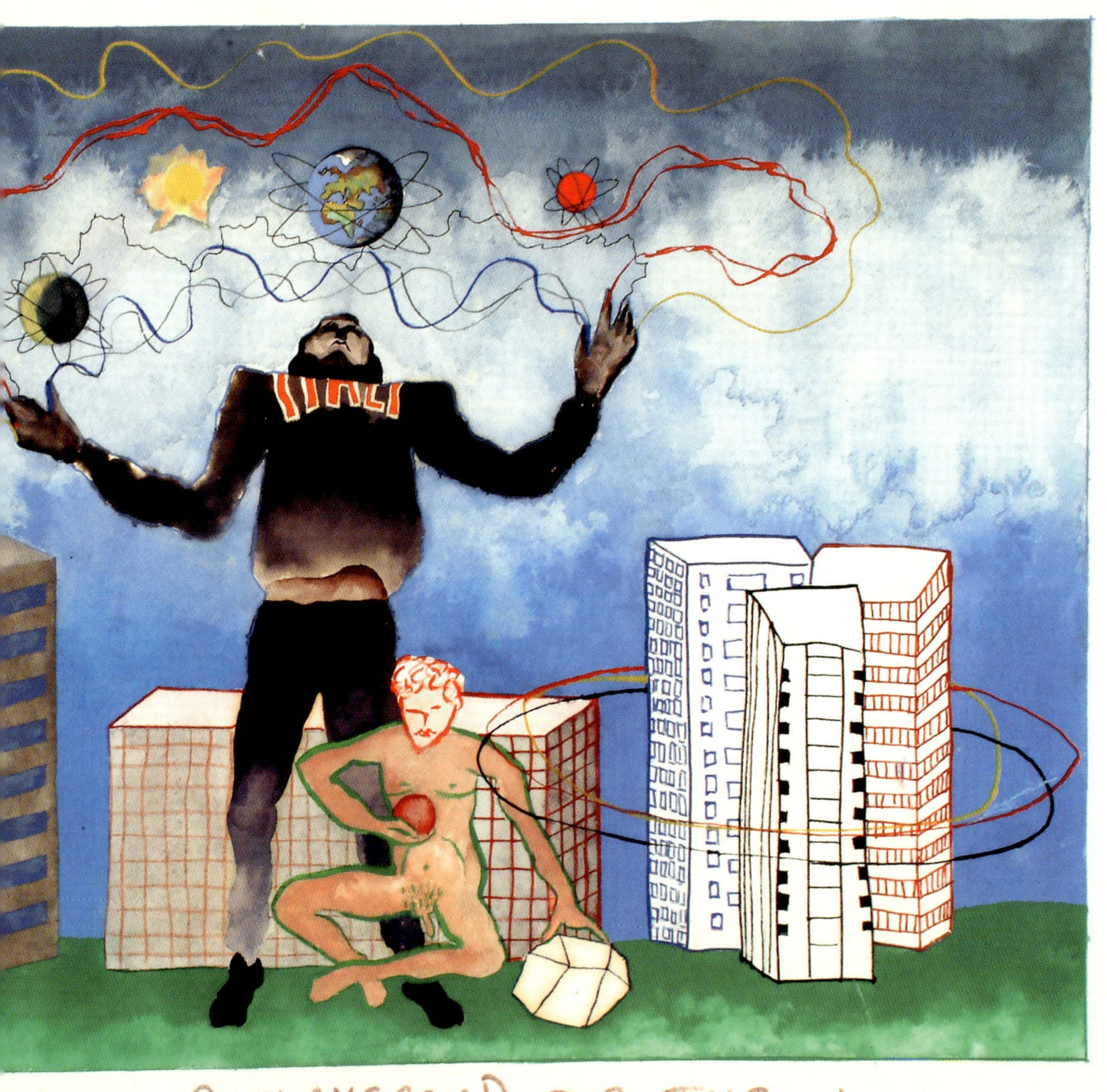

RISE – A PLAYGROUND FOR THE JUGGLER

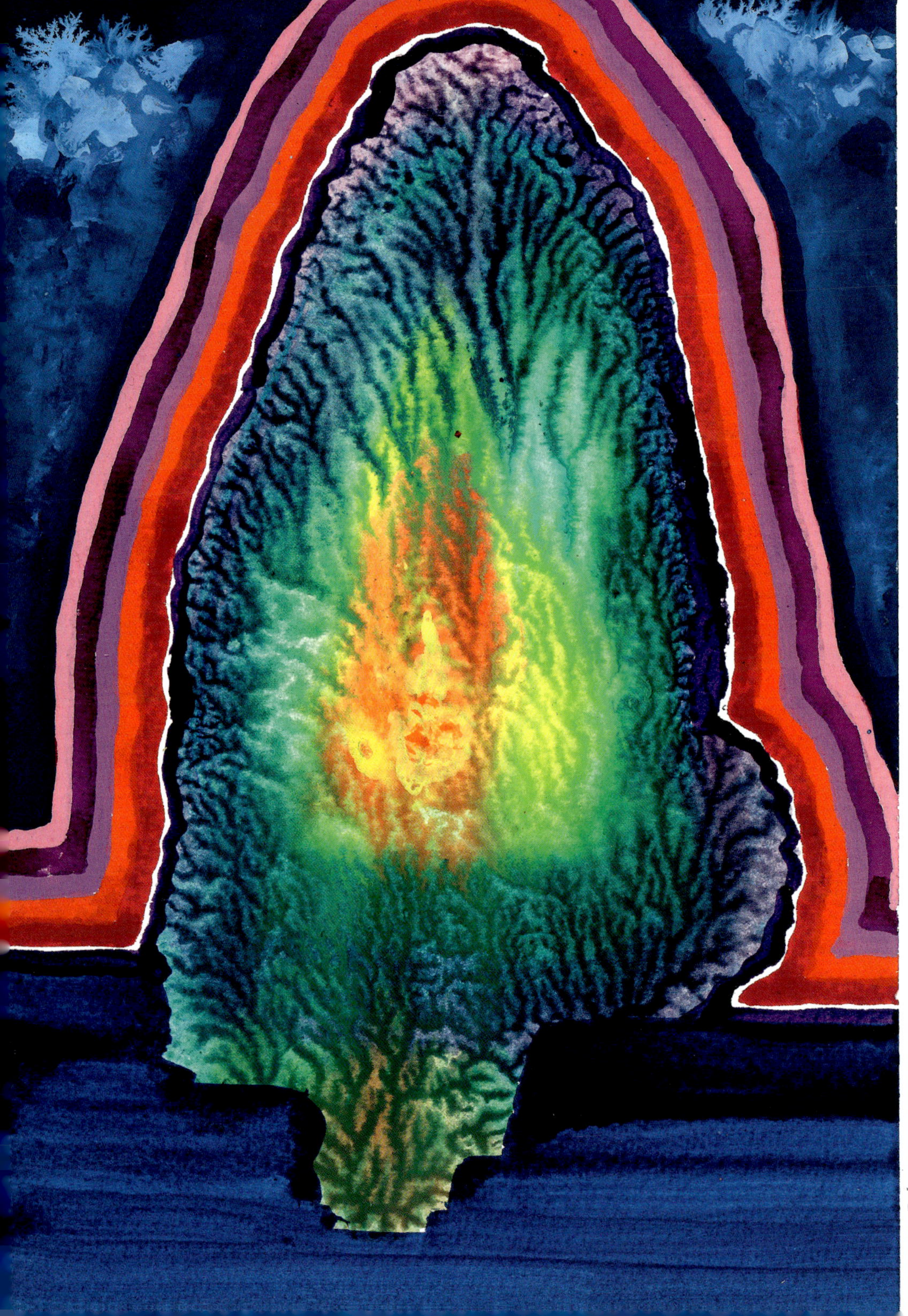

Beltane / 2010

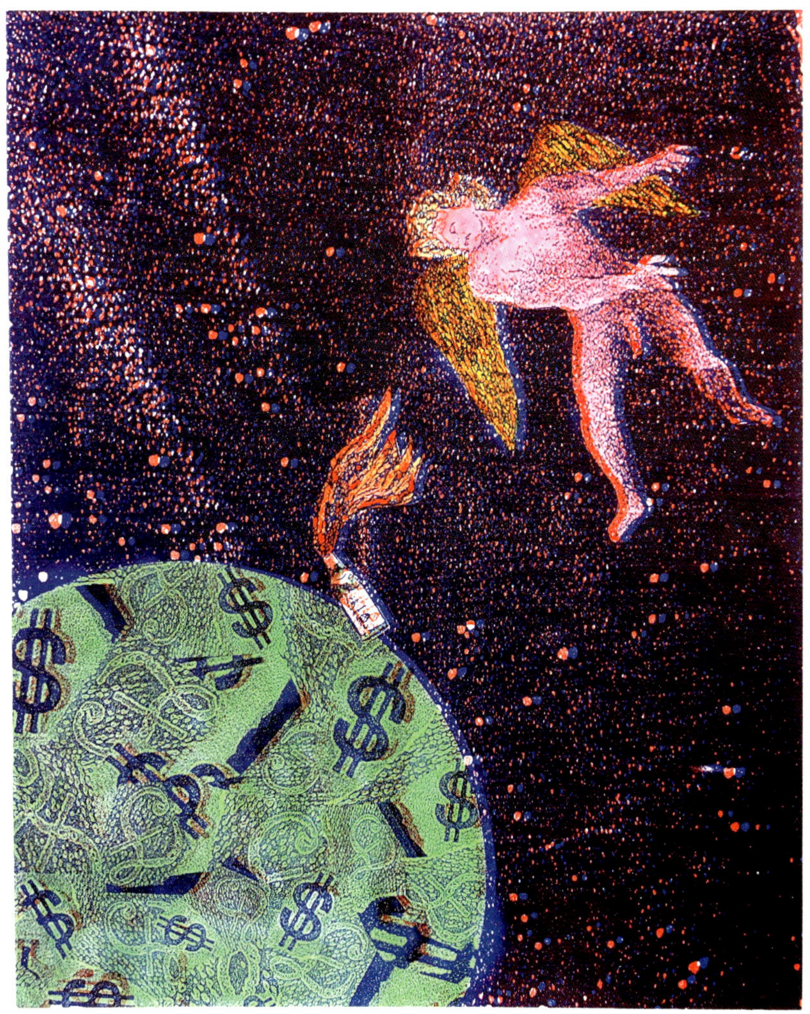

Avenging Angel (The Prince of Brass and Wand) / 1987
The avenging angel in this colour Xerox work has flown in from Titian's *Bacchus and Ariadne* (1523), where he is leaping from his chariot. Here, in an undraped and more butch incarnation, he casts his ire on the Capitalist world, spinning through the starry cosmos. This piece is a prime example of Jamie's output while working at Malcolm Garrett's Assorted iMaGes in Shoreditch, where he had been brought in as a totem and given a studio, a colour photocopier and a free rein.

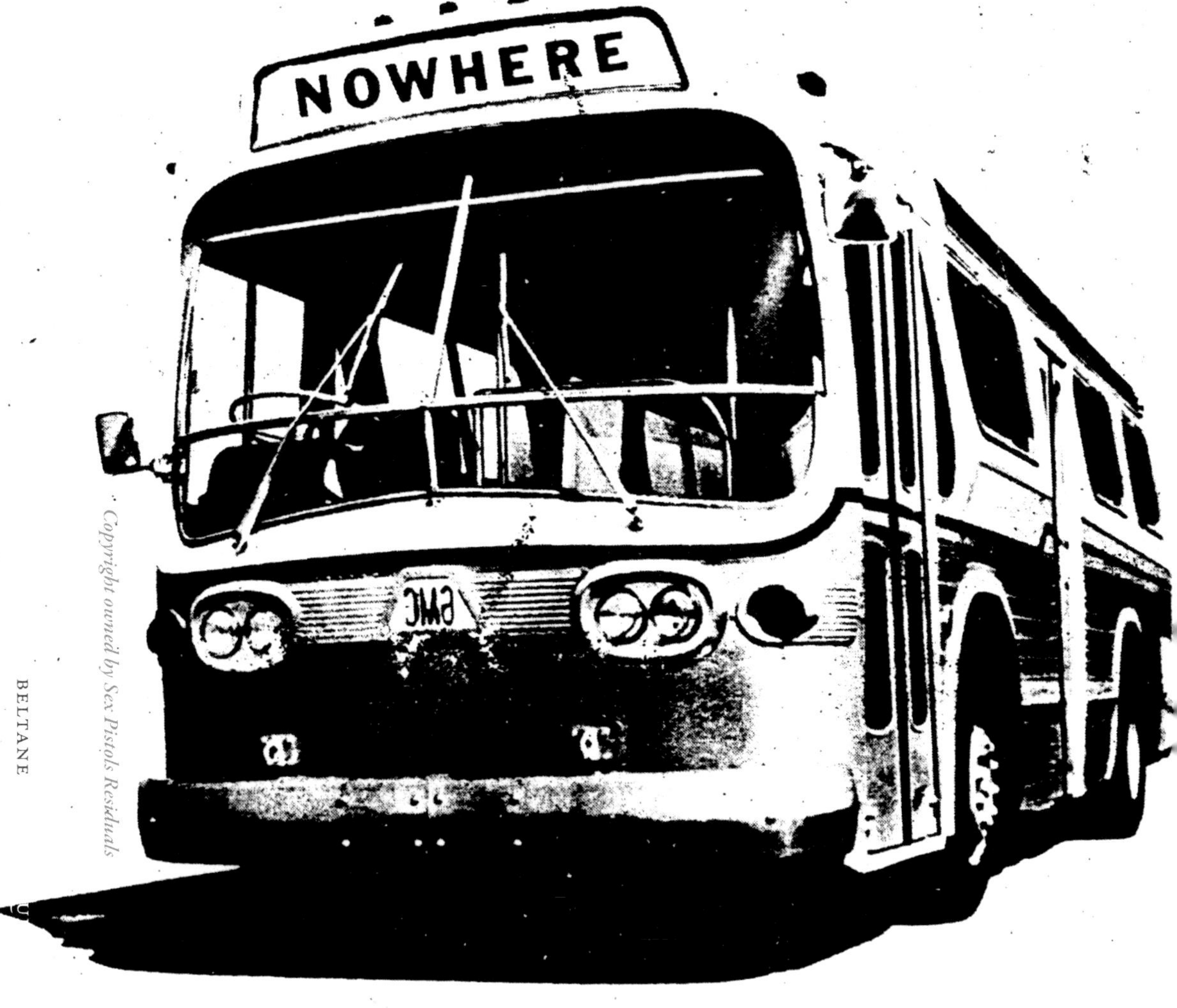

Nowhere Buses / 1974

These buses going to 'Nowhere' were first printed by Suburban Press for the San Francisco collective Point Blank and their pamphlet *Space Travel.* They then appeared in Suburban Press's *Poster Book*, before reappearing on the back cover of the *Anarchy in the UK* newspaper (designed by Jamie with Sophie Richmond). They were then repurposed for the single 'Pretty Vacant' (1977). Reappropriation was never an issue for Jamie and his Croydon cohort, who themselves declined to enforce copyright. With their infamous destinations of Nowhere and Boredom, the buses are now part of a visual canon that, along with the *Never Mind the Bollocks* album cover, the Anarchy flag and the adapted portraits of the Queen, is constantly repurposed worldwide as a symbol of disaffection and protest.

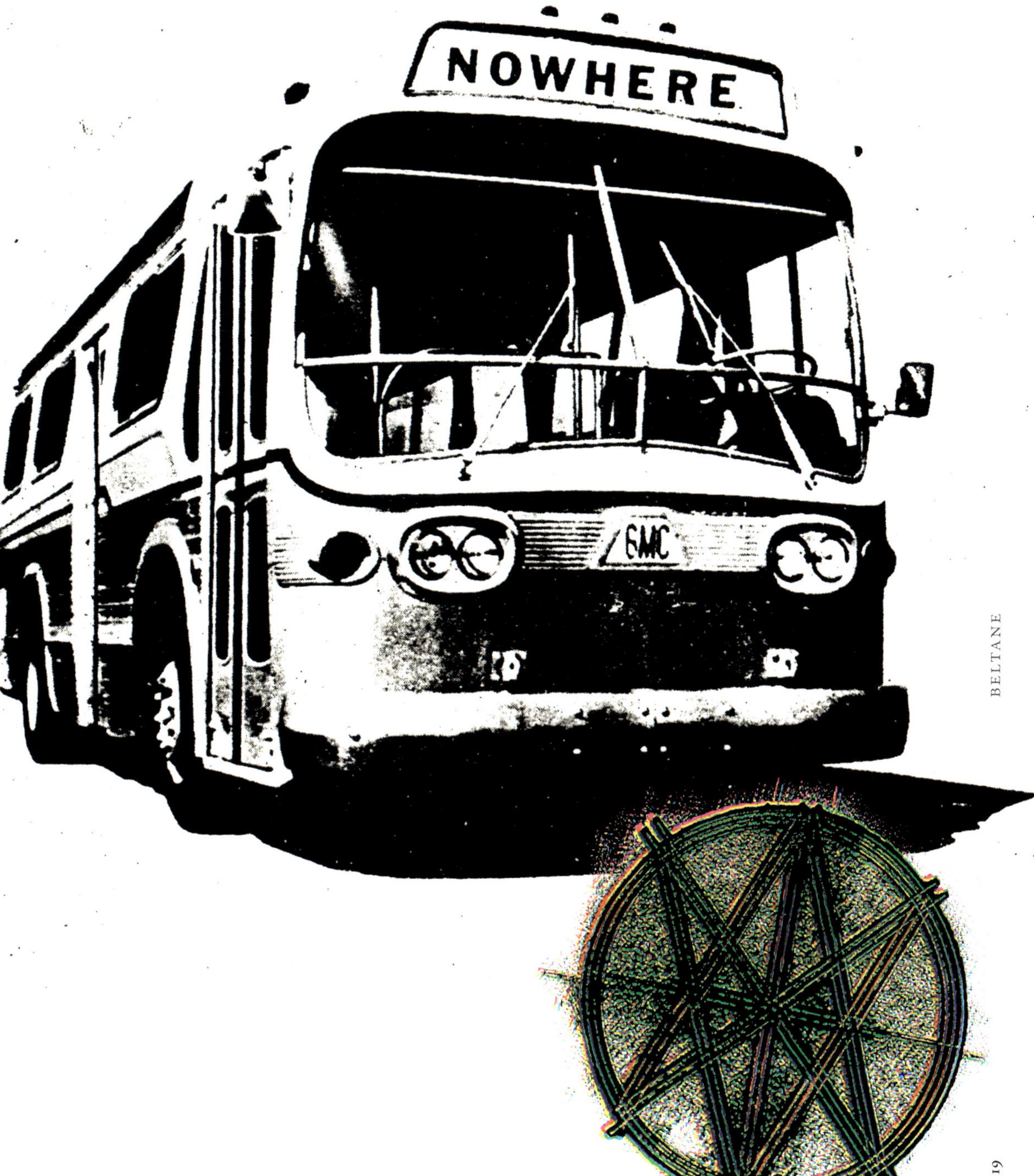
NOWHERE
GMC

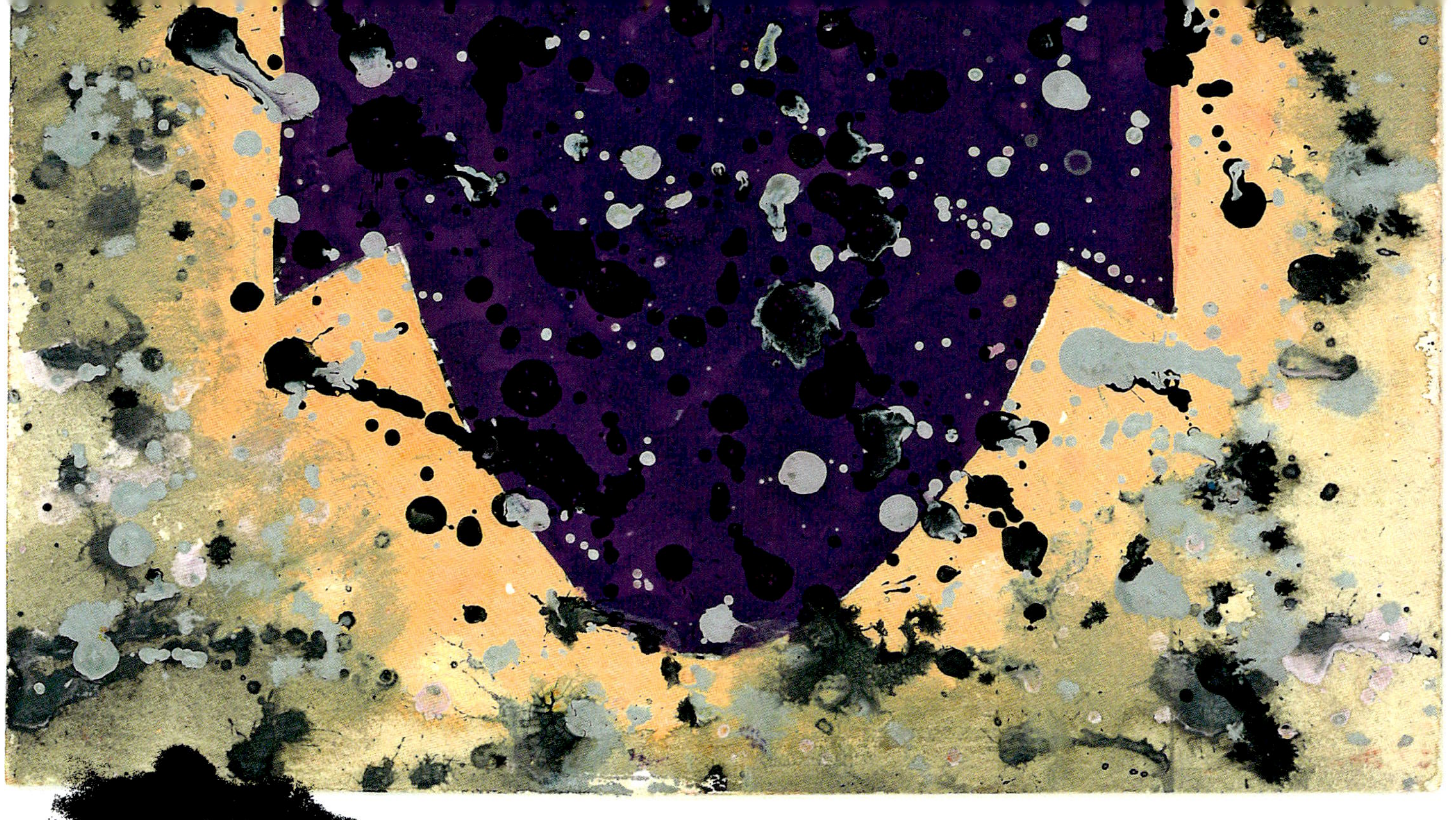

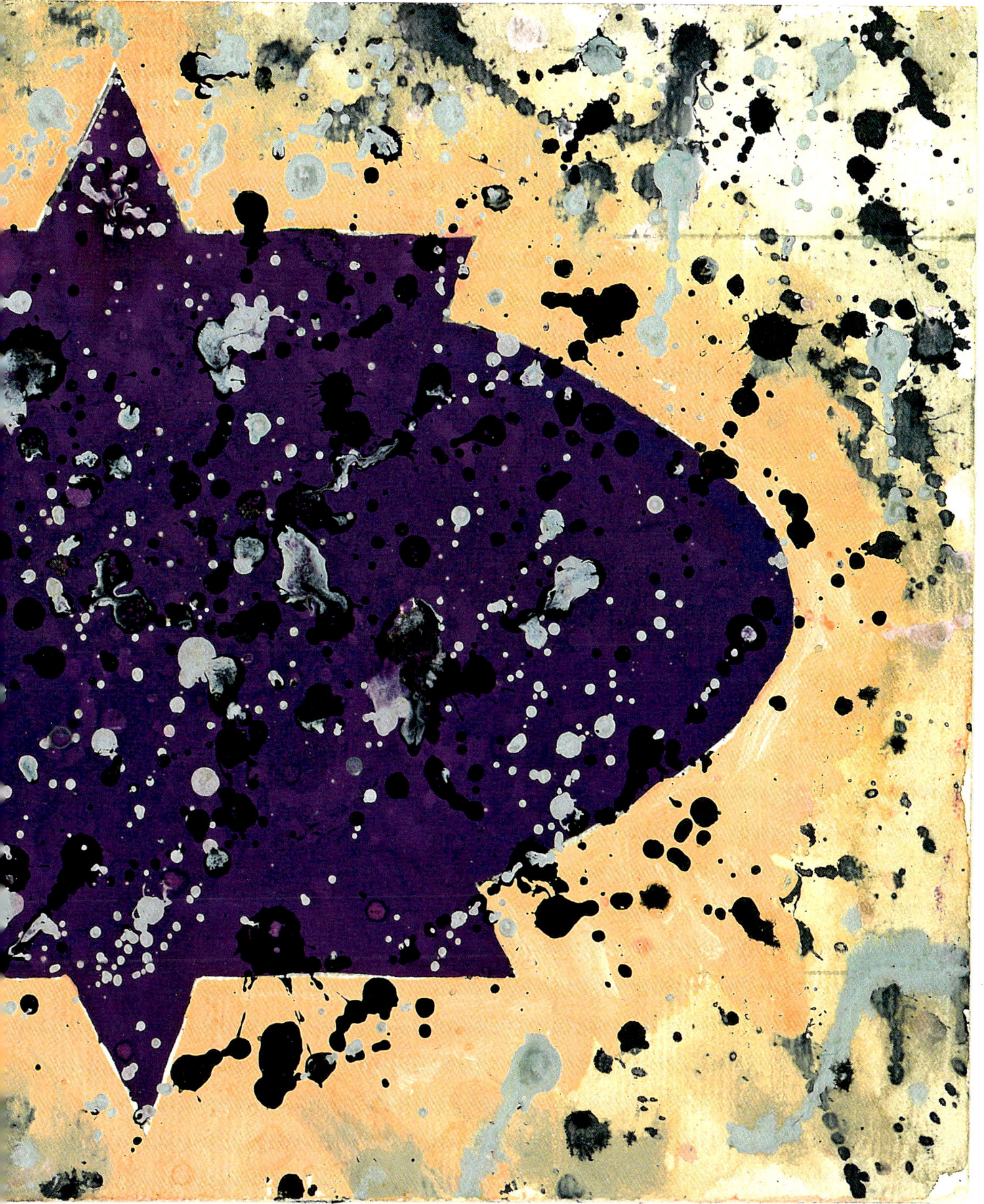

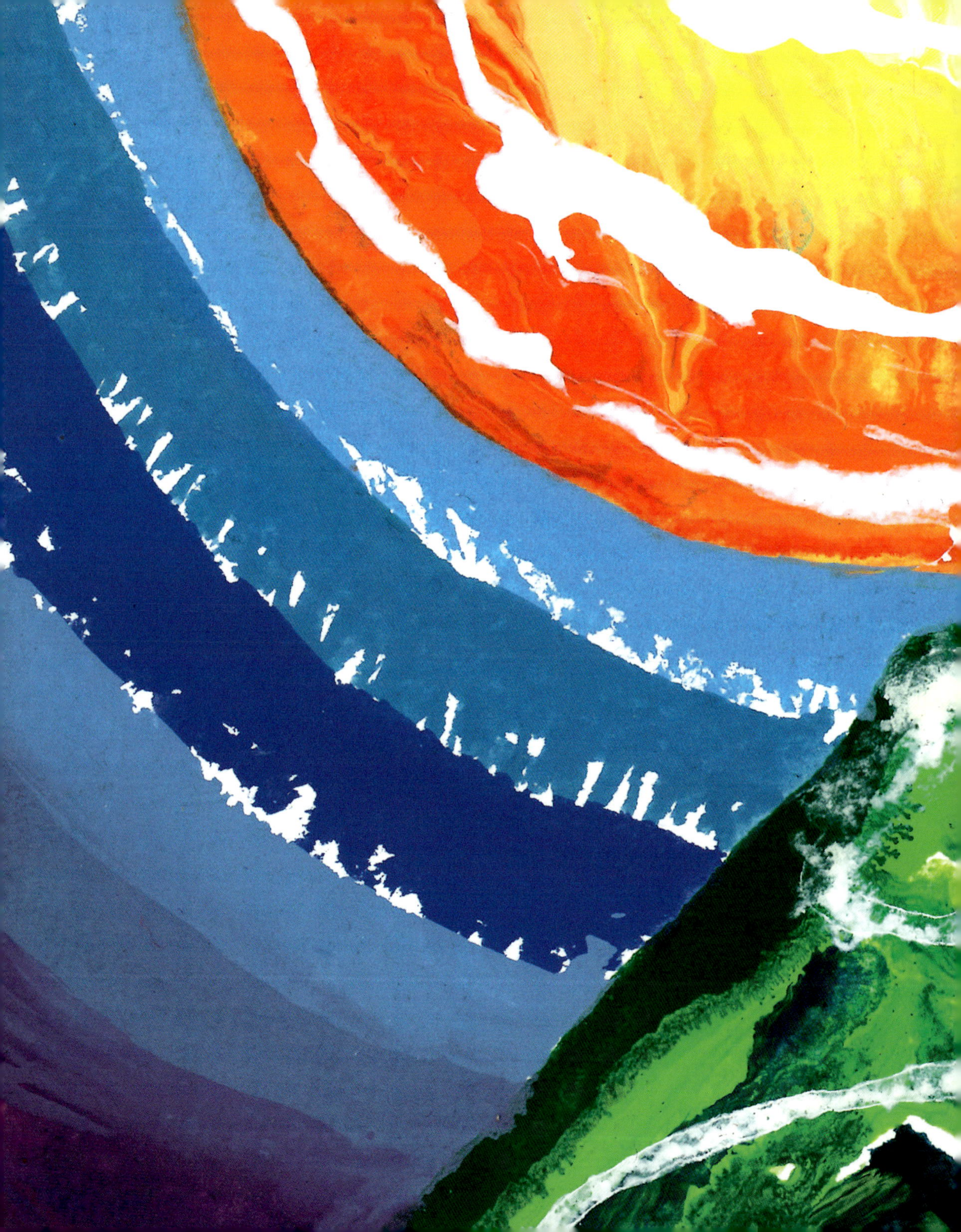

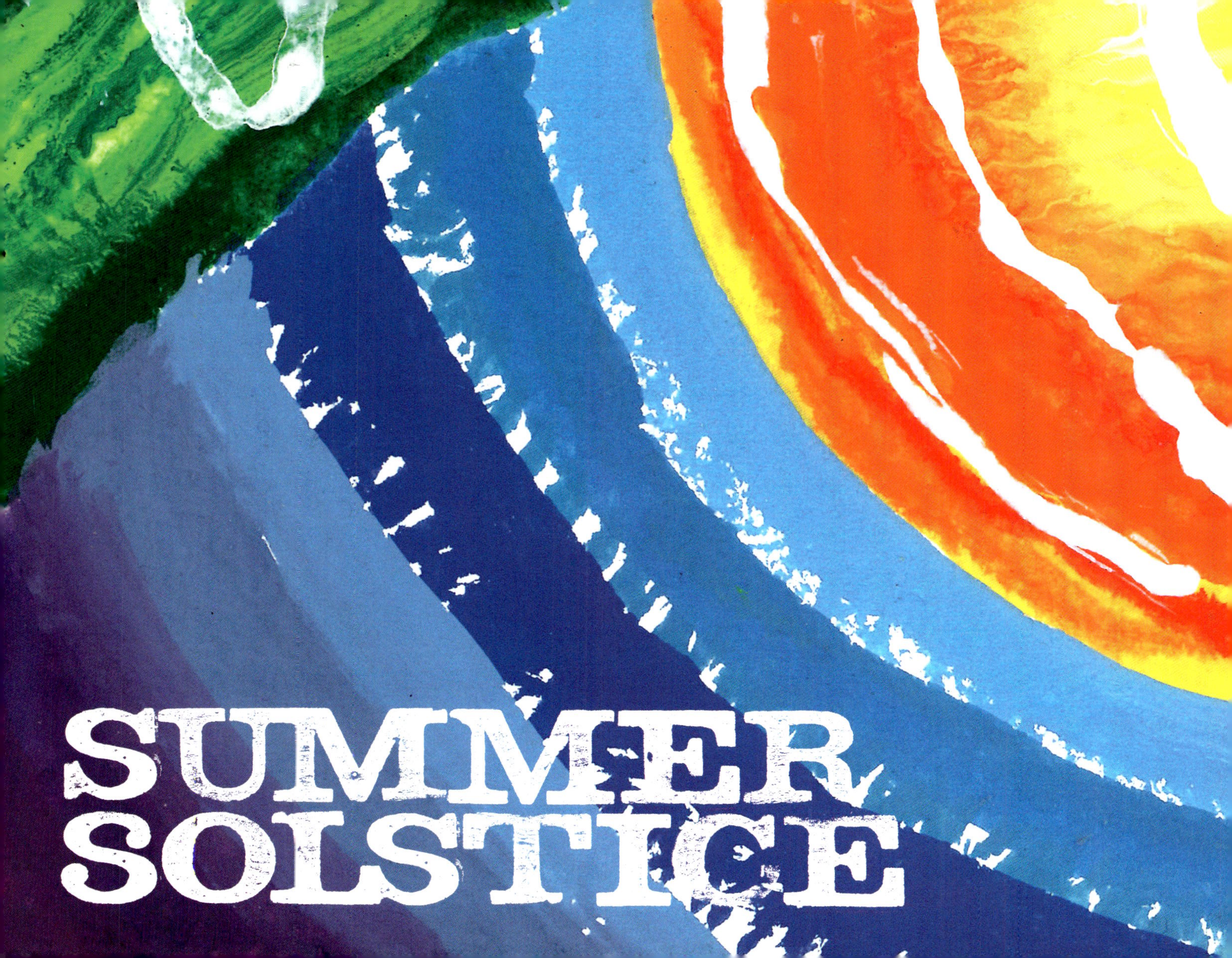
SUMMER
SOLSTICE

SUMMER SO

Previous pages
Summer Solstice / 2010

What is it that makes thousands visit Stonehenge at dawn on the Summer Solstice? If you go to Glastonbury Tor or the Stanton Drew stone circle in Somerset, or to a high place in a city, such as Primrose Hill, in London, you'll find hundreds of people there, too – standing or sitting in silence, meditating or just gazing out to the horizon, waiting for sunrise. And then, whether there's the gift of a blazing sun or only a grey light pushing its way through a bank of clouds, there are cheers of jubilation, as people start banging drums, dancing or just hugging each other and emerging in their own way out of the pre-dawn stillness.

In centuries past, the celebration of this time of year occurred a few days after the actual day of the solstice. Some of the dates in the Eightfold Year drifted forwards a few days in the Christian calendar: the rebirth of the sun at the Winter Solstice became a celebration of the birth of the son of God; the marking of the longest day of the year at the Summer Solstice became conflated with the eve of St John's Day, 24 June. In Ireland, Scotland, Wales and England, and in Europe and parts of North Africa, there were great celebrations at this time; the Summer Solstice may have seen the most important rituals of the year. There are accounts from Paris in the 12th century and London in the 16th century of bonfires in the streets, people staying up all night, minstrels playing, and children garlanded with flowers. In the countryside, wheels were set alight and sent rolling downhill.

From the Vale of Glamorgan, in Wales, we have a record of such an event in the 1820s. Men and boys gathered at the top of a hill, girls and women at the bottom. A large cartwheel was set alight and sent careering down the hillside. If the fire went out before it reached the women, this signalled a poor harvest. If it reached the bottom of the hill still ablaze, the harvest would be abundant.

Before the Christian era it's likely that religious practice included a celebration of the Summer Solstice. In fact, rolling a blazing firewheel was recorded among Pagans in 4th-century France, which means that those villagers in 19th-century Glamorgan were probably carrying out a ritual dating back thousands of years.

OLSTICE 20–21 June

Certainly, prehistoric monuments are sometimes aligned with the rising or setting sun at midsummer or midwinter. Stonehenge's dual alignment to Summer Solstice sunrise and Winter Solstice sunset is well known; and the modern-day Stonehenge Summer Solstice ritual is now one that people travel from far and wide to attend.

It may feel as though summer has not yet peaked, but, astronomically, this is summer's zenith, and the dance between the sun and the earth is at its most intense. It's time to drop into the timeless moment of the *sol stitia* – Latin for 'the standing still of the sun'. For a few days, if you observe the sunrise, you'll notice that it seems to rise at the same point on the horizon before it begins to travel back towards its nadir in December, when it sets as far northwest as it will ever go.

Now our vitality is at its peak. In these longest evenings of the year, it's time for partying. It's time to envision a healthy, dynamic and positive future for ourselves and for the planet. It's time for courage, boldness and magic.

NOTES FROM HELIGAN

'Summer Solstice was a glorious day with a deep blue sky and a shimmering heat haze, "like visible magic" as Lynsey Robinson described it. Lynsey was at Heligan representing the Sensory Trust, a charity that seeks to provide disadvantaged people in the UK with transformative sensory nature experiences. The Druids recited poetry about the Oak King and the Holly King, and the Sensory Trust brought their huge, carved poppy seeds as well as magnifying glasses and real seeds for people to examine. Lots of visitors to the gardens got involved in the ritual, symbolically sowing more seeds on open ground. The seed had germinated slowly as it had hardly rained since the sowing in May, but there was a thick carpet of young growth, ankle-deep across the field. One or two of the oldest plants had a flower, and in the bright sunshine, the petals of the corn chamomile shone brilliant white. Hoverflies skimmed past. The OVA was still invisible.'

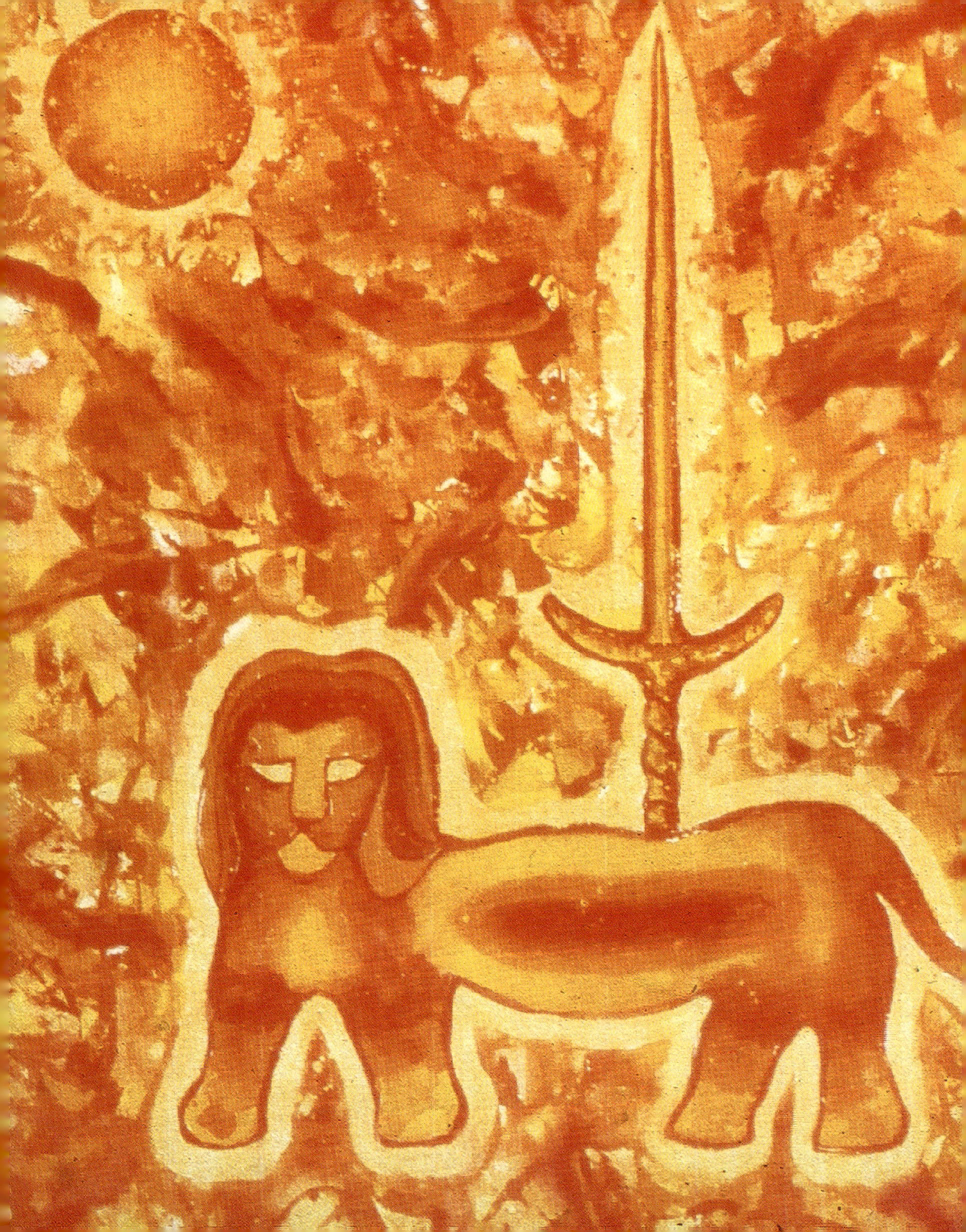

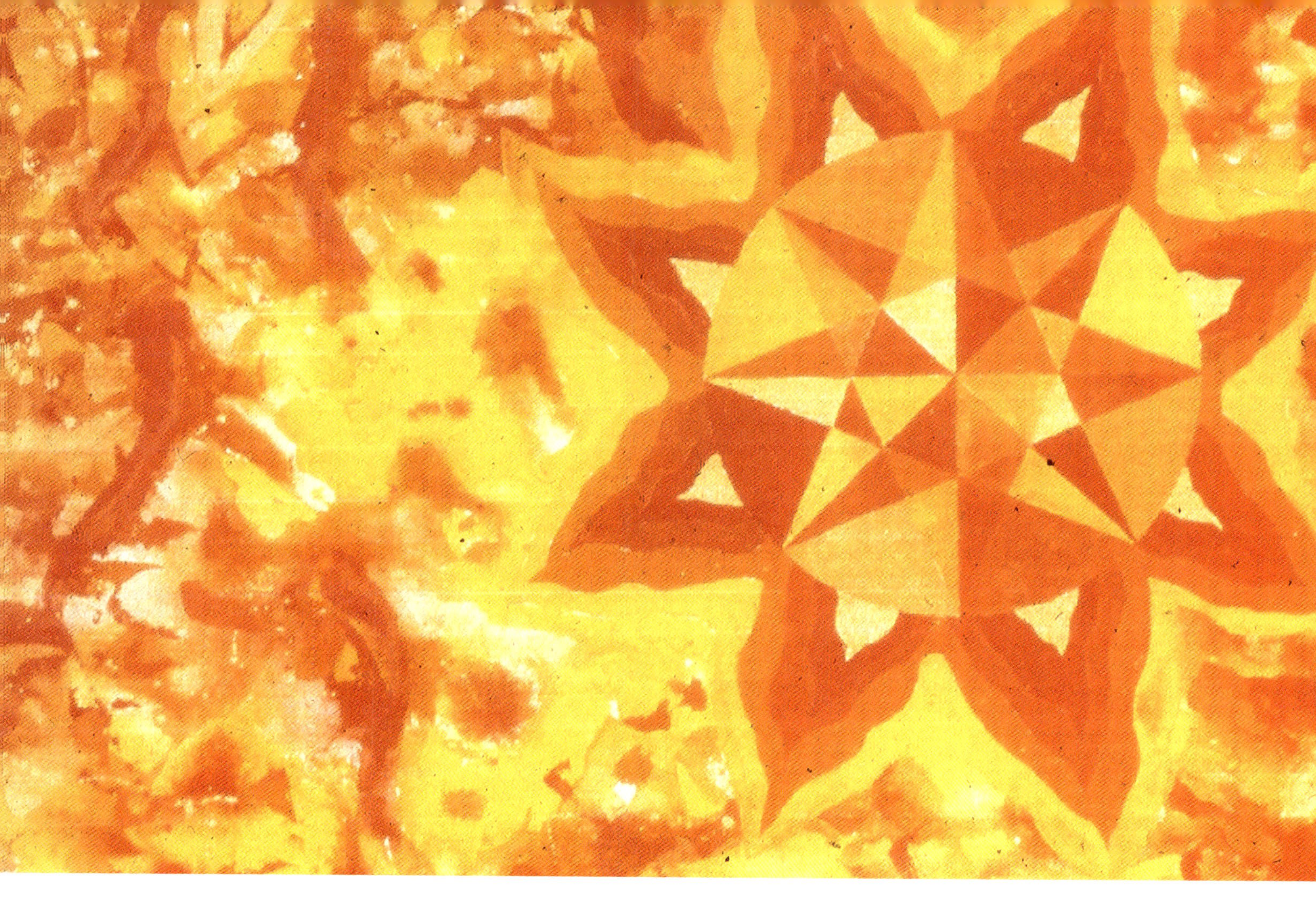

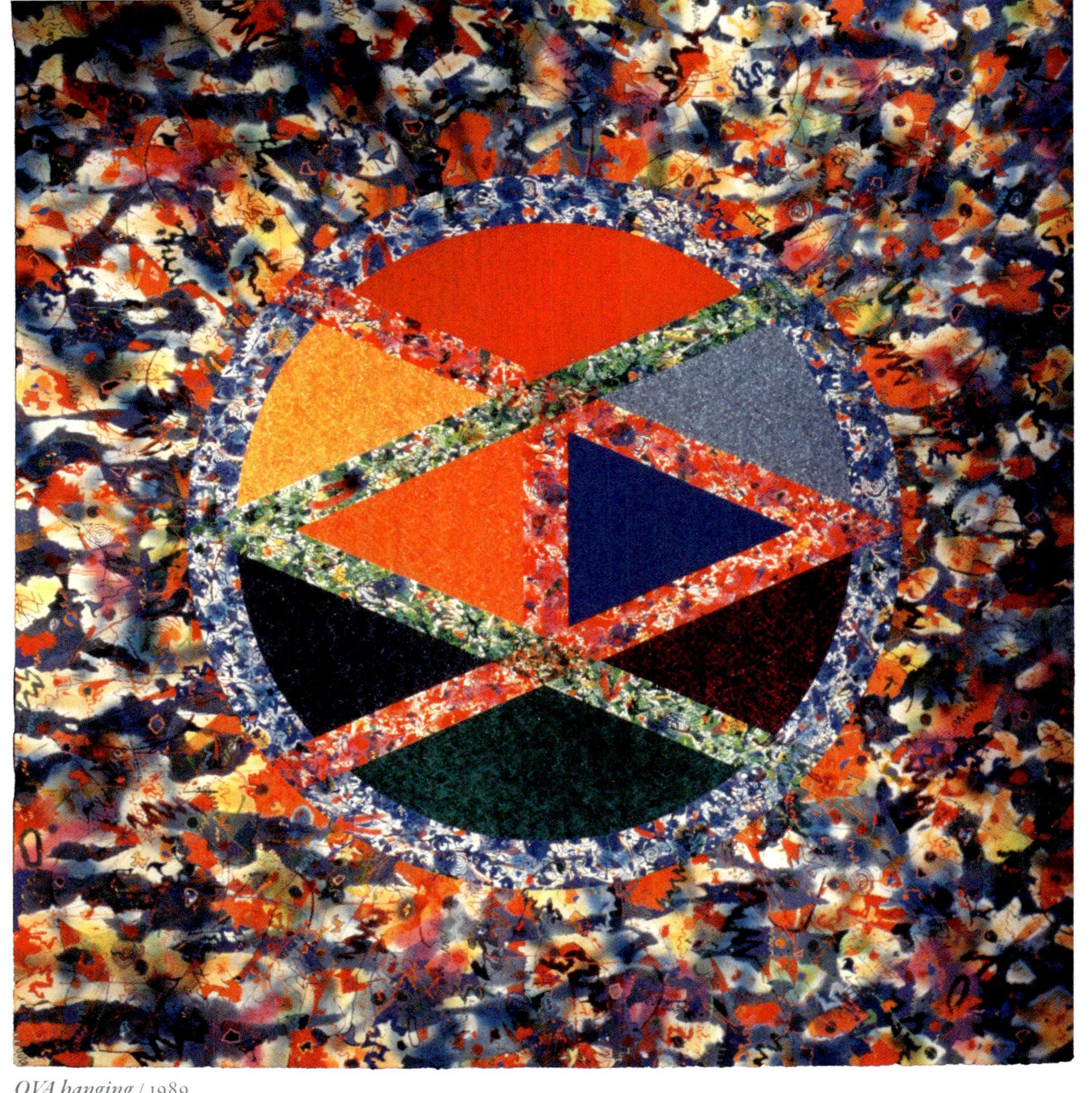

OVA hanging / 1989

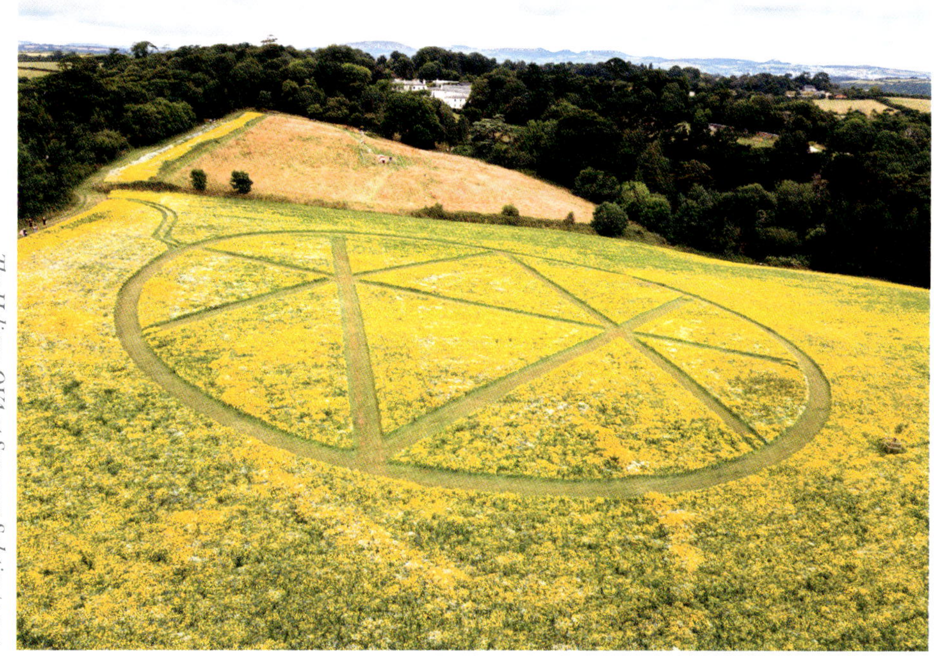

The Heligan OVA at Summer Solstice / 2022

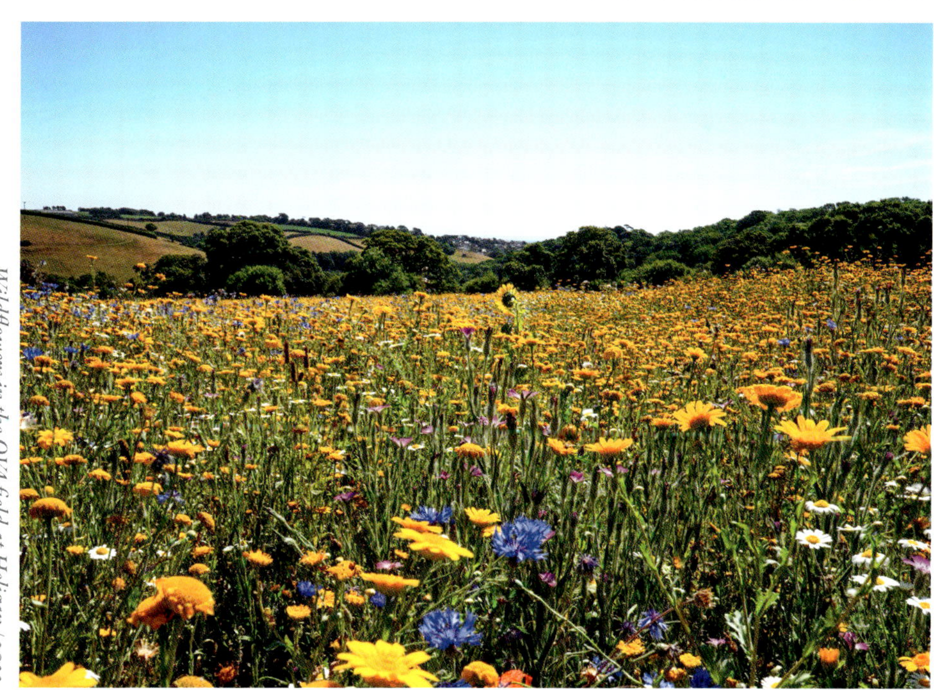

Wildflowers in the OVA field at Heligan / 2022

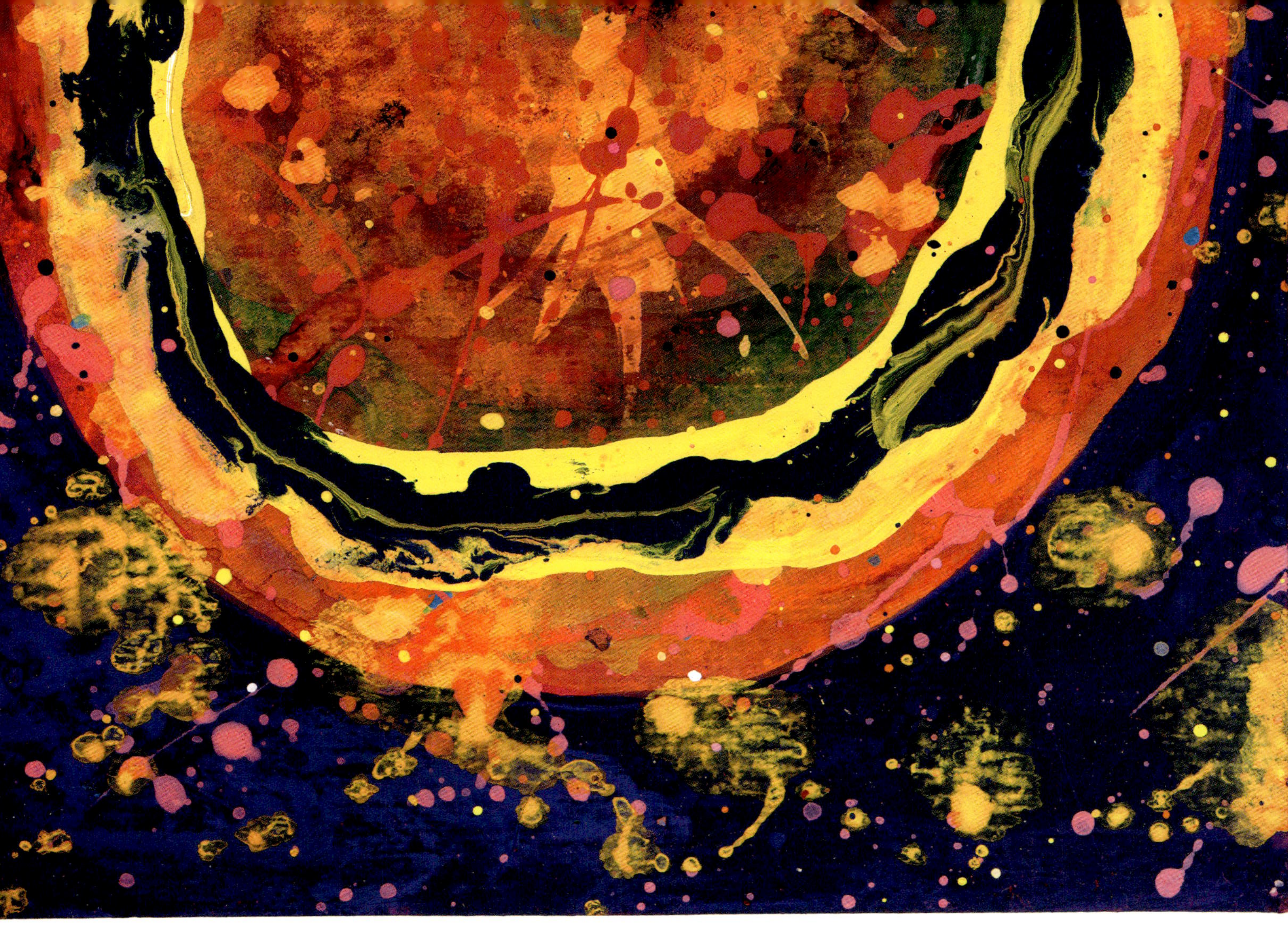

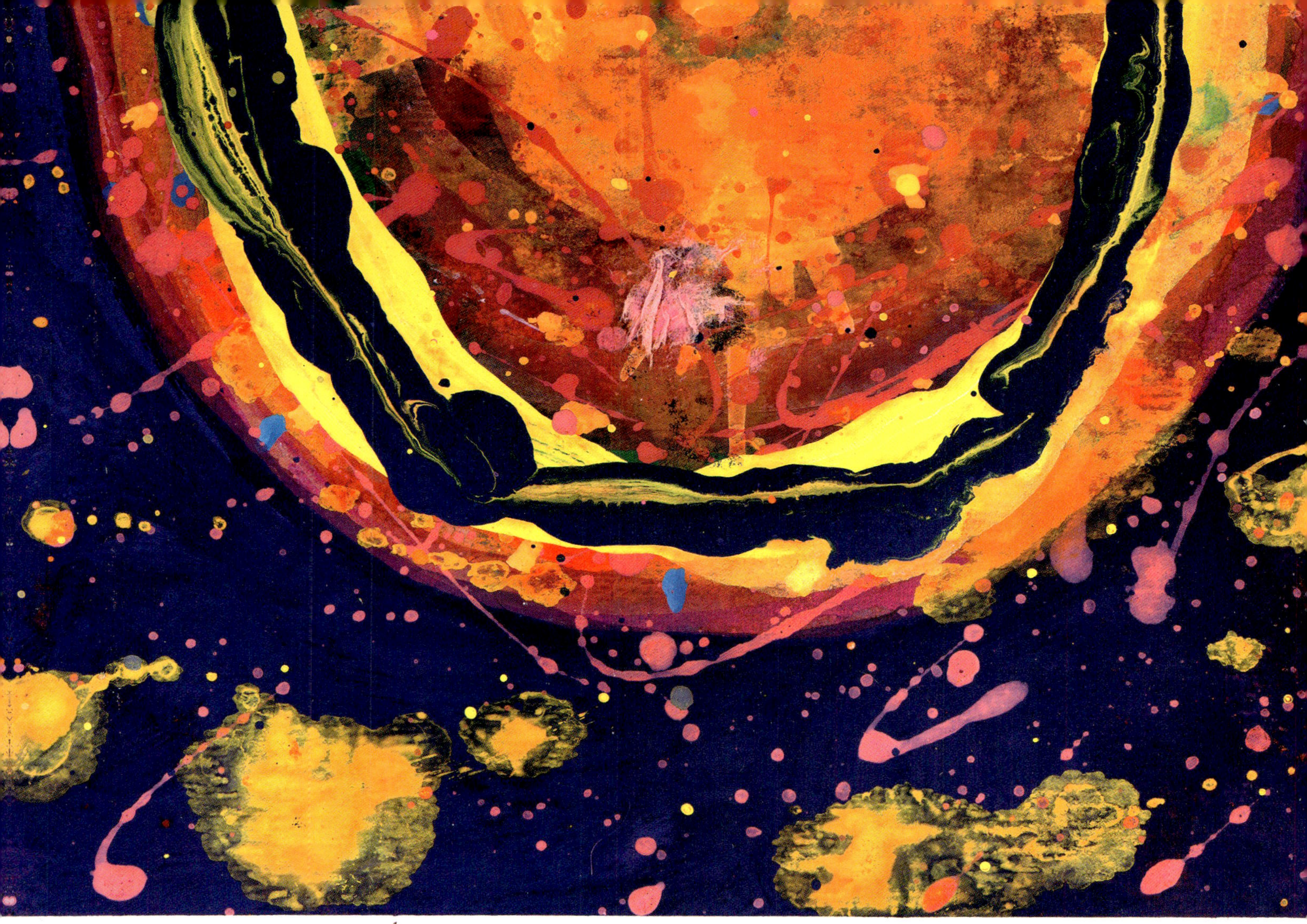

Leaving the 20th Century Ship / 1985
One of the essential themes of the *Leaving the 20th Century/How to Become Invisible* cycle was the idea of breaking away from the entrapment of what the Situationist International called the 'Spectacle' (the concept of Capital and its fake jewels). The ship is this breakaway movement made manifest – an ark for deliverance from the banal and the prison of everyday life.

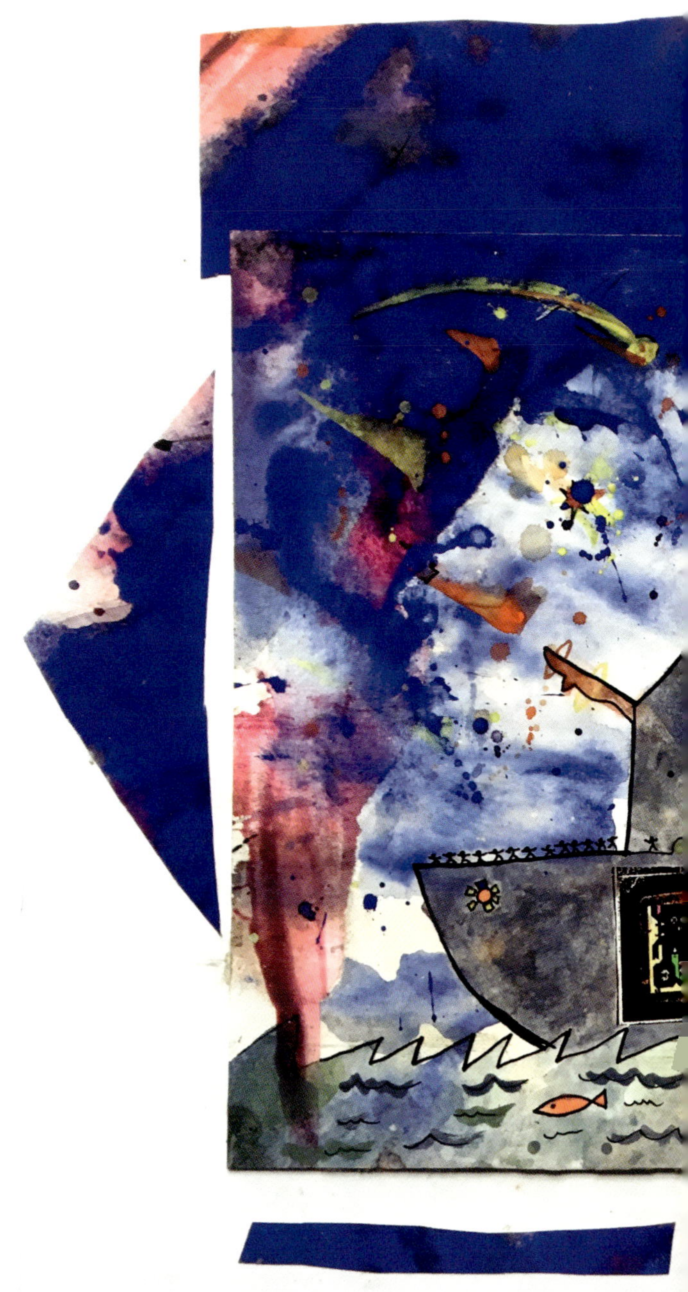

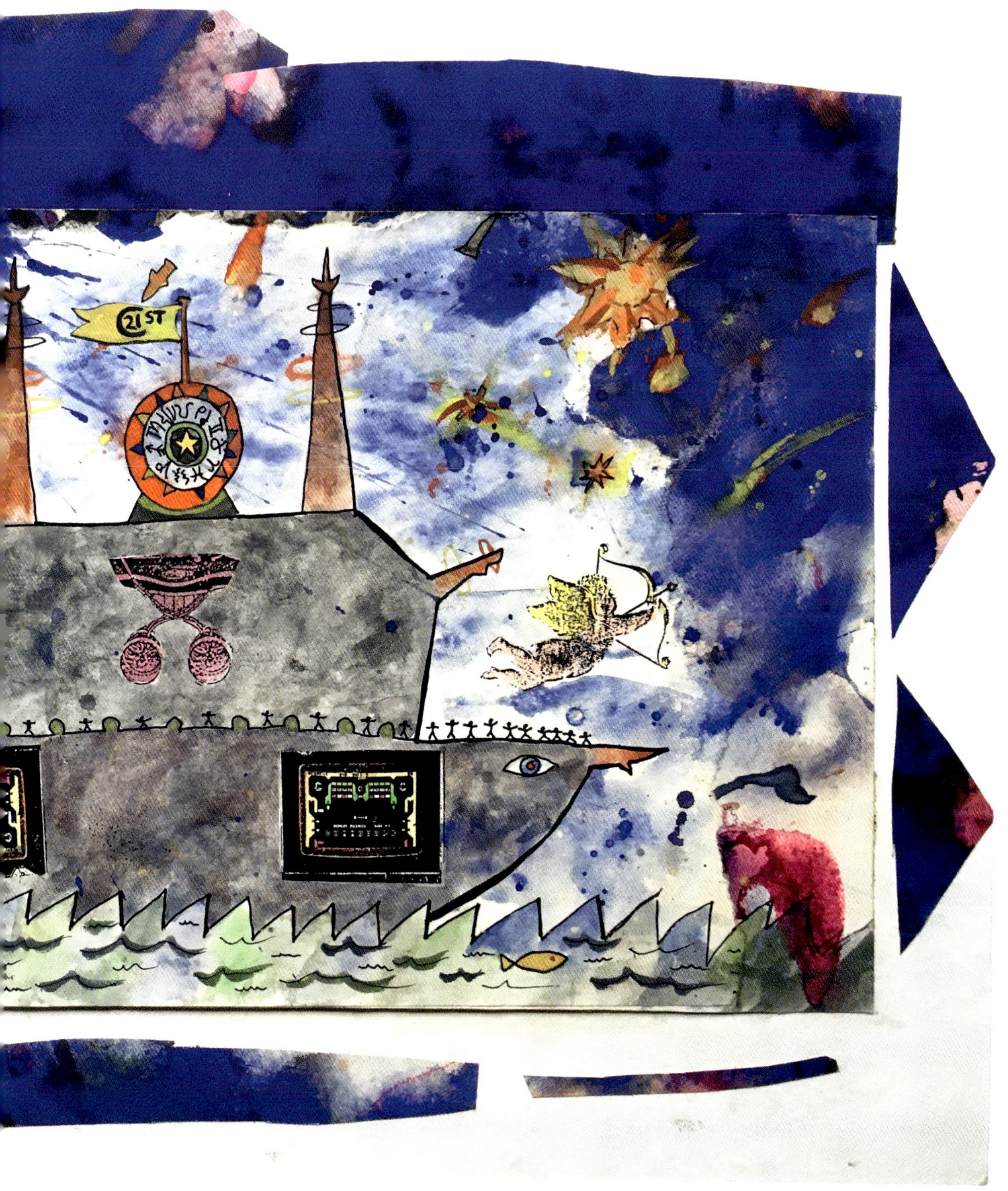
21ST

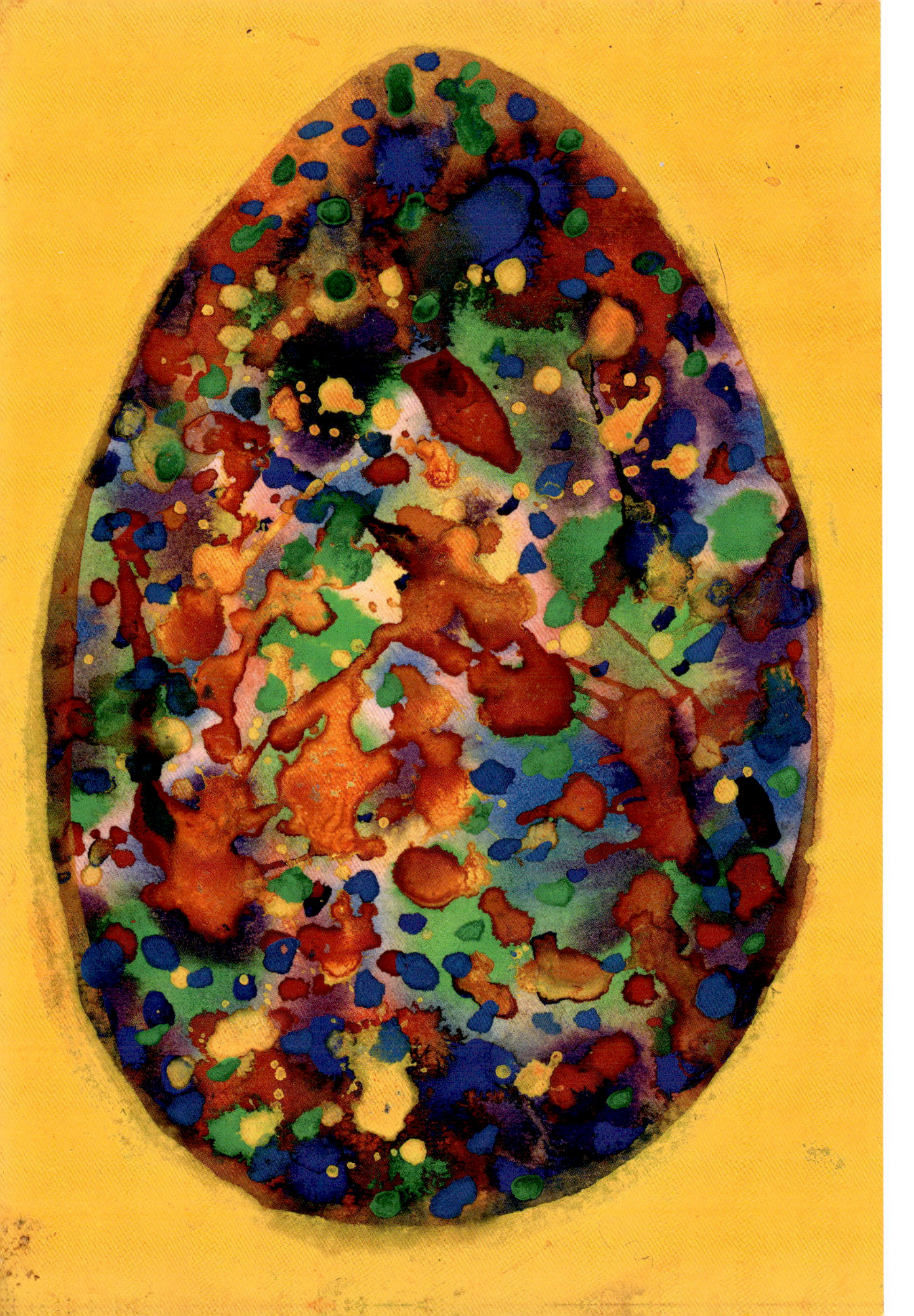

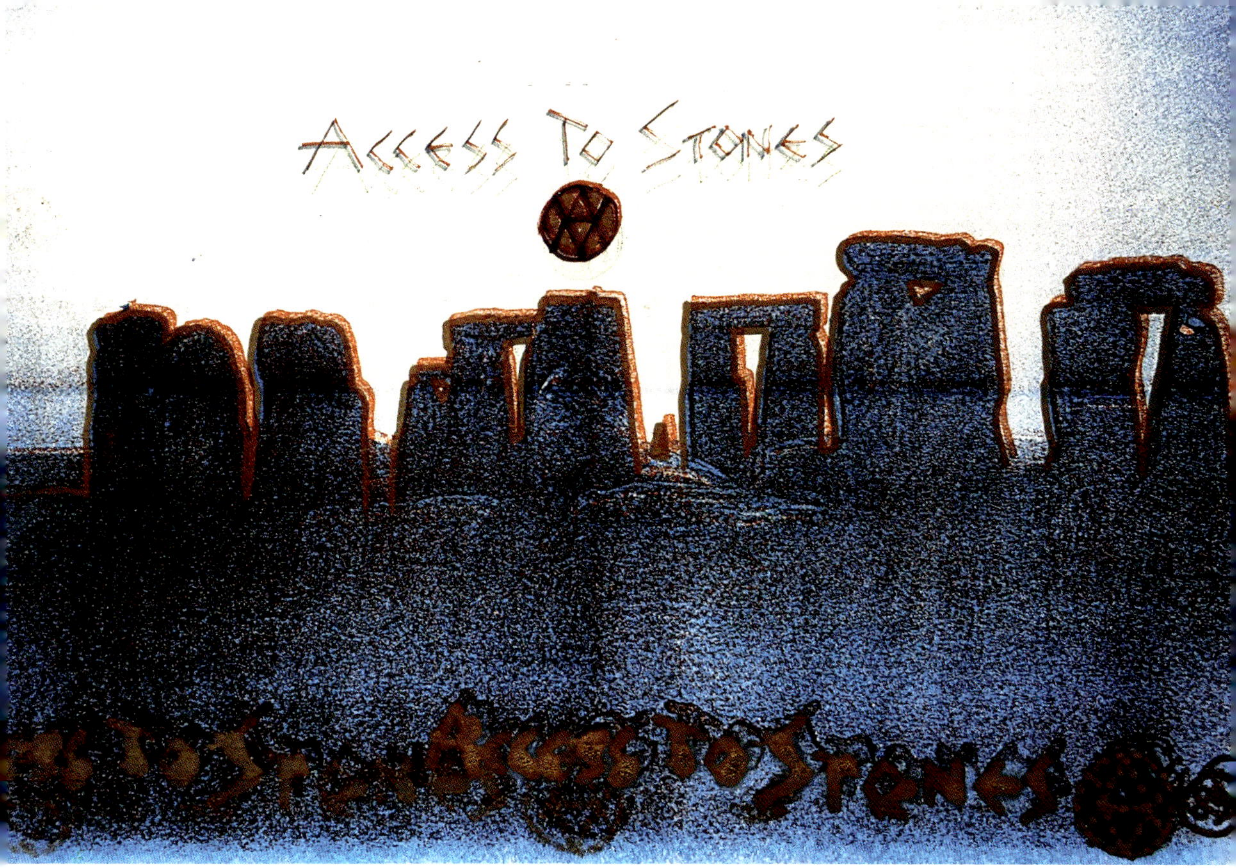

Access to Stones / 1990

This work is part of a series created in 1990 during a campaign for access to Stonehenge and other sacred sites controlled by government bodies such as English Heritage (or 'English Heretics' as Jamie liked to call them). Jamie's great-uncle George Watson MacGregor Reid had frequently encouraged the storming of fences around Stonehenge on important Druidic ritual dates when the site was privately owned by Cecil Chubb.

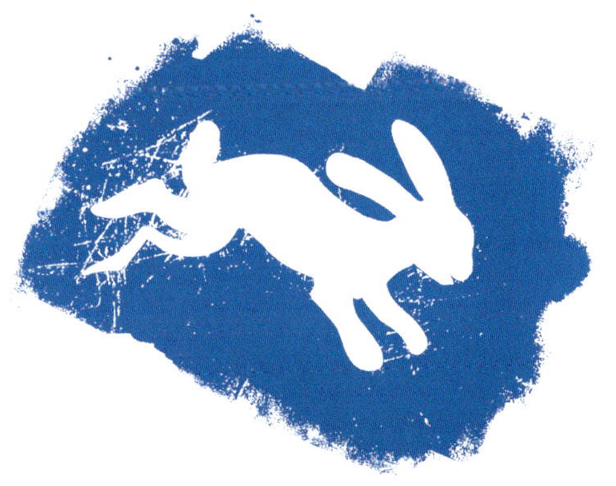

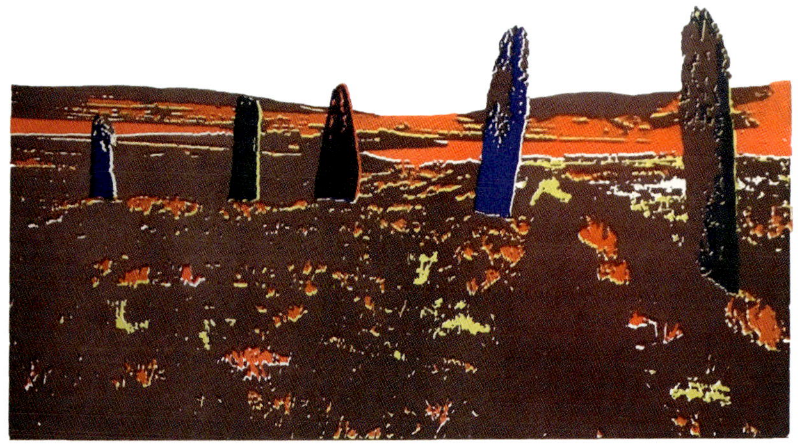

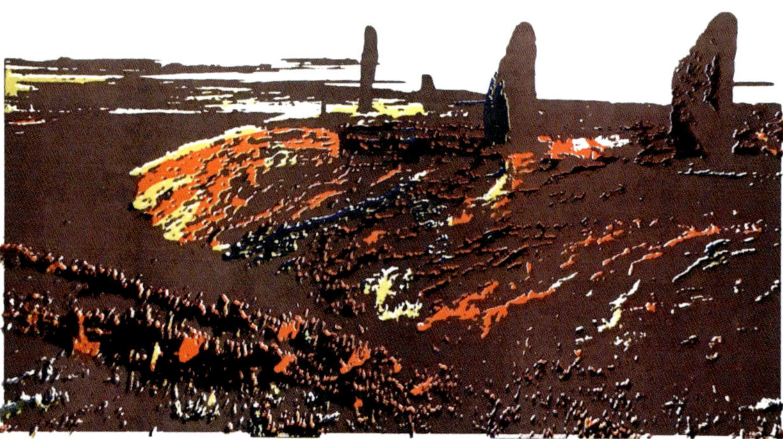

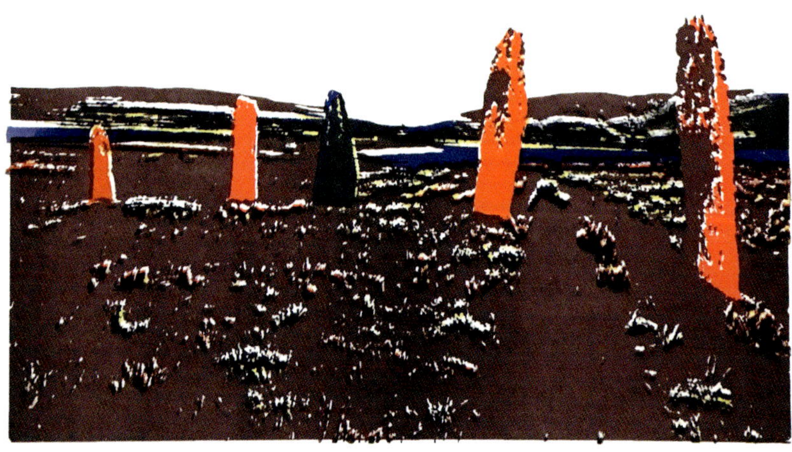

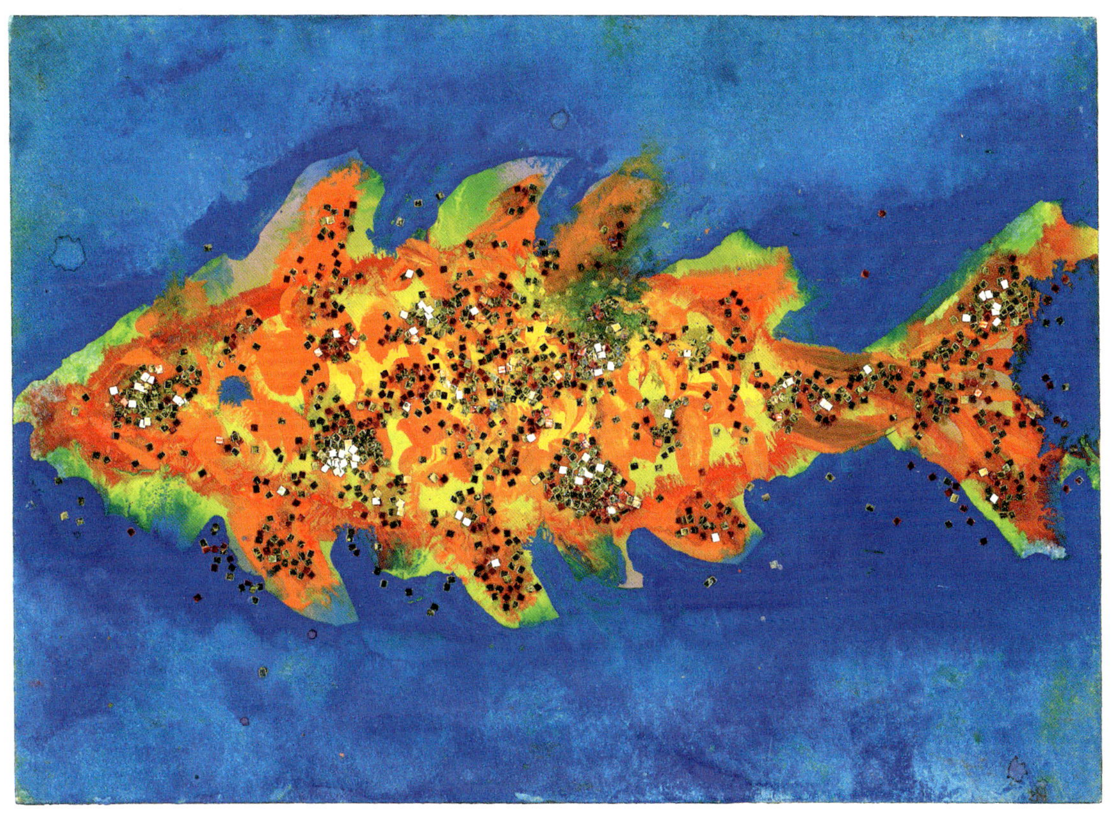

Ring of Brodgar (Day) / 1972

Jamie was very attached to his Scottish roots. The Reid family had come from Montrose and were committed to the cause of independence. In 1972, Jamie produced his first editioned work: a series of colourways of a sequence of images of the Ring of Brodgar in Orkney. The original image had been, in a typically Reidian gesture, lifted from a cigarette card. Standing stones were not only places of nature worship but sites of communal action, both always important to the artist.

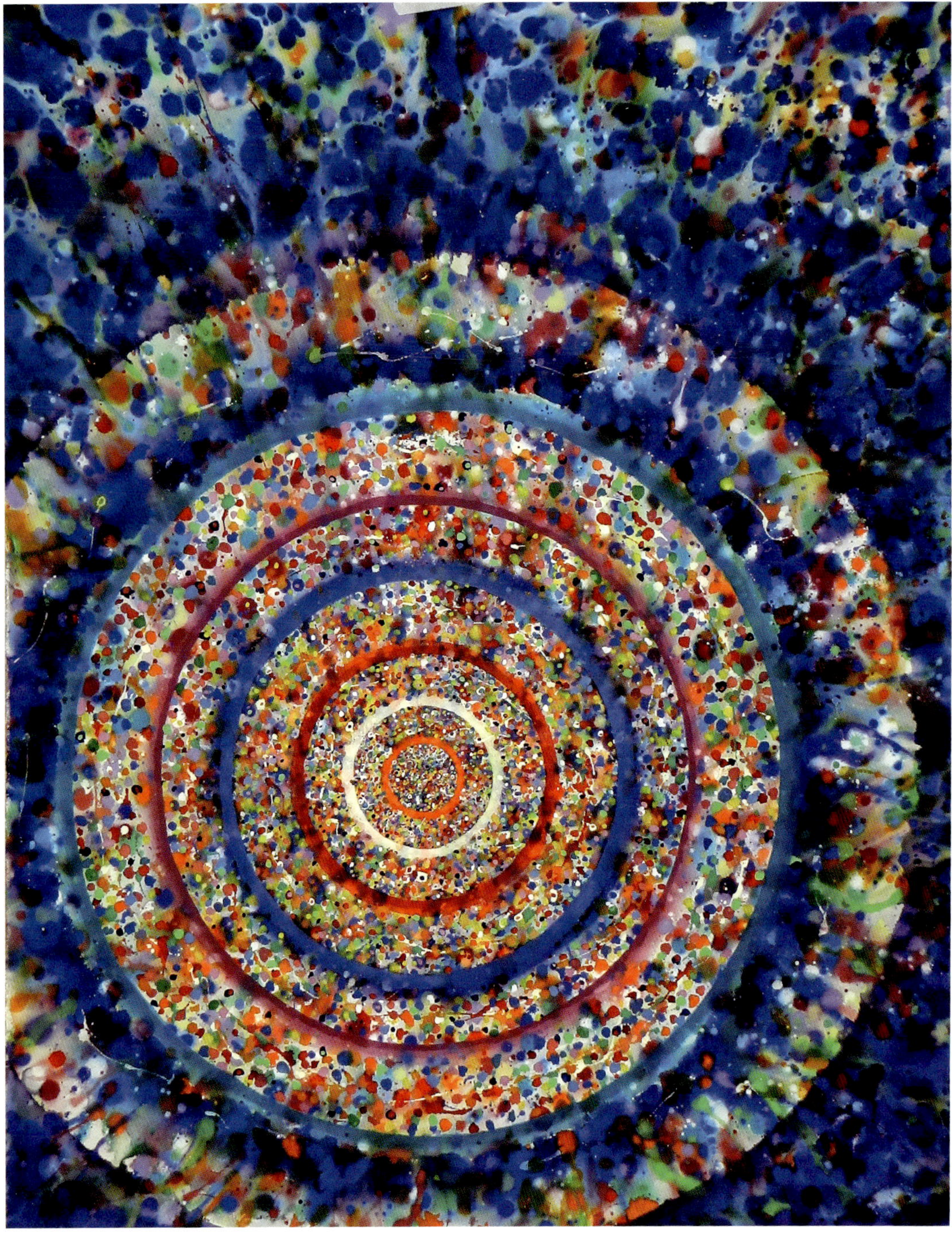

DON'T YOU REALISE HOW FUCKING
SPECIAL IT IS TO BE BORN ON A
LIVE ON PLANET EARTH.
IT IS BEYOND BELIEF
WONDROUS, UNIQUE, DIVERSE
FULL OF COLOUR & SOUND & MAGNIFICENT CREATURES, BIRDS
& INSECTS, FISH, FUNGI FLOWERS TREES
THIS IN ALL ITS GLORY & US IS CALLED
HUMANS ITS GUARDIANS
WE HAVE ABUSED THIS POSITION WITH
GREED & POLLUTION & SELFISHNESS
JUST MAYBE GAIA HAS HAVE ENOUGH
OF OUR (HUMAN) HURT & SEEKS REVENGE!

CALLING
ON OUR ANCESTORS,

ABORIGINAL PARDON
FORGIVENESS

THOSE WHO LIVED ON EARTH FOR
10,000'S OF YEARS WITH
REVERANCE & RESPECT.

ONLY TO SEE
MANKIND PLUNDER & RAPE
THIS PLANET.

PRACTICE
PENANCE & PRAYERS
& FORGIVENESS.

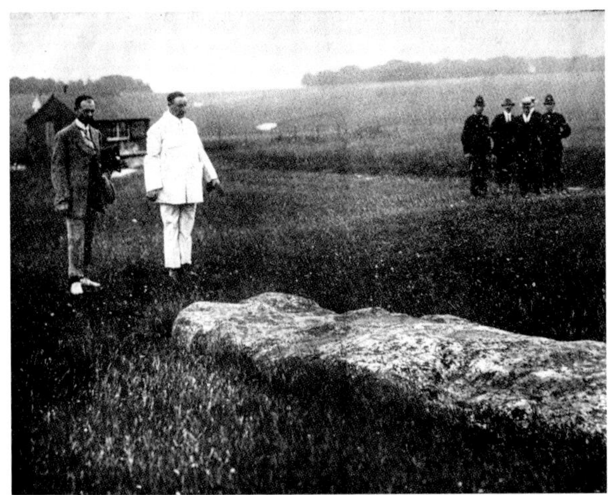

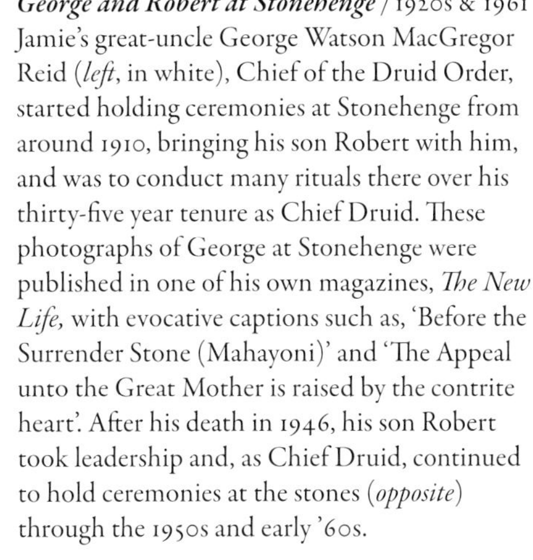

George and Robert at Stonehenge / 1920s & 1961
Jamie's great-uncle George Watson MacGregor Reid (*left*, in white), Chief of the Druid Order, started holding ceremonies at Stonehenge from around 1910, bringing his son Robert with him, and was to conduct many rituals there over his thirty-five year tenure as Chief Druid. These photographs of George at Stonehenge were published in one of his own magazines, *The New Life,* with evocative captions such as, 'Before the Surrender Stone (Mahayoni)' and 'The Appeal unto the Great Mother is raised by the contrite heart'. After his death in 1946, his son Robert took leadership and, as Chief Druid, continued to hold ceremonies at the stones (*opposite*) through the 1950s and early '60s.

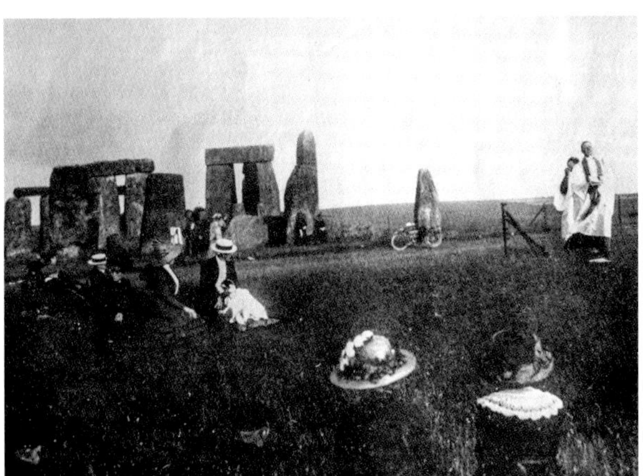

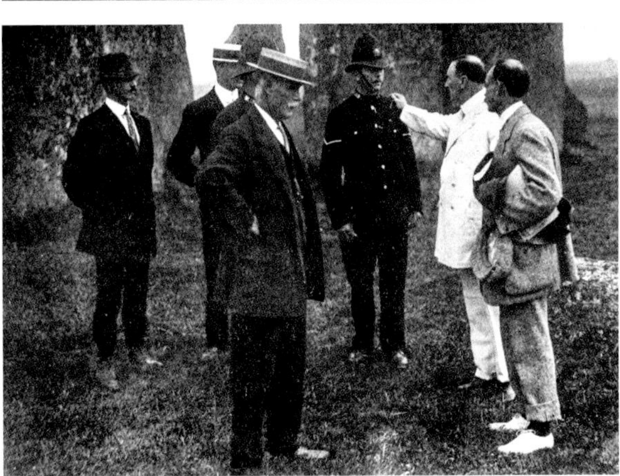

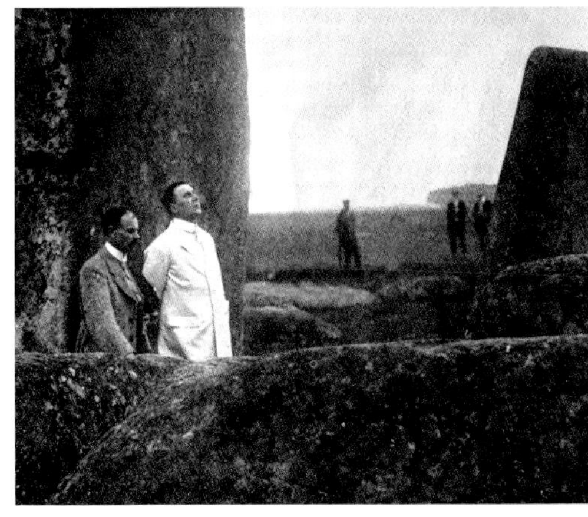

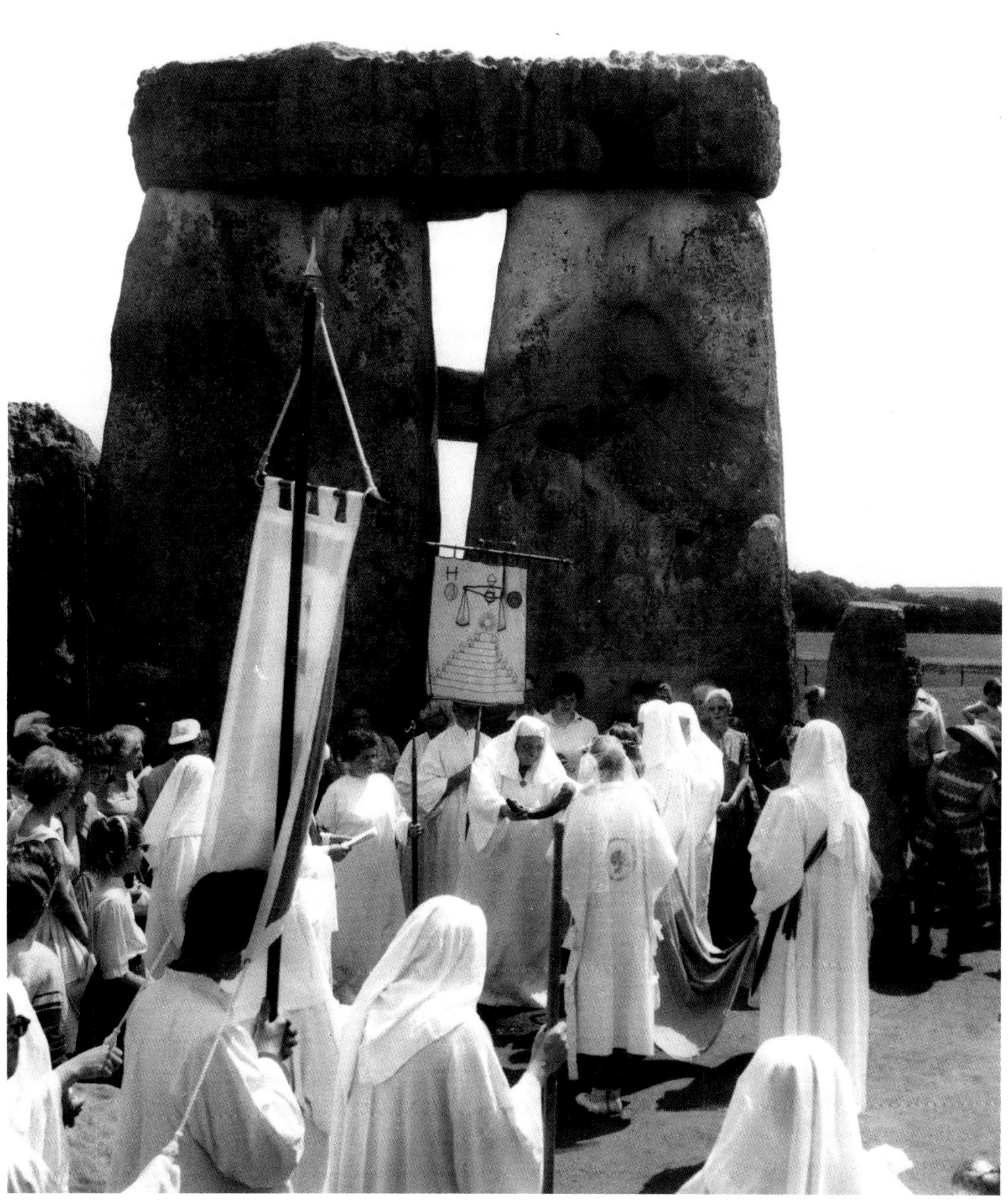

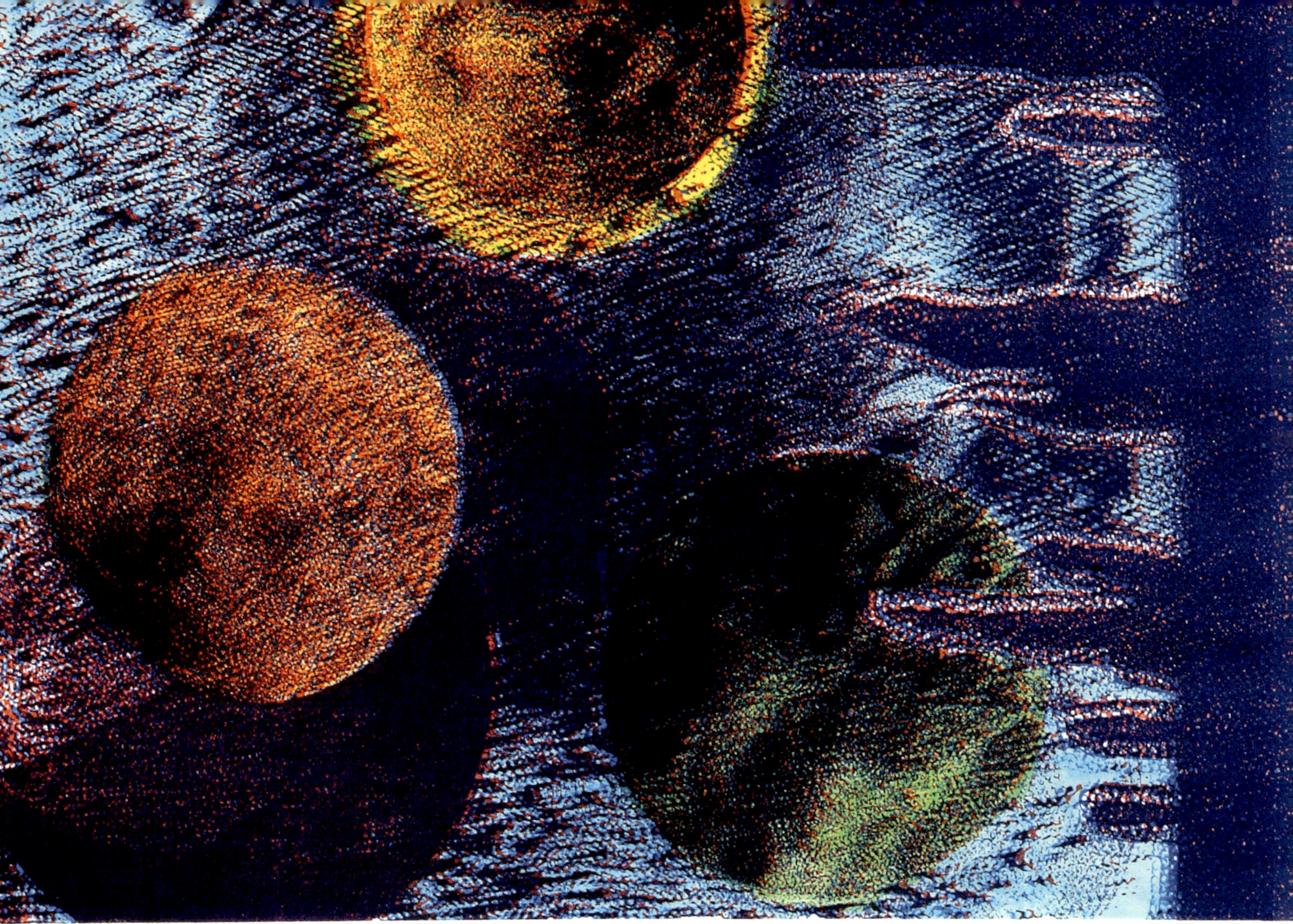

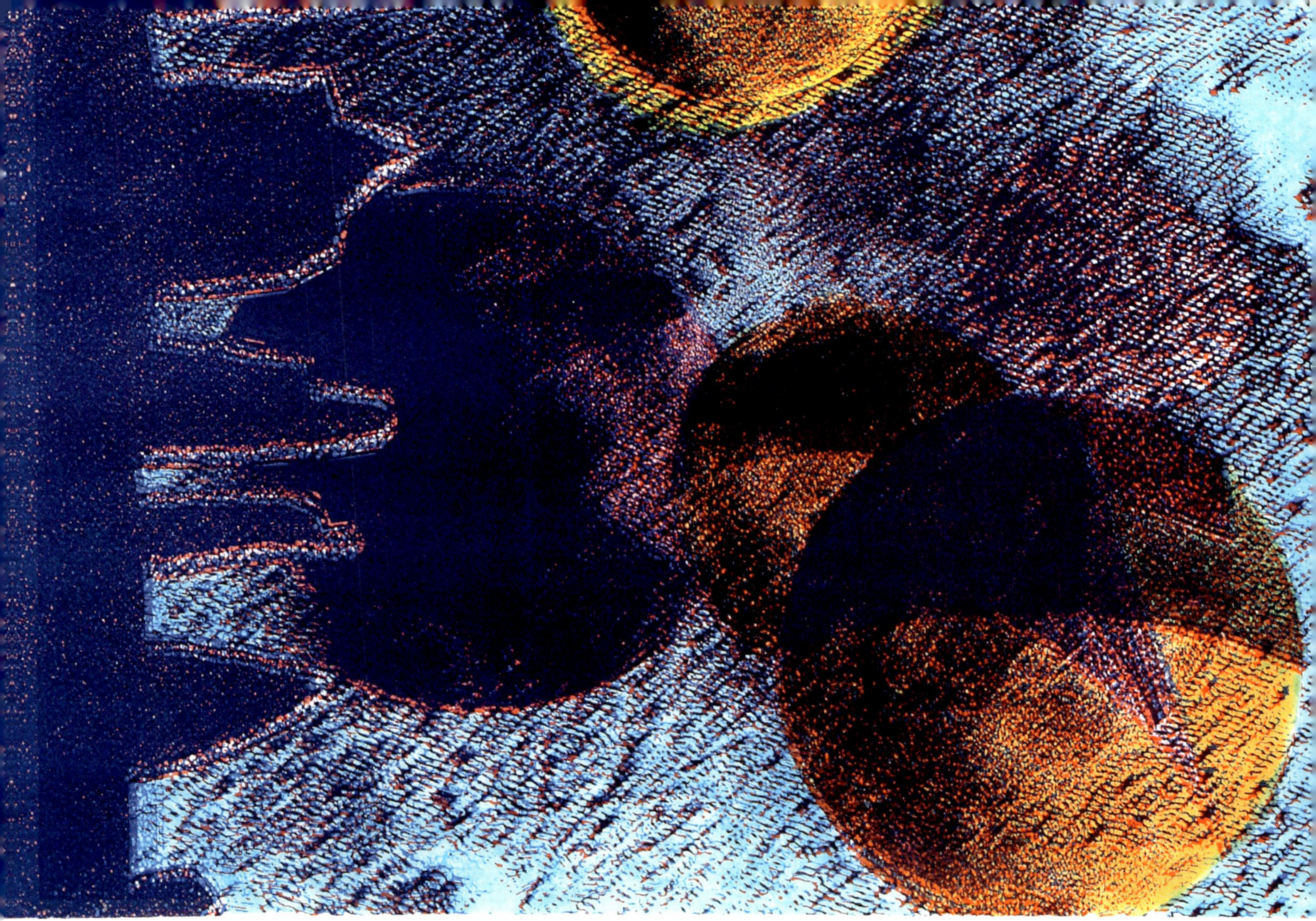

When the Earth Had Many Moons / 1990

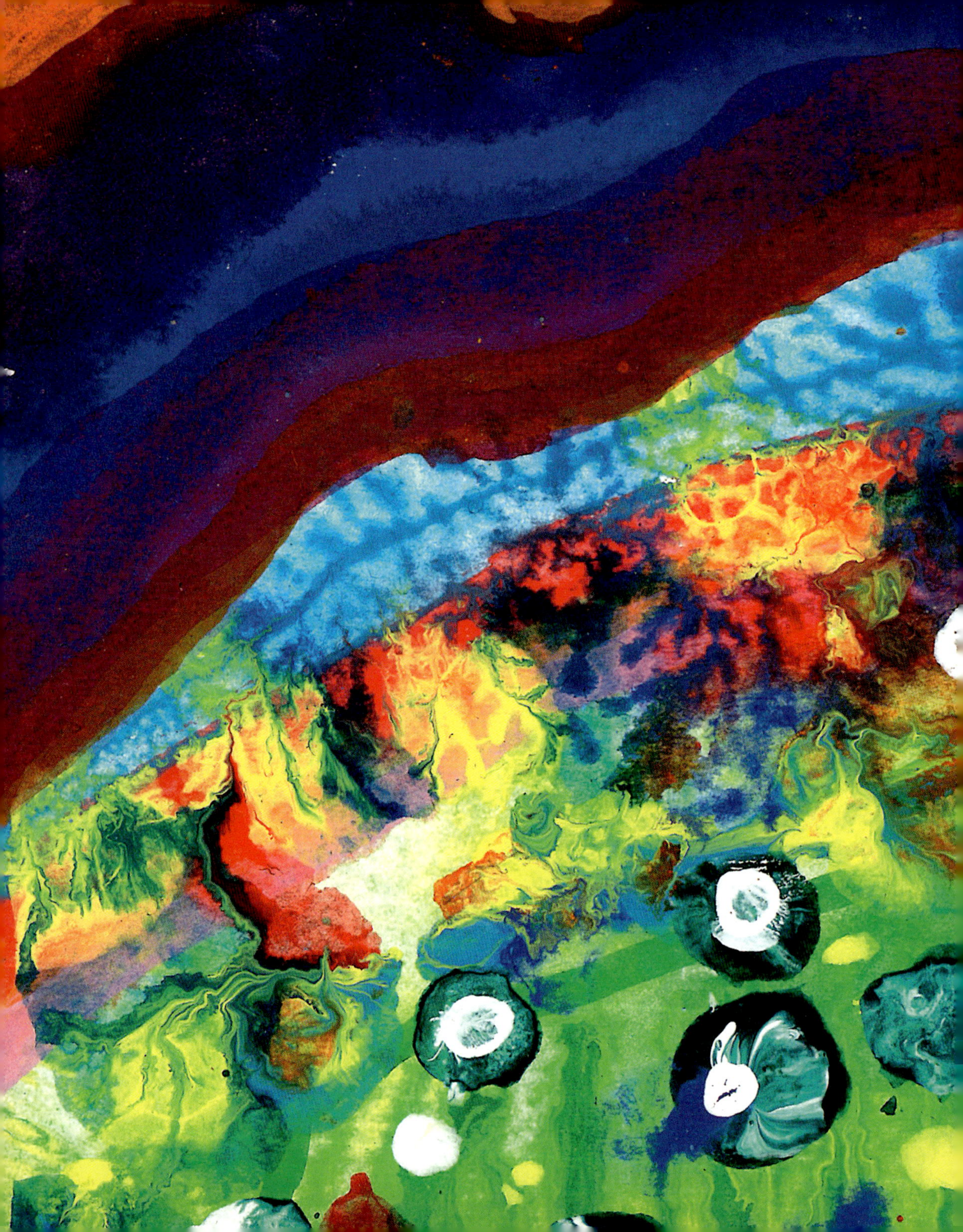

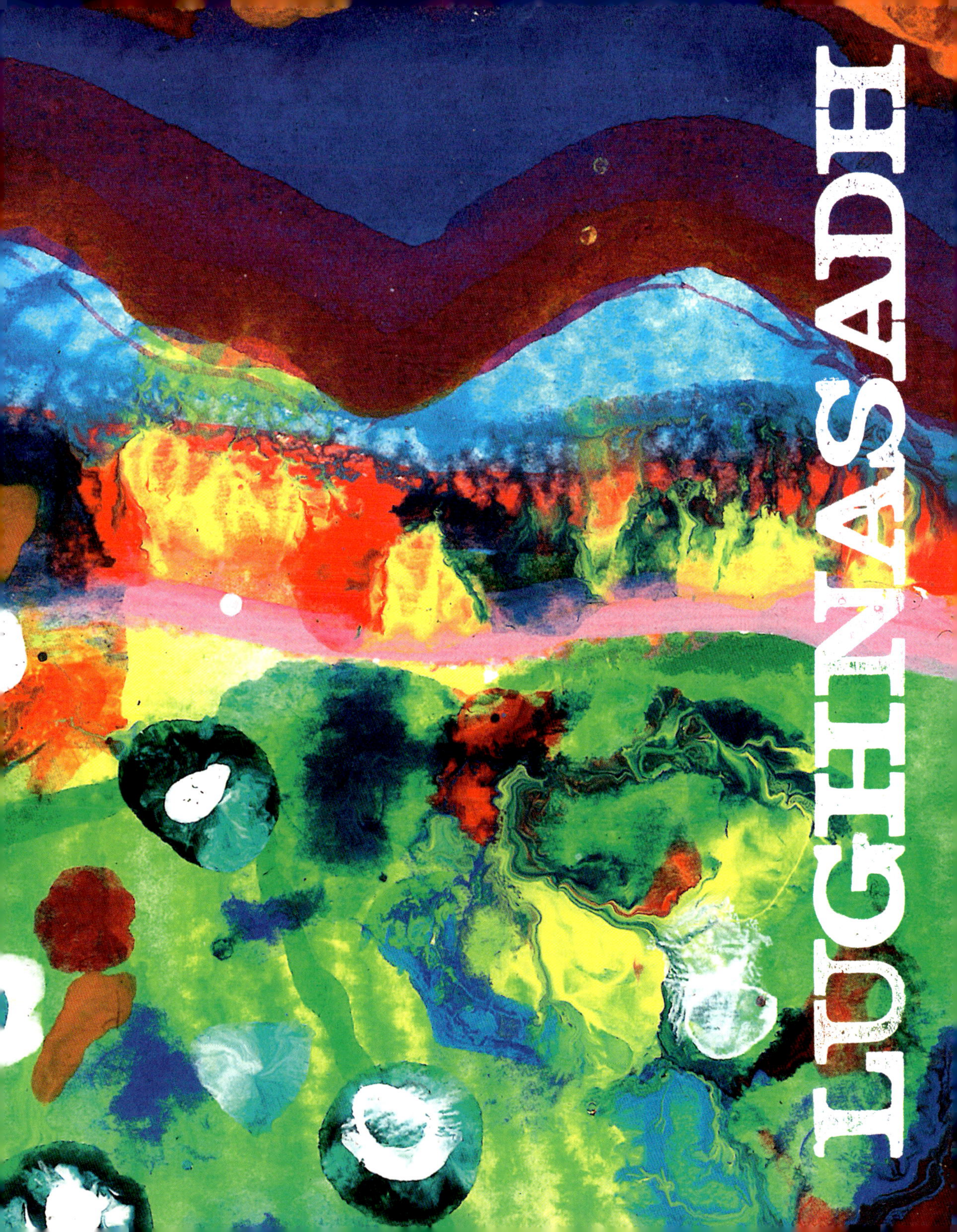
LUGHNASADH

LUGHNASA

Previous pages
Lughnasadh / 2010

Lughnasadh means 'in honour of Lugh' the sun-god. Anglo-Saxon Christians renamed the festival Loaf Mass, or Lammas, because at mass they would offer loaves baked from their first wheat harvest. Thanks to Lugh's light and heat, the crops have grown, and now it's time to start reaping the rewards of the work in the fields.

Traditionally, this was the time of gatherings – a whole month in Ireland was dedicated to socialising, with games, marriages, feasting and the last of the summer wine being enjoyed before the cold sets in. If the Beltane–Samhain axis speaks of sex and death, the ushering into and out of life, the Imbolc–Lughnasadh axis speaks of family and community, youth and ageing. The nurturing we practise at Imbolc is by now transformed into the idea of sacrifice and the start of letting go and giving away. This process of maturation and dispersion reaches its culmination at Samhain, but, for now, the focus is on community and human connection.

Our modern atomised world has eroded what once lay at the heart of every society: the virtue of generous hospitality. And Lughnasadh, with its focus on sharing and socialising, offers a perfect time for us to remember this quality and find ways to show our own hospitality.

Spring was all about potential: seeding ideas, crops and new life. Now we're at the other side of the year, and all that care and attention will – we hope – be rewarded. Spring equals promise; autumn, fulfilment.

Now it's time for dancing and for loading the plates with food because it's not going to last. The combine harvesters are already moving across the land and summer is fading. This is the first of three harvest festivals – the grain harvest. As with a sunset, you feel the beauty of the moment intensely because you know it won't last forever.

The last sheaf left standing in the field at Lughnasadh had many names: the Cailleach, the Maiden, the Neck, the Old Sow, the Frog, the Winter and plenty more. Sometimes it was bound in ribbons and given the place of honour at a feast, or taken home as a trophy and hung up until the next harvest. Often it was made into a corn doll, or a kern baby. In other places, the harvest's final

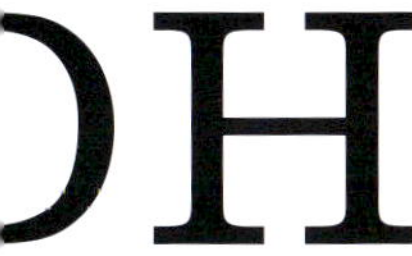

stalk was considered to be evil and farmworkers would refuse to cut it or would use it to cast a curse. John Barleycorn, the personification of barley in the old song, has been killed – cut down and turned to beer or bread.

And so dropping into the meaning of this time, we come to a strange place that combines joy and sadness. It's a time of giving something up in return for reward. A time to let go, burn the chaff in the fields, clear away the old stuff that isn't needed, whether that's emotional or material. This echoes the spring-cleaning of Imbolc at the opposite point on the Wheel.

Our harvest is the result of two processes: one of gathering what is wholesome, the sweet fruit, the promise of spring fulfilled; and another of threshing and casting aside what is rotten or useless. As we edit our lives, looking back on our failures and achievements, we might focus on our gains or our losses. The spirit of Lughnasadh calls on us to celebrate and to focus not on the declining of the year or our life, but instead on gratitude for the gifts that life has given us.

Psychologists affirm that being thankful is good for the body and mind, so now is a good time for focusing on gratitude. A time, also, for lighting a Lammas fire, like the ones in Ireland that have for centuries been lit at this time on the hilltops, to burn away the bad things that have happened and celebrate the good.

NOTES FROM HELIGAN

'This was the first celebration with the OVA in its full glory. We had marked the symbol using the simplest of methods: a central post in the ground, 50 metres of twine and a compass to orient the points of the A and V north–south, and the horizontal line east–west. We pushed through a thick sward of flowers, white, blue and gold, the odd red poppy bursting through. We heard a tale of the god Lugh and the harvest king, took part in a guided visualisation exploring our goals and skills, and made corn dollies. There was a blaze of flowers and the roaring buzz of pollinators – bumblebees, honey bees, solitary bees and hover flies. Swallows swooped, along with the moths and butterflies as the day cooled.'

Strongroom Studio (detail) / 2018

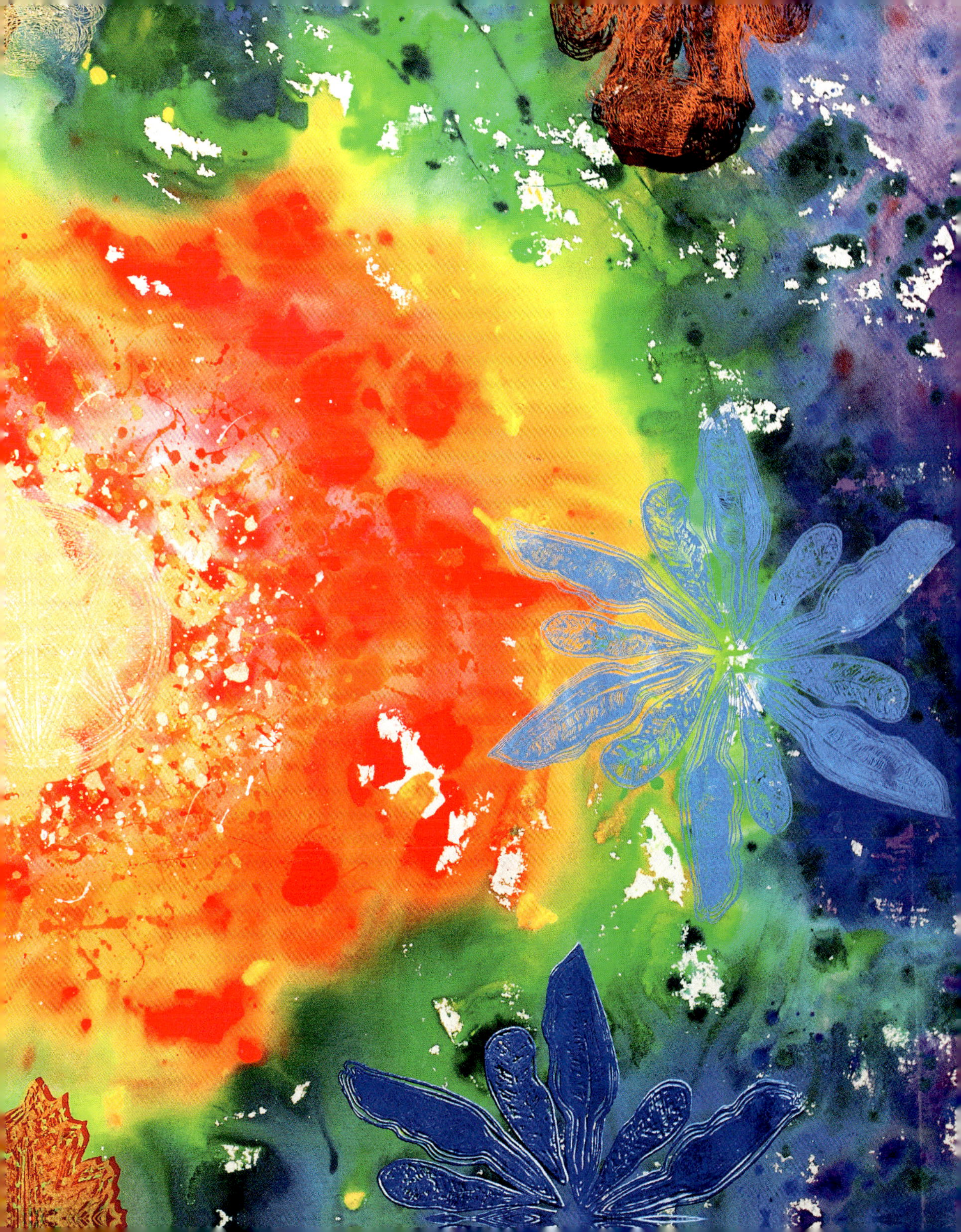

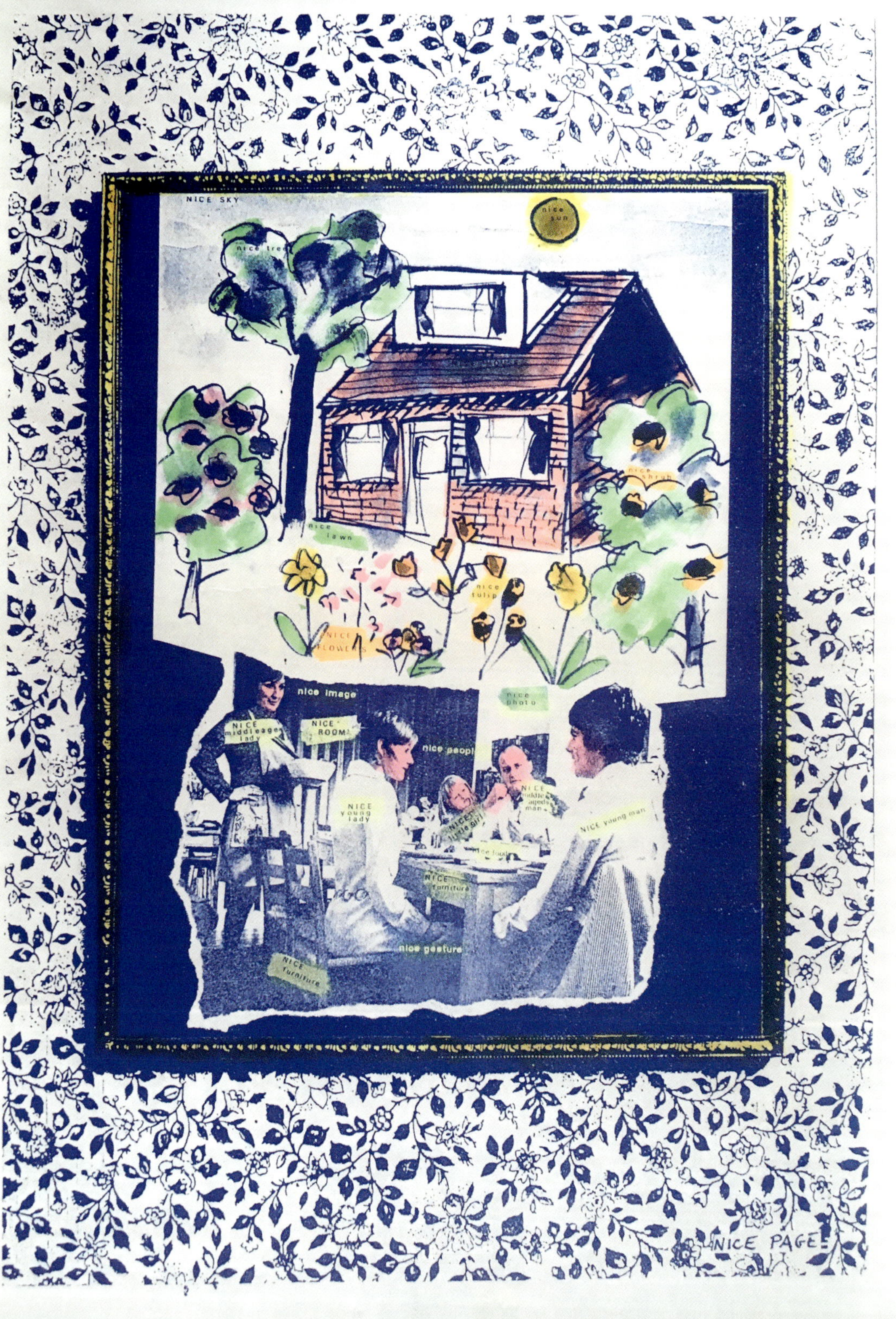
NICE SKY
nice sun
nice tre
nice shrub
nice lawn
nice tulip
NICE FLOWERS
nice image
nice photo
NICE middleage lady
NICE ROOM!
nice peopl
NICE young lady
NICE middle aged man
NICE little girl
NICE young man
NICE furniture
nice gesture
NICE furniture
NICE PAGE!

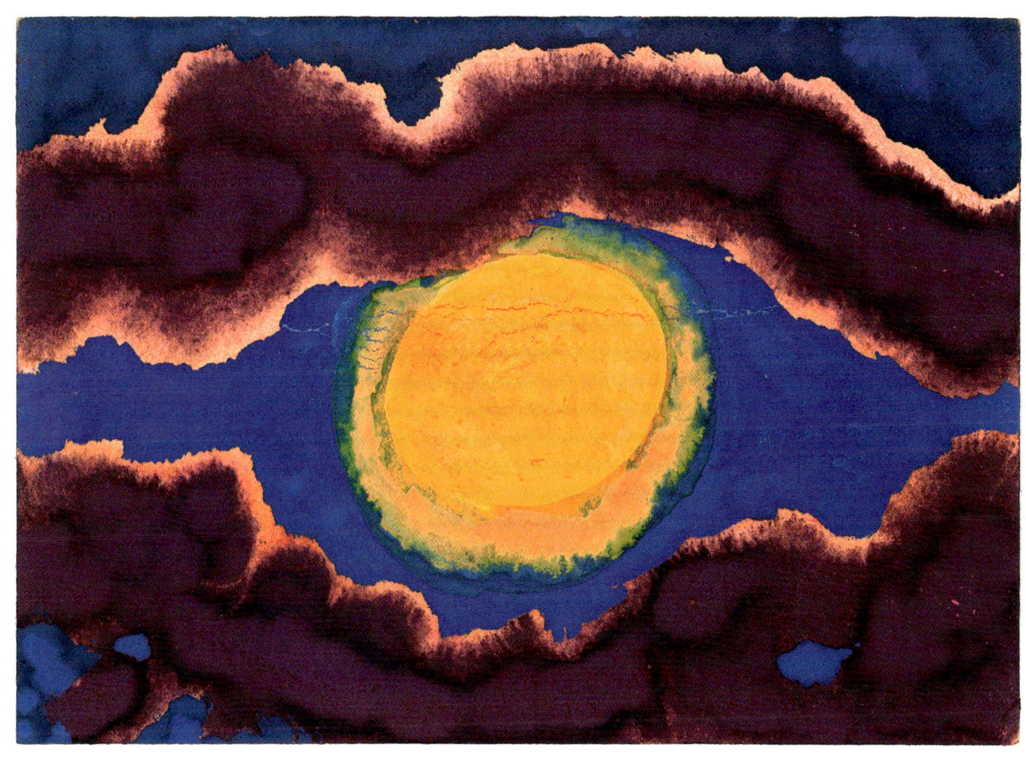

Nice Page / *c.* 1972
This work began as the collage in the lower portion of the image. Everything – room, gesture, furniture, young lady, etc – has been annotated as 'nice'. One of a series of works on this theme, the collage was repurposed by Jamie for the back cover of the Sex Pistols' single 'Holidays in the Sun' (1977). This version has been hand-coloured with felt-tip as preparation for a book about Jamie's work written by Jon Savage, initially called *Chaos in Cancerland,* and later released as *Up They Rise* (1987). This piece also appears on a background of faux brick wallpaper in the 7.5-metre *Sex Pistols Mural* (1984).

Holidays in the Sun / 1977
In this example of Situationist *détournement*, Jamie replaced the original text of a sequence of images with lyrics from the Sex Pistols' fourth single, 'Holidays in the Sun' (1977). This had been inspired by a promo trip made by the band to Berlin earlier in the year, including an obligatory visit to the Berlin Wall and the Brandenburg Gate – minus the sun. The image was used on the sleeve of the single.

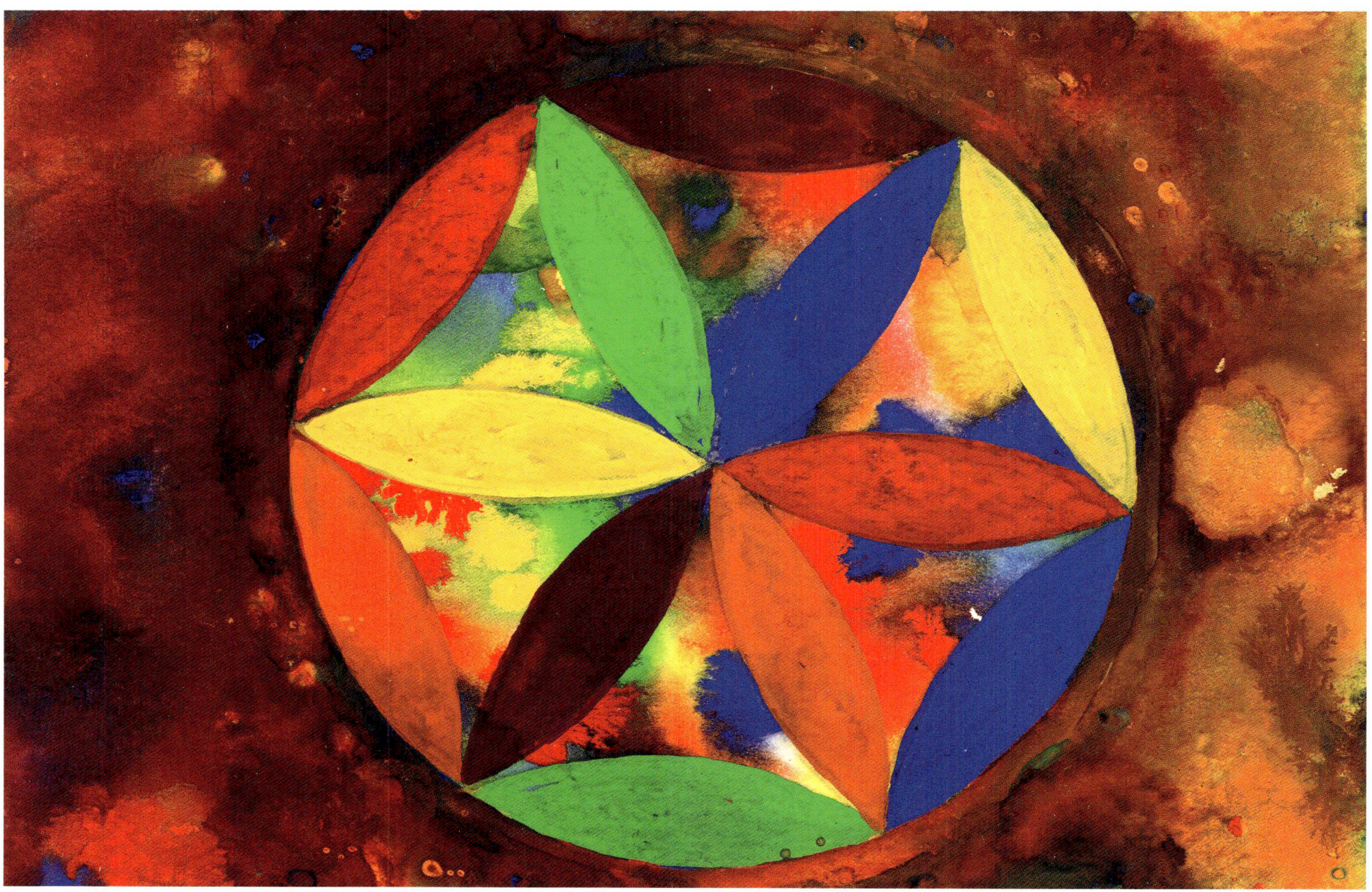

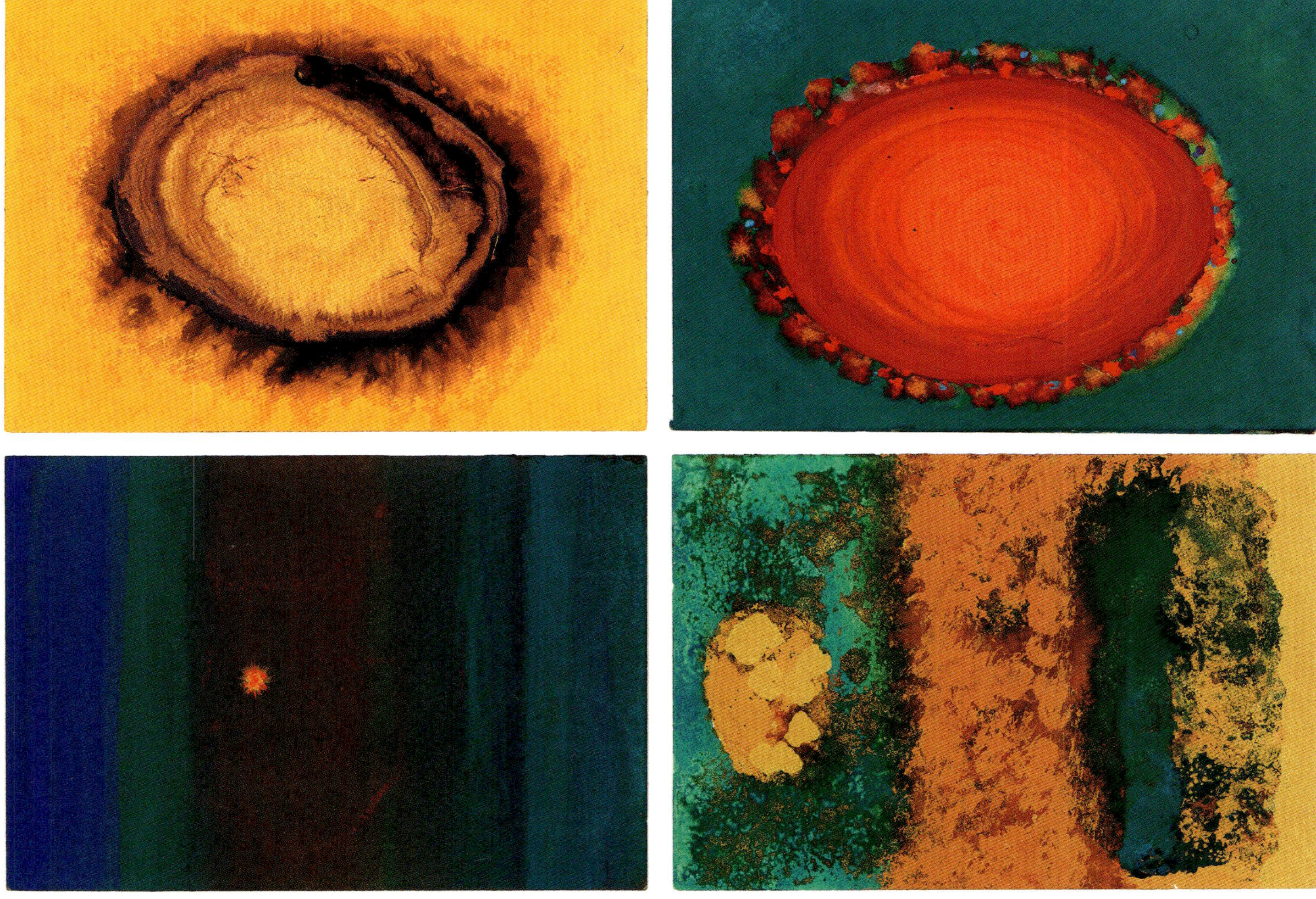

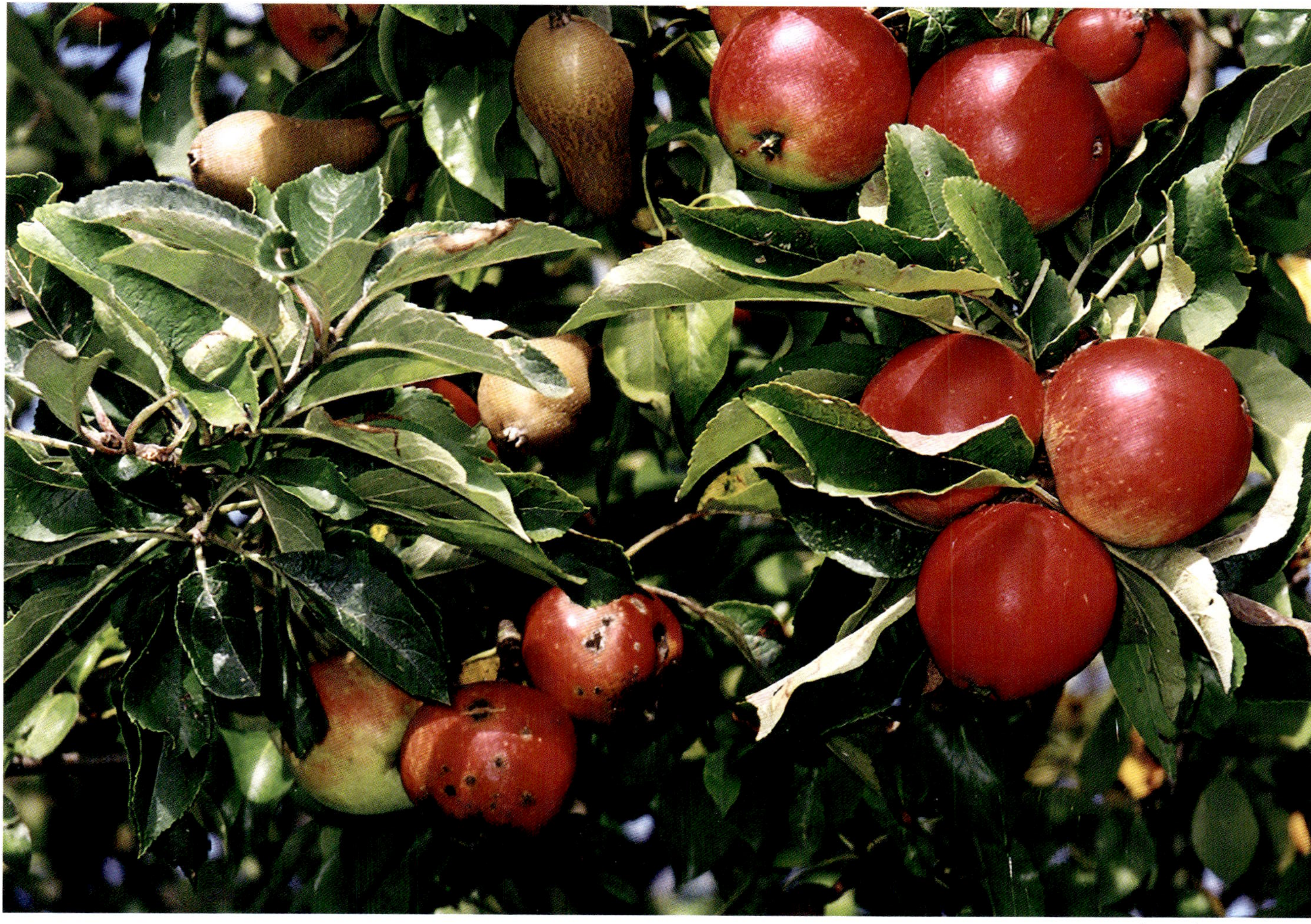

Apples and Pears / c. 2010

OUT OF THE DROSS

AND INTO THE AGE OF PIRACY

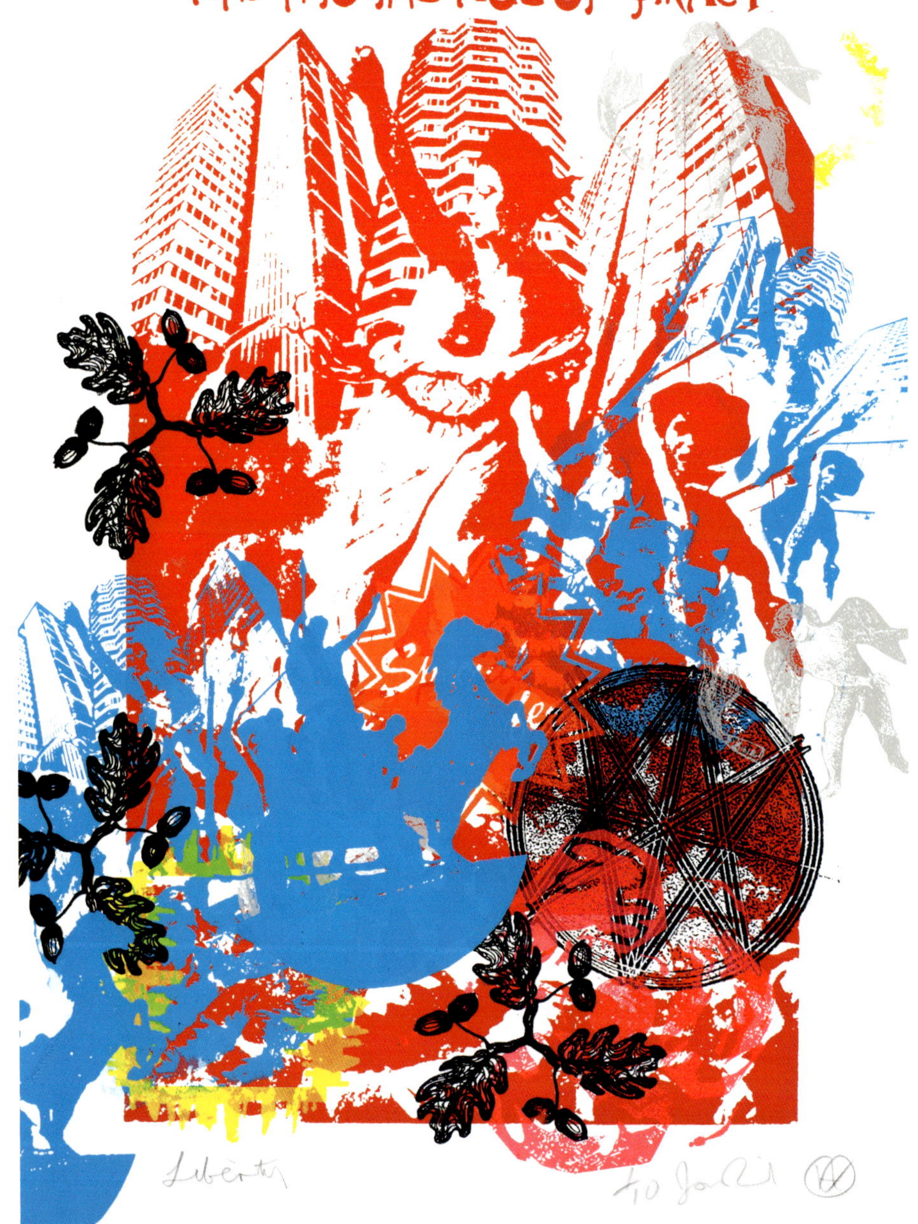

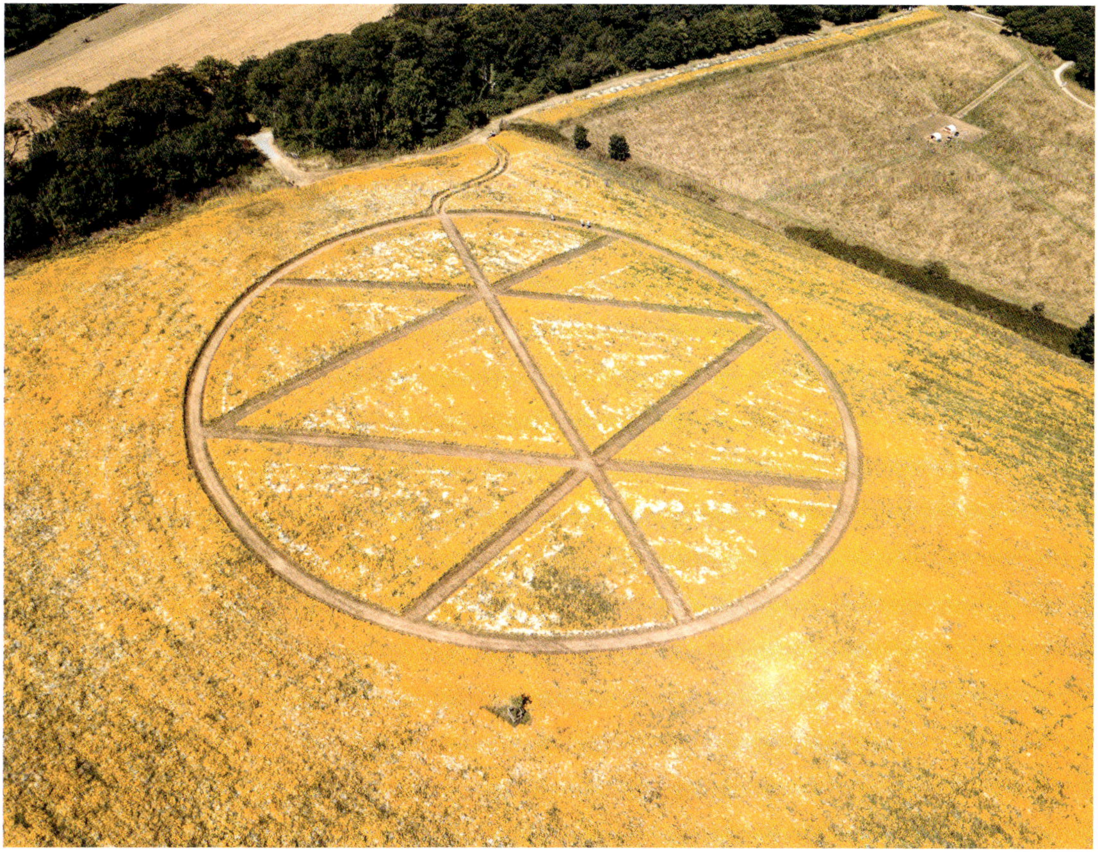

The Heligan OVA at Lughnasadh / 2022

Liberty Leading The People (After Delacroix) / 1981
The base visual of this work, derived from Delacroix's *Liberty Leading The People* (1830) but here leading the revolution in front of Croydon tower blocks, was originally a Suburban Press-era work. It was developed in 1981 as part of an advertising campaign for the single 'C30, C60, C90' by Malcolm McLaren's post-Pistols project Bow Wow Wow, which mocked the record industry's 'Home Taping Is Piracy' campaign. This version is from a series of unique prints that used original screens from the Strongroom Studios refurbishment to offer a panoply of visual references, including Boudica, the Avenging Angel and Jamie's OVA symbol.

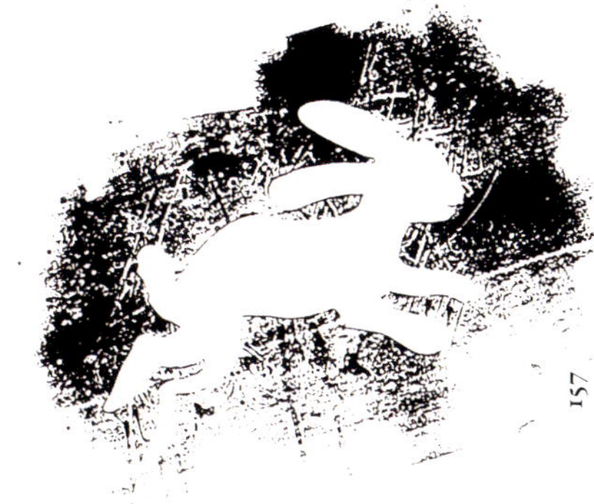

Sold Down the River / 1995

Through the mid 1990s, Jamie was involved in an 'art terrorist' collective called Visual Stress, which produced events and rituals to heal the city of Liverpool from the lasting, pernicious influence of the slave trade. He also collaborated with artist Nina Edge, who created a live artwork on the city streets entitled *Sold Down the River*, a still of which can be seen here. A few hundred people came to watch, and a few hundred more delivered a street ritual, an urban healing dance, or *vimbuza*, for the River Mersey. A giant willow woman, formed like an English corn dolly was carried to the dockside, and her clay sister was submerged in the dock – to dissolve and be reborn in the water.

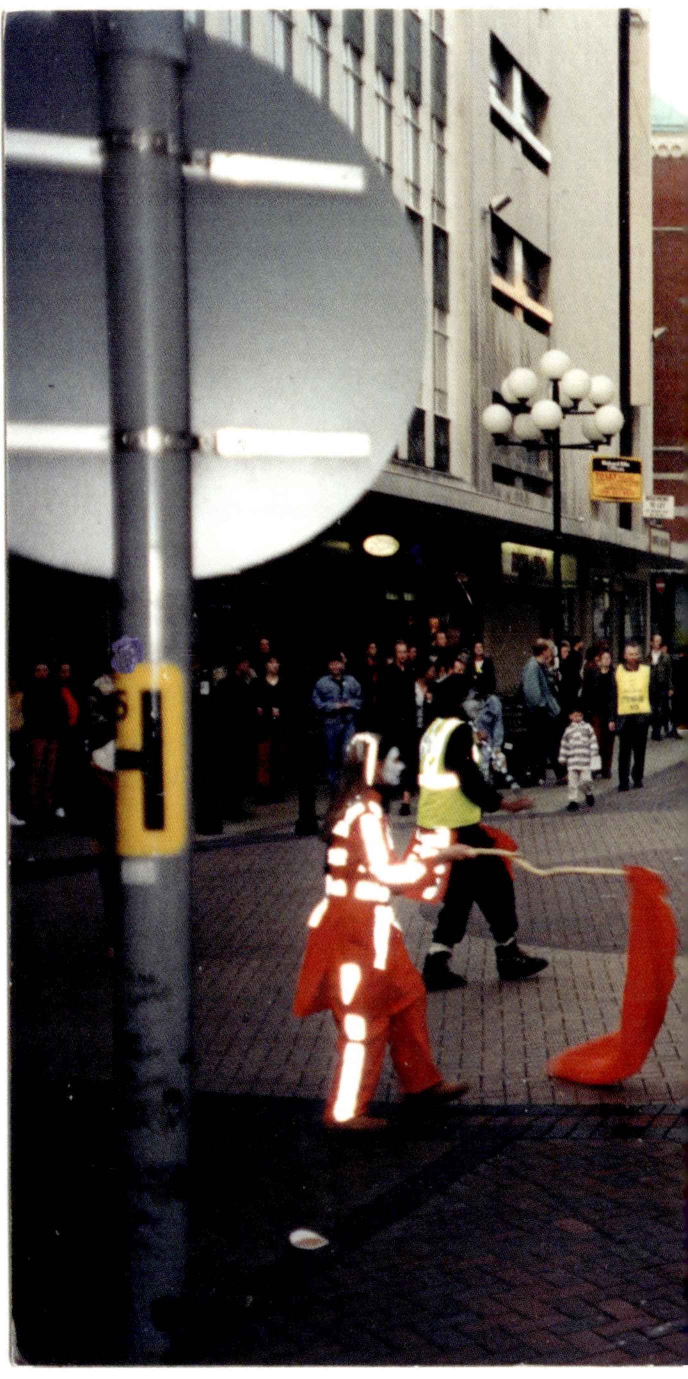

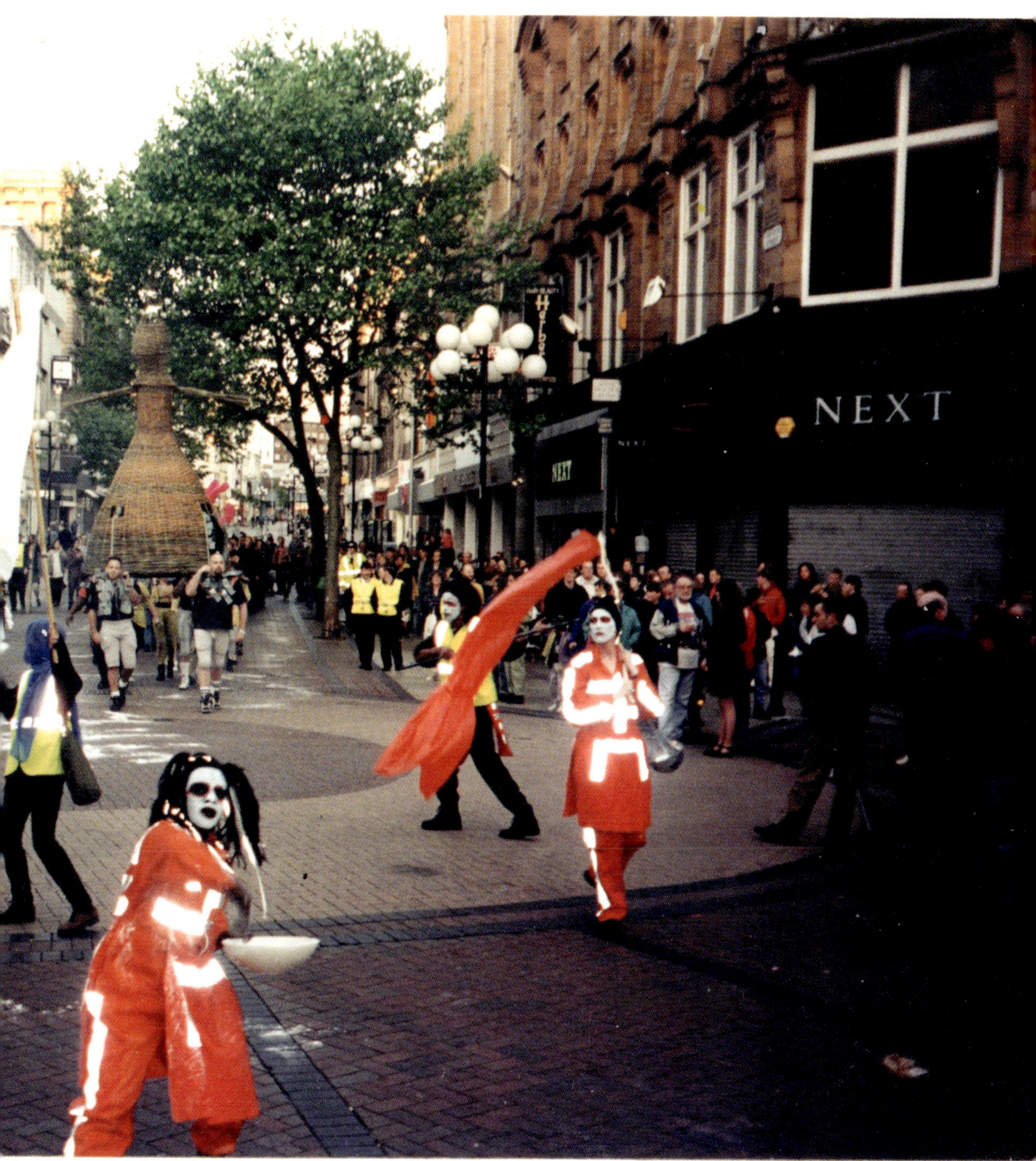
NEXT
NEXT

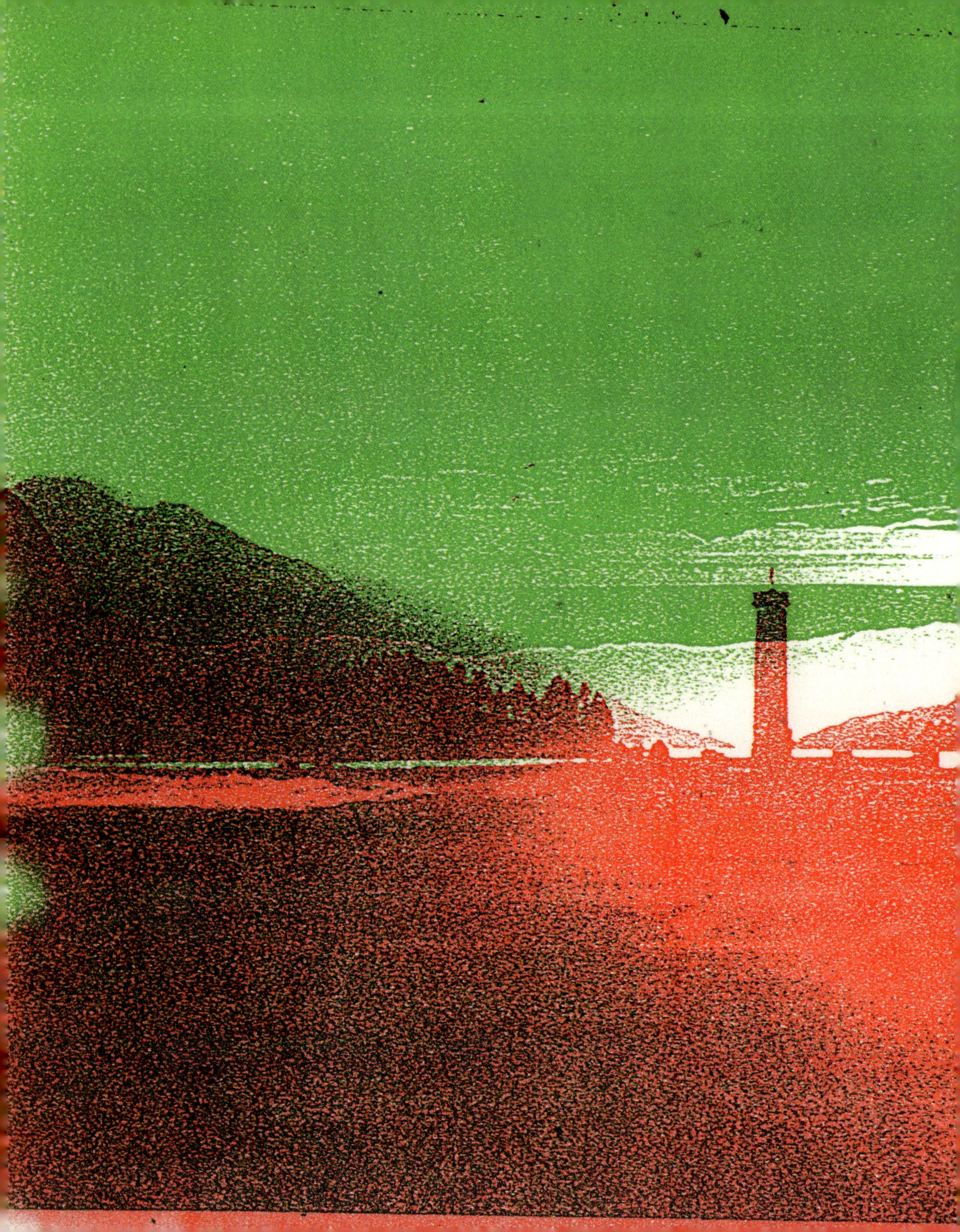

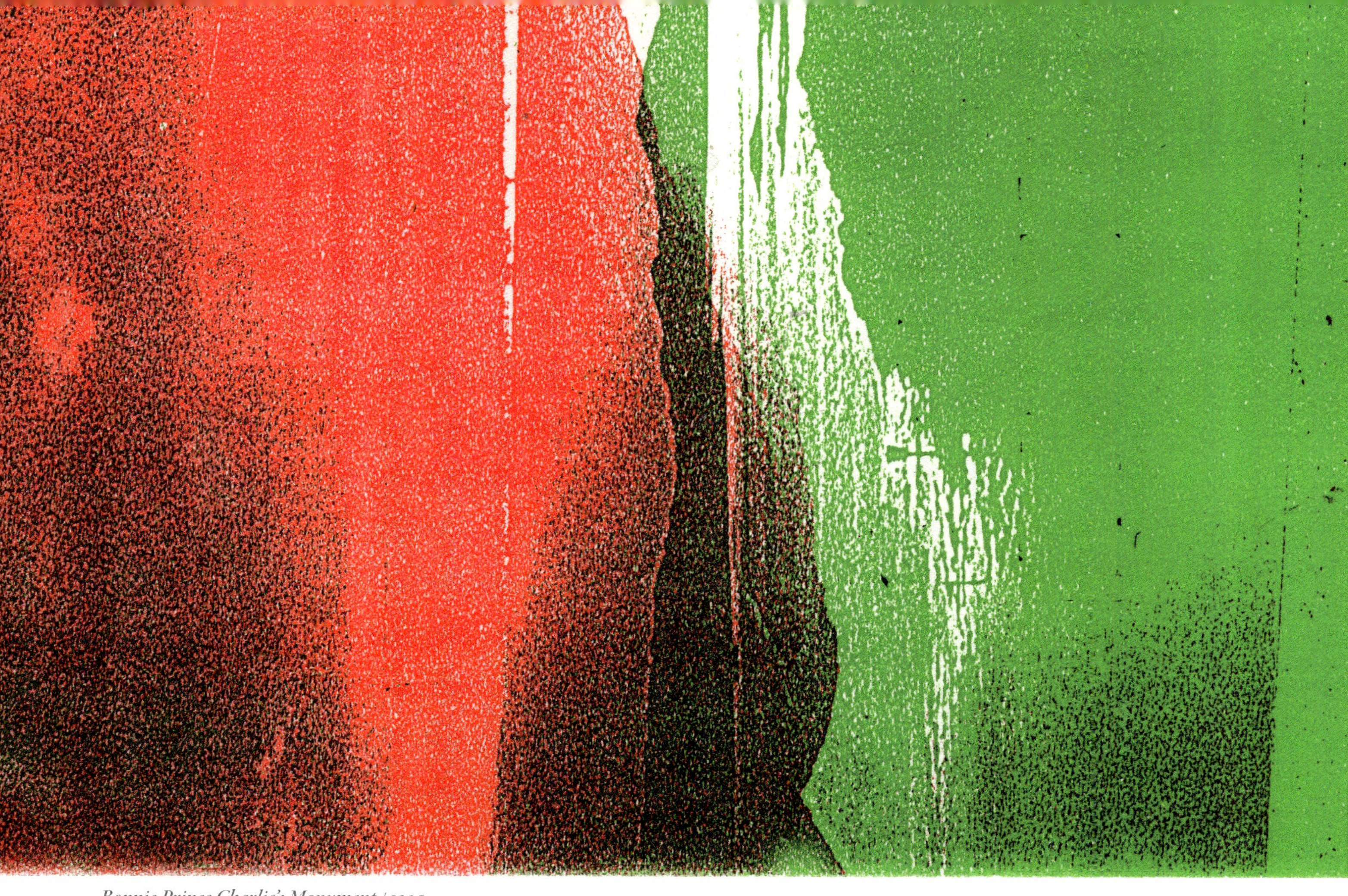

Bonnie Prince Charlie's Monument / 1990

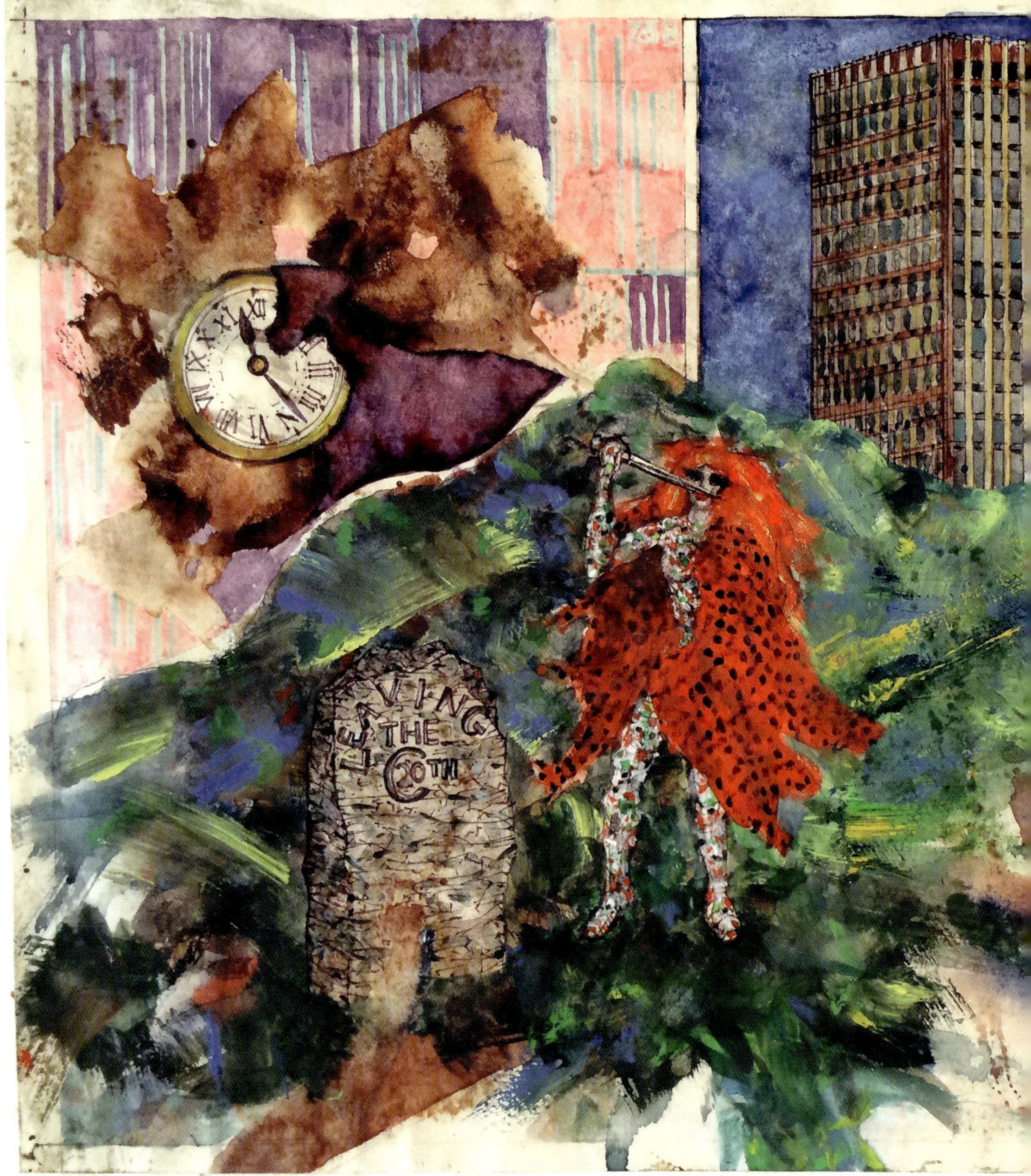
LEAVING
THE
C20TH

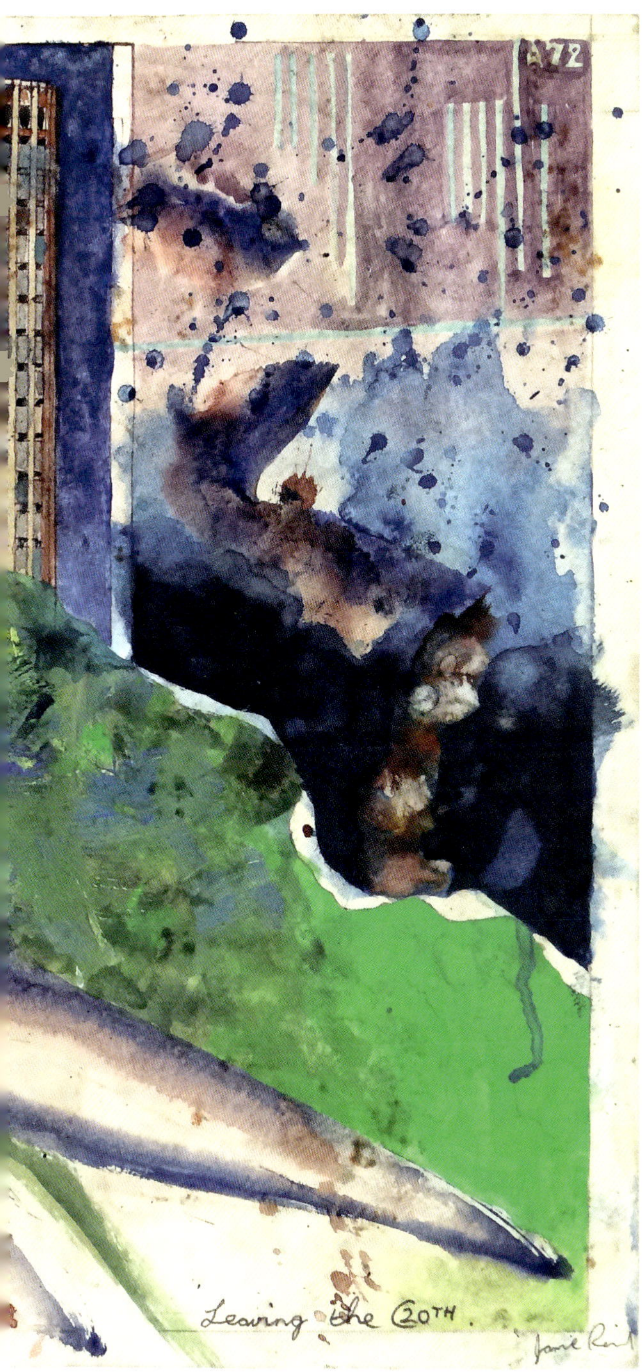

Pinkie Kissing the Dirk / 1981
In this painting from the *Leaving the 20th Century/How to Become Invisible* cycle, painted at the Place du Clichy, in Paris, lead character, Pinkie, kisses her dirk – a traditional Scottish dagger – as she makes a pledge. She stands next to a road marker, telling us she is on the right path to her destination. She wears a MacGregor tartan shawl and a multi-coloured costume, which renders her invisible. As in *Liberty Leading The People (After Delacroix)*, where the figure of Liberty is set in front of the tower blocks of Croydon (see page 156), Pinkie is seen here jumping out of the city and into a more verdant, positive and self-determined future.

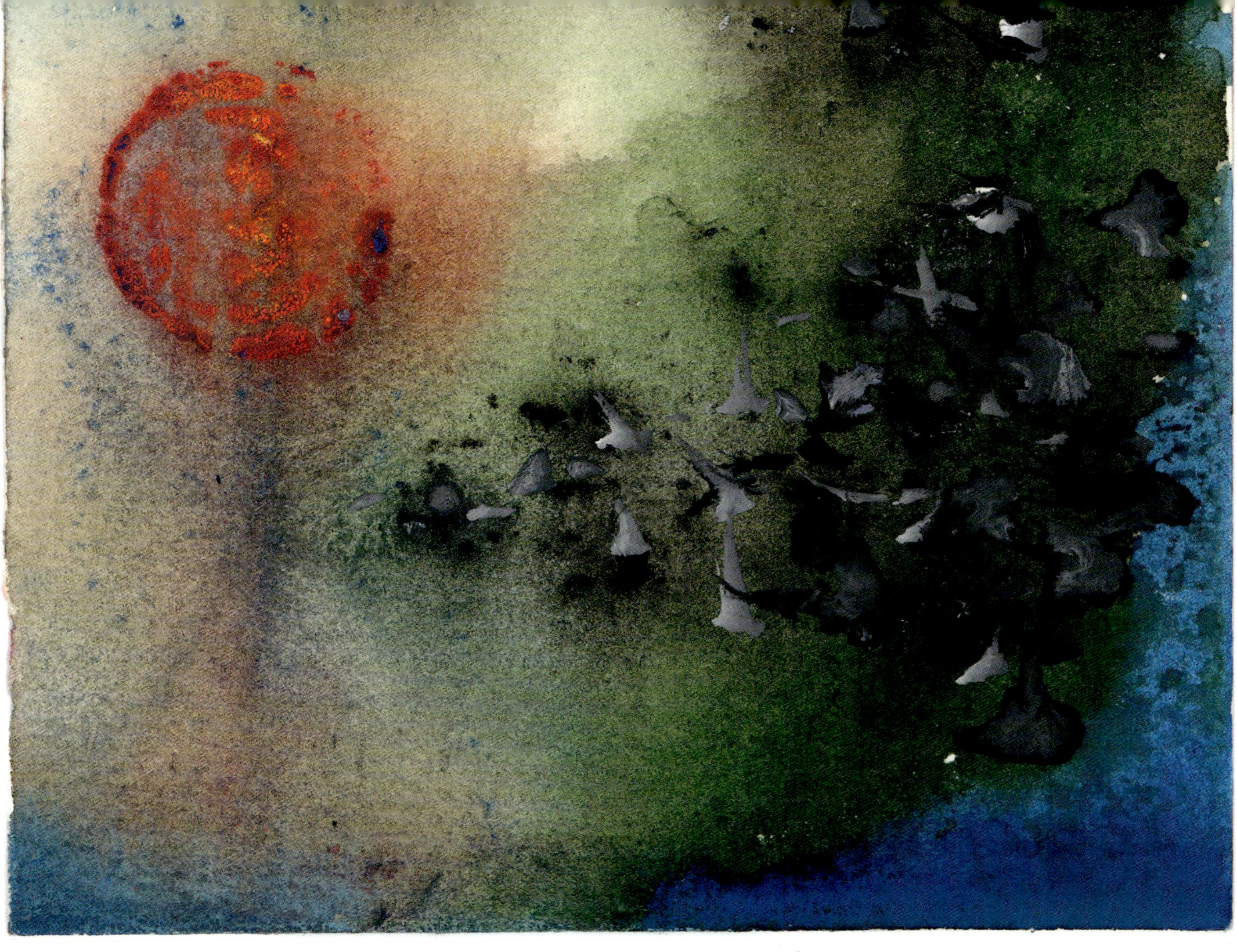

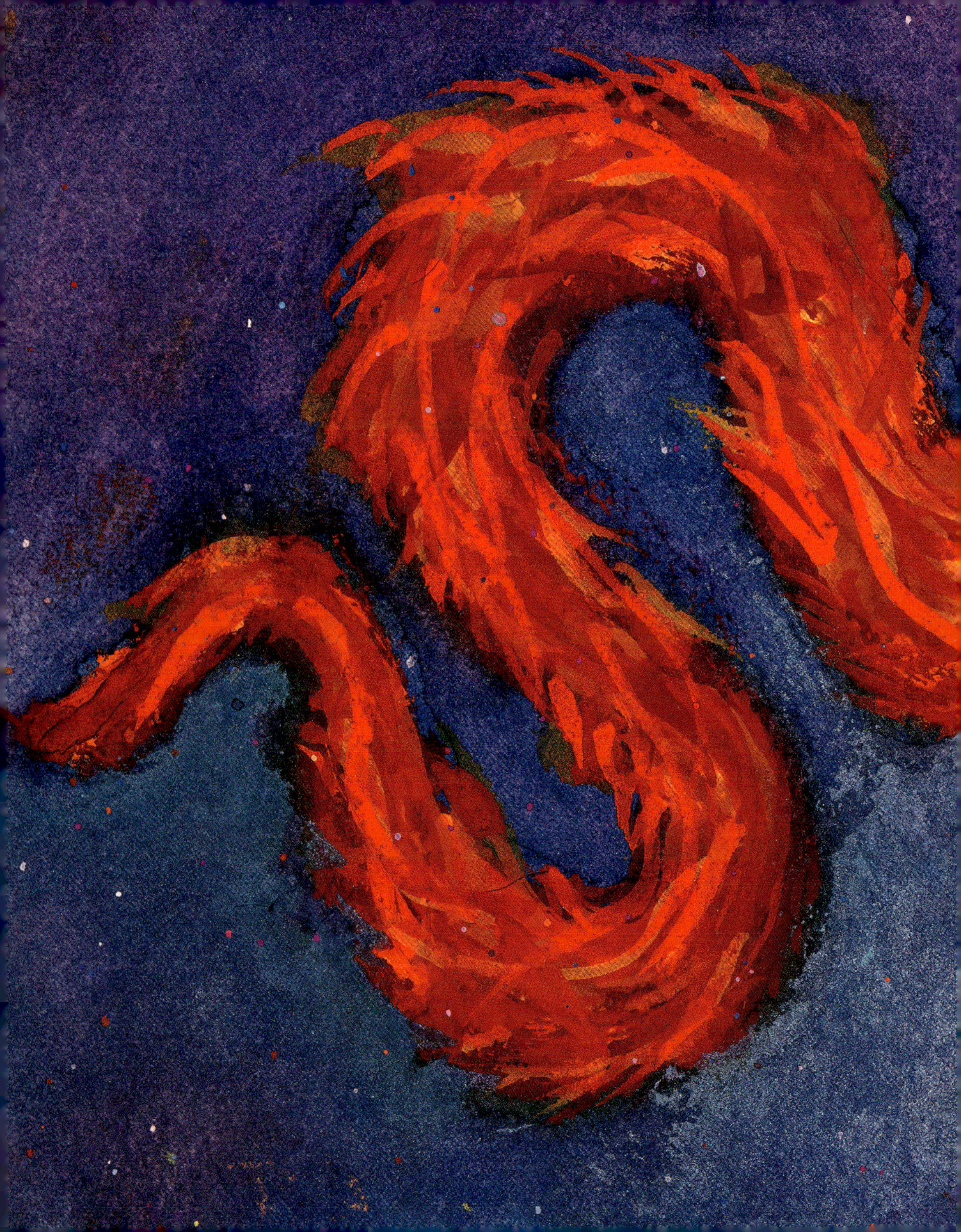

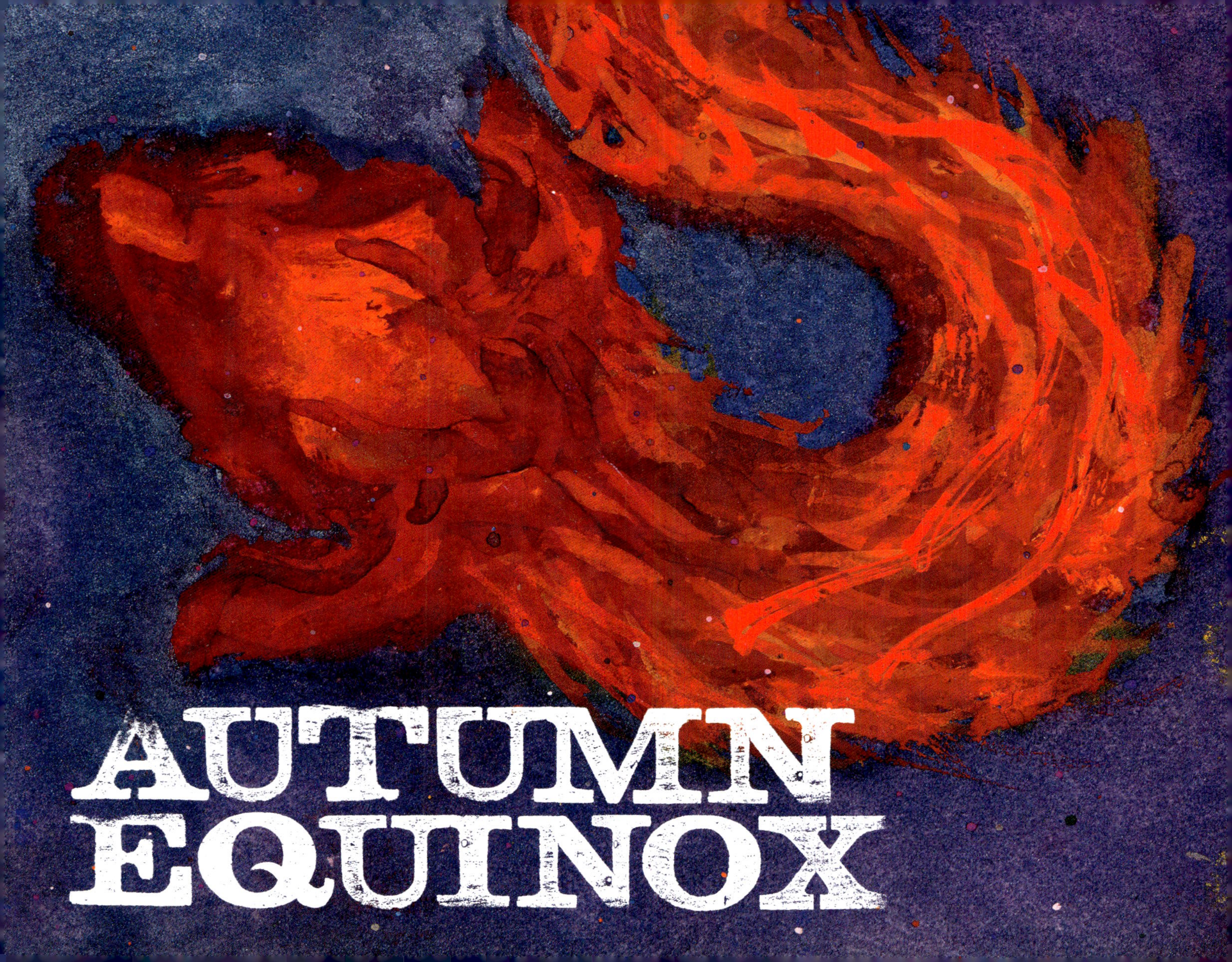
AUTUMN
EQUINOX

AUTUMN EQ

At Lughnasadh, you started cutting down, sorting out, sifting through the debris to find the gold, keeping the memories and forgetting the pain, and now – six weeks later – it's the second harvest, the Autumn Equinox. Time to complete the task.

The first harvest began with the fields, and now the maturing power of the sun has done its work in the trees and bushes. Hawthorn berries, apples and blackberries cry out to be picked, and the equinox arrives to tell us we need to get ready for the colder days, the longer nights.

This festival is associated with the setting sun, with the maturing power of old age. It is tinged by that particular feeling that autumn brings – that delicate, melancholic nostalgia. The sun is lower now, its light mellower. The leaves are just starting to turn the trees red and gold. Even the air smells different, the scent of ripe fruit borne on autumn breezes.

With these subtle changes comes a chance for deepening. If the Spring Equinox can be depicted by a figure standing, facing eastwards, arms uplifted to the sunrise, then, at Autumn Equinox, we see that same figure, seated in contemplation, gazing westwards, out to sea, as the sun sets over the water.

This is a time for recollection, for greeting oneself again – the self that was lost in the excitement of spring and the heat of summer, sowing seeds, realising dreams. Now the Autumn Equinox encourages us to switch our focus from the external world to explore our interior terrain, our dreams and our subconscious.

In the Druid Tradition, this festival is known as Alban Elfed, the Light of Water; this name honours the powerful role that the sea holds in our evolutionary story. This is where we came from and where we often long to go. It is deeply familiar to us. It is a place of solace that can also be a place of danger and death. Samhain – the time of death – is the next festival, and the dark Winter lies ahead.

Taking place a few days after the Autumn Equinox, Michaelmas is the feast of St Michael, the patron saint of the sea and fishermen. For hundreds of years, celebrations took place at this time in the Hebridean islands, with communities sharing a huge bannock and

QUINOX

22–23
September

taking part in a horse procession sunwise around the village burial ground, signalling the end of the fishing season and the harvest.

On the other side of the Wheel, we began preparing for summer at Imbolc, and from then until the Spring Equinox we prepared the ground and sowed our seeds for a new year. Now, the Autumn Equinox marks the culmination of another season of preparation: the harvesting. These two periods of preparation on opposite sides of the Wheel are perfectly balanced.

It's time to tune into all that the word 'balance' means to us: harmony, equilibrium, stability, integration. But not stasis – because after this moment we will move into the dark half of the year. From tomorrow, the nights grow shorter, but, for now, let's harvest these six weeks of gratitude.

NOTES FROM HELIGAN

'At our Autumn Equinox celebration, we showed the visitors how to clean the freshly harvested seed from the OVA field. Children from Pencalenick in Truro, a school specialising in supporting children with complex learning disabilities, cleaned their own seed and took it back with them to sow at their school. There was poetry and a recorded recital in Cornish and English. Valentine's Field was still alive with colour. We had harvested less than half of it in order to leave flowers and seed for the natural world. Clouds of goldfinches fed on the seed, and foxes hunted mice by night. Even where the harvester had been, in the understory, beneath the cut stems, was a second flush of flowers. It was not over.'

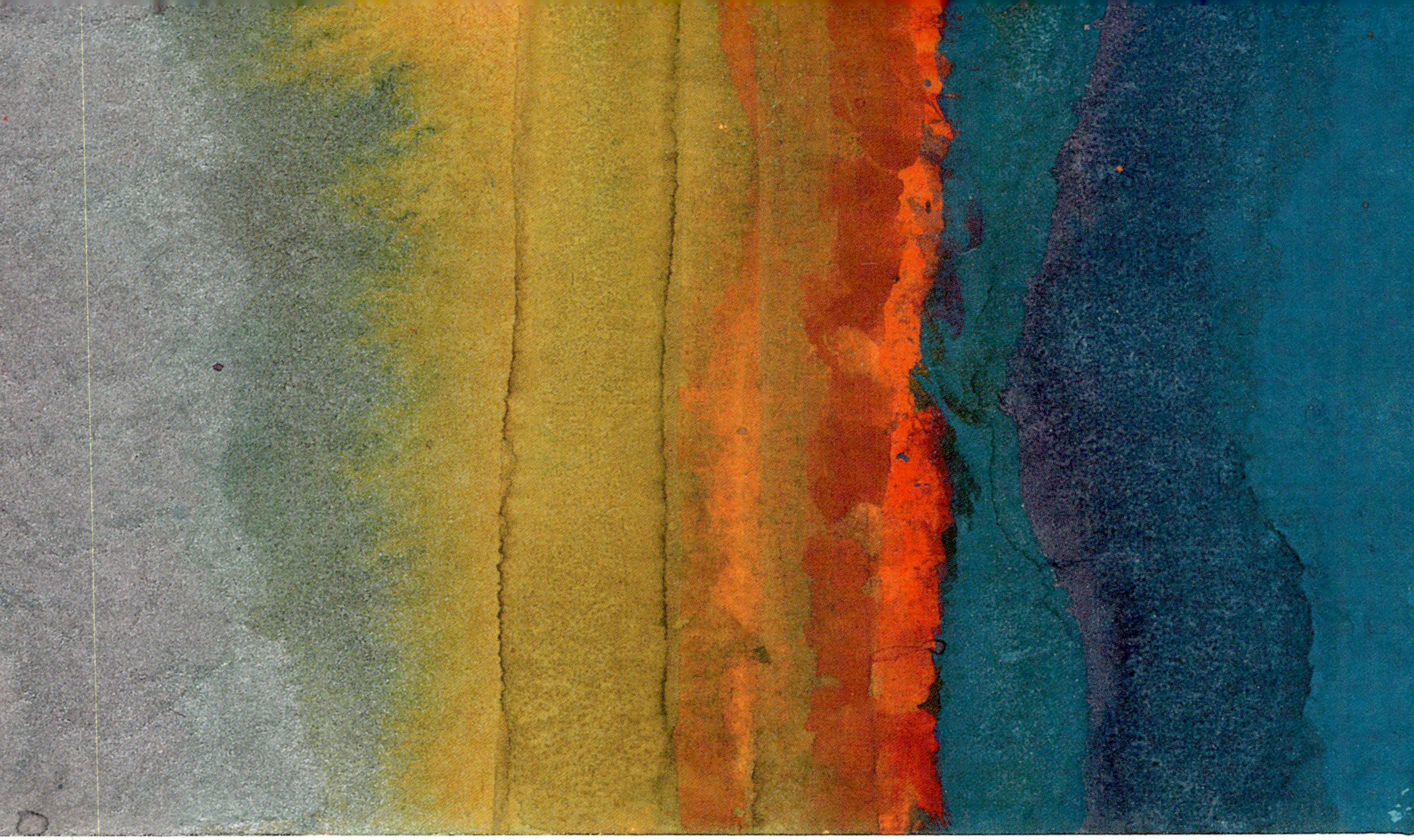

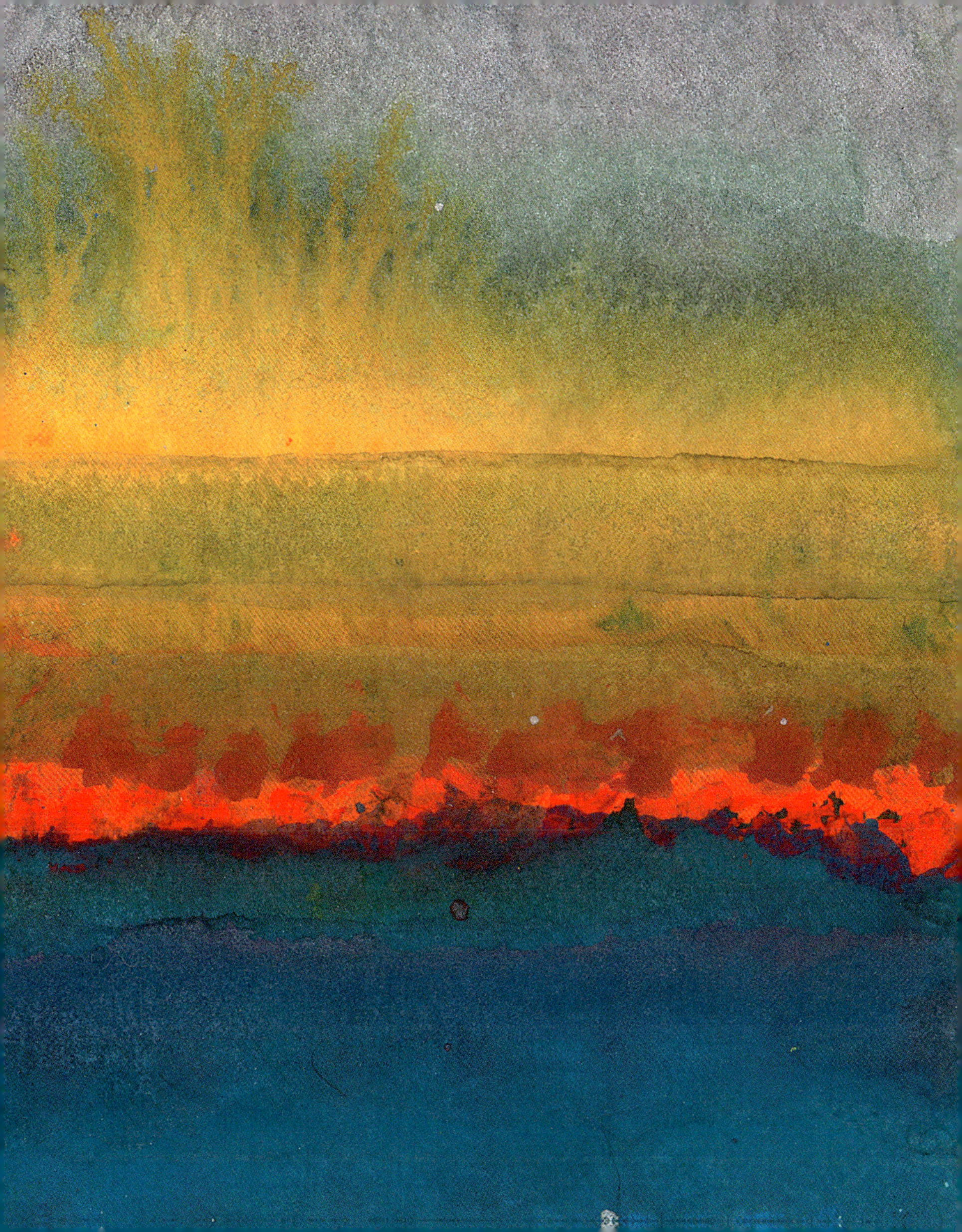

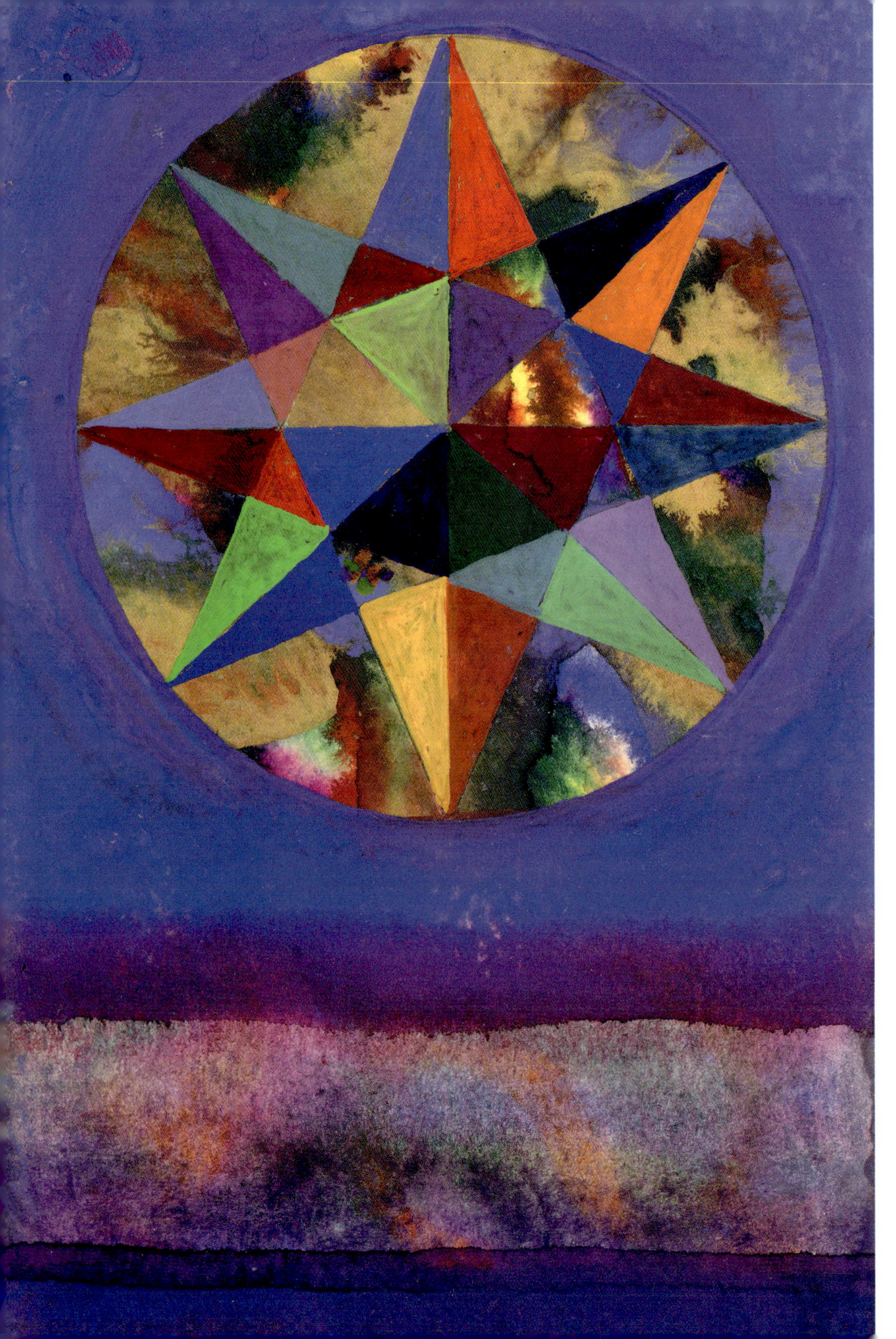

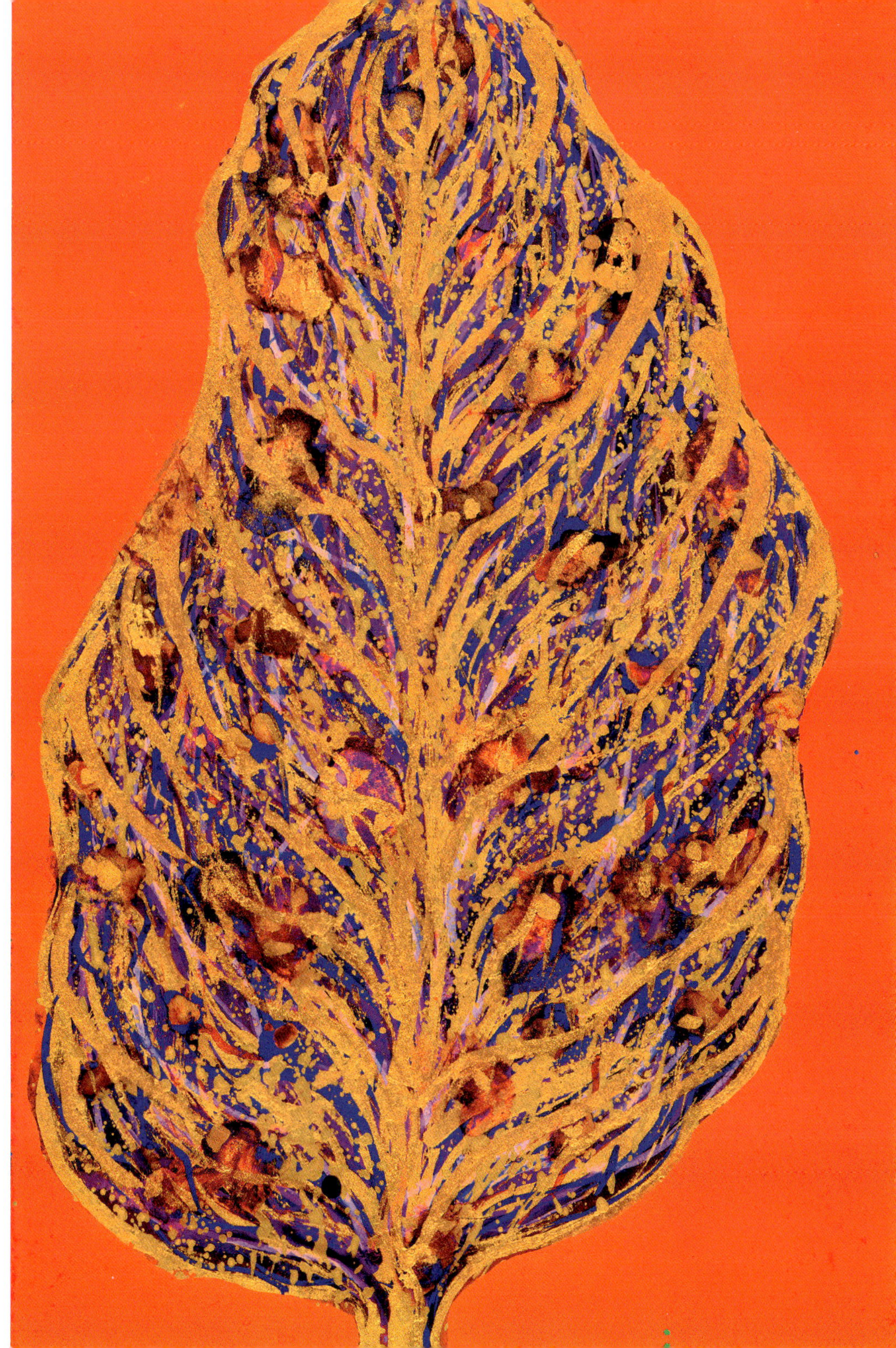

Chaos in Cancerland / 1983
This is a companion painting to *Pinkie Kissing the Dirk* (page 162) and features a crying unicorn that reappeared throughout Jamie's *Leaving the 20th Century/ How to Become Invisible* cycle. This painting and others assisted the artist and his partner at the time, Margi Clarke, in laying out the storyboard of an ambitious musical. When they were living in Paris, Jamie and Margi persuaded Polydor France to release one of the cycle's songs ('Beauty and the Thief', 1982), providing them with some much-needed funds. Despite the efforts of two very creative people and a giant, gold inflatable on-stage penis, *How to Become Invisible*, the musical, was only properly performed once and remains an enigmatic part of Jamie's canon.

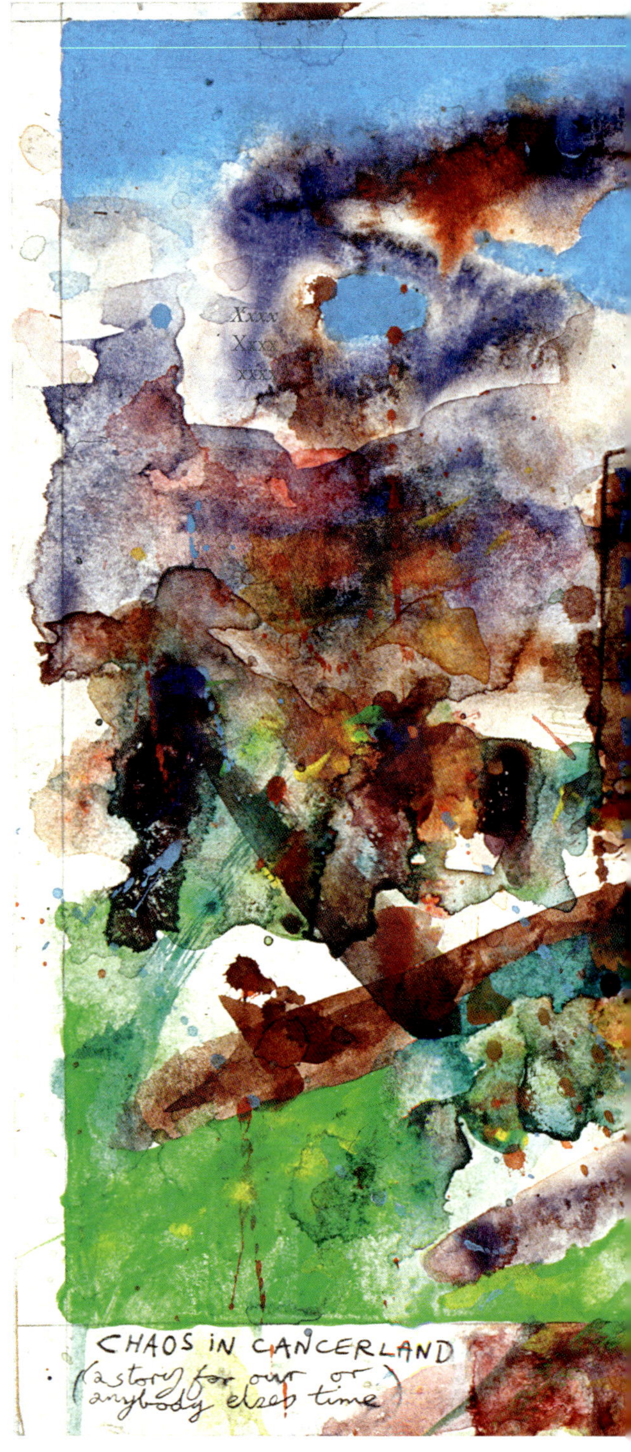

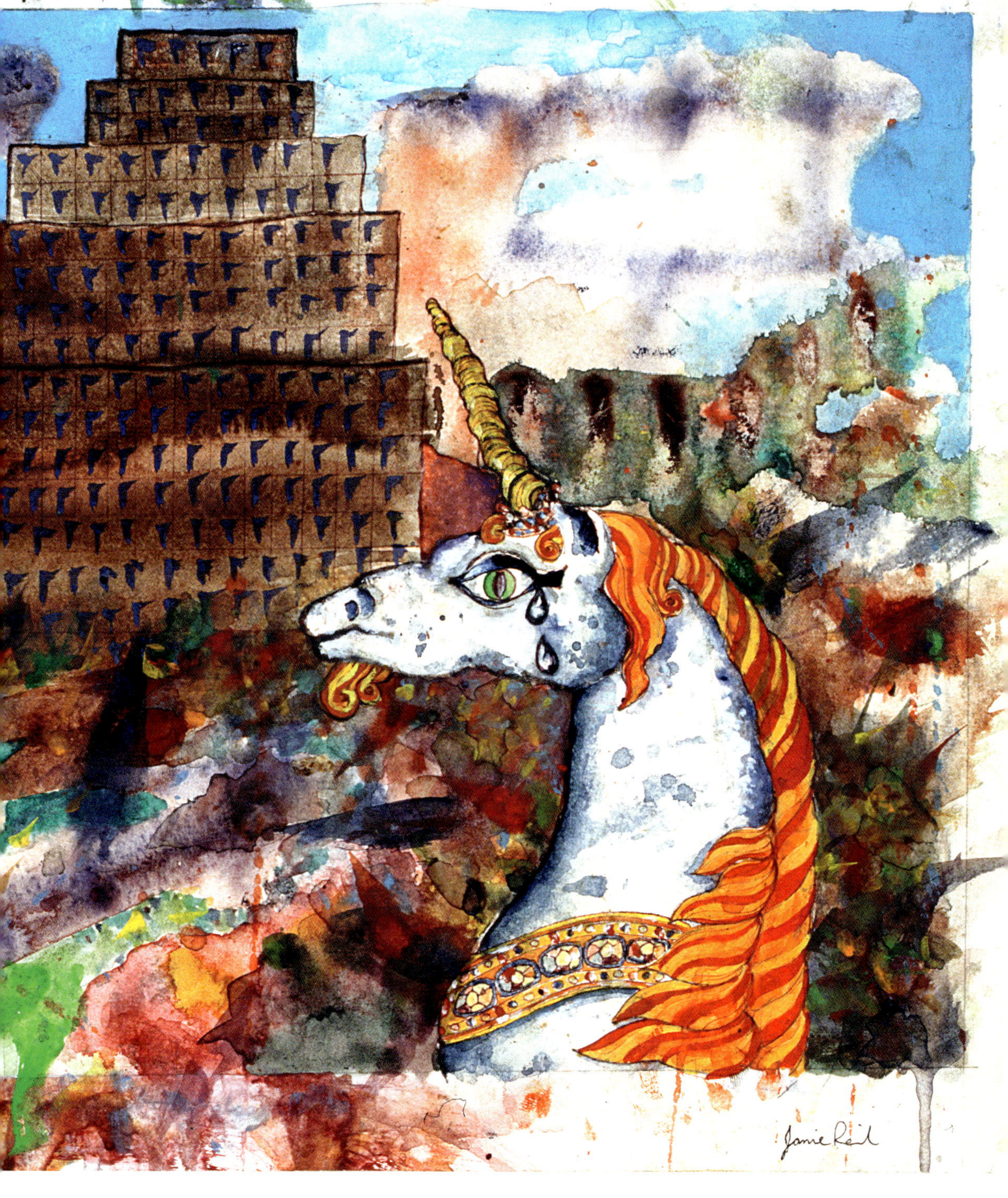
Jamie Reid

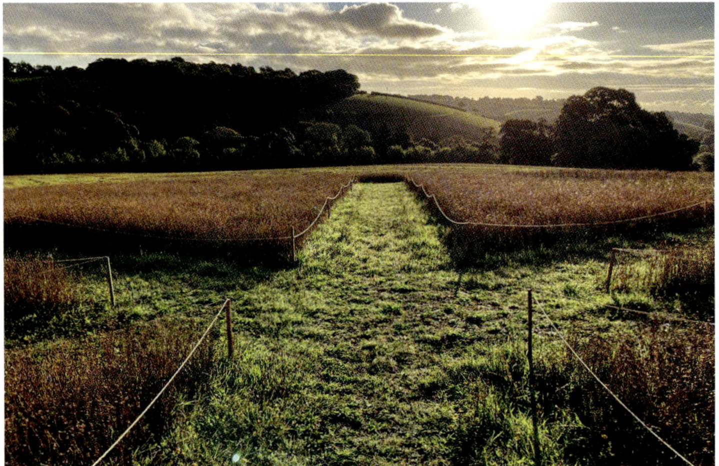

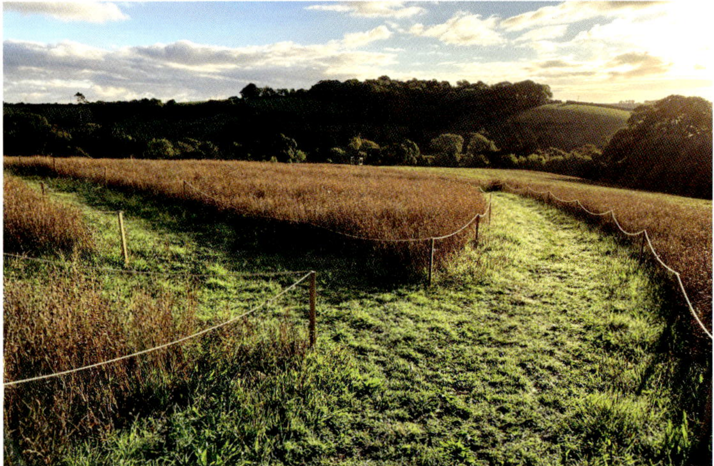

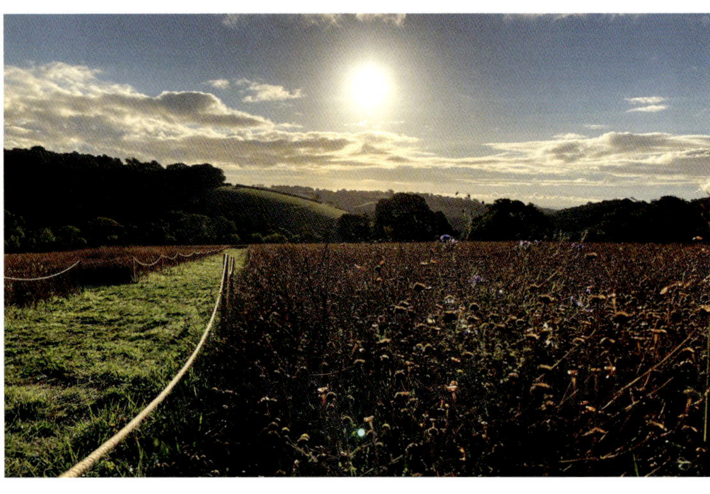

The Heligan OVA at Autumn Equinox / 2022

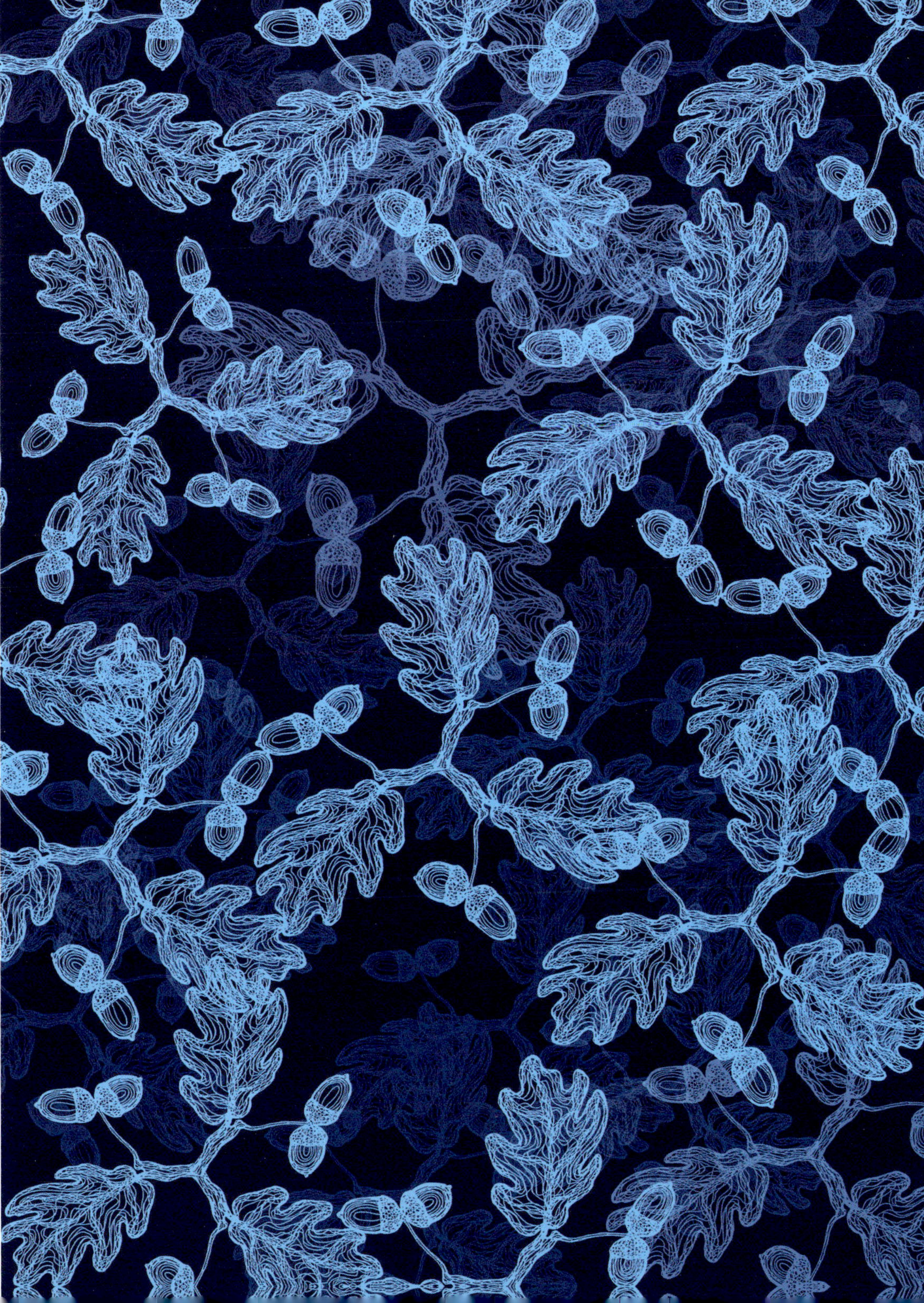

Take It You Messy Bastards / 1972
'Surely if we weren't so busy competing in this trough we could feed ourselves'. This work is from the same period as *Nice Page* (page 150), and was a product of Jamie's immersion in community politics and the exposure of local council corruption connected with extreme urban redevelopment in Croydon. Jamie's father Jack had been the City Editor of the *Daily Sketch* and, despite regularly being given insider trading tips, never invested in shares, preferring to use his position to throw light on the dealings of the city, rather than personally benefiting from them. The artwork otherwise speaks for itself.

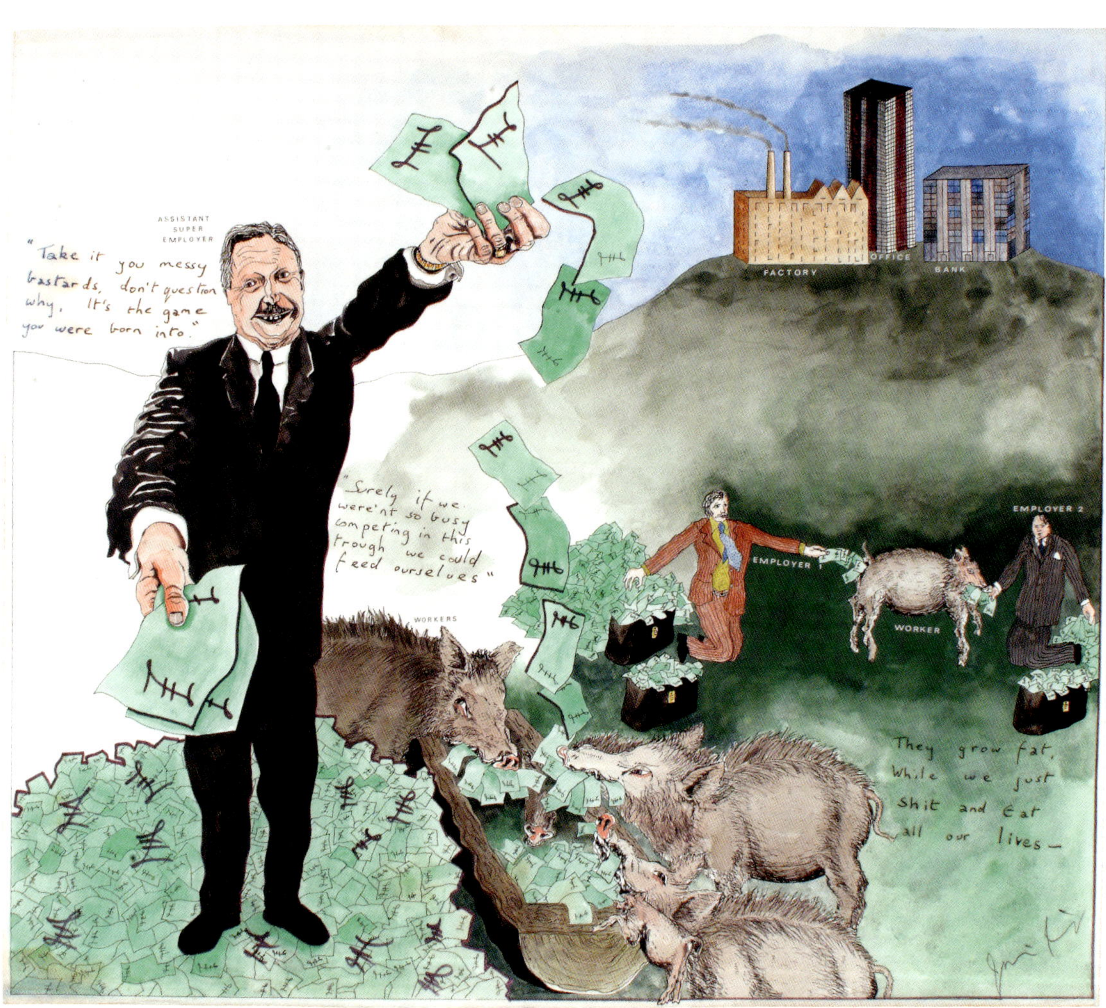

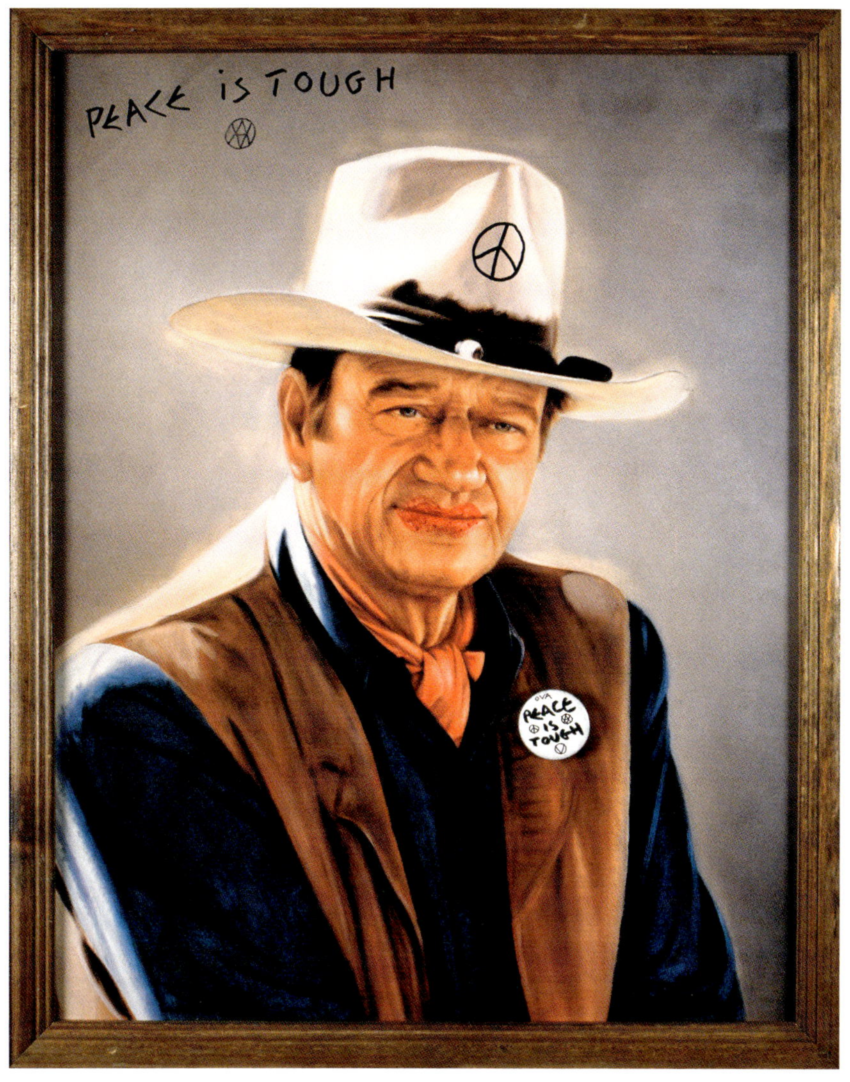

Peace Is Tough / 1993
As can be imagined, Jamie was not a fan of masculine posturing. This work was part of a commission for the cover of Greil Marcus's book, *Punk in the Fascist Bathroom* (1993), made from a found image of John Wayne, with added lipstick, pin badge and slogan. During Jamie's 2000 exhibition in Derry, Northern Ireland, this image was projected across the River Foyle onto buildings opposite, causing complaint. The following year's peace and reconciliation conference in the city was called 'Peace Is Tough', explicitly referring to the exhibition.

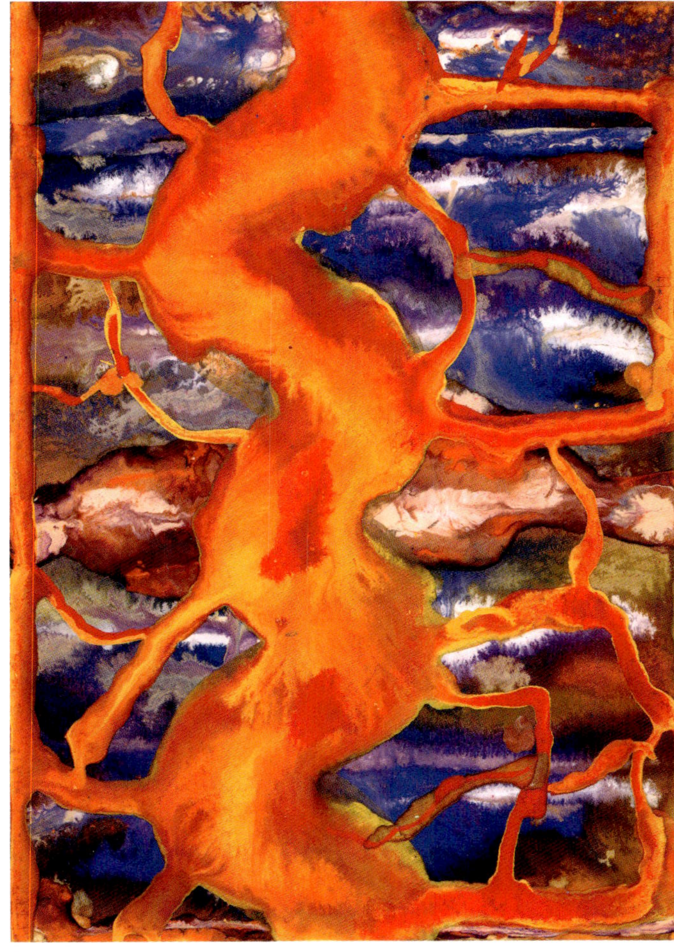

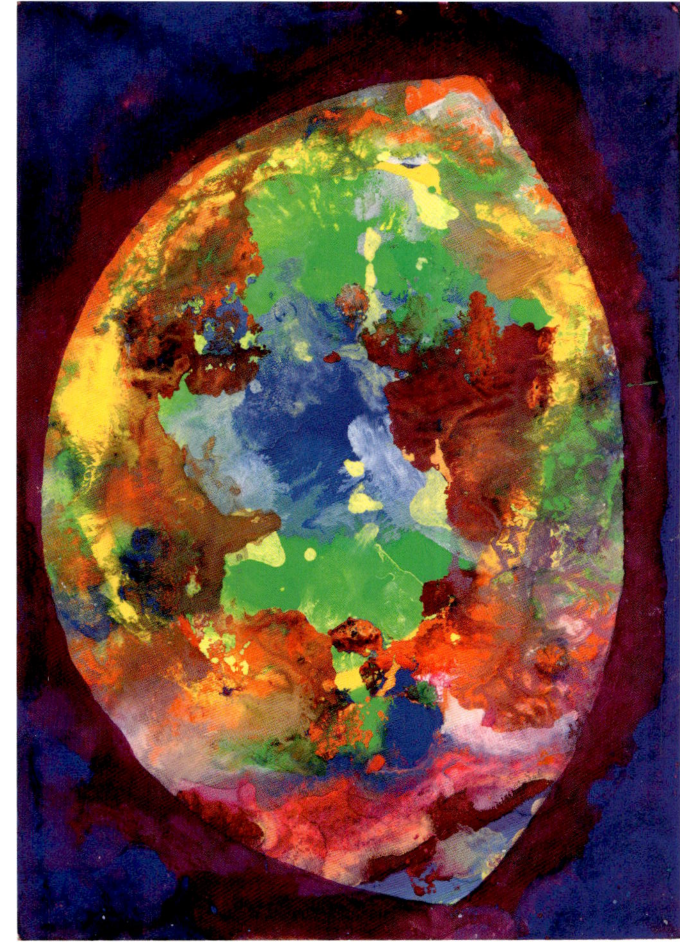

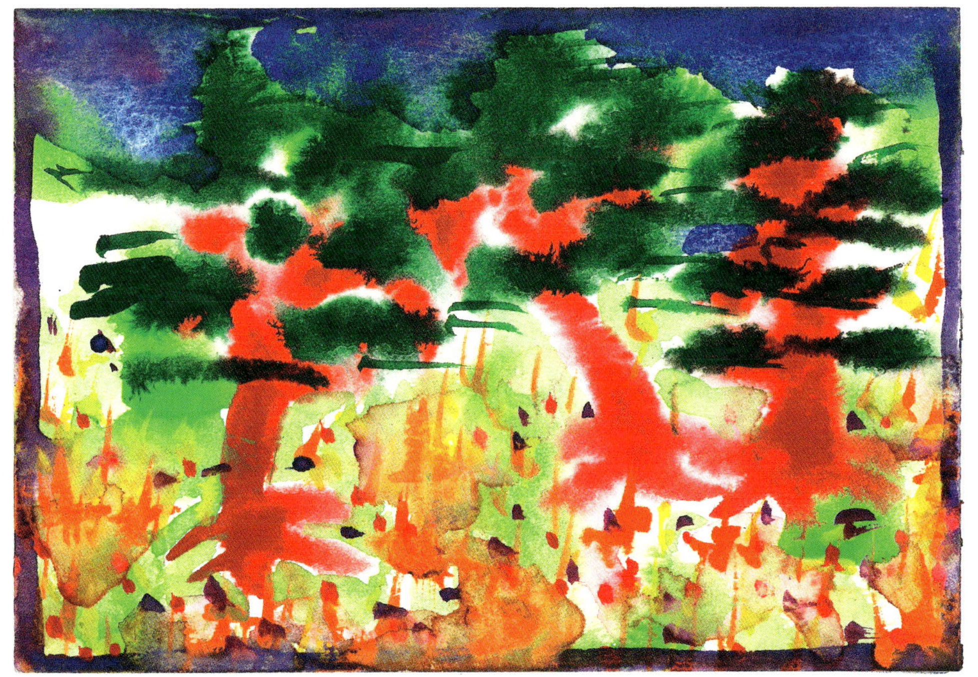

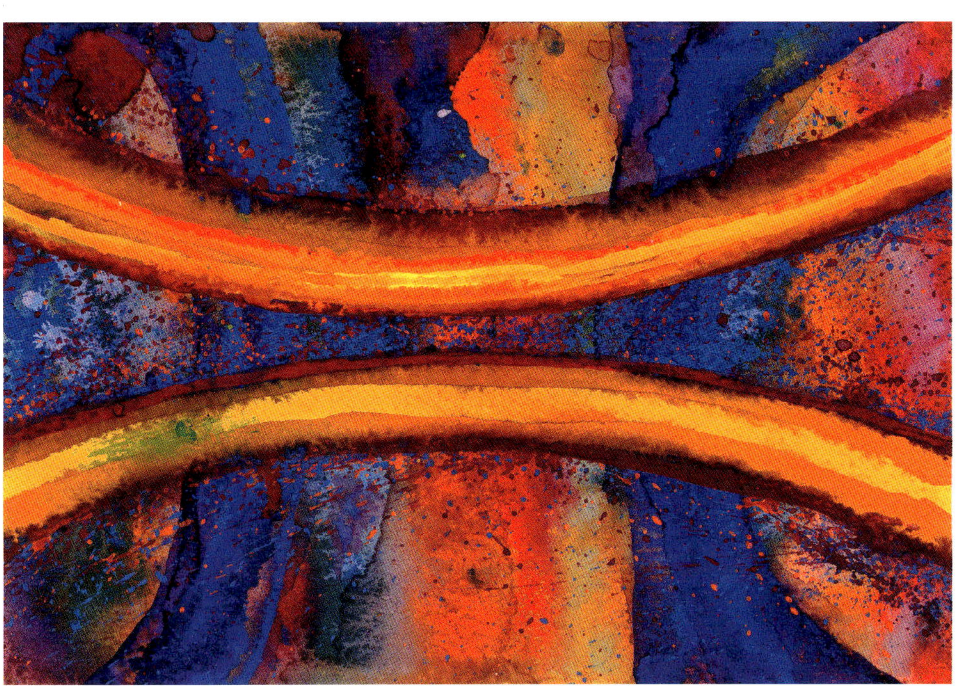

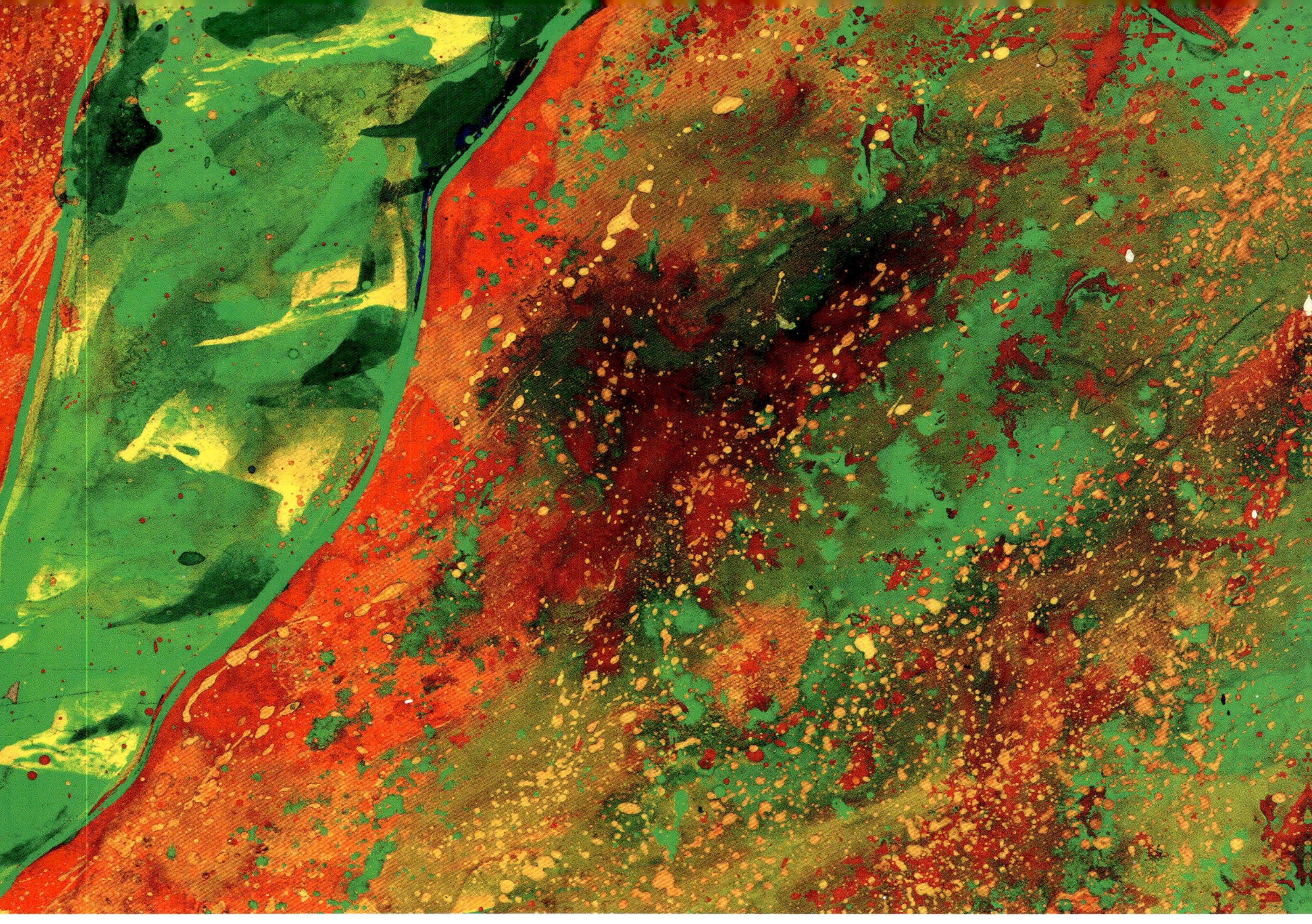

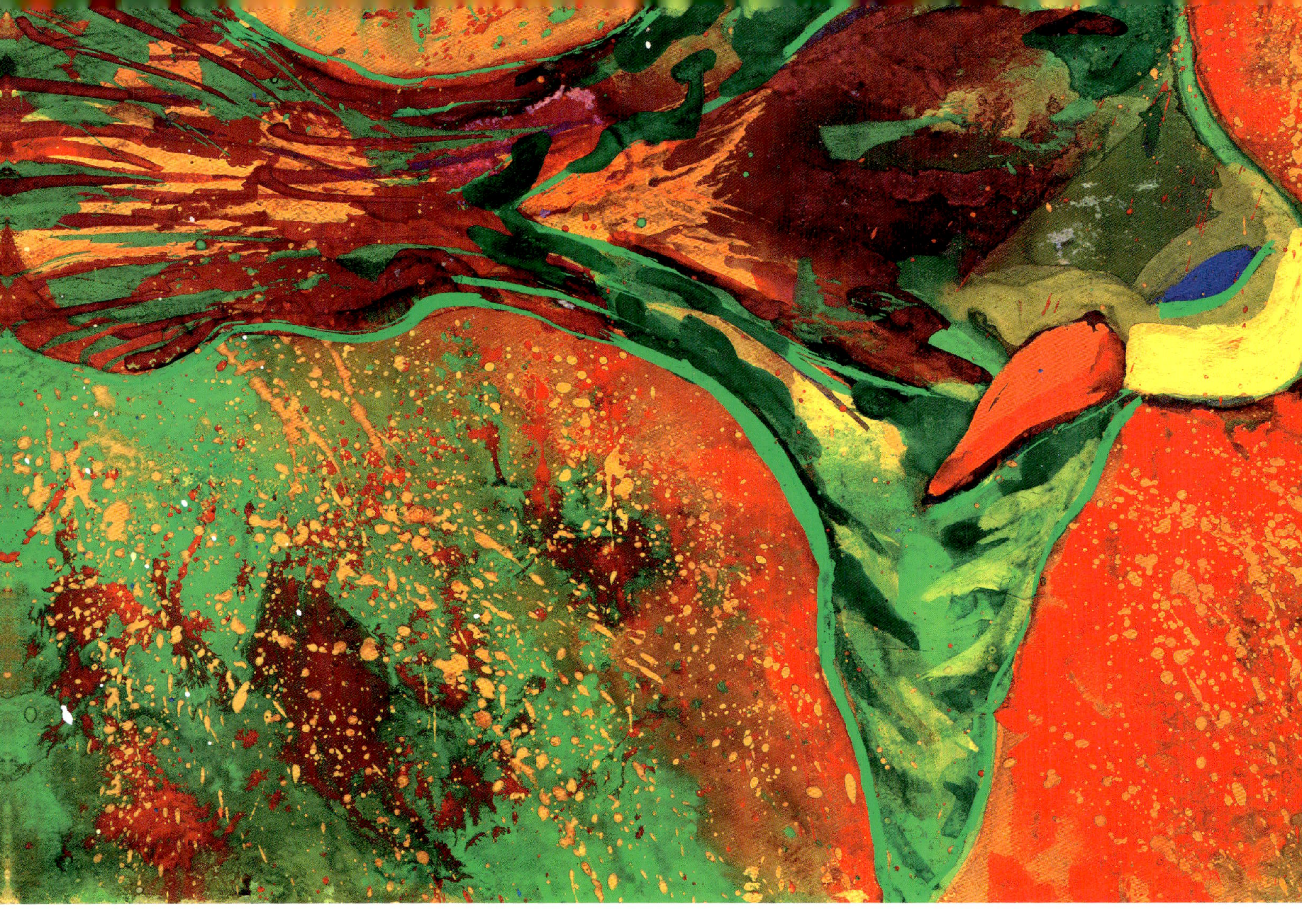

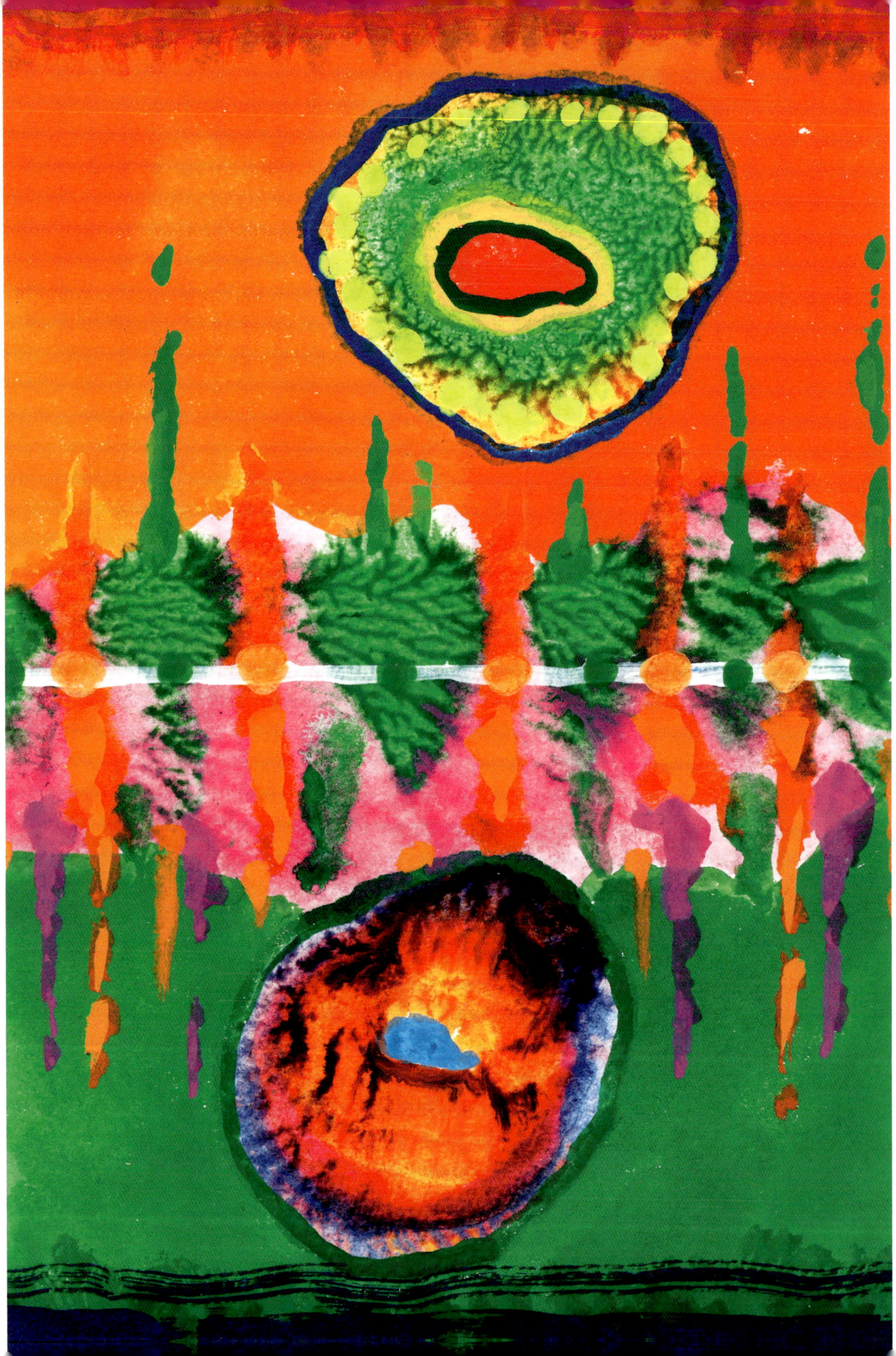

Autumn Equinox / 2010

TIME FOR MAGIC

Time for Magic

Calling on the ANCESTORS

EARTH N AIR WATER S FIRE

spin

CLAY WITH WIND

NORTH FROM EARTH ROOT

SOUTH WIND AIR BLOW RAIN

EAST TO WEST

water flows fibre

timeless fertile fish

trickle FLOOD WHICH SOUND.

learnings

ovule WHICH TREE sea INCANTATION

seasons sand see Sun

herbs from bird expansive & moon

trusting

& beast

WHICH flower CHANT in place

COMBINE Ripen rebirth

Vision Elements allingment

ALLINMENT

combine

River know-LEDGE

North East compost OVA

South west orbit

demystify

germenate grow generate

UNIVERSAL LOVE

seeding

VORTEX.

UMVH VERITY. SCHEILLIAN

MAJESTY

LOVE INFINITE

HEART

harmony reincarnate commune

healing compassion

complete

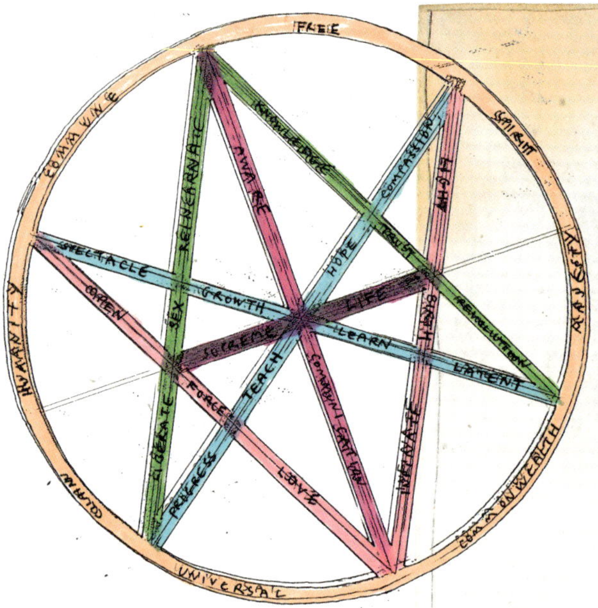

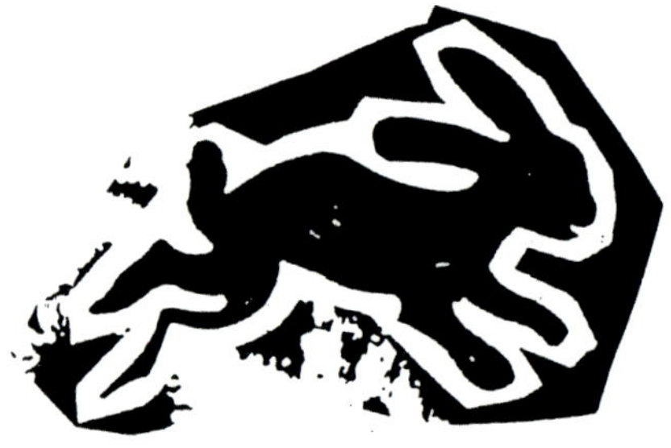

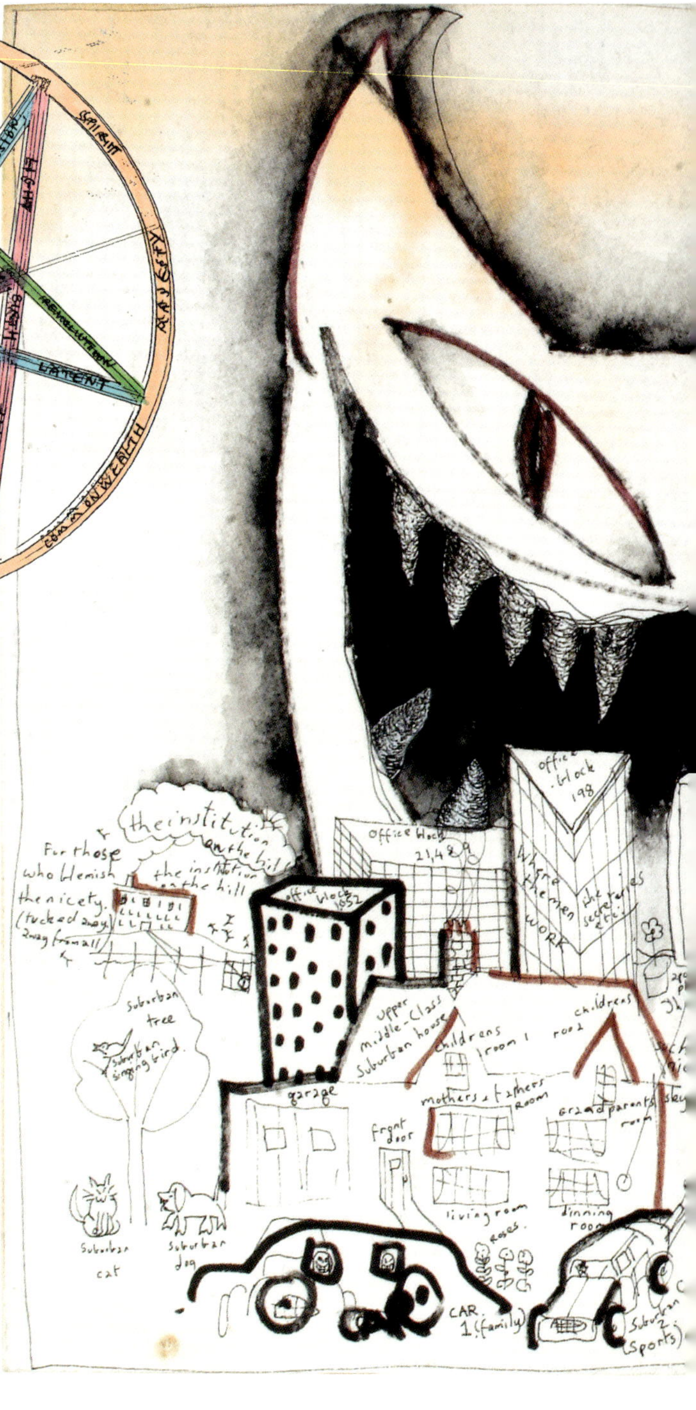

The Cat Who Ate the World | 1970

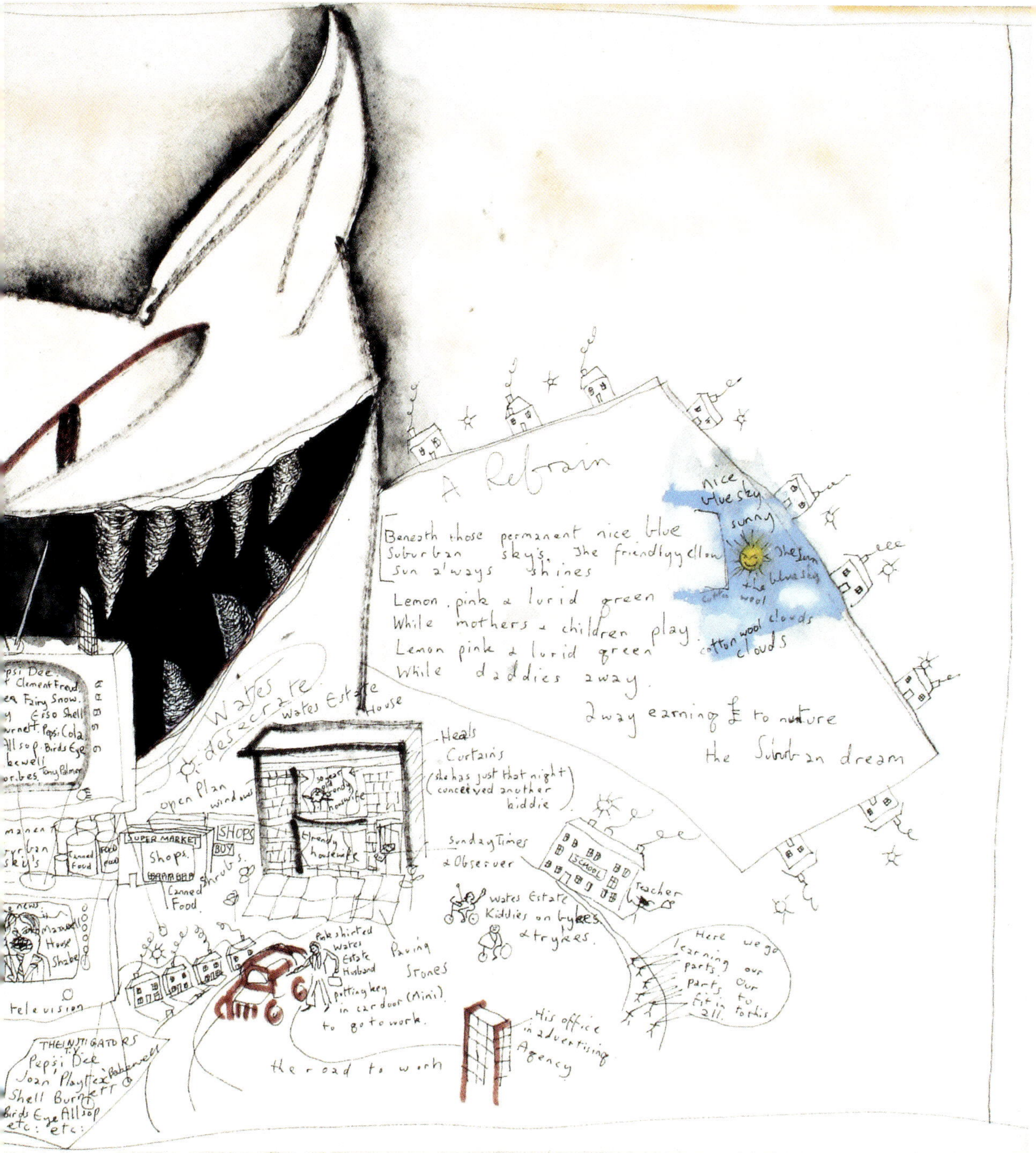

A Rebrain

Beneath those permanent nice blue
Suburban sky's. The friendlyyellow
Sun always shines

Lemon, pink & lurid green
While mothers & children play
Lemon pink & lurid green
While daddies away.

away earning £ to nature
the Suburban dream

nice blue sky
sunny
the sun
the blue sky
cotton wool
cotton wool clouds
cotton wool clouds

Wates desecrate
Wates Estate House
Heals Curtains
(she has just that night conceived another kiddie)
open Plan windows
friendly housewife
SUPER MARKET
Shops.
SHOPS
BUY
shrubs.
Canned Food
Canned Food.
Sunday Times & Observer
SCHOOL
Teacher
wates Estate Kiddies on bykes & trykes.
Here we go learning our parts. Our parts to fit in to this all.
Pink shirted Wates Estate Husband putting key in car door (Mini) to go to work.
Paving Stones
His office in advertising Agency
the road to work
television
Maxwell House
THE INSTIGATORS T.V.
Pepsi Dee
Joan Playtex Bakewell
Shell Burnett
Birds Eye Allsop
etc: etc:
Pepsi Cola
Fairy Snow
Esso Shell
Birds Eye
Tony Palmer

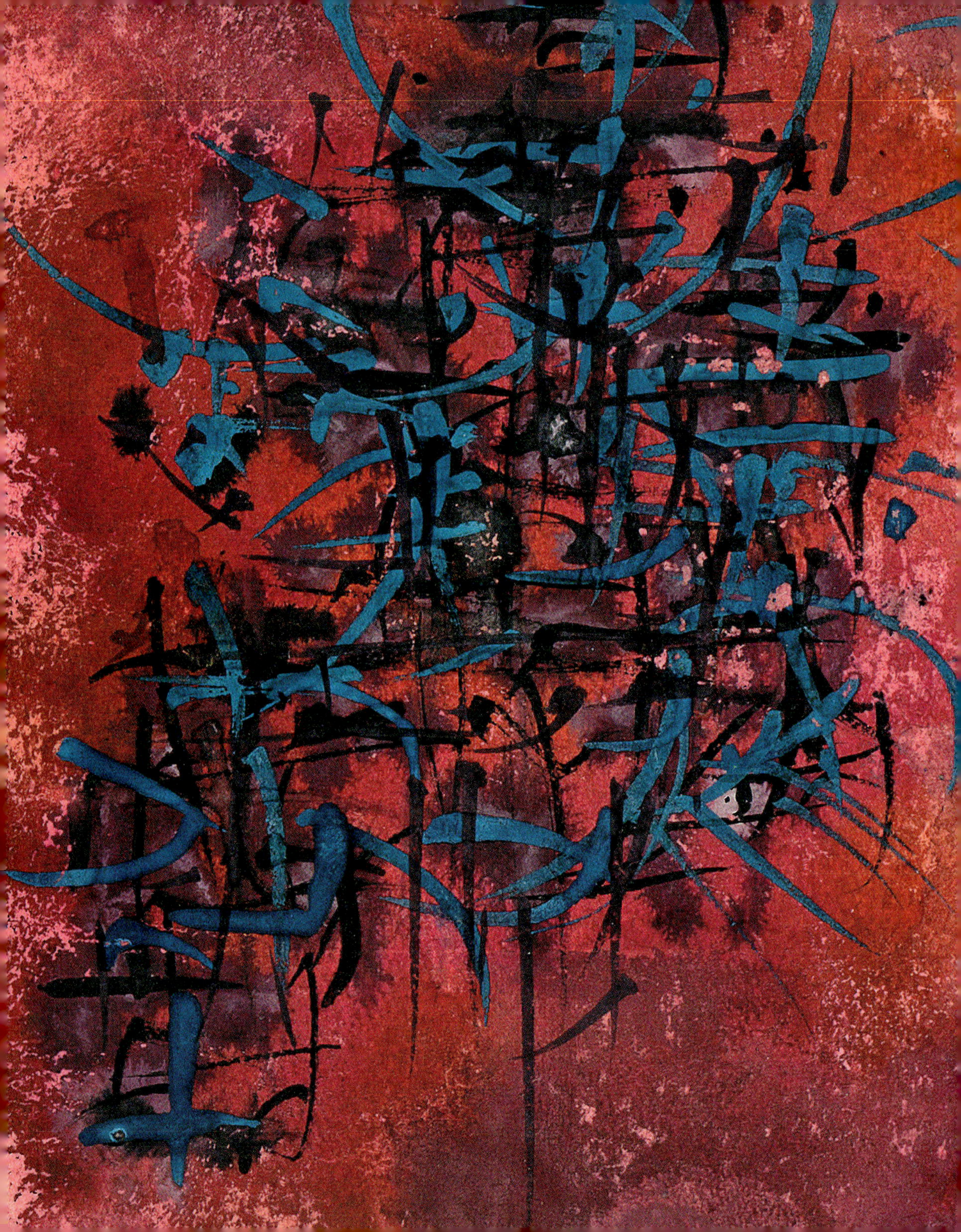

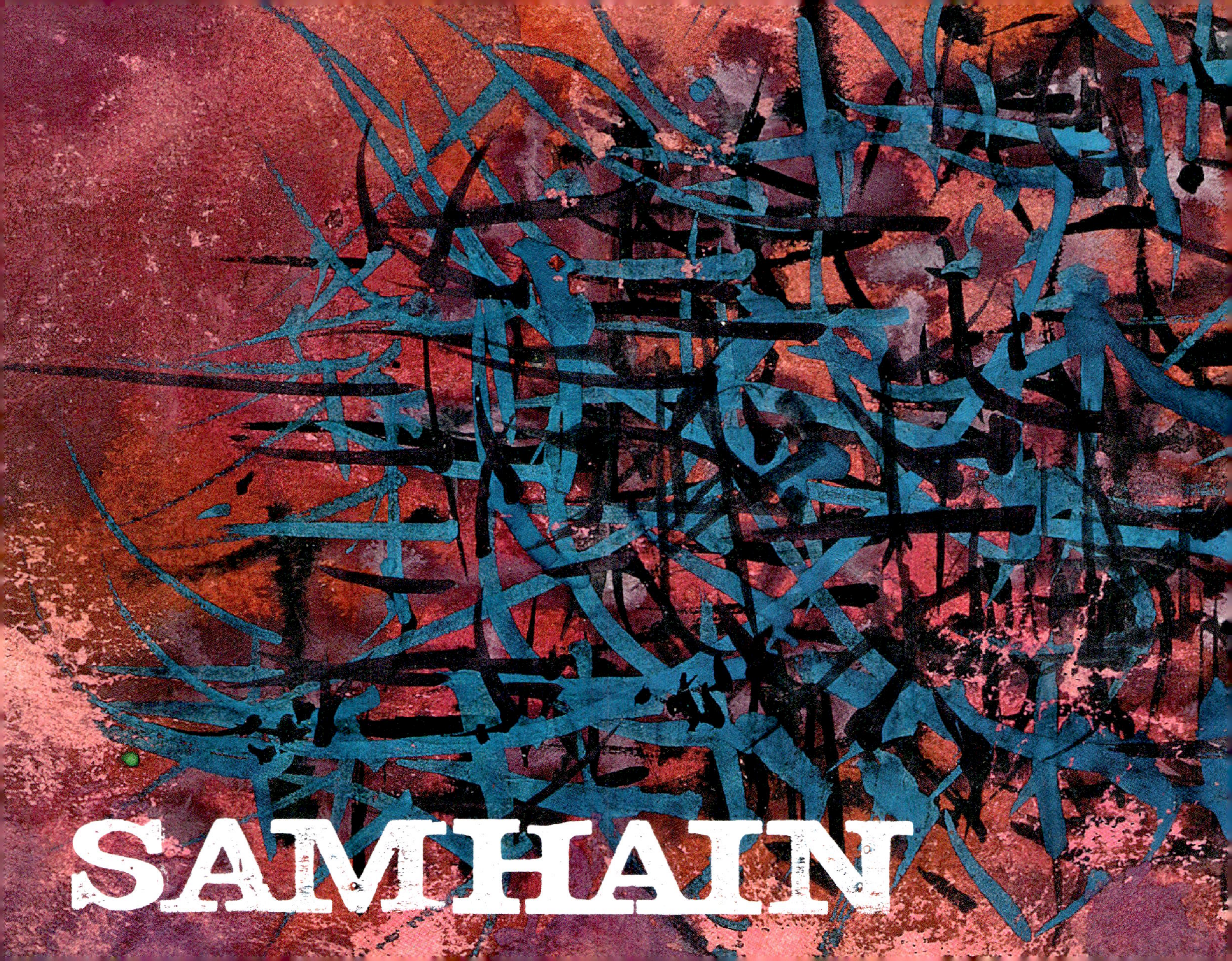
SAMHAIN

SAMHAIN

Samhain is the moment when time stops. It is the most powerful of all the festivals because it offers this quantum leap out of our reality that is defined by time and space into the Otherworld, the Afterlife. Now the fields are bare and what is left of the fruit is falling from the trees. It's the time of the third harvest – the blood harvest – when the livestock used to be slaughtered. Winter rattles at the windows and we remember our dead. They've stayed where they belong all year, but now Time's wall has been breached and there's no forgetting them, no ignoring them. They're here. We might offer them our love or our rage or our forgiveness, or perhaps all three. We might take a drink and a cake to the cemetery to share with them.

At Beltane, two fires are lit and we walk through them into life, eager for love, eager for everything. Then the Wheel turns and we face the fires of Samhain, but this time we are invited to walk, not towards the glowing centre of life, here on earth, with all its sparks and heat, but away from it, into the infinite darkness.

Samhain is probably the oldest of the festivals, rooted in tradition thousands of years old. Once, it was celebrated as a time in an ordered world when disorder and mayhem could rule for a while. Men could dress as women, women as men; raucous mischief that is watered down and commercialised today in the trick-or-treat shenanigans of Hallowe'en.

The tradition of Samhain fires was lost and then reborn as Guy Fawkes Night, shifted by a few days to 5 November. It was also reborn in the fire festivals that take place around the country at this time, alive with a tangible sense of Samhain chaos. Huge crowds are drawn to the exuberance and wildness of the bonfire nights that take place in places like Lewes and Battle, for example, and in thirty of the surrounding towns and villages in Sussex.

In Devon, at Ottery St Mary and at Hatherleigh, blazing tar barrels are heaved on shoulders in torchlit processions. In the same county, at Shebbear on Guy Fawke's night, as the church bells are rung discordantly, the locals engage in the ceremony of Turning the Devil's Boulder, stopping evil coming to the village by pushing over a great rock that the Devil dropped in the churchyard.

31 October – 2 November

Each revolution of the Wheel of the Year is a life in microcosm. We are conceived at the Winter Solstice, born at Imbolc, achieve young adulthood and find love at Beltane, reach the fullness of our lives at the Summer Solstice, and then mature into old age through the three harvests, until, at this last harvest time of Samhain, we walk through the fires and let go of our body. From the beginning of November until the Winter Solstice is the time between incarnations, a journey in-between lives, until, at the Winter Solstice, our soul incarnates again, conception occurs, and around the Wheel we go once more.

At the heart of the focus on death at Samhain is the process of shedding. Like snakes sloughing off their skin, trees dropping their leaves, we need periodically to shake ourselves free and let go of everything, from unhelpful habits and relationships to the clutter that accumulates from living in this over-complicated world we have created.

Samhain is a time for choosing simplicity over the urge to accumulate. It's a time for liberation, for the freedom that comes to us when we let go of taking and start to give instead, when we let go of the delusion that the earth belongs to us and instead take on board the magnificence of the reverse: that we belong to the earth, to nature, to life.

NOTES FROM HELIGAN

'For our Samhain celebration, we shifted our focus from human needs to those of the animals. The Heligan cattle were led into Valentine's Field to graze down the remnants of the harvest, helping to return fertility to the soil. The OVA itself was protected, its drying stems left standing. Crows called overhead in a blustery sky. Even in November, the vivid blue cornflowers chimed like tiny bells against the green field. The cows lay on the marigolds and chewed corn chamomile. Occasionally, one of them would amble over to the edge of the OVA, gaze inwards, then move on. It was a particularly beautiful way to mark the day. We set our intentions and acted mindfully.'

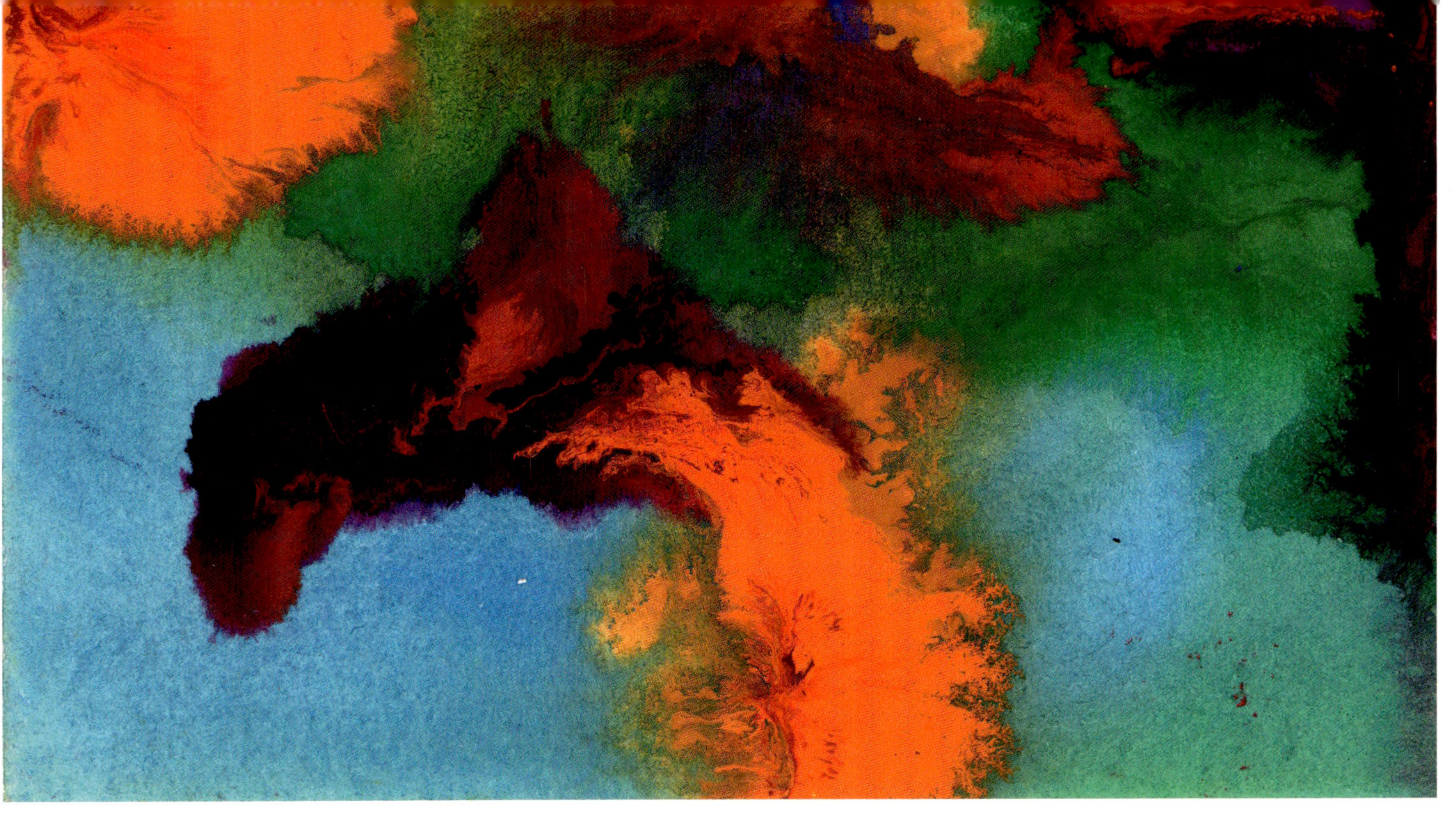

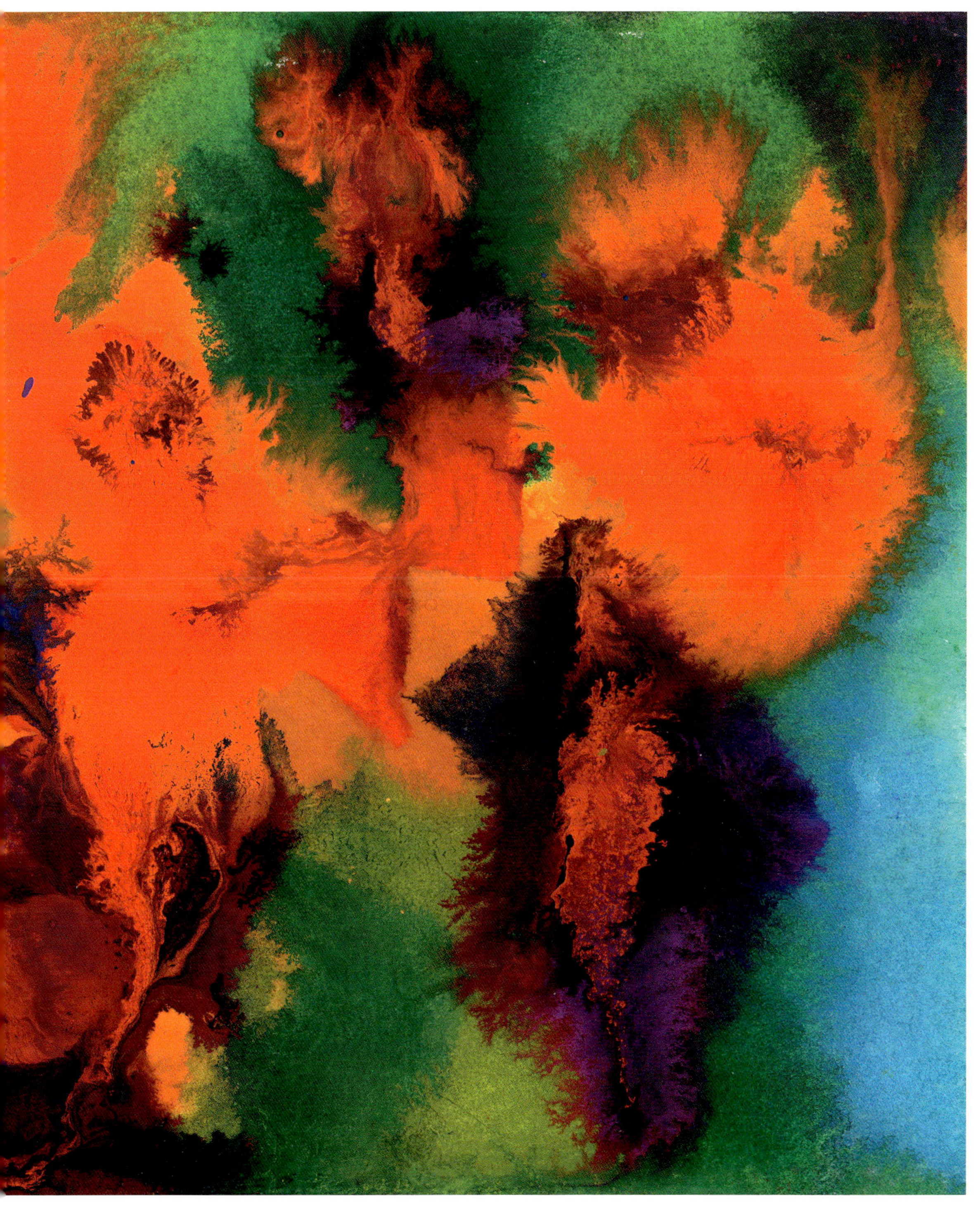

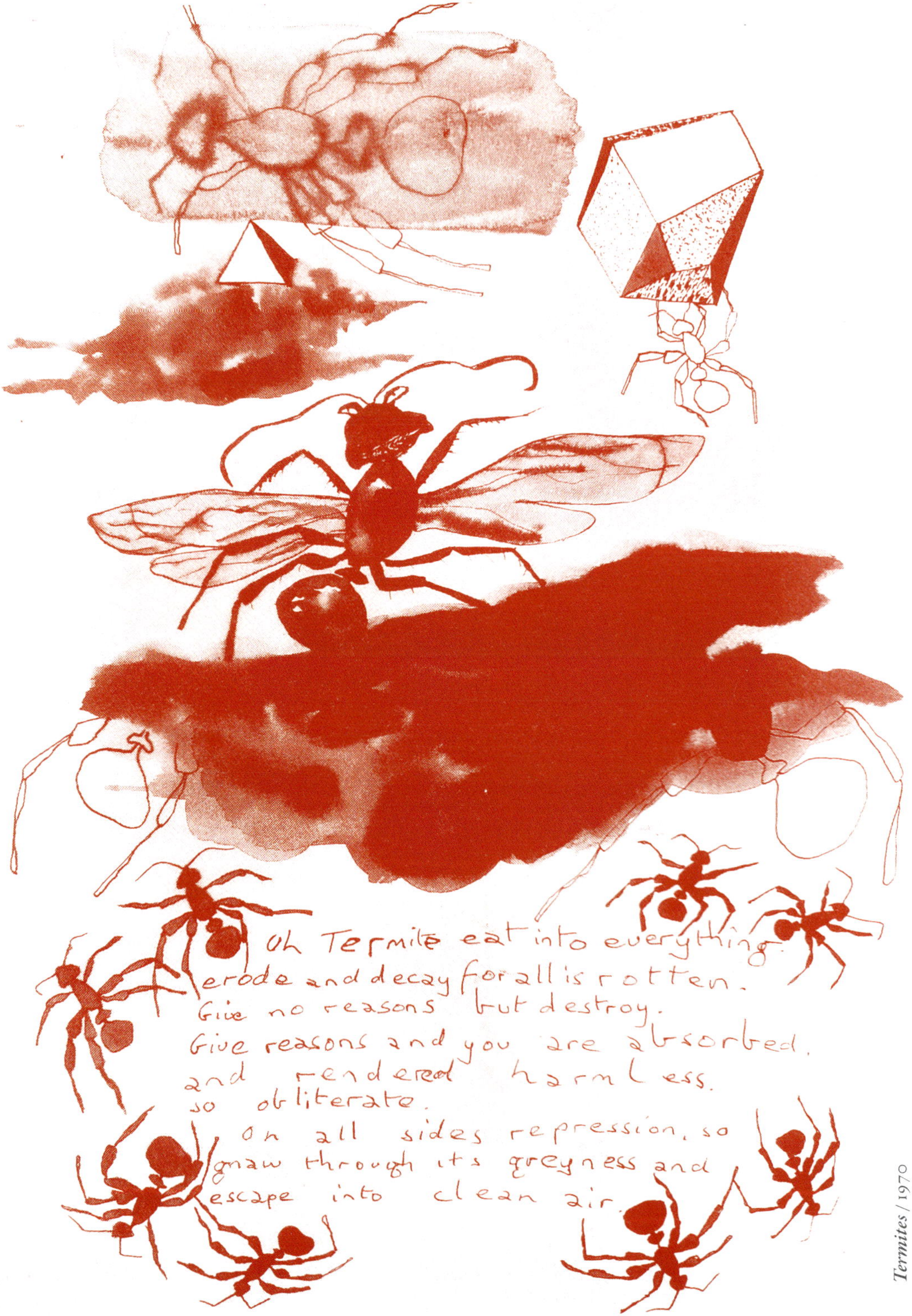

Oh Termite eat into everything
erode and decay for all is rotten.
Give no reasons but destroy.
Give reasons and you are absorbed.
and rendered harmless.
so obliterate.
On all sides repression, so
gnaw through its greyness and
escape into clean air.

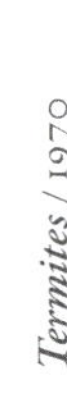

Termites / 1970

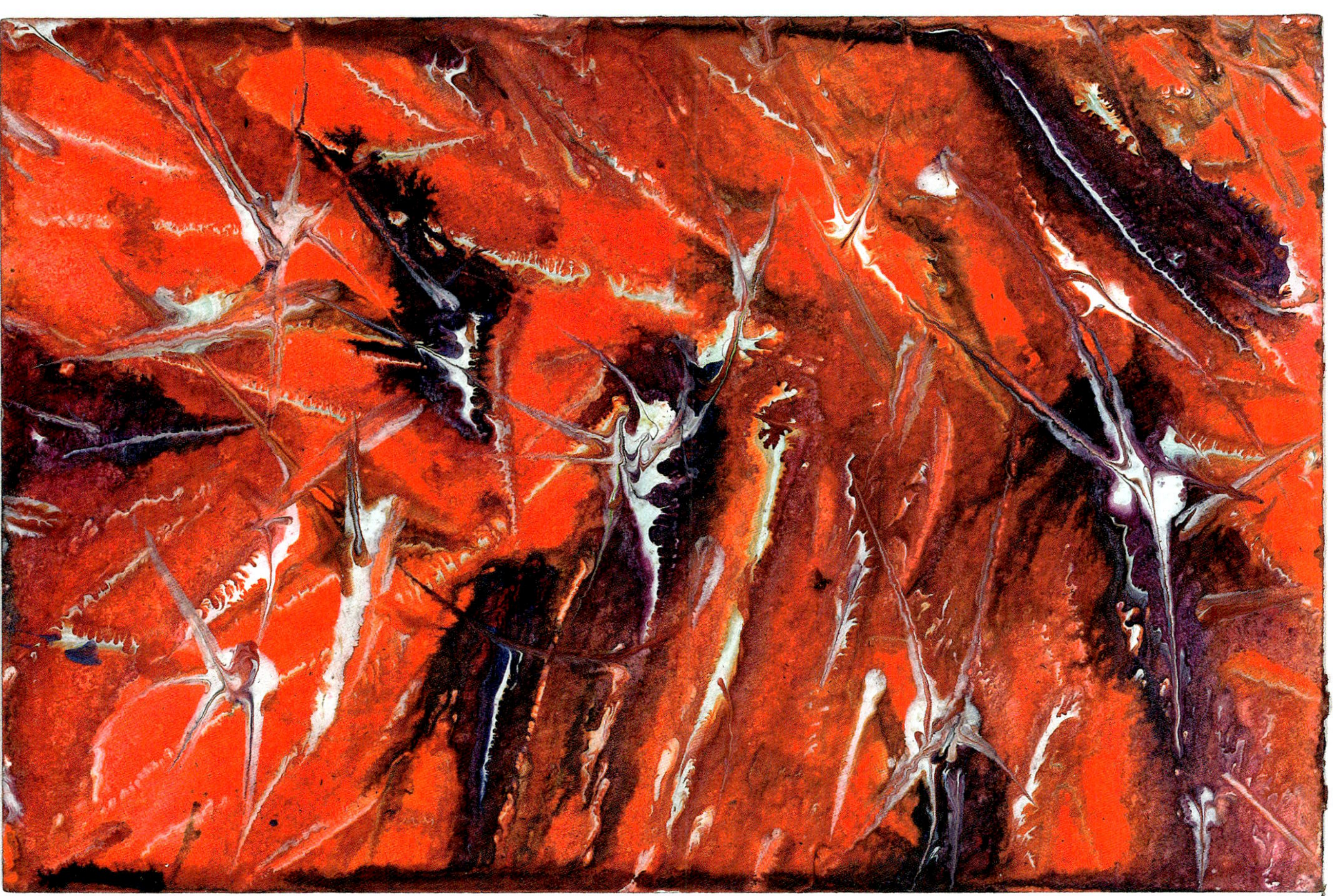

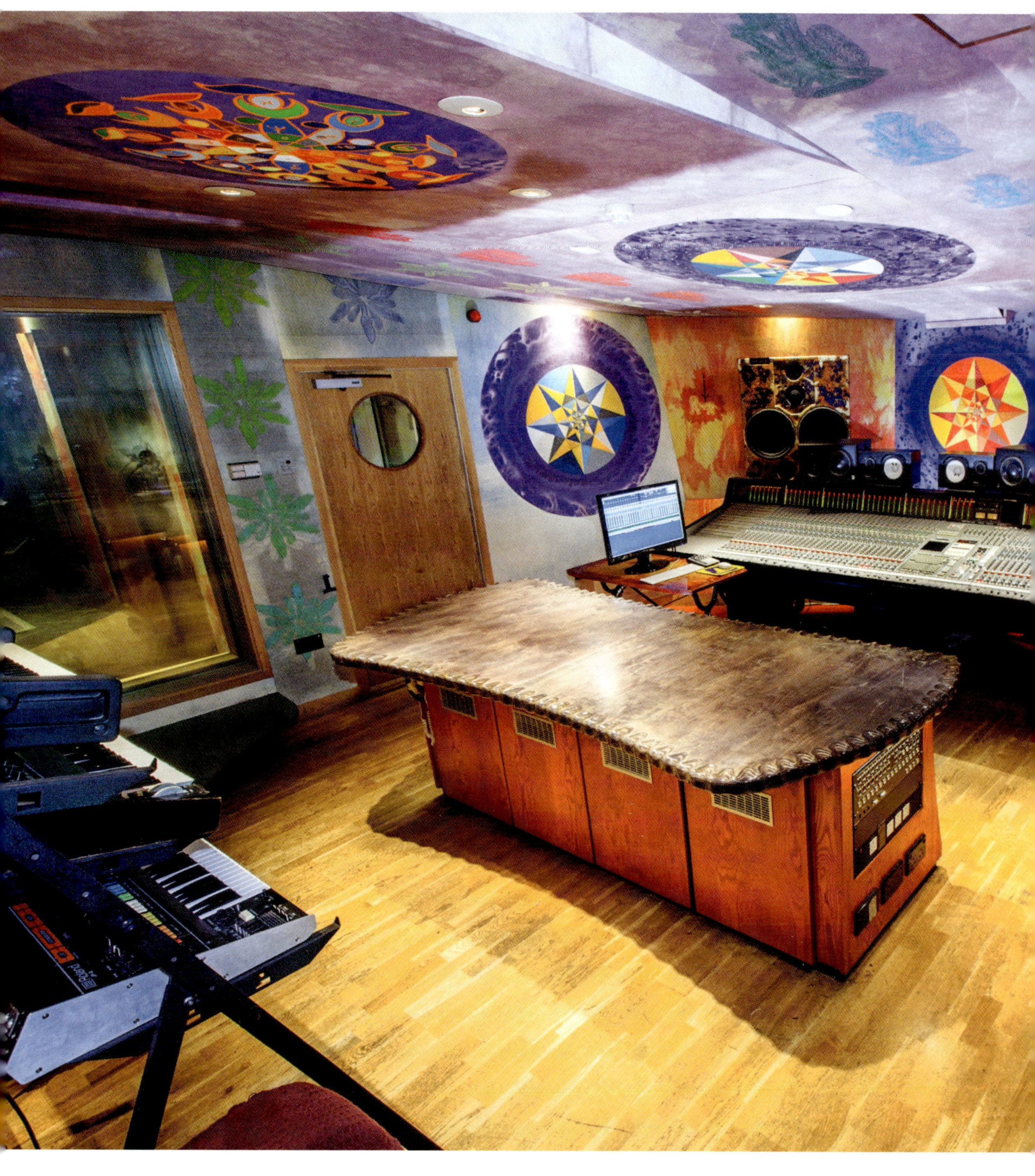

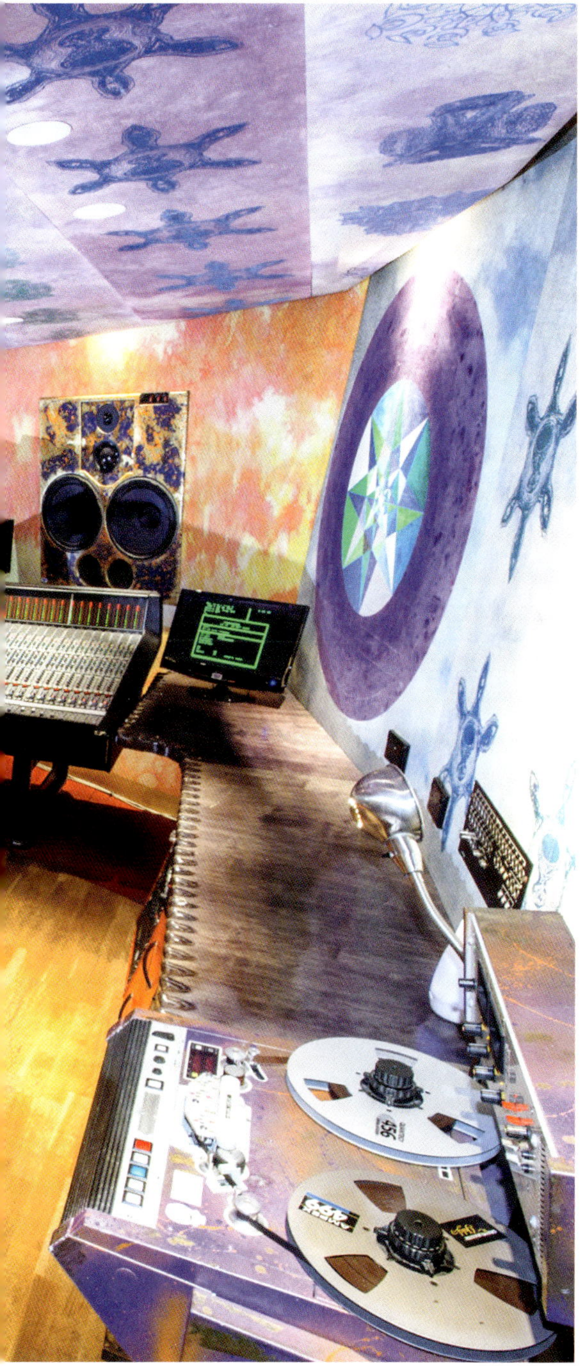

Strongroom Studio 3 –
The Four Elements Studio / 2018

Jamie was working out of his studio on Curtain Road, Shoreditch, when he was asked to refurbish a recording studio in the same Victorian building. This was Studio 2 of the developing Strongroom recording studios, which had suffered flood damage (coincidentally after a session with the record producer Flood…). Strongroom owner Richard Boote offered no brief other than to make it interesting, and 'just told Jamie to get on with it'. Drafting in help from friend and designer Mike Nicholls, Jamie began to cover all the walls in colour and magical symbols, such as his OVA, a chalice, a flaming sword and a spiralling shell, which reflected William Blake's poetry: 'To see a World in a Grain of Sand. And a Heaven in a Wild Flower'. Boote was so happy with the results that he encouraged Jamie to continue to work as Strongroom grew, eventually filling what was to become one of the largest music studio complexes in Europe with Jamie's 'colour magic'. Wall coverings, curtains, desks and other furniture erupted in a style unseen elsewhere. The Strongroom is an incredible installation that truly equals Simon Rodia's Watts Towers in dedication, scale and individual creative energy, yet it remains largely unseen and unknown because of the private nature of the environment.

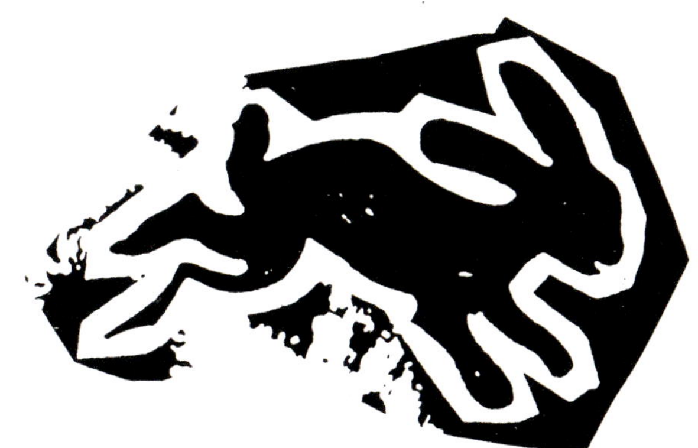

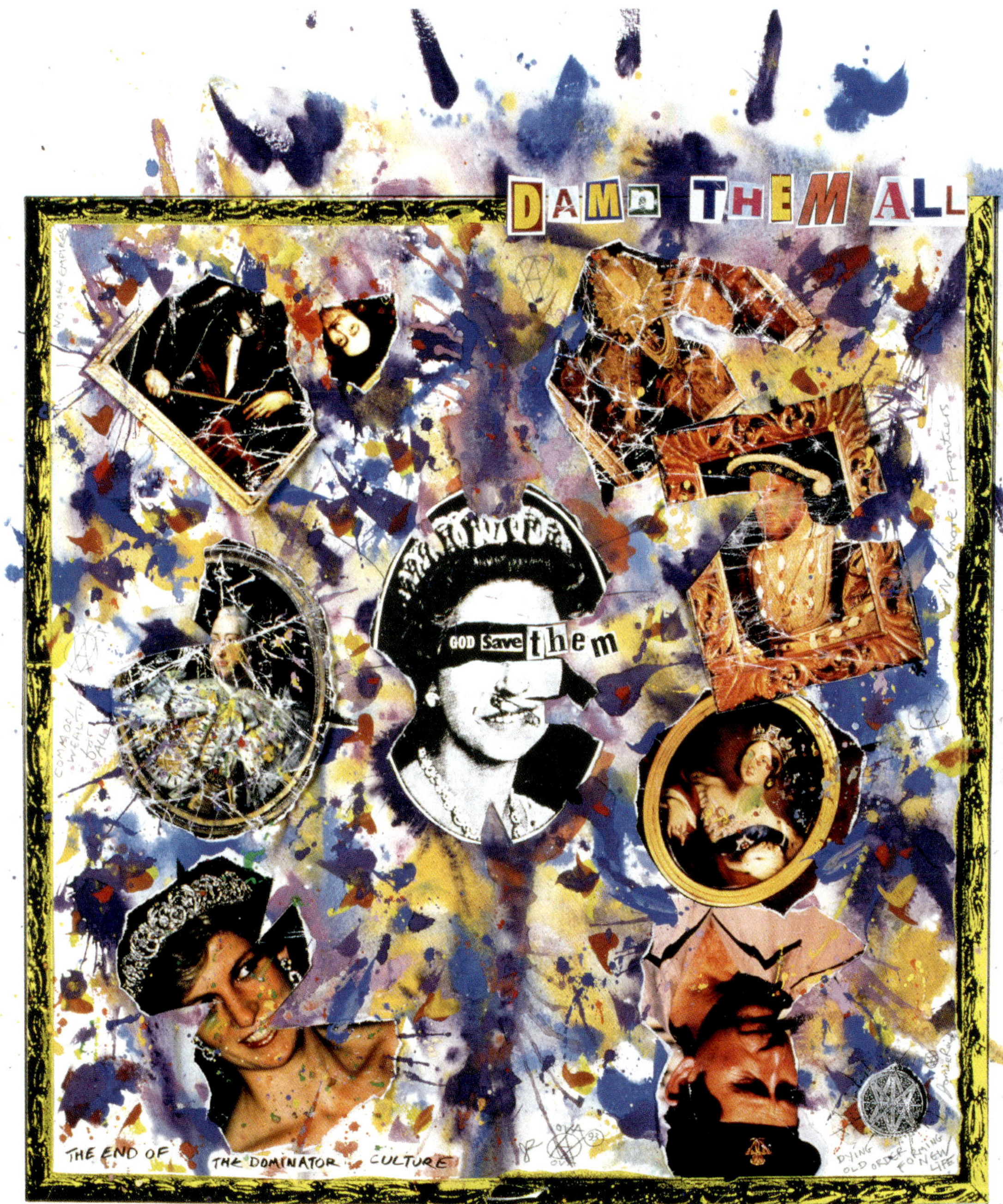
DAMn THEM ALL
GOD Save them
No more Frontiers
THE END OF THE DOMINATOR CULTURE
DYING OLD ORDER FORMING NEW LIFE

Damn Them All / 1993

Like *Stop Demonising Our Future* (page 109), this was a commission for the *Guardian*. This one appeared on billboards as well as on the cover of their Saturday supplement. Jamie believed that the monarchy in all its forms is an outdated system of exploitation that needs to end, and that corruption and violence flow from the Crown – both now and in the past. He was also quick to point out that two recent British Prime Ministers – David Cameron and Boris Johnson – claim direct lineage to the Hanoverian dynasty.

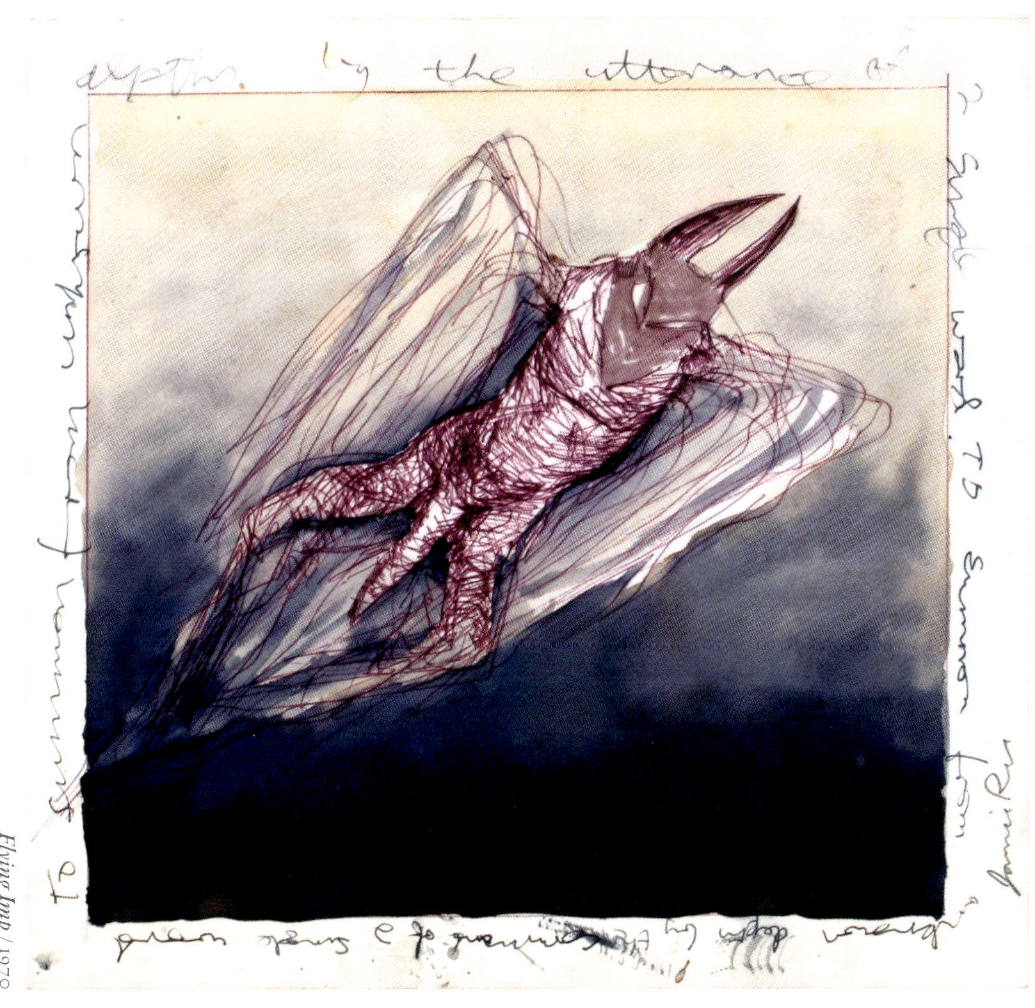

Flying Imp / 1970

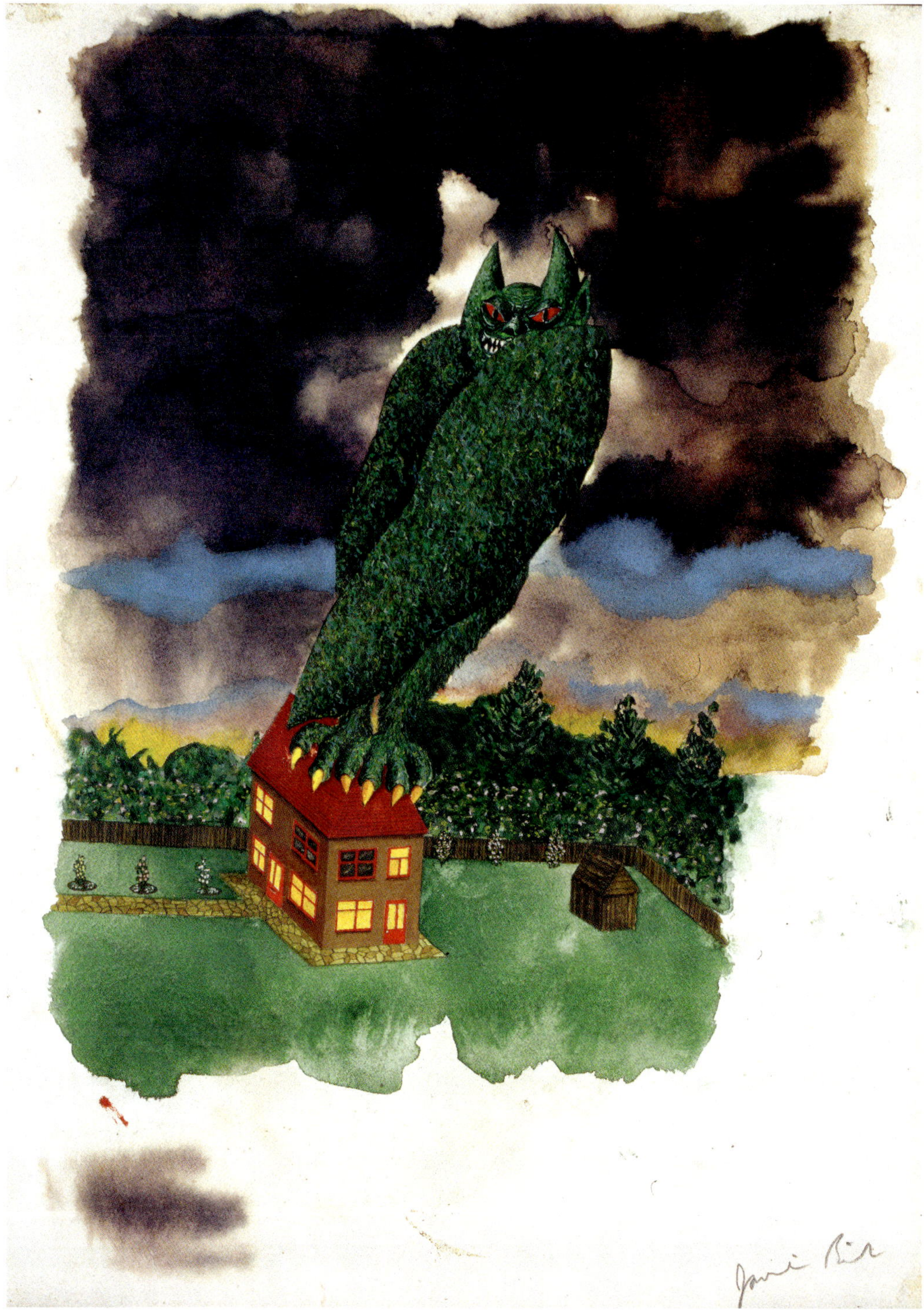

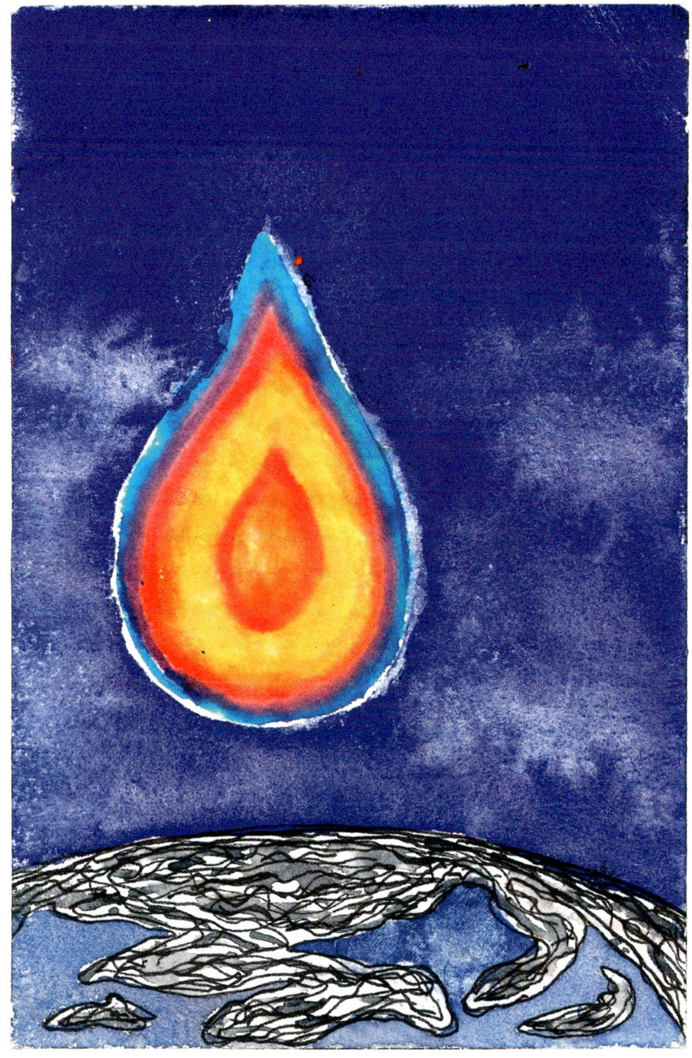

Monster on Nice Roof / 1972
This is the original painting that was adapted for the Sex Pistols in 1976 (see page 52) and rejected. Worked in gouache, the image betrays the underlying horror of suburbia felt by the artist who was its very product. Jamie said that, in theory, suburbia was a good idea – everyone had their own small plot of land – but in practice it led to choking conformity, expressed here as something dreadful and oppressive.

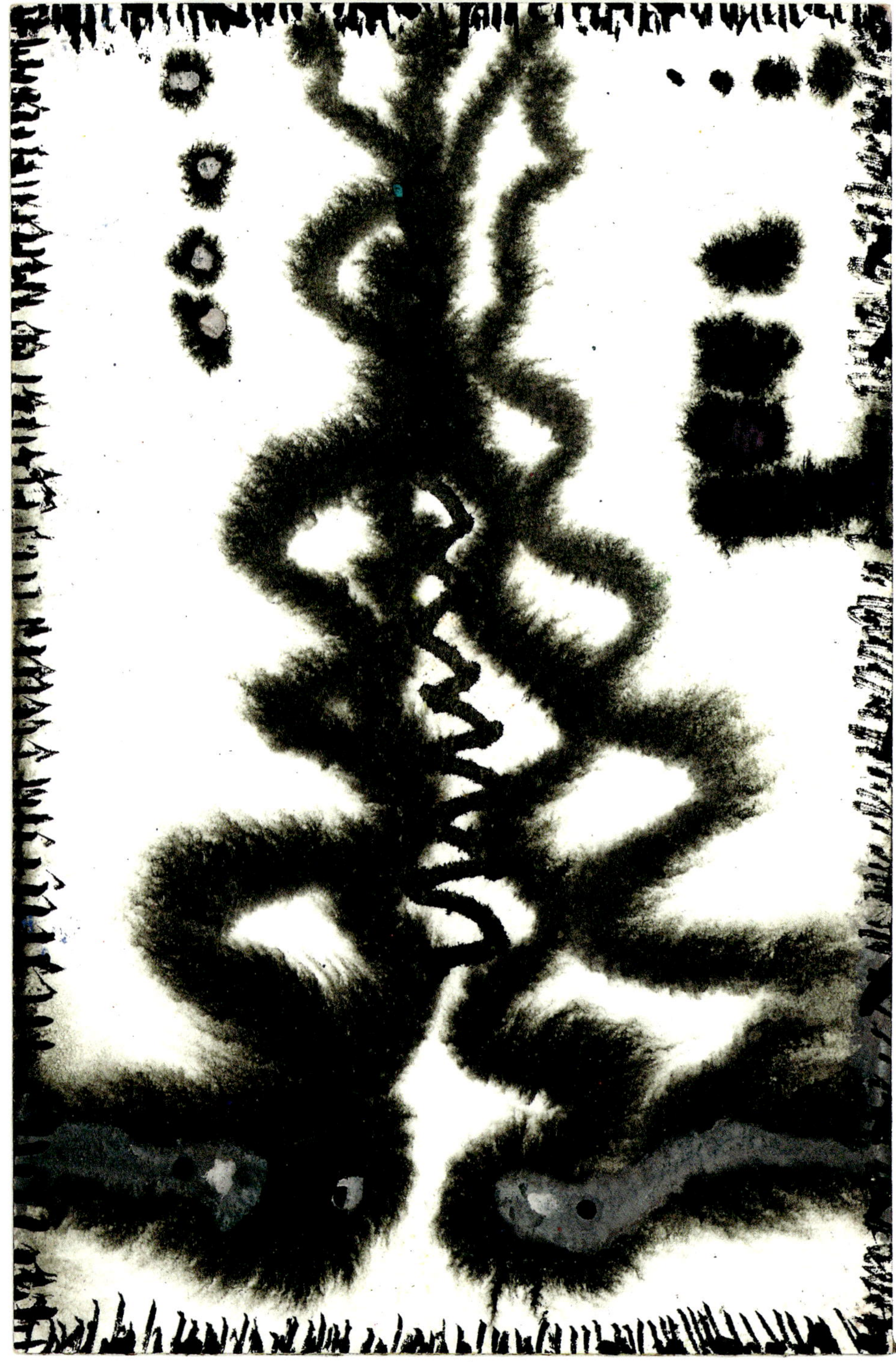

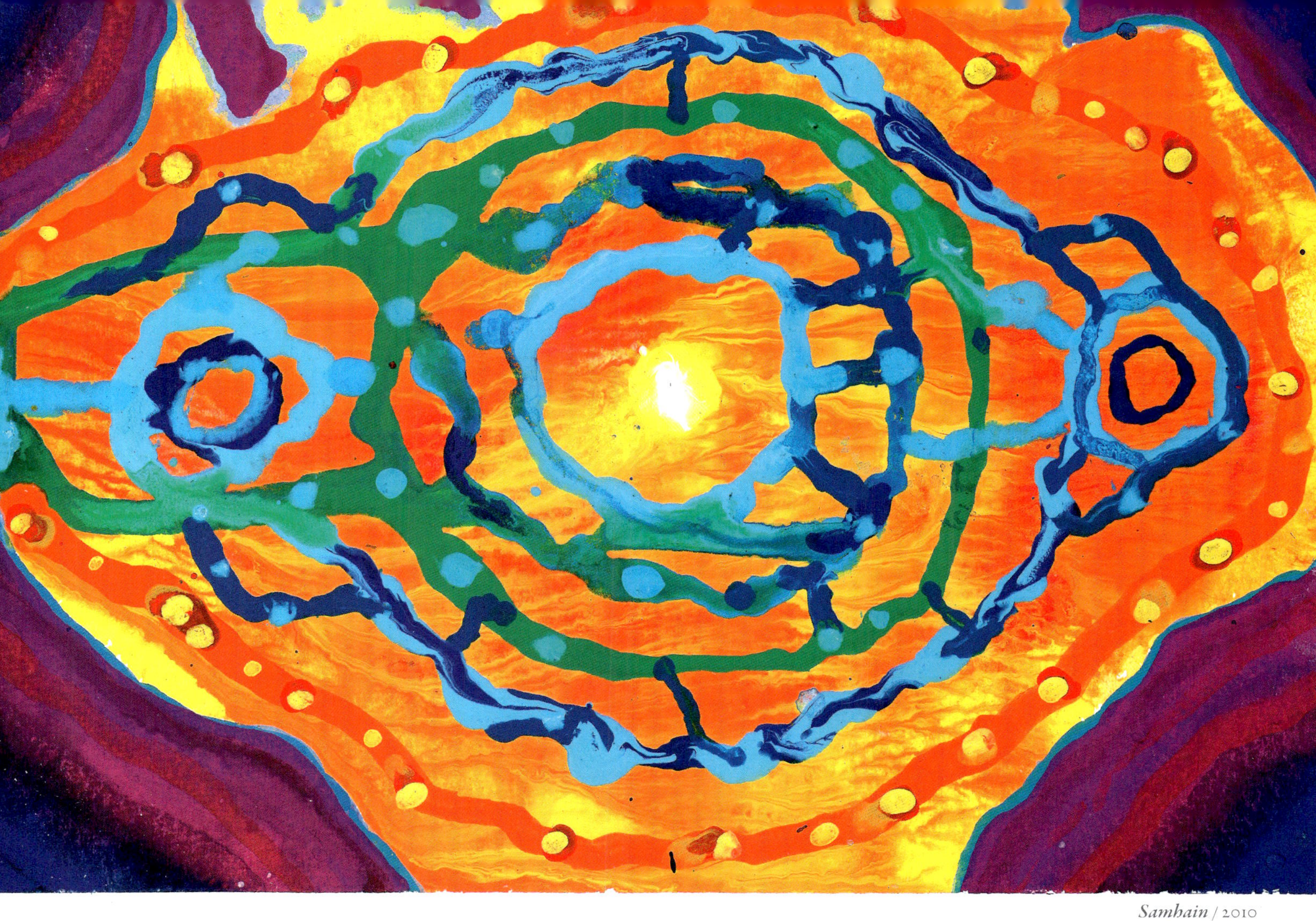

Samhain / 2010

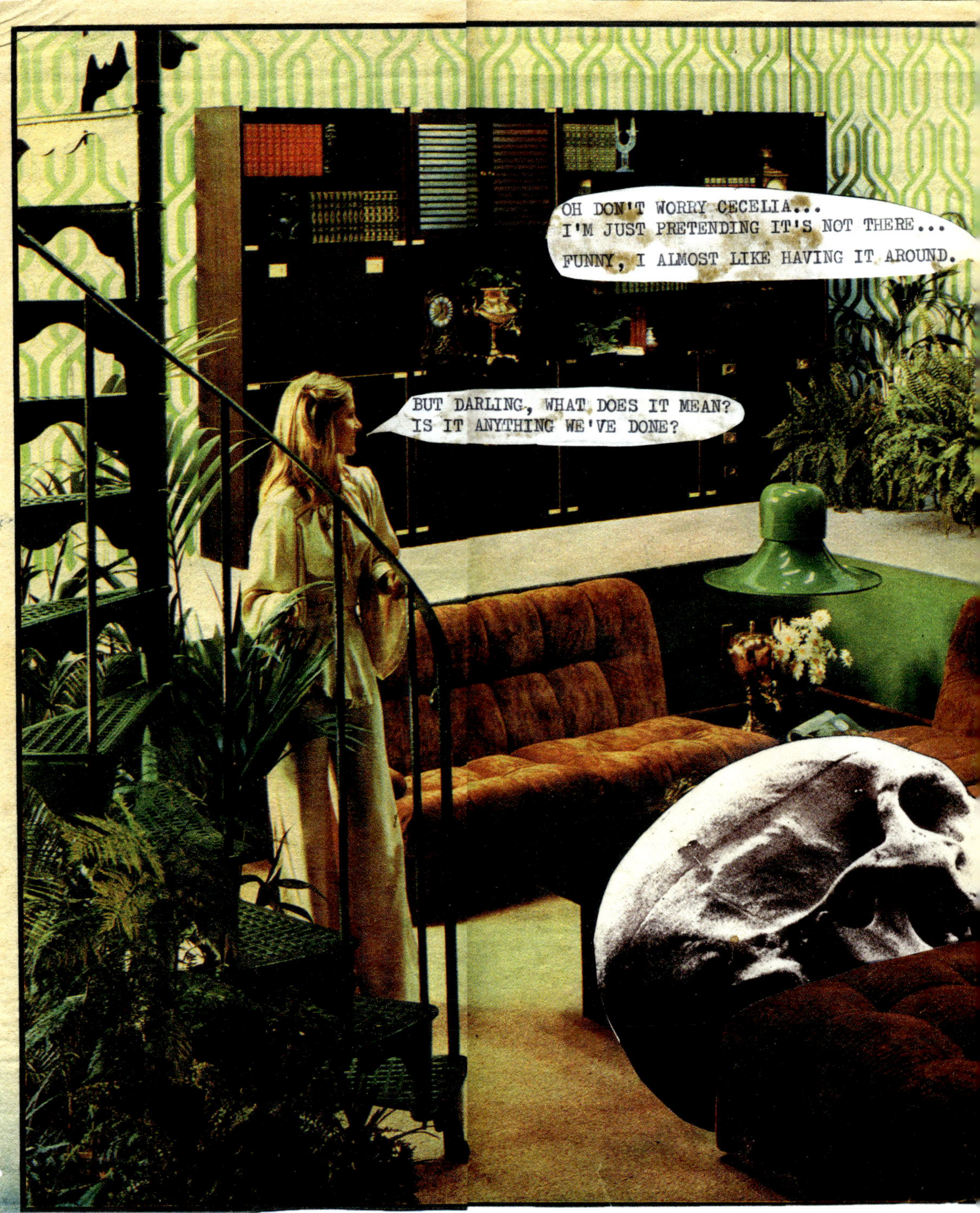

OH DON'T WORRY CECELIA...
I'M JUST PRETENDING IT'S NOT THERE...
FUNNY, I ALMOST LIKE HAVING IT AROUND.
BUT DARLING, WHAT DOES IT MEAN?
IS IT ANYTHING WE'VE DONE?

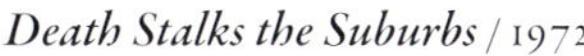

Death Stalks the Suburbs / 1972
This collage is a dark twin of Richard Hamilton's *Just What is it that Makes Today's Homes so Different, so Appealing?* (1956), with the shadow of death becoming ever more apparent to the inhabitants of the suburban house that is portrayed elsewhere with an enormous demon lurking on its roof. This work also appeared in a slightly different guise in Suburban Press's *Poster Book*, with the added text 'Death stalks the suburbs'. As with much of Jamie's graphic work, humour is used to great effect. Cecilia and her partner have become increasingly aware of the enormous skull replacing their pouffe, but seem reconciled to its malign appearance: 'Funny, I almost like having it around.'

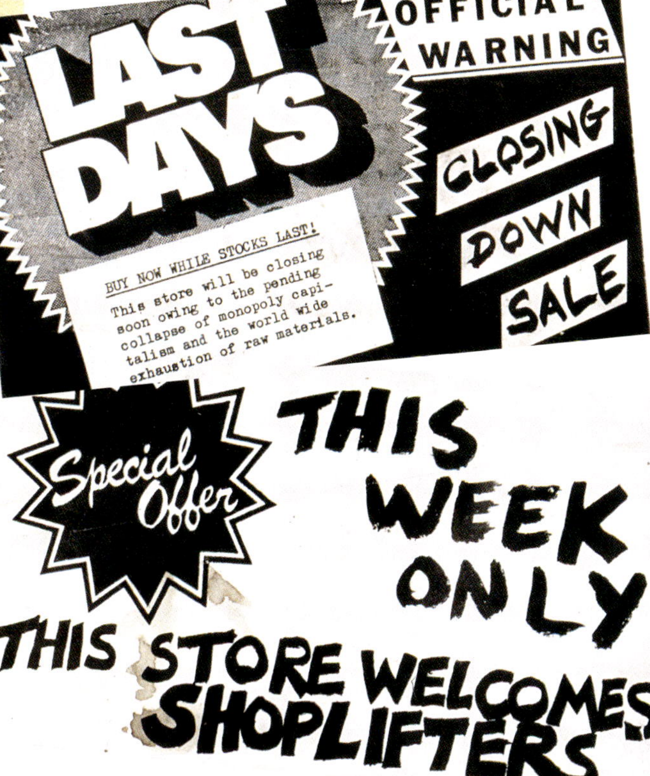

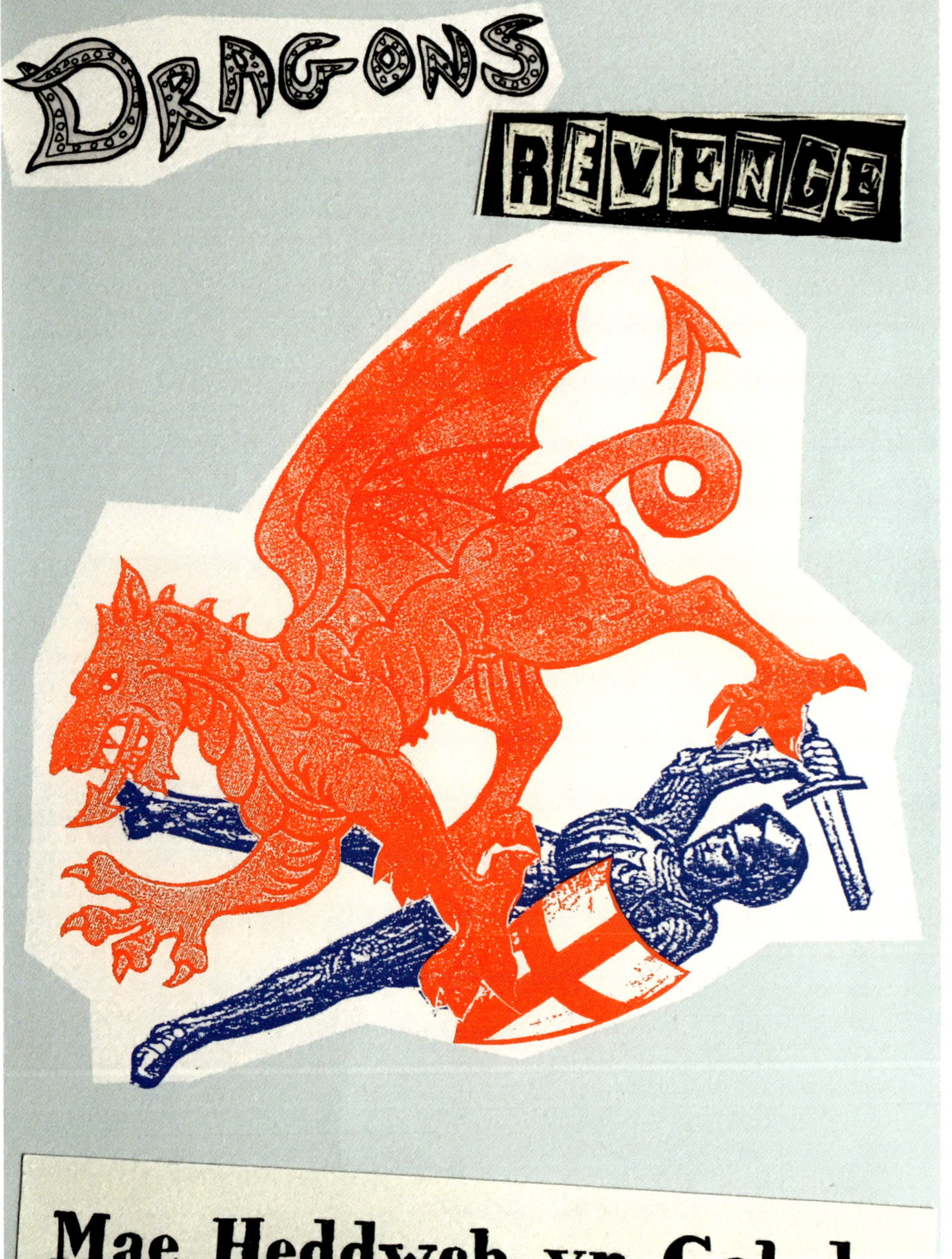

Dragons Revenge / 2020

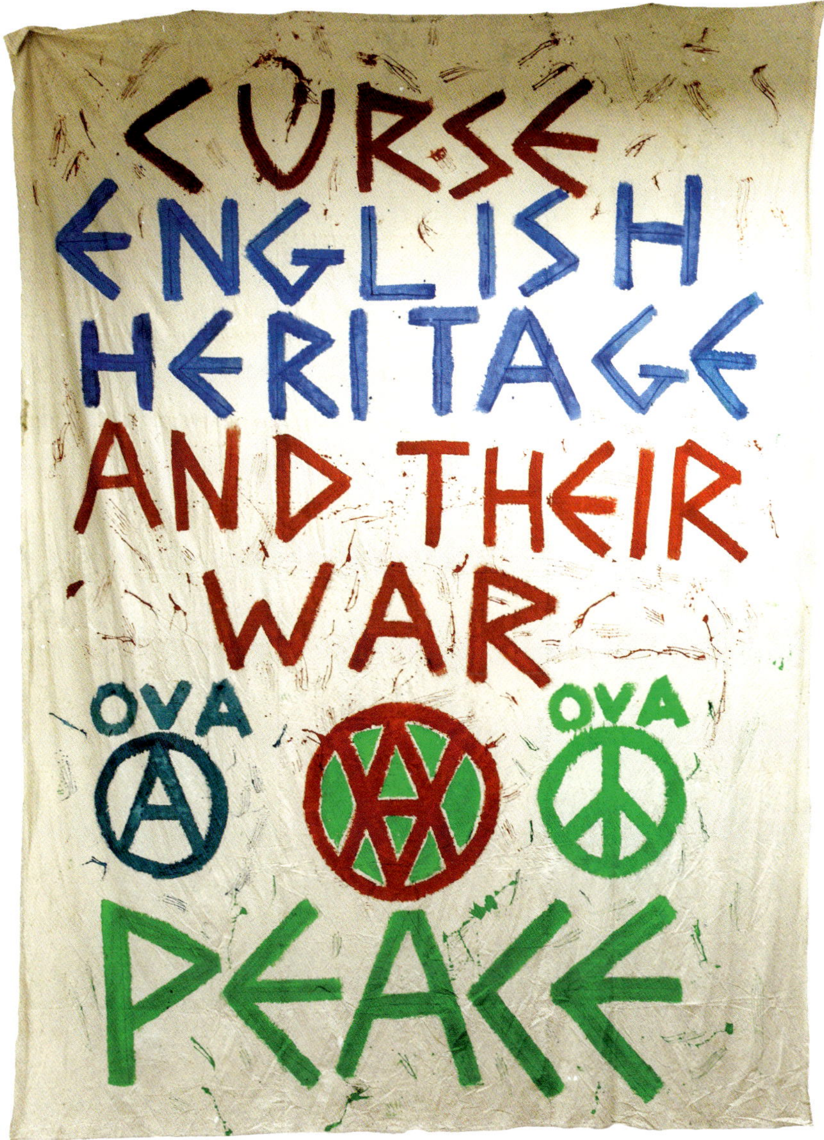

Curse English Heritage / 1991
Produced for a demonstration for public access to Stonehenge at the solstices, this hanging exhibits all the pace and vitriol of Jamie's work with the Sex Pistols. Making the link with the anarchy symbol explicit, the OVA is also aligned with the symbol for the Campaign for Nuclear Disarmament. CND had been very active in Jamie's hometown of Croydon in the 1960s, and his brother Bruce had participated in the Spies for Peace affair, breaking into a secret nuclear bunker in 1963.

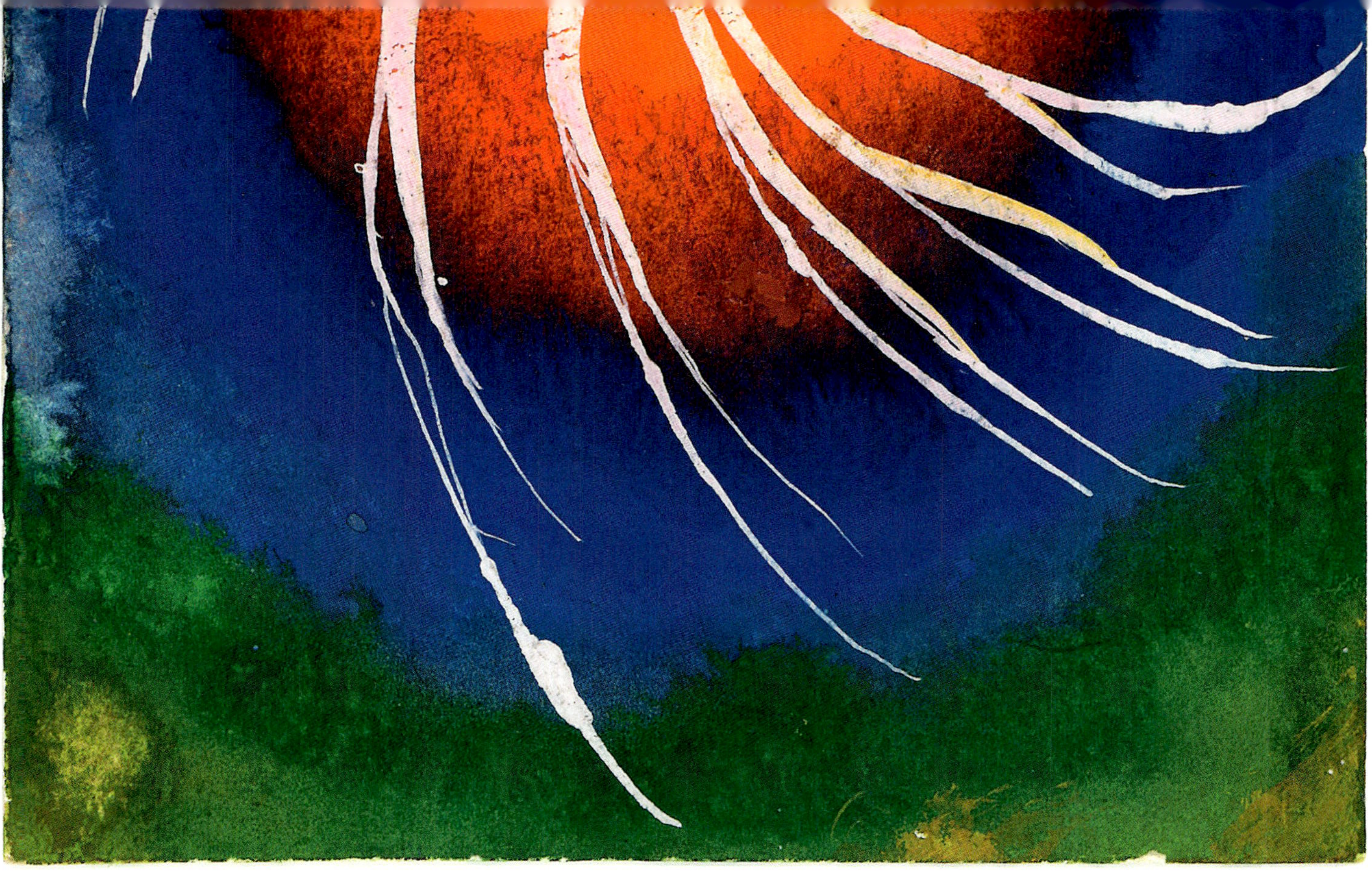

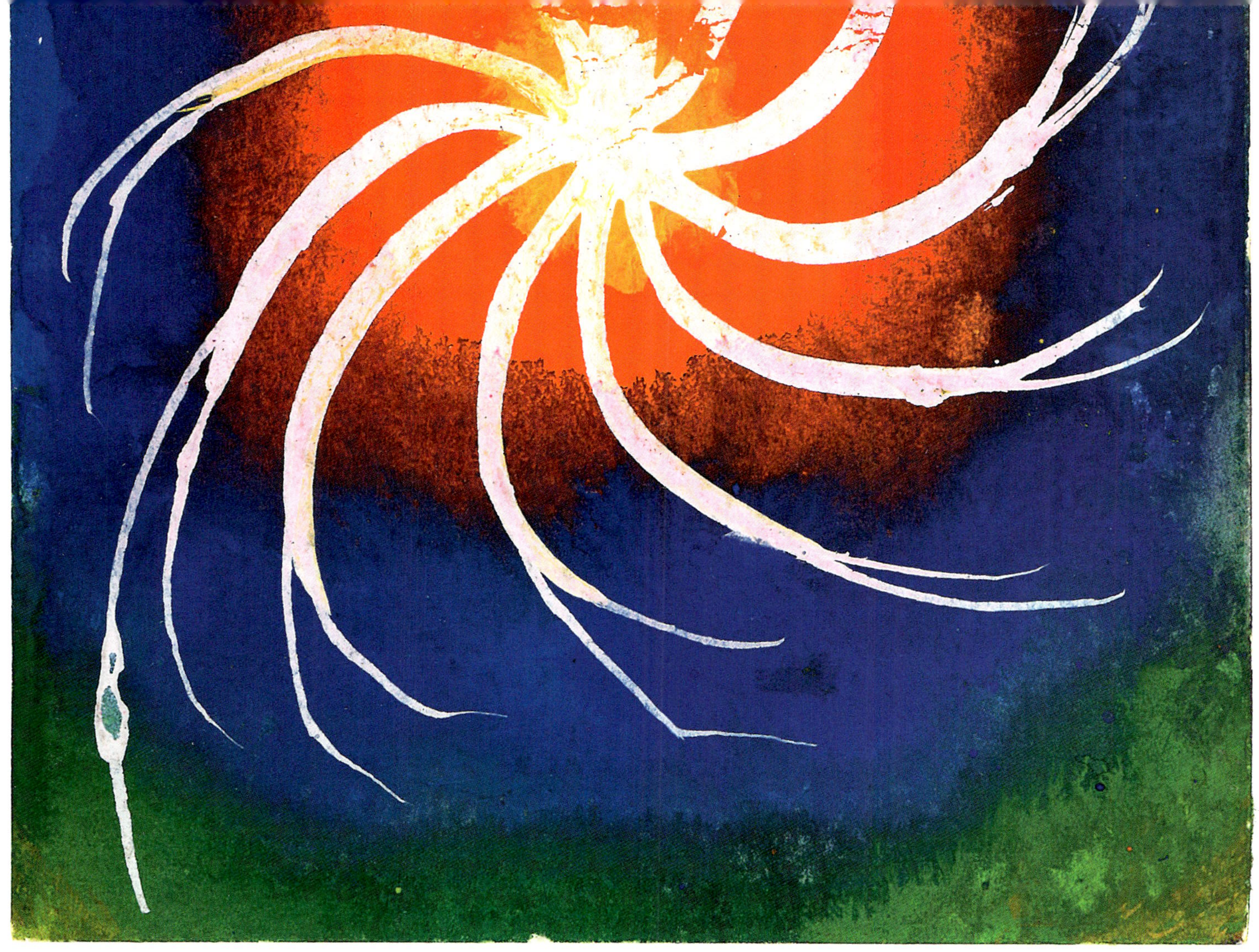

Universal Majesty Verity Love Infinite (UMVLI) / 1989

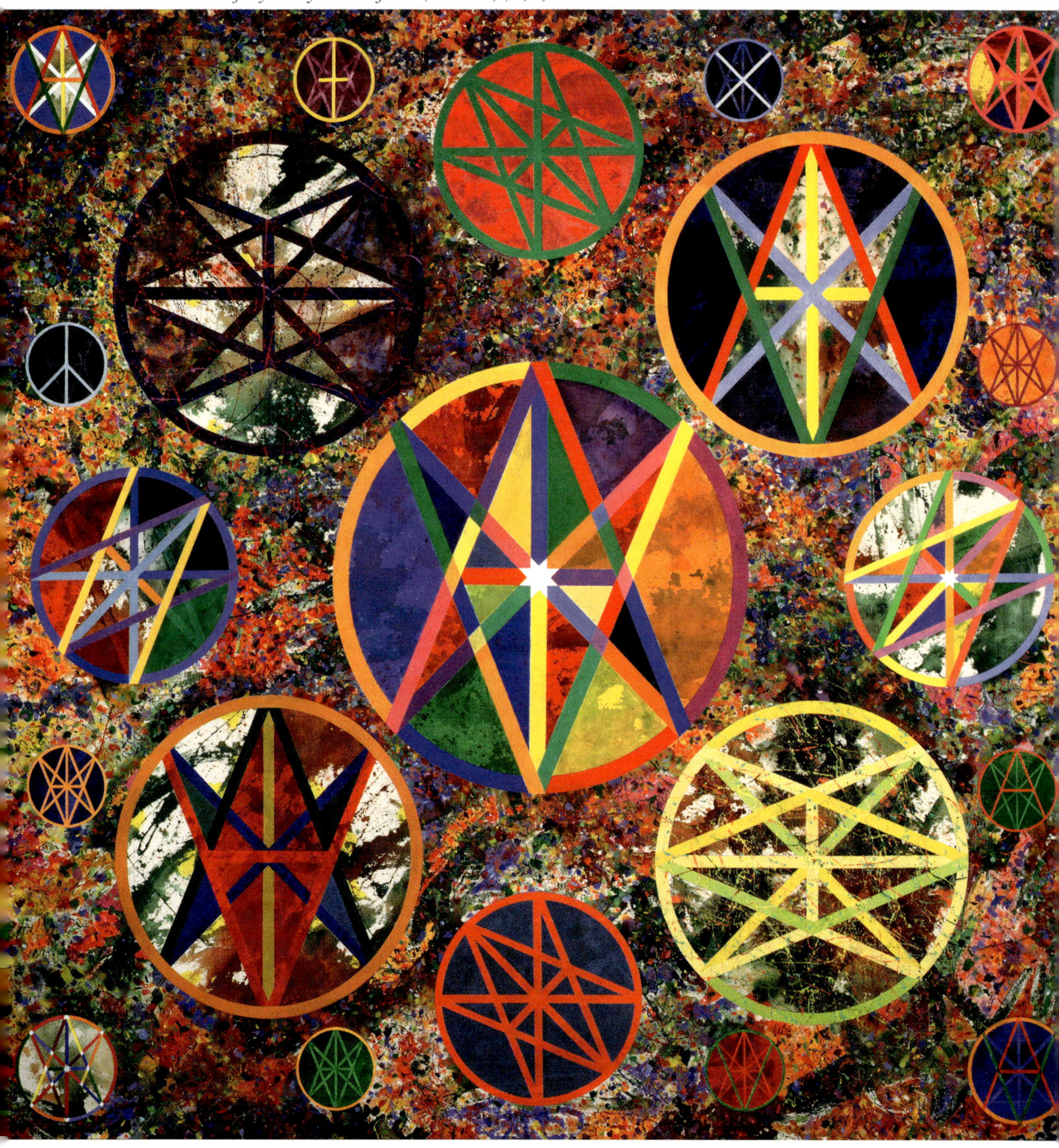

INDEX

S

T

U

V

W

PICTURE CREDITS

Page 9 copyright © John Marchant 2024

Page 15, 33, 68 and 140 copyright © Druid Order A.D.U.B. 2024

Pages 16, 40, 52, 118–19, 152 and 198 copyright © Sex Pistols Residuals 2024

Page 23 (photograph of hand only) copyright © Giles Duley 2024

Pages 76–7, 148–9 and 196–7 copyright © Rob Kelly 2024

Page 90 copyright © Greg Martin 2024

Page 91 Keystone Press / Alamy Stock Photo

Page 104 (photograph of Sid Vicious only) copyright © Bob Gruen/www.bobgruen.com

Pages 129, 157, 176 copyright © Heligan Gardens LTD 2024

Page 141 Keystone Press /Alamy Stock Photo

ACKNOWLEDGEMENTS

Stephen would like to thank Jamie and John for their faith, Fiona and Josse for their endless patience, perseverance and forbearance, and Jackie for always being there to deal with the Filth and the Fury x

John would like to thank Adam Stout, Alasdair Moore, Alison McKenna, Andrew Wilson (Dr), Anita Camarata, Bob Gruen, Clair Stevens, Colin Fallows, David Loxley, Earl Delaney, Fiona Robertson, Giles Duley, Greg Martin, Josse Pickard, Julien Temple, Malcolm Garrett, Margi Clarke, Maria Hughes, Mary MacGregor Reid, Matt Shaw, Nigel Kershaw, Nina Edge, Paul Stolper, Philip Carr-Gomm, Rhys Mwyn, Richard Boote, Richard Norris, Richard Scott, Rikard Osterlund, Rob Kelly, Rowan Reid, Sarah Philips, Sophie Richmond, Stephen Ellcock, Steve Lowe, Susan Winter, The Arcova Trust, The Florence Institute, VMM

The Jamie Reid Archive is administered by John Marchant Gallery, and includes well over a thousand items across more than fifty years of creativity and activism. John curated Jamie's major show in New York in 1997 and they maintained a close working relationship until the artist's passing in 2023. Find out more at: johnmarchantgallery.com/jra

Season
greetings
all love
Jamie

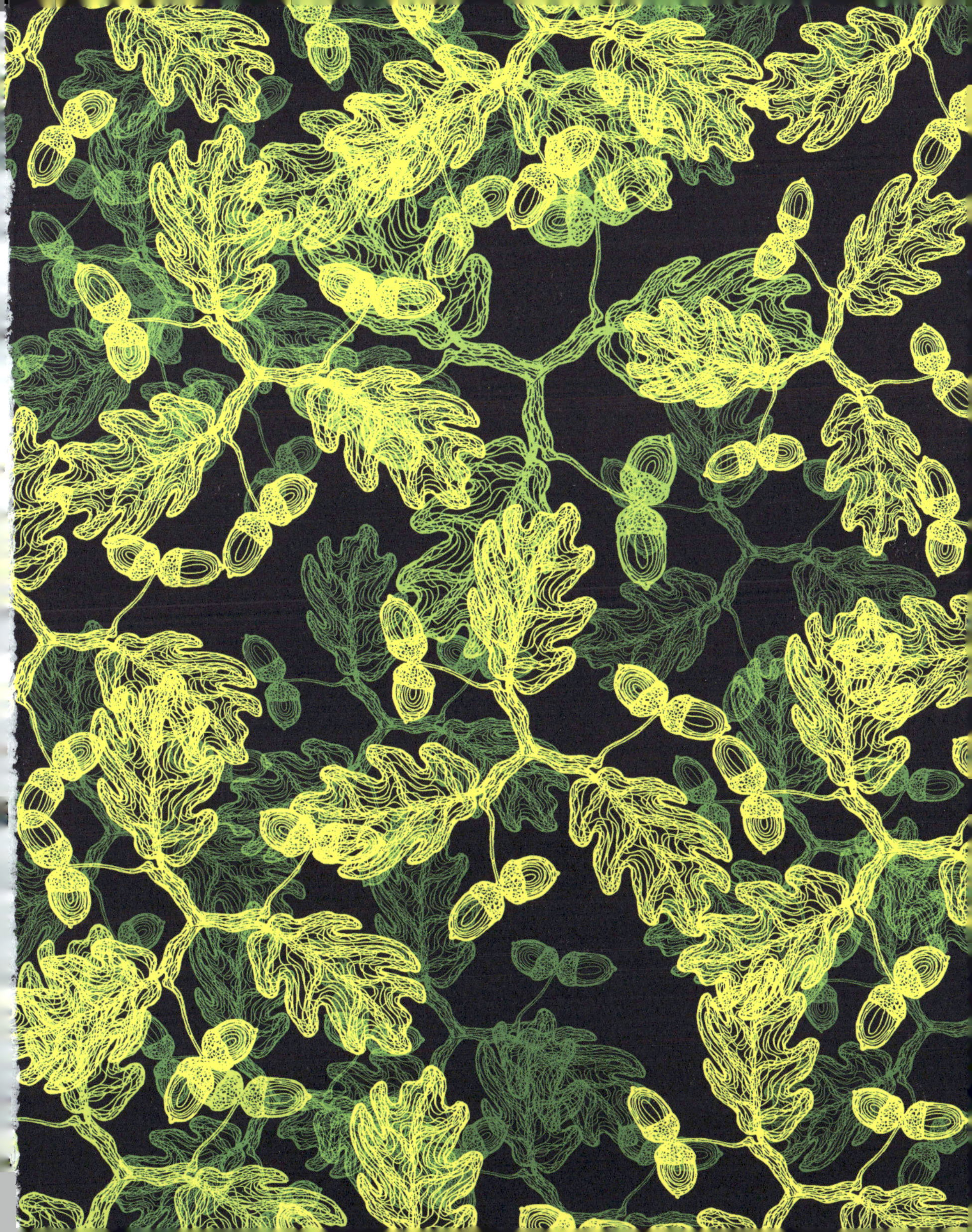

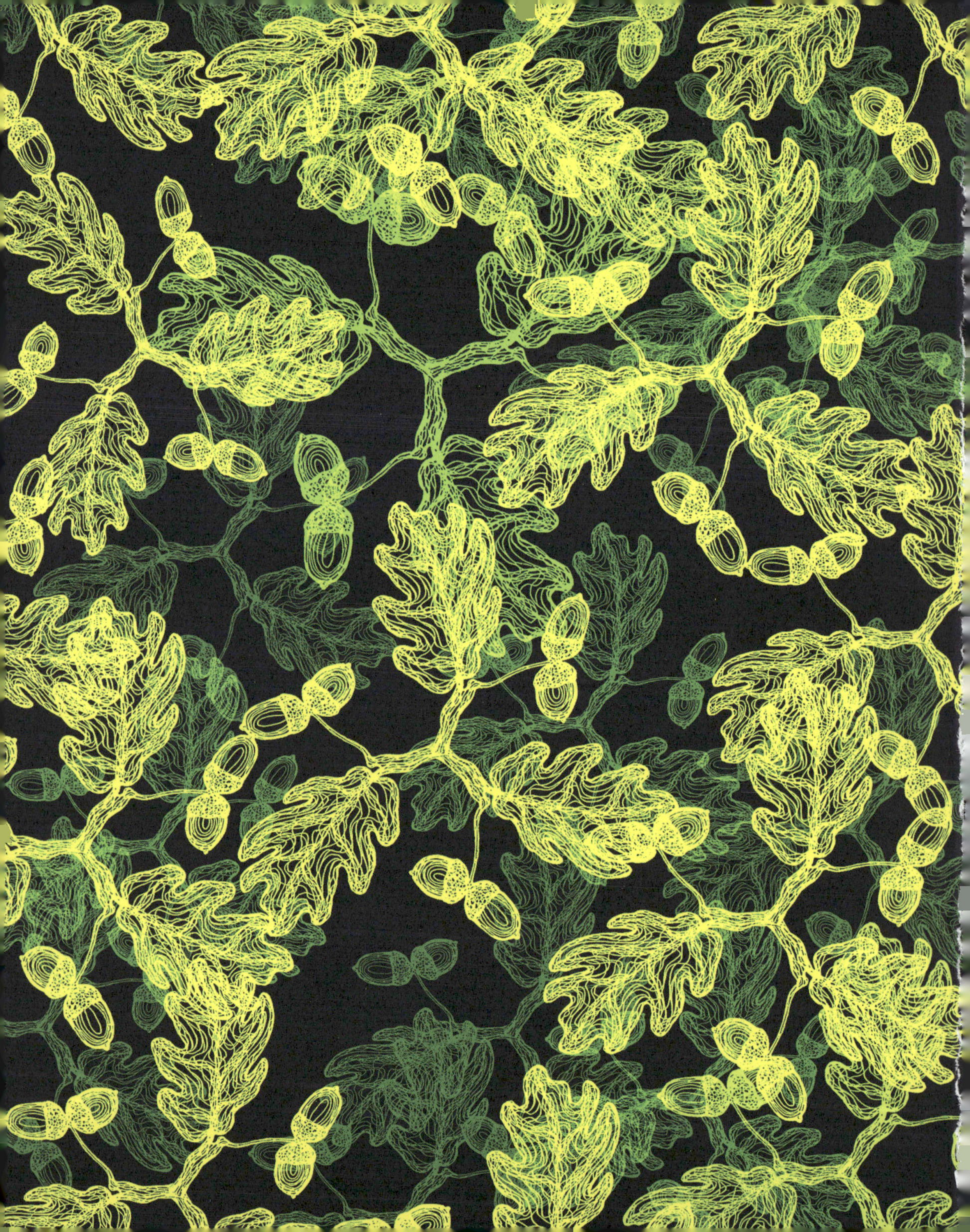